ALL GLORY TO ŚRĪ GURU AND GAURĀṄGA

ŚRĪMAD BHĀGAVATAM

of

KṚṢṆA-DVAIPĀYANA VYĀSA

कुन्त्युवाच

नमस्ये पुरुषं त्वाद्यमीश्वरं प्रकृतेः परम् ।
अलक्ष्यं सर्वभूतानामन्तर्बहिरवस्थितम् ॥

kunty uvāca
namasye puruṣaṁ tvādyam
īśvaraṁ prakṛteḥ param
alakṣyaṁ sarva-bhūtānām
antar bahir avasthitam (p. 18)

Books by His Divine Grace A. C. Bhaktivedanta Swami Prabhupāda

Bhagavad-gītā As It Is
Śrīmad-Bhāgavatam (completed by disciples)
Śrī Caitanya-caritāmṛta
Kṛṣṇa, the Supreme Personality of Godhead
Teachings of Lord Caitanya
The Nectar of Devotion
The Nectar of Instruction
Śrī Īśopaniṣad
Light of the Bhāgavata
Easy Journey to Other Planets
Teachings of Lord Kapila, the Son of Devahūti
Teachings of Queen Kuntī
Message of Godhead
The Science of Self-Realization
The Perfection of Yoga
Beyond Birth and Death
On the Way to Kṛṣṇa
Rāja-vidyā: The King of Knowledge
Elevation to Kṛṣṇa Consciousness
Kṛṣṇa Consciousness: The Matchless Gift
Kṛṣṇa Consciousness: The Topmost Yoga System
Perfect Questions, Perfect Answers
Life Comes from Life
The Nārada-bhakti-sūtra (completed by disciples)
The Mukunda-mālā-stotra (completed by disciples)
Geetār-gan (Bengali)
Vairāgya-vidyā (Bengali)
Buddhi-yoga (Bengali)
Bhakti-ratna-boli (Bengali)
Back to Godhead magazine (founder)

Books compiled from the teachings of His Divine Grace A. C. Bhaktivedanta Swami Prabhupāda after his lifetime

Search for Liberation
A Second Chance
The Journey of Self-Discovery
Civilization and Transcendence
The Laws of Nature
Renunciation Through Wisdom
The Quest for Enlightenment
Dharma, the Way of Transcendence
Beyond Illusion and Doubt
The Hare Kṛṣṇa Challenge

Available from: www.krishna.com

ŚRĪMAD BHĀGAVATAM

First Canto
"Creation"

(Part Two—Chapters 8-12)

With the Original Sanskrit Text,
Its Roman Transliteration, Synonyms,
Translation and Elaborate Purports

by

His Divine Grace
A.C. Bhaktivedanta Swami Prabhupāda
Founder-*Ācārya* of the International Society for Krishna Consciousness

THE BHAKTIVEDANTA BOOK TRUST

Readers interested in the subject matter of this book are invited by the International Society for Krishna Consciousness to correspond with its Secretary at one of the following addresses:

ISKCON Reader Services
P. O. Box 730
Watford, WD25 8ZE, United Kingdom
Tel: +44 (0)1923 857244
Website: www.iskcon.org.uk

Karuna Bhavan
Bankhouse Road, Lesmahagow
Lanarkshire, ML11 0ES
Scotland, United Kingdom
Tel: +44 (0)1555 894790
Fax: +44 (0)1555 894526
E-mail: karunabhavan@aol.com
Website: www.gouranga.cc

The Bhaktivedanta Book Trust
P. O. Box 380
Riverstone, NSW
Australia 2765
Tel: +61 (0)2 96276306
Fax: +61 (0)2 96276052

The Bhaktivedanta Book Trust
Hare Krishna Land
Juhu, Mumbai 400 049, India
Tel: +91 (0)22 26202921
Fax: +91 (0)22 26200357
E-mail: bbtmumbai@pamho.net
Website: www.bbtindia.net

www.krishna.com

ISBN 0-89213-401-1
ISBN 0-89213-430-5 (30-volume set)

Printed in India

Table of Contents

Appendixes

Preface

We must know the present need of human society. And what is that need? Human society is no longer bounded by geographical limits to particular countries or communities. Human society is broader than in the Middle Ages, and the world tendency is toward one state or one human society. The ideals of spiritual communism, according to *Śrīmad-Bhāgavatam*, are based more or less on the oneness of the entire human society, nay, on the entire energy of living beings. The need is felt by great thinkers to make this a successful ideology. *Śrīmad-Bhāgavatam* will fill this need in human society. It begins, therefore, with the aphorism of Vedānta philosophy (*janmādy asya yataḥ*) to establish the ideal of a common cause.

Human society, at the present moment, is not in the darkness of oblivion. It has made rapid progress in the field of material comforts, education and economic development throughout the entire world. But there is a pinprick somewhere in the social body at large, and therefore there are large-scale quarrels, even over less important issues. There is need of a clue as to how humanity can become one in peace, friendship and prosperity with a common cause. *Śrīmad-Bhāgavatam* will fill this need, for it is a cultural presentation for the re-spiritualization of the entire human society.

Śrīmad-Bhāgavatam should be introduced also in the schools and colleges, for it is recommended by the great student devotee Prahlāda Mahārāja in order to change the demonic face of society.

kaumāra ācaret prājño
dharmān bhāgavatān iha
durlabhaṁ mānuṣaṁ janma
tad apy adhruvam arthadam
(*Bhāg.* 7.6.1)

Disparity in human society is due to lack of principles in a godless civilization. There is God, or the Almighty One, from whom everything emanates, by whom everything is maintained and in whom everything is merged to rest. Material science has tried to find the ultimate source of creation very insufficiently, but it is a fact that there is one ultimate source of everything that be. This ultimate source is explained rationally and authoritatively in the beautiful *Bhāgavatam* or *Śrīmad-Bhāgavatam.*

Śrīmad-Bhāgavatam is the transcendental science not only for knowing the ultimate source of everything but also for knowing our relation with Him and our duty towards perfection of the human society on the basis of this perfect knowledge. It is powerful reading matter in the Sanskrit language, and it is now rendered into English elaborately so that simply by a careful reading one will know God perfectly well, so much so that the reader will be sufficiently educated to defend himself from the onslaught of atheists. Over and above this, the reader will be able to convert others to accept God as a concrete principle.

Śrīmad-Bhāgavatam begins with the definition of the ultimate source. It is a bona fide commentary on the *Vedānta-sūtra* by the same author, Śrīla Vyāsadeva, and gradually it develops into nine cantos up to the highest state of God realization. The only qualification one needs to study this great book of transcendental knowledge is to proceed step by step cautiously and not jump forward haphazardly as with an ordinary book. It should be gone through chapter by chapter, one after another. The reading matter is so arranged with its original Sanskrit text, its English transliteration, synonyms, translation and purports so that one is sure to become a God realized soul at the end of finishing the first nine cantos.

The Tenth Canto is distinct from the first nine cantos, because it deals directly with the transcendental activities of the Personality of Godhead Śrī Kṛṣṇa. One will be unable to capture the effects of the Tenth Canto without going through the first nine cantos. The book is complete in twelve cantos, each independent, but it is good for all to read them in small installments one after another.

I must admit my frailties in presenting *Śrīmad-Bhāgavatam*, but still I am hopeful of its good reception by the thinkers and leaders of society on the strength of the following statement of *Śrīmad-Bhāgavatam.*

tad-vāg-visargo janatāgha-viplavo
yasmin pratiślokam abaddhavaty api

nāmāny anantasya yaśo 'ṅkitāni yac
chṛṇvanti gāyanti gṛṇanti sādhavaḥ
(*Bhāg.* 1.5.11)

"On the other hand, that literature which is full with descriptions of the transcendental glories of the name, fame, form and pastimes of the unlimited Supreme Lord is a transcendental creation meant to bring about a revolution in the impious life of a misdirected civilization. Such transcendental literatures, even though irregularly composed, are heard, sung and accepted by purified men who are thoroughly honest."

Oṁ tat sat

A. C. Bhaktivedanta Swami

Introduction

"This *Bhāgavata Purāṇa* is as brilliant as the sun, and it has arisen just after the departure of Lord Kṛṣṇa to His own abode, accompanied by religion, knowledge, etc. Persons who have lost their vision due to the dense darkness of ignorance in the age of Kali shall get light from this *Purāṇa*." (*Śrīmad-Bhāgavatam* 1.3.43)

The timeless wisdom of India is expressed in the *Vedas*, ancient Sanskrit texts that touch upon all fields of human knowledge. Originally preserved through oral tradition, the *Vedas* were first put into writing five thousand years ago by Śrīla Vyāsadeva, the "literary incarnation of God." After compiling the *Vedas*, Vyāsadeva set forth their essence in the aphorisms known as *Vedānta-sūtras*. *Śrīmad-Bhāgavatam* is Vyāsadeva's commentary on his own *Vedānta-sūtras*. It was written in the maturity of his spiritual life under the direction of Nārada Muni, his spiritual master. Referred to as "the ripened fruit of the tree of Vedic literature," *Śrīmad-Bhāgavatam* is the most complete and authoritative exposition of Vedic knowledge.

After compiling the *Bhāgavatam*, Vyāsa impressed the synopsis of it upon his son, the sage Śukadeva Gosvāmī. Śukadeva Gosvāmī subsequently recited the entire *Bhāgavatam* to Mahārāja Parīkṣit in an assembly of learned saints on the bank of the Ganges at Hastināpura (now Delhi). Mahārāja Parīkṣit was the emperor of the world and was a great *rājarṣi* (saintly king). Having received a warning that he would die within a week, he renounced his entire kingdom and retired to the bank of the Ganges to fast until death and receive spiritual enlightenment. The *Bhāgavatam* begins with Emperor Parīkṣit's sober inquiry to Śukadeva Gosvāmī:

> "You are the spiritual master of great saints and devotees. I am therefore begging you to show the way of perfection for all persons, and especially for one who is about to die. Please let me know what a man should hear, chant, remember and worship, and also what he should not do. Please explain all this to me."

Śukadeva Gosvāmī's answer to this question, and numerous other questions posed by Mahārāja Parīkṣit, concerning everything from the nature of the self to the origin of the universe, held the assembled sages in rapt attention continuously for the seven days leading to the King's death. The sage Sūta Gosvāmī, who was present on the bank of the Ganges when Śukadeva Gosvāmī first recited *Śrīmad-Bhāgavatam*, later repeated the *Bhāgavatam* before a gathering of sages in the forest of Naimiṣāraṇya. Those sages, concerned about the spiritual welfare of the people in general, had gathered to perform a long, continuous chain of sacrifices to counteract the degrading influence of the incipient age of Kali. In response to the sages' request that he speak the essence of Vedic wisdom, Sūta Gosvāmī repeated from memory the entire eighteen thousand verses of *Śrīmad-Bhāgavatam*, as spoken by Śukadeva Gosvāmī to Mahārāja Parīkṣit.

The reader of *Śrīmad-Bhāgavatam* hears Sūta Gosvāmī relate the questions of Mahārāja Parīkṣit and the answers of Śukadeva Gosvāmī. Also, Sūta Gosvāmī sometimes responds directly to questions put by Śaunaka Ṛṣi, the spokesman for the sages gathered at Naimiṣāraṇya. One therefore simultaneously hears two dialogues: one between Mahārāja Parīkṣit and Śukadeva Gosvāmī on the bank of the Ganges, and another at Naimiṣāraṇya between Sūta Gosvāmī and the sages at Naimiṣāraṇya Forest, headed by Śaunaka Ṛṣi. Furthermore, while instructing King Parīkṣit, Śukadeva Gosvāmī often relates historical episodes and gives accounts of lengthy philosophical discussions between such great souls as the saint Maitreya and his disciple Vidura. With this understanding of the history of the *Bhāgavatam*, the reader will easily be able to follow its intermingling of dialogues and events from various sources. Since philosophical wisdom, not chronological order, is most important in the text, one need only be attentive to the subject matter of *Śrīmad-Bhāgavatam* to appreciate fully its profound message.

The translator of this edition compares the *Bhāgavatam* to sugar candy—wherever you taste it, you will find it equally sweet and relishable. Therefore, to taste the sweetness of the *Bhāgavatam*, one may begin by reading any of its volumes. After such an introductory taste, however, the serious reader is best advised to go back to Volume One of the First Canto and then proceed through the *Bhāgavatam*, volume after volume, in its natural order.

This edition of the *Bhāgavatam* is the first complete English translation of this important text with an elaborate commentary, and it is the first widely available to the English-speaking public. It is the product of the scholarly and devotional effort of His Divine Grace A. C. Bhaktivedanta Swami Prabhupāda, the world's most distinguished teacher of Indian religious and philosophical thought. His consummate Sanskrit scholarship and intimate familiarity with Vedic culture and thought as well as the modern way of life combine to reveal to the West a magnificent exposition of this important classic.

Readers will find this work of value for many reasons. For those interested in the classical roots of Indian civilization, it serves as a vast reservoir of detailed information on virtually every one of its aspects. For students of comparative philosophy and religion, the *Bhāgavatam* offers a penetrating view into the meaning of India's profound spiritual heritage. To sociologists and anthropologists, the *Bhāgavatam* reveals the practical workings of a peaceful and scientifically organized Vedic culture, whose institutions were integrated on the basis of a highly developed spiritual world view. Students of literature will discover the *Bhāgavatam* to be a masterpiece of majestic poetry. For students of psychology, the text provides important perspectives on the nature of consciousness, human behavior and the philosophical study of identity. Finally, to those seeking spiritual insight, the *Bhāgavatam* offers simple and practical guidance for attainment of the highest self-knowledge and realization of the Absolute Truth. The entire multivolume text, presented by the Bhaktivedanta Book Trust, promises to occupy a significant place in the intellectual, cultural and spiritual life of modern man for a long time to come.

—The Publishers

CHAPTER EIGHT

Prayers by Queen Kuntī and Parīkṣit Saved

TEXT 1

सूत उवाच

अथ ते सम्परेतानां स्वानामुदकमिच्छताम् ।
दातुं सकृष्णा गङ्गायां पुरस्कृत्य ययुः स्त्रियः ॥ १ ॥

sūta uvāca
atha te samparetānāṁ
svānām udakam icchatām
dātuṁ sakṛṣṇā gaṅgāyāṁ
puraskṛtya yayuḥ striyaḥ

sūtaḥ uvāca—Sūta said; *atha*—thus; *te*—the Pāṇḍavas; *sam-paretānām*—of the dead; *svānām*—of the relatives; *udakam*—water; *icchatām*—willing to have; *dātum*—to deliver; *sa-kṛṣṇāḥ*—along with Draupadī; *gaṅgāyām*—on the Ganges; *puraskṛtya*—putting in the front; *yayuḥ*—went; *striyaḥ*—the women.

TRANSLATION

Sūta Gosvāmī said: Thereafter the Pāṇḍavas, desiring to deliver water to the dead relatives who had desired it, went to the Ganges with Draupadī. The ladies walked in front.

PURPORT

To date it is the custom in Hindu society to go to the Ganges or any other sacred river to take bath when death occurs in the family. Each of the family members pours out a potful of the Ganges water for the departed soul and walks in a procession, with the ladies in the front. The

Pāṇḍavas also followed the rules more than five thousand years ago. Lord Kṛṣṇa, being a cousin of the Pāṇḍavas, was also amongst the family members.

TEXT 2

ते निनीयोदकं सर्वे विलप्य च भृशं पुनः ।
आप्लुता हरिपादाब्जरजःपूतसरिज्जले ॥ २ ॥

te ninīyodakaṁ sarve
vilapya ca bhṛśaṁ punaḥ
āplutā hari-pādābja-
rajaḥ-pūta-sarij-jale

te—all of them; *ninīya*—having offered; *udakam*—water; *sarve*—every one of them; *vilapya*—having lamented; *ca*—and; *bhṛśam*—sufficiently; *punaḥ*—again; *āplutāḥ*—took bath; *hari-pādābja*—the lotus feet of the Lord; *rajaḥ*—dust; *pūta*—purified; *sarit*—of the Ganges; *jale*—in the water.

TRANSLATION

Having lamented over them and sufficiently offered Ganges water, they bathed in the Ganges, whose water is sanctified due to being mixed with the dust of the lotus feet of the Lord.

TEXT 3

तत्रासीनं कुरुपतिं धृतराष्ट्रं सहानुजम् ।
गान्धारीं पुत्रशोकार्तां पृथां कृष्णां च माधवः ॥ ३ ॥

tatrāsīnaṁ kuru-patiṁ
dhṛtarāṣṭraṁ sahānujam
gāndhārīṁ putra-śokārtāṁ
pṛthāṁ kṛṣṇāṁ ca mādhavaḥ

tatra—there; *āsīnam*—sitting; *kuru-patim*—the King of the Kurus; *dhṛtarāṣṭram*—Dhṛtarāṣṭra; *saha-anujam*—with his younger brothers; *gāndhārīm*—Gāndhārī; *putra*—son; *śoka-artām*—overtaken by bereavement; *pṛthām*—Kuntī; *kṛṣṇām*—Draupadī; *ca*—also; *mādhavaḥ*—Lord Śrī Kṛṣṇa.

TRANSLATION

There sat the King of the Kurus, Mahārāja Yudhiṣṭhira, along with his younger brothers and Dhṛtarāṣṭra, Gāndhārī, Kuntī and Draupadī, all overwhelmed with grief. Lord Kṛṣṇa was also there.

PURPORT

The Battle of Kurukṣetra was fought between family members, and thus all affected persons were also family members like Mahārāja Yudhiṣṭhira and brothers, Kuntī, Draupadī, Subhadrā, Dhṛtarāṣṭra, Gāndhārī and her daughters-in-law, etc. All the principal dead bodies were in some way or other related with each other, and therefore the family grief was combined. Lord Kṛṣṇa was also one of them as a cousin of the Pāṇḍavas and nephew of Kuntī, as well as brother of Subhadrā, etc. The Lord, therefore, was equally sympathetic toward all of them, and therefore he began to pacify them befittingly.

TEXT 4

सान्त्वयामास मुनिभिर्हतबन्धूञ् शुचार्पितान् ।
भूतेषु कालस्य गतिं दर्शयन्नप्रतिक्रियाम् ॥ ४ ॥

sāntvayām āsa munibhir
hata-bandhūñ śucārpitān
bhūteṣu kālasya gatiṁ
darśayan na pratikriyām

sāntvayām āsa—pacified; *munibhiḥ*—along with the *munis* present there; *hata-bandhūn*—those who lost their friends and relatives; *śucārpitān*—all shocked and affected; *bhūteṣu*—unto the living beings; *kālasya*—of the supreme law of the Almighty; *gatim*—reactions; *darśayan*—demonstrated; *na*—no; *pratikriyām*—remedial measures.

TRANSLATION

Citing the stringent laws of the Almighty and their reactions upon living beings, Lord Śrī Kṛṣṇa and the munis began to pacify those who were shocked and affected.

PURPORT

The stringent laws of nature, under the order of the Supreme Personality of Godhead, cannot be altered by any living entity. The living entities are eternally under the subjugation of the almighty Lord. The Lord makes all the laws and orders, and these laws and orders are generally called *dharma* or religion. No one can create any religious formula. Bona fide religion is to abide by the orders of the Lord. The Lord's orders are clearly declared in the *Bhagavad-gītā*. Everyone should follow Him only or His orders, and that will make all happy, both materially and spiritually. As long as we are in the material world, our duty is to follow the orders of the Lord, and if by the grace of the Lord we are liberated from the clutches of the material world, then in our liberated stage also we can render transcendental loving service unto the Lord. In our material stage we can see neither ourselves nor the Lord for want of spiritual vision. But when we are liberated from material affection and are situated in our original spiritual form we can see both ourselves and the Lord face to face. *Mukti* means to be reinstated in one's original spiritual status after giving up the material conception of life. Therefore, human life is specifically meant for qualifying ourselves for this spiritual liberty. Unfortunately, under the influence of illusory material energy, we accept this spot-life of only a few years as our permanent existence and thus become illusioned by possessing so-called country, home, land, children, wife, community, wealth, etc., which are false representations created by *māyā* (illusion). And under the dictation of *māyā*, we fight with one another to protect these false possessions. By cultivating spiritual knowledge, we can realize that we have nothing to do with all this material paraphernalia. Then at once we become free from material attachment. This clearance of the misgivings of material existence at once takes place by association with the Lord's devotees, who are able to inject the transcendental sound into the depths of the bewildered heart and thus make one practically liberated from all lamentation and illusion. That is a summary of the pacifying measures for those affected by the reaction of stringent material laws, exhibited in the forms of birth, death, old age and disease, which are insoluble factors of material existence. The victims of war, namely, the family members of the Kurus, were lamenting the problems of death, and the Lord pacified them on the basis of knowledge.

TEXT 5

साधयित्वाजातशत्रोः स्वं राज्यं कितवैर्हृतम् ।
घातयित्वासतो राज्ञः कचस्पर्शक्षतायुषः ॥ ५ ॥

sādhayitvājāta-śatroḥ
svaṁ rājyaṁ kitavair hṛtam
ghātayitvāsato rājñaḥ
kaca-sparśa-kṣatāyuṣaḥ

sādhayitvā—having executed; *ajāta-śatroḥ*—of one who has no enemy; *svam rājyam*—own kingdom; *kitavaiḥ*—by the clever (Duryodhana and party); *hṛtam*—usurped; *ghātayitvā*—having killed; *asataḥ*—the unscrupulous; *rājñaḥ*—of the queen's; *kaca*—bunch of hair; *sparśa*—roughly handled; *kṣata*—decreased; *āyuṣaḥ*—by the duration of life.

TRANSLATION

The clever Duryodhana and his party cunningly usurped the kingdom of Yudhiṣṭhira, who had no enemy. By the grace of the Lord, the recovery was executed, and the unscrupulous kings who joined with Duryodhana were killed by Him. Others also died, their duration of life having decreased for their rough handling of the hair of Queen Draupadī.

PURPORT

In the glorious days, or before the advent of the age of Kali, the *brāhmaṇas*, the cows, the women, the children and the old men were properly given protection.

1. The protection of the *brāhmaṇas* maintains the institution of *varṇa* and *āśrama*, the most scientific culture for attainment of spiritual life.

2. The protection of cows maintains the most miraculous form of food, i.e., milk for maintaining the finer tissues of the brain for understanding higher aims of life.

3. The protection of women maintains the chastity of society, by which we can get a good generation for peace, tranquillity and progress of life.

4. The protection of children gives the human form of life its best chance to prepare the way of liberty from material bondage. Such protection of children begins from the very day of begetting a child by the purificatory process of *garbhādhāna-saṁskāra*, the beginning of pure life.

5. The protection of the old men gives them a chance to prepare themselves for better life after death.

This complete outlook is based on factors leading to successful humanity as against the civilization of polished cats and dogs. The killing of the above-mentioned innocent creatures is totally forbidden because even by insulting them one loses one's duration of life. In the age of Kali they are not properly protected, and therefore the duration of life of the present generation has shortened considerably. In the *Bhagavad-gītā* it is stated that when the women become unchaste for want of proper protection, there are unwanted children called *varṇa-saṅkara*. To insult a chaste woman means to bring about disaster in the duration of life. Duḥśāsana, a brother of Duryodhana, insulted Draupadī, an ideal chaste lady, and therefore the miscreants died untimely. These are some of the stringent laws of the Lord mentioned above.

TEXT 6.

याजयित्वाश्वमेधैस्तं त्रिभिरुत्तमकल्पकैः ।
तद्यशः पावनं दिक्षु शतमन्योरिवातनोत् ॥ ६ ॥

yājayitvāśvamedhais taṁ
tribhir uttama-kalpakaiḥ
tad-yaśaḥ pāvanaṁ dikṣu
śata-manyor ivātanot

yājayitvā—by performing; *aśvamedhaiḥ*—*yajña* in which a horse is sacrificed; *tam*—him (King Yudhiṣṭhira); *tribhiḥ*—three; *uttama*—best; *kalpakaiḥ*—supplied with proper ingredients and performed by able priests; *tat*—that; *yaśaḥ*—fame; *pāvanam*—virtuous; *dikṣu*—all directions; *śata-manyoḥ*—Indra, who performed one hundred such sacrifices; *iva*—like; *atanot*—spread.

TRANSLATION

Lord Śrī Kṛṣṇa caused three well-performed aśvamedha-yajñas [horse sacrifices] to be conducted by Mahārāja Yudhiṣṭhira and thus caused his virtuous fame to be glorified in all directions, like that of Indra, who had performed one hundred such sacrifices.

PURPORT

This is something like the preface to the performances of *aśvamedha-yajña* by Mahārāja Yudhiṣṭhira. The comparison of Mahārāja Yudhiṣṭhira to the King of heaven is significant. The King of heaven is thousands and thousands of times greater than Mahārāja Yudhiṣṭhira in opulence, yet the fame of Mahārāja Yudhiṣṭhira was not less. The reason is that Mahārāja Yudhiṣṭhira was a pure devotee of the Lord, and by His grace only was King Yudhiṣṭhira on the level of the King of heaven, even though he performed only three *yajñas* whereas the King of heaven performed hundreds. That is the prerogative of the devotee of the Lord. The Lord is equal to everyone, but a devotee of the Lord is more glorified because he is always in touch with the all-great. The sun rays are equally distributed, but still there are some places which are always dark. This is not due to the sun but to the receptive power. Similarly, those who are cent percent devotees of the Lord get the full-fledged mercy of the Lord, which is always equally distributed everywhere.

TEXT 7

आमन्त्र्य पाण्डुपुत्रांश्च शैनेयोद्धवसंयुतः ।
द्वैपायनादिभिर्विप्रैः पूजितैः प्रतिपूजितः ॥ ७ ॥

āmantrya pāṇḍu-putrāṁś ca
śaineyoddhava-saṁyutaḥ
dvaipāyanādibhir vipraiḥ
pūjitaiḥ pratipūjitaḥ

āmantrya—inviting; *pāṇḍu-putrān*—all the sons of Pāṇḍu; *ca*—also; *śaineya*—Sātyaki; *uddhava*—Uddhava; *saṁyutaḥ*—accompanied; *dvaipāyana-ādibhiḥ*—by the *ṛṣis* like Vedavyāsa; *vipraiḥ*—by the *brāhmaṇas; pūjitaiḥ*—being worshiped; *pratipūjitaḥ*—the Lord also reciprocated equally.

TRANSLATION

Lord Śrī Kṛṣṇa then prepared for His departure. He invited the sons of Pāṇḍu, after having been worshiped by the brāhmaṇas, headed by Śrīla Vyāsadeva. The Lord also reciprocated greetings.

PURPORT

Apparently Lord Śrī Kṛṣṇa was a *kṣatriya* and was not worshipable by the *brāhmaṇas.* But the *brāhmaṇas* present there, headed by Śrīla Vyāsadeva, all knew Him to be the Personality of Godhead, and therefore they worshiped Him. The Lord reciprocated the greetings just to honor the social order that a *kṣatriya* is obedient to the orders of the *brāhmaṇas.* Although Lord Śrī Kṛṣṇa was always offered the respects due the Supreme Lord from all responsible quarters, the Lord never deviated from the customary usages between the four orders of society. The Lord purposely observed all these social customs so that others would follow Him in the future.

TEXT 8

गन्तुं कृतमतिर्ब्रह्मन् द्वारकां रथमास्थितः ।
उपलेभेऽभिधावन्तीमुत्तरां भयविह्वलाम् ॥ ८ ॥

gantuṁ kṛtamatir brahman
dvārakāṁ ratham āsthitaḥ
upalebhe 'bhidhāvantīm
uttarāṁ bhaya-vihvalām

gantum—just desiring to start; *kṛtamatiḥ*—having decided; *brahman*—O *brāhmaṇa; dvārakām*—towards Dvārakā; *ratham*—on the chariot; *āsthitaḥ*—seated; *upalebhe*—saw; *abhidhāvantīm*—coming hurriedly; *uttarām*—Uttarā; *bhaya-vihvalām*—being afraid.

TRANSLATION

As soon as He seated Himself on the chariot to start for Dvārakā, He saw Uttarā hurrying toward Him in fear.

PURPORT

All the members of the family of the Pāṇḍavas were completely dependent on the protection of the Lord, and therefore the Lord protected all of them in all circumstances. The Lord protects everyone, but one who depends completely upon Him is especially looked after by the Lord. The father is more attentive to the little son who is exclusively dependent on the father.

TEXT 9

उत्तरोवाच
पाहि पाहि महायोगिन्देवदेव जगत्पते ।
नान्यं त्वदभयं पश्ये यत्र मृत्युः परस्परम् ॥ ९ ॥

uttarovāca
pāhi pāhi mahā-yogin
deva-deva jagat-pate
nānyaṁ tvad abhayaṁ paśye
yatra mṛtyuḥ parasparam

uttarā uvāca—Uttarā said; *pāhi pāhi*—protect, protect; *mahā-yogin*—the greatest mystic; *deva-deva*—the worshipable of the worshiped; *jagat-pate*—O Lord of the universe; *na*—not; *anyam*—anyone else; *tvat*—than You; *abhayam*—fearlessness; *paśye*—do I see; *yatra*—where there is; *mṛtyuḥ*—death; *parasparam*—in the world of duality.

TRANSLATION

Uttarā said: O Lord of lords, Lord of the universe! You are the greatest of mystics. Please protect me, for there is no one else who can save me from the clutches of death in this world of duality.

PURPORT

This material world is the world of duality, in contrast with the oneness of the absolute realm. The world of duality is composed of matter and spirit, whereas the absolute world is complete spirit without any tinge of the material qualities. In the dual world everyone is falsely trying to become the master of the world, whereas in the absolute world the

Lord is the absolute Lord, and all others are His absolute servitors. In the world of duality everyone is *envious* of all others, and death is inevitable due to the dual existence of matter and spirit. The Lord is the only shelter of fearlessness for the surrendered soul. One cannot save himself from the cruel hands of death in the material world without having surrendered himself at the lotus feet of the Lord.

TEXT 10

अभिद्रवति मामीश शरस्तप्तायसो विभो ।
कामं दहतु मां नाथ मा मे गर्भो निपात्यताम् ॥१०॥

abhidravati mām īśa
śaras taptāyaso vibho
kāmaṁ dahatu māṁ nātha
mā me garbho nipātyatām

abhidravati—coming towards; *mām*—me; *īśa*—O Lord; *śaraḥ*—the arrow; *tapta*—fiery; *ayasaḥ*—iron; *vibho*—O great one; *kāmam*—desire; *dahatu*—let it burn; *mām*—me; *nātha*—O protector; *mā*—not; *me*—my; *garbhaḥ*—embryo; *nipātyatām*—be aborted.

TRANSLATION

O my Lord, You are all-powerful. A fiery iron arrow is coming towards me fast. My Lord, let it burn me personally, if You so desire, but please do not let it burn and abort my embryo. Please do me this favor, my Lord.

PURPORT

This incident took place after the death of Abhimanyu, the husband of Uttarā. Abhimanyu's widow, Uttarā, should have followed the path of her husband, but because she was pregnant, and Mahārāja Parīkṣit, a great devotee of the Lord, was lying in embryo, she was responsible for his protection. The mother of a child has a great responsibility in giving all protection to the child, and therefore Uttarā was not ashamed to express this frankly before Lord Kṛṣṇa. Uttarā was the daughter of a great king, the wife of a great hero, and student of a great devotee, and later she was the mother of a good king also. She was fortunate in every respect.

TEXT 11

सूत उवाच
उपधार्य वचस्तस्या भगवान् भक्तवत्सलः ।
अपाण्डवमिदं कर्तुं द्रौणेरस्त्रमबुध्यत ॥११॥

sūta uvāca
upadhārya vacas tasyā
bhagavān bhakta-vatsalaḥ
apāṇḍavam idaṁ kartuṁ
drauṇer astram abudhyata

sūtaḥ uvāca—Sūta Gosvāmī said; *upadhārya*—by hearing her patiently; *vacaḥ*—words; *tasyāḥ*—her; *bhagavān*—the Personality of Godhead; *bhakta-vatsalaḥ*—He who is very much affectionate towards His devotees; *apāṇḍavam*—without the existence of the Pāṇḍavas' descendants; *idam*—this; *kartum*—to do it; *drauneḥ*—of the son of Droṇācārya; *astram*—weapon; *abudhyata*—understood.

TRANSLATION

Sūta Gosvāmī said: Having patiently heard her words, Lord Śrī Kṛṣṇa, who is always very affectionate to His devotees, could at once understand that Aśvatthāmā, the son of Droṇācārya, had thrown the brahmāstra to finish the last life in the Pāṇḍava family.

PURPORT

The Lord is impartial in every respect, but still He is inclined towards His devotees because there is a great necessity of this for everyone's well-being. The Pāṇḍava family was a family of devotees, and therefore the Lord wanted them to rule the world. That was the reason He vanquished the rule of the company of Duryodhana and established the rule of Mahārāja Yudhiṣṭhira. Therefore, He also wanted to protect Mahārāja

Parīkṣit, who was lying in embryo. He did not like the idea that the world should be without the Pāṇḍavas, the ideal family of devotees.

TEXT 12

तर्ह्येवाथ मुनिश्रेष्ठ पाण्डवाः पञ्च सायकान् ।
आत्मनोऽभिमुखान्दीप्तानालक्ष्यास्त्राण्युपाददुः॥१२॥

tarhy evātha muni-śreṣṭha
pāṇḍavāḥ pañca sāyakān
ātmano 'bhimukhān dīptān
ālakṣyāstrāṇy upādaduḥ

tarhi—then; *eva*—also; *atha*—therefore; *muni-śreṣṭha*—O chief amongst the *munis; pāṇḍavāḥ*—all the sons of Pāṇḍu; *pañca*—five; *sāyakān*—weapons; *ātmanaḥ*—own selves; *abhimukhān*—towards; *dīptān*—glaring; *ālakṣya*—seeing it; *astrāṇi*—weapons; *upādaduḥ*—took up.

TRANSLATION

O foremost among the great thinkers [munis] [Śaunaka], seeing the glaring brahmāstra proceeding towards them, the Pāṇḍavas took up their five respective weapons.

PURPORT

The *brahmāstras* are finer than the nuclear weapons. Aśvatthāmā discharged the *brahmāstra* simply to kill the Pāṇḍavas, namely the five brothers headed by Mahārāja Yudhiṣṭhira and their only grandson, who was lying within the womb of Uttarā. Therefore the *brahmāstra*, more effective and finer than the atomic weapons, was not as blind as the atomic bombs. When the atomic bombs are discharged they do not discriminate between the target and others. Mainly the atomic bombs do harm to the innocent because there is no control. The *brahmāstra* is not like that. It marks out the target and proceeds accordingly without harming the innocent.

TEXT 13

व्यसनं वीक्ष्य तत्तेषामनन्यविषयात्मनाम् ।
सुदर्शनेन स्वास्त्रेण स्वानां रक्षां व्यधाद्विभुः ॥१३॥

vyasanaṁ vīkṣya tat teṣām
ananya-viṣayātmanām
sudarśanena svāstreṇa
svānāṁ rakṣāṁ vyadhād vibhuḥ

vyasanam—great danger; *vīkṣya*—having observed; *tat*—that; *teṣām*—their; *ananya*—no other; *viṣaya*—means; *ātmanām*—thus inclined; *sudarśanena*—by the wheel of Śrī Kṛṣṇa; *sva-astreṇa*—by the weapon; *svānām*—of His own devotees; *rakṣām*—protection; *vyadhāt*—did it; *vibhuḥ*—the Almighty.

TRANSLATION

The almighty Personality of Godhead, Śrī Kṛṣṇa, having observed that a great danger was befalling His unalloyed devotees, who were fully surrendered souls, at once took up His Sudarśana disc to protect them.

PURPORT

The *brahmāstra*, the supreme weapon released by Aśvatthāmā, was something similar to the nuclear weapon but with more radiation and heat. This *brahmāstra* is the product of a more subtle science, being the product of a finer sound, a *mantra* recorded in the *Vedas*. Another advantage of this weapon is that it is not blind like the nuclear weapon because it can be directed only to the target and nothing else. Aśvatthāmā released the weapon just to finish all the male members of Pāṇḍu's family; therefore in one sense it was more dangerous than the atomic bombs because it could penetrate even the most protected place and would never miss the target. Knowing all this, Lord Śrī Kṛṣṇa at once took up His personal weapon to protect His devotees, who did not know anyone other than Kṛṣṇa. In the *Bhagavad-gītā* the Lord has clearly promised that His devotees are never to be vanquished. And He behaves according to the quality or degree of the devotional service rendered by the devotees. Here the word *ananya-viṣayātmanām* is significant. The Pāṇḍavas were cent percent dependent on the protection of the Lord, although they were all great warriors themselves. But the Lord neglects even the greatest warriors and also vanquishes them in no time. When the Lord saw that there was no time for the Pāṇḍavas to counteract the *brahmāstra* of Aśvatthāmā, He took up His weapon even at the risk of breaking His own vow. Although the Battle of Kurukṣetra was almost finished, still, according to His vow, He should not have taken up His own weapon. But the emergency was more important than the vow. He is better known as the *bhakta-vatsala*, or the lover of His devotee, and thus He preferred to continue as *bhakta-vatsala* than to be a worldly moralist who never breaks his solemn vow.

TEXT 14

अन्तःस्थः सर्वभूतानामात्मा योगेश्वरो हरिः ।
स्वमाययावृणोद्गर्भं वैराट्याः कुरुतन्तवे ॥१४॥

antaḥsthaḥ sarva-bhūtānām
ātmā yogeśvaro hariḥ
sva-māyayāvṛṇod garbhaṁ
vairāṭyāḥ kuru-tantave

antaḥsthaḥ—being within; *sarva*—all; *bhūtānām*—of the living beings; *ātmā*—soul; *yoga-īśvaraḥ*—the Lord of all mysticism; *hariḥ*—the Supreme Lord; *sva-māyayā*—by the personal energy; *āvṛṇot*—covered; *garbham*—embryo; *vairāṭyāḥ*—of Uttarā; *kuru-tantave*—for the progeny of Mahārāja Kuru.

TRANSLATION

The Lord of supreme mysticism, Śrī Kṛṣṇa, resides within everyone's heart as the Paramātmā. As such, just to protect the progeny of the Kuru dynasty, He covered the embryo of Uttarā by His personal energy.

PURPORT

The Lord of supreme mysticism can simultaneously reside within everyone's heart, or even within the atoms, by His Paramātmā feature,

His plenary portion. Therefore, from within the body of Uttarā He covered the embryo to save Mahārāja Parīkṣit and protect the progeny of Mahārāja Kuru, of whom King Pāṇḍu was also a descendant. Both the sons of Dhṛtarāṣṭra and those of Pāṇḍu belonged to the same dynasty of Mahārāja Kuru; therefore both of them were generally known as Kurus. But when there were differences between the two families, the sons of Dhṛtarāṣṭra were known as Kurus whereas the sons of Pāṇḍu were known as Pāṇḍavas. Since the sons and grandsons of Dhṛtarāṣṭra were all killed in the Battle of Kurukṣetra, the last son of the dynasty is designated as the son of the Kurus.

TEXT 15

यद्यप्यस्त्रं ब्रह्मशिरस्त्वमोघं चाप्रतिक्रियम् ।
वैष्णवं तेज आसाद्य समशाम्यद् भृगूद्वह ॥१५॥

yadyapy astraṁ brahma-śiras
tv amoghaṁ cāpratikriyam
vaiṣṇavaṁ teja āsādya
samaśāmyad bhṛgūdvaha

yadyapi—although; *astram*—weapon; *brahma-śiraḥ*—supreme; *tu*—but; *amogham*—without check; *ca*—and; *apratikriyam*—not to be counteracted; *vaiṣṇavam*—in relation with Viṣṇu; *tejaḥ*—strength; *āsādya*—being confronted with; *samaśāmyat*—was neutralized; *bhṛgu-udvaha*—O glory of the family of Bhṛgu.

TRANSLATION

O Śaunaka, although the supreme brahmāstra weapon released by Aśvatthāmā was irresistible and without check or counteraction, it was neutralized and foiled when confronted by the strength of Viṣṇu [Lord Kṛṣṇa].

PURPORT

In the *Bhagavad-gītā* it is said that the *brahmajyoti,* or the glowing transcendental effulgence, is resting on Lord Śrī Kṛṣṇa. In other words, the glowing effulgence known as *brahma-tejas* is nothing but the rays of the Lord, just as the sun rays are rays of the sun disc. So this Brahma weapon also, although materially irresistible, could not surpass the supreme strength of the Lord. The weapon called *brahmāstra*, released by Aśvatthāmā, was neutralized and foiled by Lord Śrī Kṛṣṇa by His own energy; that is to say, He did not wait for any other's help because He is absolute.

TEXT 16

मा मंस्था ह्येतदाश्चर्यं सर्वाश्चर्यमयेऽच्युते ।
य इदं मायया देव्या सृजत्यवति हन्त्यजः ॥१६॥

mā maṁsthā hy etad āścaryaṁ
sarvāścaryamaye 'cyute
ya idaṁ māyayā devyā
sṛjaty avati hanty ajaḥ

mā—do not; *maṁsthāḥ*—think; *hi*—certainly; *etat*—all these; *āścaryam*—wonderful; *sarva*—all; *āścarya-maye*—in the all-mysterious; *acyute*—the infallible; *yaḥ*—one who; *idam*—this (creation); *māyayā*—by His energy; *devyā*—transcendental; *sṛjati*—creates; *avati*—maintains; *hanti*—annihilates; *ajaḥ*—unborn.

TRANSLATION

O brāhmaṇas, do not think this to be especially wonderful in the activities of the mysterious and infallible Personality of Godhead. By His own transcendental energy, He maintains and annihilates all material things, although He Himself is unborn.

PURPORT

The activities of the Lord are always inconceivable to the tiny brain of the living entities. Nothing is impossible for the Supreme Lord, but all His actions are wonderful for us, and thus He is always beyond the range of our conceivable limits. The Lord is the all-powerful, all-perfect Personality of Godhead. The Lord is cent percent perfect, whereas others, namely Nārāyaṇa, Brahmā, Śiva, the demigods and all other living beings, possess only different percentages of such perfection. No one is equal to or greater than Him. He is unrivaled.

TEXT 17

ब्रह्मतेजोविनिर्मुक्तैरात्मजैः सह कृष्णया ।
प्रयाणाभिमुखं कृष्णमिदमाह पृथा सती ॥१७॥

brahma-tejo-vinirmuktair
ātmajaiḥ saha kṛṣṇayā
prayāṇābhimukhaṁ kṛṣṇam
idam āha pṛthā satī

brahma-tejaḥ—the radiation of the *brahmāstra; vinirmuktaiḥ*—being saved from; *ātma-jaiḥ*—along with her sons; *saha*—with; *kṛṣṇayā*—Draupadī; *prayāṇa*—outgoing; *abhimukham*—towards; *kṛṣṇam*—unto Lord Kṛṣṇa; *idam*—this; *āha*—said; *pṛthā*—Kuntī; *satī*—chaste, devoted to the Lord.

TRANSLATION

Thus saved from the radiation of the brahmāstra, Kuntī, the chaste devotee of the Lord, and her five sons and Draupadī addressed Lord Kṛṣṇa as He started for home.

PURPORT

Kuntī is described herein as *satī*, or chaste, due to her unalloyed devotion to Lord Śrī Kṛṣṇa. Her mind will now be expressed in the following prayers for Lord Kṛṣṇa. A chaste devotee of the Lord does not look to others, namely any other living being or demigod, even for deliverance from danger. That was all along the characteristic of the whole family of the Pāṇḍavas. They knew nothing except Kṛṣṇa, and therefore the Lord was also always ready to help them in all respects and in all circumstances. That is the transcendental nature of the Lord. He reciprocates the dependence of the devotee. One should not, therefore, look for help from imperfect living beings or demigods, but one should look for all help from Lord Kṛṣṇa, who is competent to save His devotees. Such a chaste devotee also never asks the Lord for help, but the Lord, out of His own accord, is always anxious to render it.

TEXT 18

कुन्त्युवाच

नमस्ये पुरुषं त्वाद्यमीश्वरं प्रकृतेः परम् ।
अलक्ष्यं सर्वभूतानामन्तर्बहिरवस्थितम् ॥१८॥

kunty uvāca
namasye puruṣaṁ tvādyam
īśvaraṁ prakṛteḥ param
alakṣyaṁ sarva-bhūtānām
antar bahir avasthitam

kuntī uvāca—Śrīmatī Kuntī said; *namasye*—let me bow down; *puruṣam*—the Supreme Person; *tvā*—You; *ādyam*—the original; *īśvaram*—the controller; *prakṛteḥ*—of the material cosmos; *param*—beyond; *alakṣyam*—the invisible; *sarva*—all; *bhūtānām*—of living beings; *antaḥ*—within; *bahiḥ*—without; *avasthitam*—existing.

TRANSLATION

Śrīmatī Kuntī said: O Kṛṣṇa, I offer my obeisances unto You because You are the original personality and are unaffected by the qualities of the material world. You are existing both within and without everything, yet You are invisible to all.

PURPORT

Śrīmatī Kuntīdevī was quite aware that Kṛṣṇa is the original Personality of Godhead, although He was playing the part of her nephew. Such an enlightened lady could not commit a mistake by offering obeisances unto her nephew. Therefore, she addressed Him as the original *puruṣa* beyond the material cosmos. Although all living entities are also transcendental, they are neither original nor infallible. The living entities are apt to fall down under the clutches of material nature, but the Lord is never like that. In the *Vedas*, therefore, He is described as the chief among all living entities (*nityo nityānāṁ cetanaś cetanānām*). Then again He is addressed as *īśvara*, or the controller. The living entities or the demigods like Candra and Sūrya are also to some extent *īśvara*, but none of them is the supreme *īśvara*, or the ultimate controller. He is the *parameśvara*, or the Supersoul. He is both within and without. Although He was present before Śrīmatī Kuntī as her nephew, He was also within her and everyone else. In the *Bhagavad-gītā* (15.15) the Lord says, "I am situated in everyone's heart, and only due to Me one remembers, forgets and is cognizant, etc. Through all the *Vedas* I am to be known because I am the compiler of the *Vedas*, and I am the teacher of the *Vedānta.*" Queen Kuntī affirms that the Lord, although both within and without all living beings, is still invisible. The Lord is, so to speak, a puzzle for the common man. Queen Kuntī experienced personally that Lord Kṛṣṇa was present before her, yet He entered within the womb of Uttarā to save her embryo from the attack of Aśvatthāmā's *brahmāstra.* Kuntī herself was puzzled about whether Śrī Kṛṣṇa is all-pervasive or localized. In fact, He is both, but He reserves the right of not being exposed to persons who are not surrendered souls. This checking curtain is called the *māyā* energy of the Supreme Lord, and it controls the limited vision of the rebellious soul. It is explained as follows.

TEXT 19

मायाजवनिकाच्छन्नमज्ञाधोक्षजमव्ययम् ।
न लक्ष्यसे मूढदृशा नटो नाट्यधरो यथा ॥१९॥

māyā-javanikācchannam
ajñādhokṣajam avyayam
na lakṣyase mūḍha-dṛśā
naṭo nāṭyadharo yathā

māyā—deluding; *javanikā*—curtain; *ācchannam*—covered by; *ajñā*—ignorant; *adhokṣajam*—beyond the range of material conception (transcendental); *avyayam*—irreproachable; *na*—not; *lakṣyase*—observed; *mūḍha-dṛśā*—by the foolish observer; *naṭaḥ*—artist; *nāṭya-dharaḥ*—dressed as a player; *yathā*—as.

TRANSLATION

Being beyond the range of limited sense perception, You are the eternally irreproachable factor covered by the curtain of deluding

energy. You are invisible to the foolish observer, exactly as an actor dressed as a player is not recognized.

PURPORT

In the *Bhagavad-gītā* Lord Śrī Kṛṣṇa affirms that less intelligent persons mistake Him to be an ordinary man like us, and thus they deride Him. The same is confirmed herein by Queen Kuntī. The less intelligent persons are those who rebel against the authority of the Lord. Such persons are known as *asuras.* The *asuras* cannot recognize the Lord's authority. When the Lord Himself appears amongst us, as Rāma, Nṛsiṁha, Varāha or in His original form as Kṛṣṇa, He performs many wonderful acts which are humanly impossible. As we shall find in the Tenth Canto of this great literature, Lord Śrī Kṛṣṇa exhibited His humanly impossible activities even from the days of His lying on the lap of His mother. He killed the Pūtanā witch, although she smeared her breast with poison just to kill the Lord. The Lord sucked her breast like a natural baby, and He sucked out her very life also. Similarly, He lifted the Govardhana Hill, just as a boy picks up a frog's umbrella, and stood several days continuously just to give protection to the residents of Vṛndāvana. These are some of the superhuman activities of the Lord described in the authoritative Vedic literatures like the *Purāṇas, Itihāsas* (histories) and *Upaniṣads.* He has delivered wonderful instructions in the shape of the *Bhagavad-gītā.* He has shown marvelous capacities as a hero, as a householder, as a teacher and as a renouncer. He is accepted as the Supreme Personality of Godhead by such authoritative personalities as Vyāsa, Devala, Asita, Nārada, Madhva, Śaṅkara, Rāmānuja, Śrī Caitanya Mahāprabhu, Jīva Gosvāmī, Viśvanātha Cakravartī, Bhaktisiddhānta Sarasvatī and all other authorities of the line. He Himself has declared as much in many places of the authentic literatures. And yet there is a class of men with demoniac mentality who are always reluctant to accept the Lord as the Supreme Absolute Truth. This is partially due to their poor fund of knowledge and partially due to their stubborn obstinacy, which results from various misdeeds in the past and present. Such persons could not recognize Lord Śrī Kṛṣṇa even when He was present before them. Another difficulty is that those who depend more on their imperfect senses cannot realize Him as the Supreme Lord. Such persons are like the modern scientist. They want to know everything by their experimental knowledge. But it is not possible to know the Supreme Person by imperfect experimental knowledge. He is described herein as *adhokṣaja*, or beyond the range of experimental knowledge. All our senses are imperfect. We claim to observe everything and anything, but we must admit that we can observe things under certain material conditions only, which are also beyond our control. The Lord is beyond the observation of sense perception. Queen Kuntī accepts this deficiency of the conditioned soul, especially of the woman class, who are less intelligent. For less intelligent men there must be such things as temples, mosques or churches so that they may begin to recognize the authority of the Lord and hear about Him from authorities in such holy places. For less intelligent men, this beginning of spiritual life is essential, and only foolish men decry the establishment of such places of worship, which are required to raise the standard of spiritual attributes for the mass of people. For less intelligent persons, bowing down before the authority of the Lord, as generally done in the temples, mosques or churches, is as beneficial as it is for the advanced devotees to meditate upon Him by active service.

TEXT 20

तथा परमहंसानां मुनीनाममलात्मनाम् ।
भक्तियोगविधानार्थं कथं पश्येम हि स्त्रियः ॥२०॥

tathā paramahaṁsānāṁ
munīnām amalātmanām
bhakti-yoga-vidhānārthaṁ
kathaṁ paśyema hi striyaḥ

tathā—besides that; *paramahaṁsānām*—of the advanced transcendentalists; *munīnām*—of the great philosophers or mental speculators; *amala-ātmanām*—those whose minds are competent to discern between spirit and matter; *bhakti-yoga*—the science of devotional service; *vidhāna-artham*—for executing; *katham*—how; *paśyema*—can observe; *hi*—certainly; *striyaḥ*—women.

TRANSLATION

You Yourself descend to propagate the transcendental science of devotional service unto the hearts of the advanced

transcendentalists and mental speculators, who are purified by being able to discriminate between matter and spirit. How, then, can we women know You perfectly?

PURPORT

Even the greatest philosophical speculators cannot have access to the region of the Lord. It is said in the *Upaniṣads* that the Supreme Truth, the Absolute Personality of Godhead, is beyond the range of the thinking power of the greatest philosopher. He is unknowable by great learning or by the greatest brain. He is knowable only by one who has His mercy. Others may go on thinking about Him for years together, yet He is unknowable. This very fact is corroborated by the Queen, who is playing the part of an innocent woman. Women in general are unable to speculate like philosophers, but they are blessed by the Lord because they believe at once in the superiority and almightiness of the Lord, and thus they offer obeisances without reservation. The Lord is so kind that He does not show special favor only to one who is a great philosopher. He knows the sincerity of purpose. For this reason only, women generally assemble in great number in any sort of religious function. In every country and in every sect of religion it appears that the women are more interested than the men. This simplicity of acceptance of the Lord's authority is more effective than showy insincere religious fervor.

TEXT 21

कृष्णाय वासुदेवाय देवकीनन्दनाय च ।
नन्दगोपकुमाराय गोविन्दाय नमो नमः ॥२१॥

kṛṣṇāya vāsudevāya
devakī-nandanāya ca
nanda-gopa-kumārāya
govindāya namo namaḥ

kṛṣṇāya—the Supreme Lord; *vāsudevāya*—unto the son of Vasudeva; *devakī-nandanāya*—unto the son of Devakī; *ca*—and; *nanda-gopa*—Nanda and the cowherd men; *kumārāya*—unto their son; *govindāya*—unto the Personality of Godhead, who enlivens the cows and the senses; *namaḥ*—respectful obeisances; *namaḥ*—obeisances.

TRANSLATION

Let me therefore offer my respectful obeisances unto the Lord, who has become the son of Vasudeva, the pleasure of Devakī, the boy of Nanda and the other cowherd men of Vṛndāvana, and the enlivener of the cows and the senses.

PURPORT

The Lord, being thus unapproachable by any material assets, out of unbounded and causeless mercy descends on the earth as He is in order to show His special mercy upon His unalloyed devotees and to diminish the upsurges of the demoniac persons. Queen Kuntī specifically adores the incarnation or descent of Lord Kṛṣṇa above all other incarnations because in this particular incarnation He is more approachable. In the Rāma incarnation He remained a king's son from His very childhood, but in the incarnation of Kṛṣṇa, although He was the son of a king, He at once left the shelter of His real father and mother (King Vasudeva and Queen Devakī) just after His appearance and went to the lap of Yaśodāmāyī to play the part of an ordinary cowherd boy in the blessed Vrajabhūmi, which is very sanctified because of His childhood pastimes. Therefore Lord Kṛṣṇa is more merciful than Lord Rāma. He was undoubtedly very kind to Kuntī's brother Vasudeva and the family. Had He not become the son of Vasudeva and Devakī, Queen Kuntī could not claim Him to be her nephew and thus address Kṛṣṇa in parental affection. But Nanda and Yaśodā are more fortunate because they could relish the Lord's childhood pastimes, which are more attractive than all other pastimes. There is no parallel to His childhood pastimes as exhibited at Vrajabhūmi, which are the prototypes of His eternal affairs in the original Kṛṣṇaloka described as the *cintāmaṇi-dhāma* in the *Brahma-saṁhitā*. Lord Śrī Kṛṣṇa descended Himself at Vrajabhūmi with all His transcendental entourage and paraphernalia. Śrī Caitanya Mahāprabhu therefore confirmed that no one is as fortunate as the residents of Vrajabhūmi, and specifically the cowherd girls, who dedicated their everything for the satisfaction of the Lord. His pastimes with Nanda and Yaśodā and His pastimes with the cowherd men and especially with the cowherd boys and the cows have caused Him to be known as Govinda. Lord Kṛṣṇa as Govinda is more inclined to the *brāhmaṇas* and the cows, indicating thereby that human prosperity depends more on these two items, namely brahminical culture and cow protection. Lord Kṛṣṇa is never satisfied where these are lacking.

TEXT 22

नमः पङ्कजनाभाय नमः पङ्कजमालिने ।
नमः पङ्कजनेत्राय नमस्ते पङ्कजाङ्घ्रये ॥२२॥

namaḥ paṅkaja-nābhāya
namaḥ paṅkaja-māline
namaḥ paṅkaja-netrāya
namas te paṅkajāṅghraye

namaḥ—all respectful obeisances; *paṅkaja-nābhāya*—unto the Lord who has a specific depression resembling a lotus flower in the center of His abdomen; *namaḥ*—obeisances; *paṅkaja-māline*—one who is always decorated with a garland of lotus flowers; *namaḥ*—obeisances; *paṅkaja-netrāya*—one whose glance is as cooling as a lotus flower; *namaḥ te*—respectful obeisances unto You; *paṅkaja-aṅghraye*—unto You, the soles of whose feet are engraved with lotus flowers (and who are therefore said to possess lotus feet).

TRANSLATION

My respectful obeisances are unto You, O Lord, whose abdomen is marked with a depression like a lotus flower, who are always decorated with garlands of lotus flowers, whose glance is as cool as the lotus and whose feet are engraved with lotuses.

PURPORT

Here are some of the specific symbolical marks on the spiritual body of the Personality of Godhead which distinguish His body from the bodies of all others. They are all special features of the body of the Lord. The Lord may appear as one of us, but He is always distinct by His specific bodily features. Śrīmatī Kuntī claims herself unfit to see the Lord because of her being a woman. This is claimed because women, *śūdras* (the laborer class) and the *dvija-bandhus*, or the wretched descendants of the higher three classes, are unfit by intelligence to understand transcendental subject matter concerning the spiritual name, fame, attributes, forms, etc., of the Supreme Absolute Truth. Such persons, although they are unfit to enter into the spiritual affairs of the Lord, can see Him as the *arcā-vigraha,* who descends on the material world just to distribute favors to the fallen souls, including the above-mentioned women, *śūdras* and *dvija-bandhus.* Because such fallen souls cannot see anything beyond matter, the Lord condescends to enter into each and every one of the innumerable universes as the Garbhodakaśāyī Viṣṇu, who grows a lotus stem from the lotuslike depression in the center of His transcendental abdomen, and thus Brahmā, the first living being in the universe, is born. Therefore, the Lord is known as the Paṅkajanābhi. The Paṅkajanābhi Lord accepts the *arcā-vigraha* (His transcendental form) in different elements, namely a form within the mind, a form made of wood, a form made of earth, a form made of metal, a form made of jewel, a form made of paint, a form drawn on sand, etc. All such forms of the Lord are always decorated with garlands of lotus flowers, and there should be a soothing atmosphere in the temple of worship to attract the burning attention of the nondevotees always engaged in material wranglings. The meditators worship a form within the mind. Therefore, the Lord is merciful even to the women, *śūdras* and *dvija-bandhus,* provided they agree to visit the temple of worship in different forms made for them. Such temple visitors are not idolaters, as alleged by some men with a poor fund of knowledge. All the great *ācāryas* established such temples of worship in all places just to favor the less intelligent, and one should not pose himself as transcending the stage of temple worship while one is actually in the category of the *śūdras* and the women or less. One should begin to see the Lord from His lotus feet, gradually rising to the thighs, waist, chest and face. One should not try to look at the face of the Lord without being accustomed to seeing the lotus feet of the Lord. Śrīmatī Kuntī, because of her being the aunt of the Lord, did not begin to see the Lord from the lotus feet because the Lord might feel ashamed, and thus Kuntīdevī, just to save a painful situation for the Lord, began to see the Lord just above His lotus feet, i.e., from the waist of the Lord, gradually rising to the face, and then down to the lotus feet. In the round, everything there is in order.

TEXT 23

यथा हृषीकेश खलेन देवकी
कंसेन रुद्धातिचिरं शुचार्पिता ।

विमोचिताहं च सहात्मजा विभो
त्वयैव नाथेन मुहुर्विपद्गणात् ॥२३॥

yathā hṛṣīkeśa khalena devakī
kaṁsena ruddhāticiraṁ śucārpitā
vimocitāhaṁ ca sahātmajā vibho
tvayaiva nāthena muhur vipad-gaṇāt

yathā—as it were; *hṛṣīkeśa*—the master of the senses; *khalena*—by the envious; *devakī*—Devakī (the mother of Śrī Kṛṣṇa); *kaṁsena*—by King Kaṁsa; *ruddhā*—imprisoned; *ati-ciram*—for a long time; *śuca-arpitā*—distressed; *vimocitā*—released; *aham ca*—also myself; *saha-ātma-jā*—along with my children; *vibho*—O great one; *tvayā eva*—by Your Lordship; *nāthena*—as the protector; *muhuḥ*—constantly; *vipat-gaṇāt*—from a series of dangers.

TRANSLATION

O Hṛṣīkeśa, master of the senses and Lord of lords, You have released Your mother, Devakī, who was long imprisoned and distressed by the envious King Kaṁsa, and me and my children from a series of constant dangers.

PURPORT

Devakī, the mother of Kṛṣṇa and sister of King Kaṁsa, was put into prison along with her husband, Vasudeva, because the envious King was afraid of being killed by Devakī's eighth son (Kṛṣṇa). He killed all the sons of Devakī who were born before Kṛṣṇa, but Kṛṣṇa escaped the danger of child-slaughter because He was transferred to the house of Nanda Mahārāja, Lord Kṛṣṇa's foster father. Kuntīdevī, along with her children, was also saved from a series of dangers. But Kuntīdevī was shown far more favor because Lord Kṛṣṇa did not save the other children of Devakī, whereas He saved the children of Kuntīdevī. This was done because Devakī's husband, Vasudeva, was living, whereas Kuntīdevī was a widow, and there was none to help her except Kṛṣṇa. The conclusion is that Kṛṣṇa endows more favor to a devotee who is in greater dangers. Sometimes He puts His pure devotees in such dangers because in that condition of helplessness the devotee becomes more attached to the Lord. The more the attachment is there for the Lord, the more success is there for the devotee.

TEXT 24

विषान्महाग्नेः पुरुषाददर्शना-
दसत्सभाया वनवासकृच्छ्रतः ।
मृधे मृधेऽनेकमहारथास्त्रतो
द्रौण्यस्त्रतश्चास्म हरेऽभिरक्षिताः ॥२४॥

viṣān mahāgneḥ puruṣāda-darśanād
asat-sabhāyā vana-vāsa-kṛcchrataḥ
mṛdhe mṛdhe 'neka-mahārathāstrato
drauṇy-astratas cāsma hare 'bhirakṣitāḥ

viṣāt—from poison; *mahā-agneḥ*—from the great fire; *puruṣa-ada*—the man-eaters; *darśanāt*—by combating; *asat*—vicious; *sabhāyāḥ*—assembly; *vana-vāsa*—exiled to the forest; *kṛcchrataḥ*—sufferings; *mṛdhe mṛdhe*—again and again in battle; *aneka*—many; *mahā-ratha*—great generals; *astrataḥ*—weapons; *drauṇi*—the son of Droṇācārya; *astrataḥ*—from the weapon of; *ca*—and; *āsma*—indicating past tense; *hare*—O my Lord; *abhirakṣitāḥ*—protected completely.

TRANSLATION

My dear Kṛṣṇa, Your Lordship has protected us from a poisoned cake, from a great fire, from cannibals, from the vicious assembly, from sufferings during our exile in the forest and from the battle where great generals fought. And now You have saved us from the weapon of Aśvatthāmā.

PURPORT

The list of dangerous encounters is submitted herein. Devakī was once put into difficulty by her envious brother, otherwise she was well. But Kuntīdevī and her sons were put into one difficulty after another for years and years together. They were put into trouble by Duryodhana and his party due to the kingdom, and each and every time the sons of Kuntī were saved by the Lord. Once Bhīma was administered poison in a cake, once they were put into the house made of shellac and set afire, and once Draupadī was dragged out, and attempts were made to insult her by stripping her naked in the vicious assembly of the Kurus. The Lord saved Draupadī by supplying an immeasurable length of cloth, and Duryodhana's party failed to see her naked. Similarly, when they were exiled in the forest, Bhīma had to fight with the man-eater demon Hiḍimba Rākṣasa, but the Lord saved him. So it was not finished there. After all these tribulations, there was the great Battle of Kurukṣetra, and Arjuna had to meet such great generals as Droṇa, Bhīṣma and Karṇa, all powerful fighters. And at last, even when everything was done away with, there was the *brahmāstra* released by the son of Droṇācārya to kill the child within the womb of Uttarā, and so the Lord saved the only surviving descendant of the Kurus, Mahārāja Parīkṣit.

TEXT 25

विपदः सन्तु ताः शश्वत्तत्र तत्र जगद्गुरो ।
भवतो दर्शनं यत्स्यादपुनर्भवदर्शनम् ॥२५॥

vipadaḥ santu tāḥ śaśvat
tatra tatra jagad-guro
bhavato darśanaṁ yat syād
apunar bhava-darśanam

vipadaḥ—calamities; *santu*—let there be; *tāḥ*—all; *śaśvat*—again and again; *tatra*—there; *tatra*—and there; *jagat-guro*—O Lord of the universe; *bhavataḥ*—Your; *darśanam*—meeting; *yat*—that which; *syāt*—is; *apunaḥ*—not again; *bhava-darśanam*—seeing repetition of birth and death.

TRANSLATION

I wish that all those calamities would happen again and again so that we could see You again and again, for seeing You means that we will no longer see repeated births and deaths.

PURPORT

Generally the distressed, the needy, the intelligent and the inquisitive, who have performed some pious activities, worship or begin to worship the Lord. Others, who are thriving on misdeeds only, regardless of status, cannot approach the Supreme due to being misled by the illusory energy. Therefore, for a pious person, if there is some calamity there is no other alternative than to take shelter of the lotus feet of the Lord. Constantly remembering the lotus feet of the Lord means preparing for liberation from birth and death. Therefore, even though there are so-called calamities, they are welcome because they give us an opportunity to remember the Lord, which means liberation.

One who has taken shelter of the lotus feet of the Lord, which are accepted as the most suitable boat for crossing the ocean of nescience, can achieve liberation as easily as one leaps over the holes made by the hoofs of a calf. Such persons are meant to reside in the abode of the Lord, and they have nothing to do with a place where there is danger in every step.

This material world is certified by the Lord in the *Bhagavad-gītā* as a dangerous place full of calamities. Less intelligent persons prepare plans to adjust to those calamities without knowing that the nature of this place is itself full of calamities. They have no information of the abode of the Lord, which is full of bliss and without trace of calamity. The duty of the sane person, therefore, is to be undisturbed by worldly calamities, which are sure to happen in all circumstances. Suffering all sorts of unavoidable misfortunes, one should make progress in spiritual realization because that is the mission of human life. The spirit soul is transcendental to all material calamities; therefore, the so-called calamities are called false. A man may see a tiger swallowing him in a dream, and he may cry for this calamity. Actually there is no tiger and there is no suffering; it is simply a case of dreams. In the same way, all calamities of life are said to be dreams. If someone is lucky enough to get in contact with the Lord by devotional service, it is all gain. Contact with the Lord by any one of the nine devotional services is always a forward step on the path going back to Godhead.

TEXT 26

जन्मैश्वर्यश्रुतश्रीभिरेधमानमदः पुमान् ।
नैवार्हत्यभिधातुं वै त्वामकिञ्चनगोचरम् ॥२६॥

janmaiśvarya-śruta-śrībhir
edhamāna-madaḥ pumān
naivārhaty abhidhātuṁ vai
tvām akiñcana-gocaram

janma—birth; *aiśvarya*—opulence; *śruta*—education; *śrībhiḥ*—by the possession of beauty; *edhamāna*—progressively increasing; *madaḥ*—intoxication; *pumān*—the human being; *na*—never; *eva*—ever; *arhati*—deserves; *abhidhātum*—to address in feeling; *vai*—certainly; *tvām*—You; *akiñcana-gocaram*—one who is approached easily by the materially exhausted man.

TRANSLATION

My Lord, Your Lordship can easily be approached, but only by those who are materially exhausted. One who is on the path of [material] progress, trying to improve himself with respectable parentage, great opulence, high education and bodily beauty, cannot approach You with sincere feeling.

PURPORT

Being materially advanced means taking birth in an aristocratic family and possessing great wealth, an education and attractive personal beauty. All materialistic men are mad after possessing all these material opulences, and this is known as the advancement of material civilization. But the result is that by possessing all these material assets one becomes artificially puffed up, intoxicated by such temporary possessions. Consequently, such materially puffed up persons are incapable of uttering the holy name of the Lord by addressing Him feelingly, "O Govinda, O Kṛṣṇa." It is said in the *śāstras* that by once uttering the holy name of the Lord, the sinner gets rid of a quantity of sins that he is unable to commit. Such is the power of uttering the holy name of the Lord. There is not the least exaggeration in this statement. Actually the Lord's holy name has such powerful potency. But there is a quality to such utterances also. It depends on the quality of feeling. A helpless man can feelingly utter the holy name of the Lord, whereas a man who utters the same holy name in great material satisfaction cannot be so sincere. A materially puffed up person may utter the holy name of the Lord occasionally, but he is incapable of uttering the name in quality. Therefore, the four principles of material advancement, namely 1) high parentage, 2) good wealth, 3) high education and 4) attractive beauty, are, so to speak, disqualifications for progress on the path of spiritual advancement. The material covering of the pure spirit soul is an external feature, as much as fever is an external feature of the unhealthy body. The general process is to decrease the degree of the fever and not to aggravate it by maltreatment. Sometimes it is seen that spiritually advanced persons become materially impoverished. This is no discouragement. On the other hand, such impoverishment is a good sign as much as the falling of temperature is a good sign. The principle of life should be to decrease the degree of material intoxication which leads one to be more and more illusioned about the aim of life. Grossly illusioned persons are quite unfit for entrance into the kingdom of God.

TEXT 27

नमोऽकिंचनवित्ताय निवृत्तगुणवृत्तये ।
आत्मारामाय शान्ताय कैवल्यपतये नमः ॥२७॥

namo 'kiñcana-vittāya
nivṛtta-guṇa-vṛttaye
ātmārāmāya śāntāya
kaivalya-pataye namaḥ

namaḥ—all obeisances unto You; *akiñcana-vittāya*—unto the property of the materially impoverished; *nivṛtta*—completely transcendental to the actions of the material modes; *guṇa*—material modes; *vṛttaye*—affection; *ātma-ārāmāya*—one who is self-satisfied; *śāntāya*—the most gentle; *kaivalya-pataye*—unto the master of the monists; *namaḥ*—bowing down.

TRANSLATION

My obeisances are unto You, who are the property of the materially impoverished. You have nothing to do with the actions and reactions of the material modes of nature. You are self-satisfied, and therefore You are the most gentle and are master of the monists.

PURPORT

A living being is finished as soon as there is nothing to possess. Therefore a living being cannot be, in the real sense of the term, a renouncer. A living being renounces something for gaining something more valuable. A student sacrifices his childish proclivities to gain better education. A servant gives up his job for a better job. Similarly, a devotee renounces the material world not for nothing but for something tangible in spiritual value. Śrīla Rūpa Gosvāmī, Sanātana Gosvāmī and Śrīla Raghunātha dāsa Gosvāmī and others gave up their worldly pomp and prosperity for the sake of the service of the Lord. They were big men in the worldly sense. The Gosvāmīs were ministers in the government service of Bengal, and Śrīla Raghunātha dāsa Gosvāmī was the son of a big *zamindar* of his time. But they left everything to gain something superior to what they previously possessed. The devotees are generally without material prosperity, but they have a very secret treasure-house in the lotus feet of the Lord. There is a nice story about Śrīla Sanātana Gosvāmī. He had a touchstone with him, and this stone was left in a pile of refuse. A needy man took it, but later on wondered why the valuable stone was kept in such a neglected place. He therefore asked him for the most valuable thing, and then he was given the holy name of the Lord. *Akiñcana* means one who has nothing to give materially. A factual devotee, or *mahātmā*, does not give anything material to anyone because he has already left all material assets. He can, however, deliver the supreme asset, namely the Personality of Godhead, because He is the only property of a factual devotee. The touchstone of Sanātana Gosvāmī, which was thrown in the rubbish, was not the property of the Gosvāmī, otherwise it would not have been kept in such a place. This specific example is given for the neophyte devotees just to convince them that material hankerings and spiritual advancement go ill together. Unless one is able to see everything as spiritual in relation with the Supreme Lord, one must always distinguish between spirit and matter. A spiritual master like Śrīla Sanātana Gosvāmī, although personally able to see everything as spiritual, set this example for us only because we have no such spiritual vision.

Advancement of material vision or material civilization is a great stumbling block for spiritual advancement. Such material advancement entangles the living being in the bondage of a material body followed by all sorts of material miseries. Such material advancement is called *anartha*, or things not wanted. Actually this is so. In the present context of material advancement one uses lipstick at a cost of fifty cents, and there are so many unwanted things which are all products of the material conception of life. By diverting attention to so many unwanted things, human energy is spoiled without achievement of spiritual realization, the prime necessity of human life. The attempt to reach the moon is another example of spoiling energy because even if the moon is reached, the problems of life will not be solved. The devotees of the Lord are called *akiñcanas* because they have practically no material assets. Such material assets are all products of the three modes of material nature. They foil spiritual energy, and thus the less we possess such products of material nature, the more we have a good chance for spiritual progress.

The Supreme Personality of Godhead has no direct connection with material activities. All His acts and deeds, which are exhibited even in this material world, are spiritual and without affection for the modes of material nature. In the *Bhagavad-gītā* the Lord says that all His acts, even His appearance and disappearance in and out of the material world, are transcendental, and one who knows this perfectly shall not take his birth again in this material world, but will go back to Godhead.

The material disease is due to hankering after and lording it over material nature. This hankering is due to an interaction of the three modes of nature, and neither the Lord nor the devotees have attachment for such false enjoyment. Therefore, the Lord and the devotees are called *nivṛtta-guṇa-vṛtti*. The perfect *nivṛtta-guṇa-vṛtti* is the Supreme Lord because He never becomes attracted by the modes of material nature, whereas the living beings have such a tendency. Some of them are entrapped by the illusory attraction of material nature.

Because the Lord is the property of the devotees, and the devotees are the property of the Lord reciprocally, the devotees are certainly transcendental to the modes of material nature. That is a natural conclusion. Such unalloyed devotees are distinct from the mixed devotees who approach the Lord for mitigation of miseries and poverty or because of inquisitiveness and speculation. The unalloyed devotees and the Lord are transcendentally attached to one another. For others, the Lord has nothing to reciprocate, and therefore He is called *ātmārāma*, self-satisfied. Self-satisfied as He is, He is the master of all monists who seek to merge into the existence of the Lord. Such monists merge within the personal effulgence of the Lord called the *brahmajyoti*, but the devotees enter into the transcendental pastimes of the Lord, which are never to be misunderstood as material.

TEXT 28

मन्ये त्वां कालमीशानमनादिनिधनं विभुम् ।
समं चरन्तं सर्वत्र भूतानां यन्मिथः कलिः ॥२८॥

manye tvāṁ kālam īśānam
anādi-nidhanaṁ vibhum
samaṁ carantaṁ sarvatra
bhūtānāṁ yan mithaḥ kaliḥ

manye—I consider; *tvām*—Your Lordship; *kālam*—the eternal time; *īśānam*—the Supreme Lord; *anādi-nidhanam*—without beginning and end; *vibhum*—all-pervading; *samam*—equally merciful; *carantam*—distributing; *sarvatra*—everywhere; *bhūtānām*—of the living beings; *yat mithaḥ*—by intercourse; *kaliḥ*—dissension.

TRANSLATION

My Lord, I consider Your Lordship to be eternal time, the supreme controller, without beginning and end, the all-pervasive one. In distributing Your mercy, You are equal to everyone. The dissensions between living beings are due to social intercourse.

PURPORT

Kuntīdevī knew that Kṛṣṇa was neither her nephew nor an ordinary family member of her paternal house. She knew perfectly well that Kṛṣṇa is the primeval Lord who lives in everyone's heart as the Supersoul, Paramātmā. Another name of the Paramātmā feature of the Lord is *kāla*, or eternal time. Eternal time is the witness of all our actions, good and bad, and thus resultant reactions are destined by Him. It is no use saying that we do not know why and for what we are suffering. We may forget the misdeed for which we may suffer at this present moment, but we must remember that Paramātmā is our constant companion, and therefore He knows everything, past, present and future. And because the Paramātmā feature of Lord Kṛṣṇa destines all actions and reactions, He is the supreme controller also. Without His sanction not a blade of grass can move. The living beings are given as much freedom as they deserve, and misuse of that freedom is the cause of suffering. The devotees of the Lord do not misuse their freedom, and therefore they are the good sons of the Lord. Others, who misuse freedom, are put into miseries destined by the eternal *kāla.* The *kāla* offers the conditioned souls both happiness and miseries. It is all predestined by eternal time. As we have miseries uncalled-for, so we may have happiness also without being asked, for they are all predestined by *kāla.* No one is therefore either an enemy or friend of the Lord. Everyone is suffering and enjoying the result of his own destiny. This destiny is made by the living beings in course of social intercourse. Everyone here wants to lord it over the material nature, and thus everyone creates his own destiny under the supervision of the Supreme Lord. He is all-pervading and therefore He can see everyone's activities. And because the Lord has no beginning or end, He is known also as the eternal time, *kāla.*

TEXT 29

न वेद कश्चिद्भगवंश्चिकीर्षितं
तवेहमानस्य नृणां विडम्बनम् ।
न यस्य कश्चिद्दयितोऽस्ति कर्हिचिद्
द्वेष्यश्च यस्मिन् विषमा मतिर्नृणाम् ॥२९॥

na veda kaścid bhagavaṁś cikīrṣitaṁ
tavehamānasya nṛṇāṁ viḍambanam
na yasya kaścid dayito 'sti karhicid
dveṣyaś ca yasmin viṣamā matir nṛṇām

na—does not; *veda*—know; *kaścit*—anyone; *bhagavan*—O Lord; *cikīrṣitam*—pastimes; *tava*—Your; *īhamānasya*—like the worldly men; *nṛṇām*—of the people in general; *viḍambanam*—misleading; *na*—never; *yasya*—His; *kaścit*—anyone; *dayitaḥ*—object of specific favor;

asti—there is; *karhicit*—anywhere; *dveṣyaḥ*—object of envy; *ca*—and; *yasmin*—unto Him; *viṣamā*—partiality; *matiḥ*—conception; *nṛṇām*—of the people.

TRANSLATION

O Lord, no one can understand Your transcendental pastimes, which appear to be human and so are misleading. You have no specific object of favor, nor do You have any object of envy. People only imagine that You are partial.

PURPORT

The Lord's mercy upon the fallen souls is equally distributed. He has no one as the specific object of hostility. The very conception of the Personality of Godhead as a human being is misleading. His pastimes *appear* to be exactly like a human being's, but actually they are transcendental and without any tinge of material contamination. He is undoubtedly known as partial to His pure devotees, but in fact He is never partial, as much as the sun is never partial to anyone. By utilizing the sun rays, sometimes even the stones become valuable, whereas a blind man cannot see the sun, although there are enough sun rays before him. Darkness and light are two opposite conceptions, but this does not mean that the sun is partial in distributing its rays. The sun rays are open to everyone, but the capacities of the receptacles differ. Foolish people think that devotional service is flattering the Lord to get special mercy. Factually the pure devotees who are engaged in the transcendental loving service of the Lord are not a mercantile community. A mercantile house renders service to someone in exchange for values. The pure devotee does not render service unto the Lord for such exchange, and therefore the full mercy of the Lord is open for him. Suffering and needy men, inquisitive persons or philosophers make temporary connections with the Lord to serve a particular purpose. When the purpose is served, there is no more relation with the Lord. A suffering man, if he is pious at all, prays to the Lord for his recovery. But as soon as the recovery is over, in most cases the suffering man no longer cares to keep any connection with the Lord. The mercy of the Lord is open for him, but he is reluctant to receive it. That is the difference between a pure devotee and a mixed devotee.

Those who are completely against the service of the Lord are considered to be in abject darkness, those who ask for the Lord's favor only at the time of necessity are partial recipients of the mercy of the Lord, and those who are cent percent engaged in the service of the Lord are full recipients of the mercy of the Lord. Such partiality in receiving the Lord's mercy is relative to the recipient, and it is not due to the partiality of the all-merciful Lord.

When the Lord descends on this material world by His all-merciful energy, He plays like a human being, and therefore it appears that the Lord is partial to His devotees only, but that is not a fact. Despite such apparent manifestation of partiality, His mercy is equally distributed. In the Battlefield of Kurukṣetra all persons who died in the fight before the presence of the Lord got salvation without the necessary qualifications because death before the presence of the Lord purifies the passing soul from the effects of all sins, and therefore the dying man gets a place somewhere in the transcendental abode. Somehow or other if someone puts himself open in the sun rays, he is sure to get the requisite benefit both by heat and by ultraviolet rays. Therefore, the conclusion is that the Lord is never partial. It is wrong for the people in general to think of Him as partial.

TEXT 30

जन्म कर्म च विश्वात्मन्नजस्याकर्तुरात्मनः ।
तिर्यङ्नृषिषु यादःसु तदत्यन्तविडम्बनम् ॥३०॥

janma karma ca viśvātmann
ajasyākartur ātmanaḥ
tiryaṅ-nṛṣiṣu yādaḥsu
tad atyanta-viḍambanam

janma—birth; *karma*—activity; *ca*—and; *viśva-ātman*—O soul of the universe; *ajasya*—of the unborn; *akartuḥ*—of the inactive; *ātmanaḥ*—of the vital energy; *tiryak*—animal; *nṛ*—human being; *ṛṣiṣu*—in the sages; *yādaḥsu*—in the water; *tat*—that; *atyanta*—veritable; *viḍambanam*—bewildering.

TRANSLATION

Of course it is bewildering, O soul of the universe, that You work, though You are inactive, and that You take birth, though You are the vital force and the unborn. You Yourself descend amongst animals, men, sages and aquatics. Verily, this is bewildering.

PURPORT

The transcendental pastimes of the Lord are not only bewildering but also apparently contradictory. In other words, they are all inconceivable to the limited thinking power of the human being. The Lord is the all-prevailing Supersoul of all existence, and yet He appears in the form of a boar amongst the animals, in the form of a human being as Rāma, Kṛṣṇa, etc., in the form of a *ṛṣi* like Nārāyaṇa, and in the form of an aquatic like a fish. Yet it is said that He is unborn, and He has nothing to do. In the *śruti mantra* it is said that the Supreme Brahman has nothing to do. No one is equal to or greater than Him. He has manifold energies, and everything is performed by Him perfectly by automatic knowledge, strength and activity. All these statements prove without any question that the Lord's activities, forms and deeds are all inconceivable to our limited thinking power, and because He is inconceivably powerful, everything is possible in Him. Therefore no one can calculate Him exactly; every action of the Lord is bewildering to the common man. He cannot be understood by the Vedic knowledge, but He can be easily understood by the pure devotees because they are intimately related with Him. The devotees therefore know that although He appears amongst the animals, He is not an animal, nor a man, nor a *ṛṣi*, nor a fish. He is eternally the Supreme Lord, in all circumstances.

TEXT 31

गोप्याददे त्वयि कृतागसि दाम तावद्
या ते दशाश्रुकलिलाञ्जनसम्भ्रमाक्षम् ।
वक्त्रं निनीय भयभावनया स्थितस्य
सा मां विमोहयति भीरपि यद्बिभेति ॥३१॥

gopy ādade tvayi kṛtāgasi dāma tāvad
yā te daśāśru-kalilāñjana-sambhramākṣam
vaktraṁ ninīya bhaya-bhāvanayā sthitasya
sā māṁ vimohayati bhīr api yad bibheti

gopī—the cowherd lady (Yaśodā); *ādade*—took up; *tvayi*—on Your; *kṛtāgasi*—creating disturbances (by breaking the butter pot); *dāma*—rope; *tāvat*—at that time; *yā*—that which; *te*—Your; *daśā*—situation; *aśru-kalila*—overflooded with tears; *añjana*—ointment; *sambhrama*—perturbed; *akṣam*—eyes; *vaktram*—face; *ninīya*—downwards; *bhaya-bhāvanayā*—by thoughts of fear; *sthitasya*—of the situation; *sā*—that; *mām*—me; *vimohayati*—bewilders; *bhīḥ api*—even fear personified; *yat*—whom; *bibheti*—is afraid.

TRANSLATION

My dear Kṛṣṇa, Yaśodā took up a rope to bind You when You committed an offense, and Your perturbed eyes overflooded with tears, which washed the mascara from Your eyes. And You were afraid, though fear personified is afraid of You. This sight is bewildering to me.

PURPORT

Here is another explanation of the bewilderment created by the pastimes of the Supreme Lord. The Supreme Lord is the Supreme in all circumstances, as already explained. Here is a specific example of the Lord's being the Supreme and at the same time a plaything in the presence of His pure devotee. The Lord's pure devotee renders service unto the Lord out of unalloyed love only, and while discharging such devotional service the pure devotee forgets the position of the Supreme Lord. The Supreme Lord also accepts the loving service of His devotees more relishably when the service is rendered spontaneously out of pure affection, without anything of reverential admiration. Generally the Lord is worshiped by the devotees in a reverential attitude, but the Lord is meticulously pleased when the devotee, out of pure affection and love, considers the Lord to be less important than himself. The Lord's pastimes in the original abode of Goloka Vṛndāvana are exchanged in that spirit. The friends of Kṛṣṇa consider Him one of them. They do not consider Him to be of reverential importance. The parents of the Lord (who are all pure devotees) consider Him a child only. The Lord accepts the chastisements of the parents more cheerfully than the prayers of the Vedic hymns. Similarly, He accepts the reproaches of His fiancées more palatably than the Vedic hymns. When Lord Kṛṣṇa was present in this material world to manifest His eternal pastimes of the transcendental realm of Goloka Vṛndāvana as an attraction for the people in general, He displayed a unique picture of subordination before His foster mother, Yaśodā. The Lord, in His naturally childish playful activities, used to spoil the stocked butter of mother Yaśodā by breaking the pots and distributing the contents to His friends and playmates, including the celebrated monkeys of Vṛndāvana, who took advantage of the Lord's munificence. Mother Yaśodā saw this, and out of her pure love she wanted to make a show of punishment for her transcendental child. She took a rope and threatened the Lord that she would tie Him up, as is generally done in the ordinary household. Seeing the rope in the hands of mother Yaśodā, the Lord bowed down His head and began to weep just like a child, and tears rolled down His cheeks, washing off the black ointment smeared about His beautiful eyes. This picture of the Lord is adored by Kuntīdevī because she is conscious of the Lord's supreme position. He is feared often by fear personified, yet He is afraid of His mother, who wanted to punish Him just in an ordinary manner. Kuntī was conscious of the exalted position of Kṛṣṇa, whereas Yaśodā was not. Therefore Yaśodā's position was more exalted than Kuntī's. Mother Yaśodā got the Lord as her child, and the Lord made her forget altogether that her child was the Lord Himself. If mother Yaśodā had been conscious of the exalted position of the Lord, she would certainly have hesitated to punish the Lord. But she was made to forget this situation because the Lord wanted to make a complete gesture of childishness before the affectionate Yaśodā. This exchange of love between the mother and the son was performed in a natural way, and Kuntī, remembering the scene, was bewildered, and she could do nothing but praise the transcendental filial love. Indirectly mother Yaśodā is praised for her unique position of love, for she could control even the all-powerful Lord as her beloved child.

TEXT 32

केचिदाहुरजं जातं पुण्यश्लोकस्य कीर्तये ।
यदोः प्रियस्यान्ववाये मलयस्येव चन्दनम् ॥३२॥

kecid āhur ajaṁ jātaṁ
puṇya-ślokasya kīrtaye
yadoḥ priyasyānvavāye
malayasyeva candanam

kecit—someone; *āhuḥ*—says; *ajam*—the unborn; *jātam*—being born; *puṇya-ślokasya*—of the great pious king; *kīrtaye*—for glorifying; *yadoḥ*—of King Yadu; *priyasya*—of the dear; *anvavāye*—in the family of; *malayasya*—Malaya hills; *iva*—as; *candanam*—sandalwood.

TRANSLATION

Some say that the Unborn is born for the glorification of pious kings, and others say that He is born to please King Yadu, one of Your dearest devotees. You appear in his family as sandalwood appears in the Malaya hills.

PURPORT

Because the Lord's appearance in this material world is bewildering, there are different opinions about the birth of the Unborn. In the *Bhagavad-gītā* the Lord says that He takes His birth in the material world, although He is the Lord of all creations and He is unborn. So there cannot be any denial of the birth of the Unborn because He Himself establishes the truth. But still there are different opinions as to why He takes His birth. That is also declared in the *Bhagavad-gītā.* He appears by His own internal potency to reestablish the principles of religion and to protect the pious and to annihilate the impious. That is the mission of the appearance of the Unborn. Still, it is said that the Lord is there to glorify the pious King Yudhiṣṭhira. Lord Śrī Kṛṣṇa certainly wanted to establish the kingdom of the Pāṇḍavas for the good of all in the world. When there is a pious king ruling over the world, the people are happy. When the ruler is impious, the people are unhappy. In the age of Kali in most cases the rulers are impious, and therefore the citizens are also continuously unhappy. But in the case of democracy, the impious citizens themselves elect their representative to rule over them, and therefore they cannot blame anyone for their unhappiness. Mahārāja Nala was also celebrated as a great pious king, but he had no connection with Lord Kṛṣṇa. Therefore Mahārāja Yudhiṣṭhira is meant here to be glorified by Lord Kṛṣṇa. He had also glorified King Yadu, having taken His birth in the family. He is known as Yādava, Yaduvīra, Yadunandana, etc., although the Lord is always independent of such obligation. He is just like the sandalwood that grows in the Malaya hills. Trees can grow anywhere and everywhere, yet because the sandalwood trees grow mostly in the area of the Malaya hills, the name sandalwood and the Malaya hills are interrelated. Therefore, the conclusion is that the Lord is ever unborn like the sun, and yet He appears as the sun rises on the eastern horizon. As the sun is never the sun of the eastern horizon, so the Lord is no one's son, but He is the father of everything that be.

TEXT 33

अपरे वसुदेवस्य देवक्यां याचितोऽभ्यगात् ।
अजस्त्वमस्य क्षेमाय वधाय च सुरद्विषाम् ॥३३॥

apare vasudevasya
devakyāṁ yācito 'bhyagāt
ajas tvam asya kṣemāya
vadhāya ca sura-dviṣām

apare—others; *vasudevasya*—of Vasudeva; *devakyām*—of Devakī; *yācitaḥ*—being prayed for; *abhyagāt*—took birth; *ajaḥ*—unborn; *tvam*—You are; *asya*—of him; *kṣemāya*—for the good; *vadhāya*—for the purpose of killing; *ca*—and; *sura-dviṣām*—of those who are envious of the demigods.

TRANSLATION

Others say that since both Vasudeva and Devakī prayed for You, You have taken Your birth as their son. Undoubtedly You are unborn, yet You take Your birth for their welfare and to kill those who are envious of the demigods.

PURPORT

It is also said that Vasudeva and Devakī, in their previous birth as Sutapa and Pṛśni, underwent a severe type of penance to get the Lord as their son, and as a result of such austerities the Lord appeared as their son. It is already declared in the *Bhagavad-gītā* that the Lord appears for the welfare of all people of the world and to vanquish the *asuras*, or the materialistic atheists.

TEXT 34

भारावतारणायान्ये भुवो नाव इवोदधौ ।
सीदन्त्या भूरिभारेण जातो ह्यात्मभुवार्थितः ॥३४॥

bhārāvatāraṇāyānye
bhuvo nāva ivodadhau
sīdantyā bhūri-bhāreṇa
jāto hy ātma-bhuvārthitaḥ

bhāra-avatāraṇāya—just to reduce the burden to the world; *anye*—others; *bhuvaḥ*—of the world; *nāvaḥ*—boat; *iva*—like; *udadhau*—on the sea; *sīdantyāḥ*—aggrieved; *bhūri*—extremely; *bhāreṇa*—by the burden; *jātaḥ*—You were born; *hi*—certainly; *ātma-bhuvā*—by Brahmā; *arthitaḥ*—being prayed for.

TRANSLATION

Others say that the world, being overburdened like a boat at sea, is much aggrieved, and that Brahmā, who is Your son, prayed for You, and so You have appeared to diminish the trouble.

PURPORT

Brahmā, or the first living being born just after the creation, is the direct son of Nārāyaṇa. Nārāyaṇa, as Garbhodakaśāyī Viṣṇu, first of all entered the material universe. Without spiritual contact, matter cannot create. This principle was followed from the very beginning of the creation. The Supreme Spirit entered the universe, and the first living being, Brahmā, was born on a lotus flower grown out of the transcendental abdomen of Viṣṇu. Viṣṇu is therefore known as Padmanābha.

Brahmā is known as *ātma-bhū* because he was begotten directly from the father without any contact of mother Lakṣmījī. Lakṣmījī was present near Nārāyaṇa, engaged in the service of the Lord, and still, without contact with Lakṣmījī, Nārāyaṇa begot Brahmā. That is the omnipotency of the Lord. One who foolishly considers Nārāyaṇa like other living beings should take a lesson from this. Nārāyaṇa is not an ordinary living being. He is the Personality of Godhead Himself, and He has all the potencies of all the senses in all parts of His transcendental body. An ordinary living being begets a child by sexual intercourse, and he has no other means to beget a child other than the one designed for him. But Nārāyaṇa, being omnipotent, is not bound to any condition of energy. He is complete and independent to do anything and everything by His various potencies, very easily and perfectly. Brahmā is therefore directly the son of the father and was not put into the womb of a mother. Therefore he is known as *ātma-bhū*. This Brahmā is in charge of further creations in the universe, secondarily reflected by the potency of the Omnipotent. Within the halo of the universe there is a transcendental planet known as Śvetadvīpa, which is the abode of the Kṣīrodakaśāyī Viṣṇu, the Paramātmā feature of the Supreme Lord. Whenever there is trouble in the universe that cannot be solved by the administrative demigods, they approach Brahmājī for a solution, and if it is not to be solved even by Brahmājī, then Brahmājī consults and prays to the Kṣīrodakaśāyī Viṣṇu for an incarnation and solution to the problems. Such a problem arose when Kaṁsa and others were ruling over the earth and the earth became too much overburdened by the misdeeds of the *asuras*. Brahmājī, along with other demigods, prayed at the shore of the Kṣīrodaka Ocean, and they were advised of the descent of Kṛṣṇa as the son of Vasudeva and Devakī. So some people say that the Lord appeared because of the prayers of Brahmājī.

TEXT 35

भवेऽस्मिन् क्लिश्यमानानामविद्याकामकर्मभिः ।
श्रवणस्मरणार्हाणि करिष्यन्निति केचन ॥३५॥

bhave 'smin kliśyamānānām
avidyā-kāma-karmabhiḥ

śravaṇa-smaraṇārhāṇi
kariṣyann iti kecana

bhave—in the material creation; *asmin*—this; *kliśyamānānām*—of those who are suffering from; *avidyā*—nescience; *kāma*—desire; *karmabhiḥ*—by execution of fruitive work; *śravaṇa*—hearing; *smaraṇa*—remembering; *arhāṇi*—worshiping; *kariṣyan*—may perform; *iti*—thus; *kecana*—others.

TRANSLATION

And yet others say that You appeared to rejuvenate the devotional service of hearing, remembering, worshiping and so on in order that the conditioned souls suffering from material pangs might take advantage and gain liberation.

PURPORT

In the *Śrīmad Bhagavad-gītā* the Lord asserts that He appears in every millennium just to reestablish the way of religion. The way of religion is made by the Supreme Lord. No one can manufacture a new path of religion, as is the fashion for certain ambitious persons. The factual way of religion is to accept the Lord as the supreme authority and thus render service unto Him in spontaneous love. A living being cannot help but render service because he is constitutionally made for that purpose. The only function of the living being is to render service to the Lord. The Lord is great, and living beings are subordinate to Him. Therefore, the duty of the living being is just to serve Him only. Unfortunately the illusioned living beings, out of misunderstanding only, become servants of the senses by material desire. This desire is called *avidyā*, or nescience. And out of such desire the living being makes different plans for material enjoyment centered about a perverted sex life. He therefore becomes entangled in the chain of birth and death by transmigrating into different bodies on different planets under the direction of the Supreme Lord. Unless, therefore, one is beyond the boundary of this nescience, one cannot get free from the threefold miseries of material life. That is the law of nature.

The Lord, however, out of His causeless mercy, because He is more merciful to the suffering living beings than they can expect, appears before them and renovates the principles of devotional service comprised of hearing, chanting, remembering, serving, worshiping, praying, cooperating and surrendering unto Him. Adoption of all the above-mentioned items, or any one of them, can help a conditioned soul get out of the tangle of nescience and thus become liberated from all material sufferings created by the living being illusioned by the external energy. This particular type of mercy is bestowed upon the living being by the Lord in the form of Lord Śrī Caitanya Mahāprabhu.

TEXT 36

शृण्वन्ति गायन्ति गृणन्त्यभीक्ष्णशः
स्मरन्ति नन्दन्ति तवेहितं जनाः ।
त एव पश्यन्त्यचिरेण तावकं
भवप्रवाहोपरमं पदाम्बुजम् ॥३६॥

śṛṇvanti gāyanti gṛṇanty abhīkṣṇaśaḥ
smaranti nandanti tavehitaṁ janāḥ
ta eva paśyanty acireṇa tāvakaṁ
bhava-pravāhoparamaṁ padāmbujam

śṛṇvanti—hear; *gāyanti*—chant; *gṛṇanti*—take; *abhīkṣṇaśaḥ*—continuously; *smaranti*—remember; *nandanti*—take pleasure; *tava*—Your; *īhitam*—activities; *janāḥ*—people in general; *te*—they; *eva*—certainly; *paśyanti*—can see; *acireṇa*—very soon; *tāvakam*—Your; *bhava-pravāha*—the current of rebirth; *uparamam*—cessation; *pada-ambujam*—lotus feet.

TRANSLATION

O Kṛṣṇa, those who continuously hear, chant and repeat Your transcendental activities, or take pleasure in others' doing so, certainly see Your lotus feet, which alone can stop the repetition of birth and death.

PURPORT

The Supreme Lord Śrī Kṛṣṇa cannot be seen by our present conditional vision. In order to see Him, one has to change his present vision by developing a different condition of life full of spontaneous love of Godhead. When Śrī Kṛṣṇa was personally present on the face of the globe, not everyone could see Him as the Supreme Personality of Godhead. Materialists like Rāvaṇa, Hiraṇyakaśipu, Kaṁsa, Jarāsandha and Śiśupāla, were highly qualified personalities by acquisition of material assets, but they were unable to appreciate the presence of the Lord. Therefore, even though the Lord may be present before our eyes, it is not possible to see Him unless we have the necessary vision. This necessary qualification is developed by the process of devotional service only, beginning with hearing about the Lord from the right sources. The *Bhagavad-gītā* is one of the popular literatures which are generally heard, chanted, repeated, etc., by the people in general, but in spite of such hearing, etc., sometimes it is experienced that the performer of such devotional service does not see the Lord eye to eye. The reason is that the first item, *śravaṇa*, is very important. If hearing is from the right sources, it acts very quickly. Generally people hear from unauthorized persons. Such unauthorized persons may be very learned by academic qualifications, but because they do not follow the principles of devotional service, hearing from them becomes a sheer waste of time. Sometimes the texts are interpreted fashionably to suit their own purposes. Therefore, first one should select a competent and bona fide speaker and then hear from him. When the hearing process is perfect and complete, the other processes become automatically perfect in their own way.

There are different transcendental activities of the Lord, and each and every one of them is competent to bestow the desired result, provided the hearing process is perfect. In the *Bhāgavatam* the activities of the Lord begin from His dealings with the Pāṇḍavas. There are many other pastimes of the Lord in connection with His dealings with the *asuras* and others. And in the Tenth Canto the sublime dealings with His conjugal associates, the *gopīs*, as well as with His married wives at Dvārakā are mentioned. Since the Lord is absolute, there is no difference in the transcendental nature of each and every dealing of the Lord. But sometimes people, in an unauthorized hearing process, take more interest in hearing about His dealings with the *gopīs*. Such an inclination indicates the lusty feelings of the hearer, so a bona fide speaker of the dealings of the Lord never indulges in such hearings. One must hear about the Lord from the very beginning, as in the *Śrīmad-Bhāgavatam* or any other scriptures, and that will help the hearer attain perfection by progressive development. One should not, therefore, consider that His dealings with the Pāṇḍavas are less important than His dealings with the *gopīs*. We must always remember that the Lord is always transcendental to all mundane attachment. In all the above-mentioned dealings of the Lord, He is the hero in all circumstances, and hearing about Him or about His devotees or combatants is conducive to spiritual life. It is said that the *Vedas* and *Purāṇas*, etc., are all made to revive our lost relation with Him. Hearing of all these scriptures is essential.

TEXT 37

अप्यद्य नस्त्वं स्वकृतेहित प्रभो
जिहाससि स्वित्सुहृदोऽनुजीविनः ।
येषां न चान्यद्भवतः पदाम्बुजात्
परायणं राजसु योजितांहसाम् ॥३७॥

apy adya nas tvaṁ sva-kṛtehita prabho
jihāsasi svit suhṛdo 'nujīvinaḥ
yeṣāṁ na cānyad bhavataḥ padāmbujāt
parāyaṇaṁ rājasu yojitāṁhasām

api—if; *adya*—today; *naḥ*—us; *tvam*—You; *sva-kṛta*—self-executed; *īhita*—all duties; *prabho*—O my Lord; *jihāsasi*—giving up; *svit*—possibly; *suhṛdaḥ*—intimate friends; *anujīvinaḥ*—living at the mercy of; *yeṣām*—of whom; *na*—nor; *ca*—and; *anyat*—anyone else; *bhavataḥ*—Your; *pada-ambujāt*—from the lotus feet; *parāyaṇam*—dependent; *rājasu*—unto the kings; *yojita*—engaged in; *aṁhasām*—enmity.

TRANSLATION

O my Lord, You have executed all duties Yourself. Are you leaving us today, though we are completely dependent on Your mercy and have no one else to protect us, now when all kings are at enmity with us?

PURPORT

The Pāṇḍavas are most fortunate because with all good luck they were entirely dependent on the mercy of the Lord. In the material world, to be dependent on the mercy of someone else is the utmost sign of misfortune, but in the case of our transcendental relation with the Lord, it is the most fortunate case when we can live completely dependent on Him. The material disease is due to thinking of becoming independent of everything. But the cruel material nature does not allow us to become independent. The false attempt to become independent of the stringent laws of nature is known as material advancement of experimental knowledge. The whole material world is moving on this false attempt of becoming independent of the laws of nature. Beginning from Rāvaṇa, who wanted to prepare a direct staircase to the planets of heaven, down to the present age, they are trying to overcome the laws of nature. They are trying now to approach distant planetary systems by electronic mechanical power. But the highest goal of human civilization is to work hard under the guidance of the Lord and become completely dependent on Him. The highest achievement of perfect civilization is to work with valor but at the same time depend completely on the Lord. The Pāṇḍavas were the ideal executors of this standard of civilization. Undoubtedly they were completely dependent on the good will of Lord Śrī Kṛṣṇa, but they were not idle parasites of the Lord. They were all highly qualified both by personal character and by physical activities. Still they always looked for the mercy of the Lord because they knew that every living being is dependent by constitutional position. The perfection of life is, therefore, to become dependent on the will of the Lord, instead of becoming falsely independent in the material world. Those who try to become falsely independent of the Lord are called *anātha*, or without any guardian, whereas those who are completely dependent on the will of the Lord are called *sanātha*, or those having someone to protect them. Therefore we must try to be *sanātha* so that we can always be protected from the unfavorable condition of material existence. By the deluding power of the external material nature we forget that the material condition of life is the most undesirable perplexity. The *Bhagavad-gītā* therefore directs us (7.19) that after many, many births one fortunate person becomes aware of the fact that Vāsudeva is all in all and that the best way of leading one's life is to surrender unto Him completely. That is the sign of a *mahātmā*. All the members of the Pāṇḍava family were *mahātmās* in household life. Mahārāja Yudhiṣṭhira was the head of these *mahātmās*, and Queen Kuntīdevī was the mother. The lessons of the *Bhagavad-gītā* and all the *Purāṇas*, specifically the *Bhāgavata Purāṇa*, are therefore inevitably connected with the history of the Pāṇḍava *mahātmās*. For them, separation from the Lord was just like the separation of a fish from water. Śrīmatī Kuntīdevī, therefore, felt such separation like a thunderbolt, and the whole prayer of the Queen is to try to persuade the Lord to stay with them. After the Battle of Kurukṣetra, although the inimical kings were killed, their sons and grandsons were still there to deal with the Pāṇḍavas. It is not only the Pāṇḍavas who were put into the condition of enmity, but all of us are always in such a condition, and the best way of living is to become completely dependent on the will of the Lord and thereby overcome all difficulties of material existence.

TEXT 38

के वयं नामरूपाभ्यां यदुभिः सह पाण्डवाः ।
भवतोऽदर्शनं यर्हि हृषीकाणामिवेशितुः ॥३८॥

ke vayaṁ nāma-rūpābhyāṁ
yadubhiḥ saha pāṇḍavāḥ
bhavato 'darśanaṁ yarhi
hṛṣīkāṇām iveśituḥ

ke—who are; *vayam*—we; *nāma-rūpābhyām*—without fame and ability; *yadubhiḥ*—with the Yadus; *saha*—along with; *pāṇḍavāḥ*—and the Pāṇḍavas; *bhavataḥ*—Your; *adarśanam*—absence; *yarhi*—as if; *hṛṣīkāṇām*—of the senses; *iva*—like; *īśituḥ*—of the living being.

TRANSLATION

As the name and fame of a particular body is finished with the disappearance of the living spirit, similarly if You do not look upon us, all our fame and activities, along with the Pāṇḍavas and Yadus, will end at once.

PURPORT

Kuntīdevī is quite aware that the existence of the Pāṇḍavas is due to Śrī Kṛṣṇa only. The Pāṇḍavas are undoubtedly well established in name and fame and are guided by the great King Yudhiṣṭhira, who is morality personified, and the Yadus are undoubtedly great allies, but without the guidance of Lord Kṛṣṇa all of them are nonentities, as much as the senses of the body are useless without the guidance of consciousness. No one should be proud of his prestige, power and fame without being guided by the favor of the Supreme Lord. The living beings are always dependent, and the ultimate dependable object is the Lord Himself. We may, therefore, invent by our advancement of material knowledge all sorts of counteracting material resources, but without being guided by the Lord all such inventions end in fiasco, however strong and stout the reactionary elements may be.

TEXT 39

नेयं शोभिष्यते तत्र यथेदानीं गदाधर ।
त्वत्पदैरङ्किता भाति स्वलक्षणविलक्षितैः ॥३९॥

neyaṁ śobhiṣyate tatra
yathedānīṁ gadādhara
tvat-padair aṅkitā bhāti
sva-lakṣaṇa-vilakṣitaiḥ

na—not; *iyam*—this land of our kingdom; *śobhiṣyate*—will appear beautiful; *tatra*—then; *yathā*—as it is now; *idānīm*—how; *gadādhara*—O Kṛṣṇa; *tvat*—Your; *padaiḥ*—by the feet; *aṅkitā*—marked; *bhāti*—is dazzling; *sva-lakṣaṇa*—Your own marks; *vilakṣitaiḥ*—by the impressions.

TRANSLATION

O Gadādhara [Kṛṣṇa], our kingdom is now being marked by the impressions of Your feet, and therefore it appears beautiful. But when You leave, it will no longer be so.

PURPORT

There are certain particular marks on the feet of the Lord which distinguish the Lord from others. The marks of a flag, thunderbolt, and instrument to drive an elephant, umbrella, lotus, disc, etc., are on the bottom of the Lord's feet. These marks are impressed upon the soft dust of the land where the Lord traverses. The land of Hastināpura was thus marked while Lord Śrī Kṛṣṇa was there with the Pāṇḍavas, and the kingdom of the Pāṇḍavas thus flourished by such auspicious signs. Kuntīdevī pointed out these distinguished features and was afraid of ill luck in the absence of the Lord.

TEXT 40

इमे जनपदाः स्वृद्धाः सुपक्वौषधिवीरुधः ।
वनाद्रिनद्युदन्वन्तो ह्येधन्ते तव वीक्षितैः ॥४०॥

ime jana-padāḥ svṛddhāḥ
supakvauṣadhi-vīrudhaḥ
vanādri-nady-udanvanto
hy edhante tava vīkṣitaiḥ

ime—all these; *jana-padāḥ*—cities and towns; *svṛddhāḥ*—flourished; *supakva*—mature; *auṣadhi*—herbs; *vīrudhaḥ*—vegetables; *vana*—forests; *adri*—hills; *nadī*—rivers; *udanvantaḥ*—seas; *hi*—certainly; *edhante*—increasing; *tava*—by You; *vīkṣitaiḥ*—seen.

TRANSLATION

All these cities and villages are flourishing in all respects because the herbs and grains are in abundance, the trees are full of fruits, the rivers are flowing, the hills are full of minerals and the oceans full of wealth. And this is all due to Your glancing over them.

PURPORT

Human prosperity flourishes by natural gifts and not by gigantic industrial enterprises. The gigantic industrial enterprises are products of a godless civilization, and they cause the destruction of the noble aims of human life. The more we go on increasing such troublesome industries to squeeze out the vital energy of the human being, the more there will be unrest and dissatisfaction of the people in general, although a few only can live lavishly by exploitation. The natural gifts such as grains and vegetables, fruits, rivers, the hills of jewels and minerals, and the seas full of pearls are supplied by the order of the Supreme, and as He desires, material nature produces them in abundance or restricts them at times. The natural law is that the human being may take advantage of these godly gifts by nature and satisfactorily flourish on them without being captivated by the exploitative motive of lording it over material nature. The more we attempt to exploit material nature according to our whims of enjoyment, the more we shall become entrapped by the reaction of such exploitative attempts. If we have sufficient grains, fruits, vegetables and herbs, then what is the necessity of running a slaughterhouse and killing poor animals? A man need not kill an animal if he has sufficient grains and vegetables to eat. The flow of river waters fertilizes the fields, and there is more than what we need. Minerals are produced in the hills, and the jewels in the ocean. If the human civilization has sufficient grains, minerals, jewels, water, milk, etc., then why should it hanker after terrible industrial enterprises at the cost of the labor of some unfortunate men? But all these natural gifts are dependent on the mercy of the Lord. What we need, therefore, is to be obedient to the laws of the Lord and achieve the perfection of human life by devotional service. The indications by Kuntīdevī are just to the point. She desires that God's mercy be bestowed upon them so that natural prosperity be maintained by His grace.

TEXT 41

अथ विश्वेश विश्वात्मन् विश्वमूर्ते स्वकेषु मे ।
स्नेहपाशमिमं छिन्धि दृढं पाण्डुषु वृष्णिषु ॥४१॥

atha viśveśa viśvātman
viśva-mūrte svakeṣu me
sneha-pāśam imaṁ chindhi
dṛḍhaṁ pāṇḍuṣu vṛṣṇiṣu

atha—therefore; *viśva-īśa*—O Lord of the universe; *viśva-ātman*—O soul of the universe; *viśva-mūrte*—O personality of the universal form; *svakeṣu*—unto my own kinsmen; *me*—my; *sneha-pāśam*—tie of affection; *imam*—this; *chindhi*—cut off; *dṛḍham*—deep; *pāṇḍuṣu*—for the Pāṇḍavas; *vṛṣṇiṣu*—for the Vṛṣṇis also.

TRANSLATION

O Lord of the universe, soul of the universe, O personality of the form of the universe, please, therefore, sever my tie of affection for my kinsmen, the Pāṇḍavas and the Vṛṣṇis.

PURPORT

A pure devotee of the Lord is ashamed to ask anything in self-interest from the Lord. But the householders are sometimes obliged to ask favors from the Lord, being bound by the tie of family affection. Śrīmatī Kuntīdevī was conscious of this fact, and therefore she prayed to the Lord to cut off the affectionate tie from her own kinsmen, the Pāṇḍavas and the Vṛṣṇis. The Pāṇḍavas are her own sons, and the Vṛṣṇis are the members of her paternal family. Kṛṣṇa was equally related to both the families. Both the families required the Lord's help because both were dependent devotees of the Lord. Śrīmatī Kuntīdevī wished Śrī Kṛṣṇa to remain with her sons the Pāṇḍavas, but by His doing so her paternal house would be bereft of the benefit. All these partialities troubled the mind of Kuntī, and therefore she desired to cut off the affectionate tie.

A pure devotee cuts off the limited ties of affection for his family and widens his activities of devotional service for all forgotten souls. The typical example is the band of six Gosvāmīs, who followed the path of Lord Caitanya. All of them belonged to the most enlightened and cultured rich families of the higher castes, but for the benefit of the mass of population they left their comfortable homes and became mendicants. To cut off all family affection means to broaden the field of activities. Without doing this, no one can be qualified as a *brāhmaṇa*, a king, a public leader or a devotee of the Lord. The Personality of Godhead, as an ideal king, showed this by example. Śrī Rāmacandra cut off the tie of affection for His beloved wife to manifest the qualities of an ideal king.

Such personalities as a *brāhmaṇa*, a devotee, a king or a public leader must be very broadminded in discharging their respective duties. Śrīmatī Kuntīdevī was conscious of this fact, and being weak she prayed to be free from such bondage of family affection. The Lord is addressed as the Lord of the universe, or the Lord of the universal mind, indicating His all-powerful ability to cut the hard knot of family affection. Therefore, it is sometimes experienced that the Lord, out of His special affinity towards a weak devotee, breaks the family affection by force of circumstances arranged by His all-powerful energy. By doing so He causes the devotee to become completely dependent on Him and thus clears the path for his going back to Godhead.

TEXT 42

त्वयि मेऽनन्यविषया मतिर्मधुपतेऽसकृत् ।
रतिमुद्वहतादद्धा गङ्गेवौघमुदन्वति ॥४२॥

tvayi me 'nanya-viṣayā
matir madhu-pate 'sakṛt
ratim udvahatād addhā
gaṅgevaugham udanvati

tvayi—unto You; *me*—my; *ananya-viṣayā*—unalloyed; *matiḥ*—attention; *madhu-pate*—O Lord of Madhu; *asakṛt*—continuously; *ratim*—attraction; *udvahatāt*—may overflow; *addhā*—directly; *gaṅgā*—the Ganges; *iva*—like; *ogham*—flows; *udanvati*—down to the sea.

TRANSLATION

O Lord of Madhu, as the Ganges forever flows to the sea without hindrance, let my attraction be constantly drawn unto You without being diverted to anyone else.

PURPORT

Perfection of pure devotional service is attained when all attention is diverted towards the transcendental loving service of the Lord. To cut off the tie of all other affections does not mean complete negation of the finer elements, like affection for someone else. This is not possible. A living being, whoever he may be, must have this feeling of affection for others because this is a symptom of life. The symptoms of life, such as desire, anger, hankerings, feelings of attraction, etc., cannot be annihilated. Only the objective has to be changed. Desire cannot be negated, but in devotional service the desire is changed only for the service of the Lord in place of desire for sense gratification. The so-called affection for family, society, country, etc., consists of different phases of sense gratification. When this desire is changed for the satisfaction of the Lord, it is called devotional service.

In the *Bhagavad-gītā* we can see that Arjuna desired not to fight with his brothers and relations just to satisfy his own personal desires. But when he heard the message of the Lord, *Śrīmad Bhagavad-gītā*, he changed his decision and served the Lord. And for his doing so, he became a famous devotee of the Lord, for it is declared in all the scriptures that Arjuna attained spiritual perfection by devotional service to the Lord in friendship. The fighting was there, the friendship was there, Arjuna was there, and Kṛṣṇa was there, but Arjuna became a different person by devotional service. Therefore, the prayers of Kuntī also indicate the same categorical changes in activities. Śrīmatī Kuntī wanted to serve the Lord without diversion, and that was her prayer. This unalloyed devotion is the ultimate goal of life. Our attention is usually diverted to the service of something which is nongodly or not in the program of the Lord. When the program is changed into the service of the Lord, that is to say when the senses are purified in relation with the service of the Lord, it is called pure unalloyed devotional service. Śrīmatī Kuntīdevī wanted that perfection and prayed for it from the Lord.

Her affection for the Pāṇḍavas and the Vṛṣṇis is not out of the range of devotional service because the service of the Lord and the service of the devotees are identical. Sometimes service to the devotee is more valuable than service to the Lord. But here the affection of Kuntīdevī for the Pāṇḍavas and the Vṛṣṇis was due to family relation. This tie of affection in terms of material relation is the relation of *māyā* because the relations of the body or the mind are due to the influence of the external energy. Relations of the soul, established in relation with the Supreme Soul, are factual relations. When Kuntīdevī wanted to cut off the family relation, she meant to cut off the relation of the skin. The skin relation is the cause of material bondage, but the relation of the soul is the cause of freedom. This relation of the soul to the soul can be established by the via medium of the relation with the Supersoul. Seeing in the darkness is not seeing. But seeing by the light of the sun means to see the sun and everything else which was unseen in the darkness. That is the way of devotional service.

TEXT 43

श्रीकृष्ण कृष्णसख वृष्ण्यृषभावनिध्रुग्
राजन्यवंशदहनानपवर्गवीर्य ।

गोविन्द गोद्विजसुरार्तिहरावतार
योगेश्वराखिलगुरो भगवन्नमस्ते ॥४३॥

śrī-kṛṣṇa kṛṣṇa-sakha vṛṣṇy-ṛṣabhāvani-dhrug-
rājanya-vaṁśa-dahanānapavarga-vīrya
govinda go-dvija-surārti-harāvatāra
yogeśvarākhila-guro bhagavan namas te

śrī-kṛṣṇa—O Śrī Kṛṣṇa; *kṛṣṇa-sakha*—O friend of Arjuna; *vṛṣṇi*—of descendants of Vṛṣṇi; *ṛṣabha*—O chief; *avani*—the earth; *dhruk*—rebellious; *rājanya-vaṁśa*—dynasties of the kings; *dahana*—O annihilator; *anapavarga*—without deterioration of; *vīrya*—prowess; *govinda*—O proprietor of Golokadhāma; *go*—of the cows; *dvija*—the *brāhmaṇas; sura*—the demigods; *arti-hara*—to relieve distress; *avatāra*—O Lord who descends; *yoga-īśvara*—O master of all mystic powers; *akhila*—universal; *guro*—O preceptor; *bhagavan*—O possessor of all opulences; *namaḥ te*—respectful obeisances unto You.

TRANSLATION

O Kṛṣṇa, O friend of Arjuna, O chief amongst the descendants of Vṛṣṇi, You are the destroyer of those political parties which are disturbing elements on this earth. Your prowess never deteriorates. You are the proprietor of the transcendental abode, and You descend to relieve the distresses of the cows, the brāhmaṇas and the devotees. You possess all mystic powers, and You are the preceptor of the entire universe. You are the almighty God, and I offer You my respectful obeisances.

PURPORT

A summary of the Supreme Lord Śrī Kṛṣṇa is made herein by Śrīmatī Kuntīdevī. The almighty Lord has His eternal transcendental abode where He is engaged in keeping *surabhi* cows. He is served by hundreds and thousands of goddesses of fortune. He descends on the material world to reclaim His devotees and to annihilate the disturbing elements in groups of political parties and kings who are supposed to be in charge of administration work. He creates, maintains and annihilates by His unlimited energies, and still He is always full with prowess and does not deteriorate in potency. The cows, the *brāhmaṇas* and the devotees of the Lord are all objects of His special attention because they are very important factors for the general welfare of living beings.

TEXT 44

सूत उवाच
पृथयेत्थं कलपदैः परिणूताखिलोदयः ।
मन्दं जहास वैकुण्ठो मोहयन्निव मायया ॥४४॥

sūta uvāca
pṛthayetthaṁ kala-padaiḥ
pariṇūtākhilodayaḥ
mandaṁ jahāsa vaikuṇṭho
mohayann iva māyayā

sūtaḥ uvāca—Sūta said; *pṛthayā*—by Pṛthā (Kuntī); *ittham*—this; *kala-padaiḥ*—by chosen words; *pariṇūta*—being worshiped; *akhila*—universal; *udayaḥ*—glories; *mandam*—mildly; *jahāsa*—smiled; *vaikuṇṭhaḥ*—the Lord; *mohayan*—captivating; *iva*—like; *māyayā*—His mystic power.

TRANSLATION

Sūta Gosvāmī said: The Lord, thus hearing the prayers of Kuntīdevī, composed in choice words for His glorification, mildly smiled. That smile was as enchanting as His mystic power.

PURPORT

Anything that is enchanting in the world is said to be a representation of the Lord. The conditioned souls, who are engaged in trying to lord it over the material world, are also enchanted by His mystic powers, but His devotees are enchanted in a different way by the glories of the Lord, and His merciful blessings are upon them. His energy is displayed in different ways, as electrical energy works in manifold capacities. Śrīmatī Kuntīdevī has prayed to the Lord just to enunciate a fragment of His glories. All His devotees worship Him in that way, by chosen words, and therefore the Lord is known as Uttamaśloka. No amount of chosen words is sufficient to enumerate the Lord's glory, and yet He is satisfied by such prayers as the father is satisfied even by the broken linguistic attempts of the growing child. The word *māyā* is used both in the sense of delusion and mercy. Herein the word *māyā* is used in the sense of the Lord's mercy upon Kuntīdevī.

TEXT 45

तां बाढमित्युपामन्त्र्य प्रविश्य गजसाह्वयम् ।
स्त्रियश्च स्वपुरं यास्यन् प्रेम्णा राज्ञा निवारितः ॥४५॥

tāṁ bāḍham ity upāmantrya
praviśya gajasāhvayam
striyaś ca sva-puraṁ yāsyan
premṇā rājñā nivāritaḥ

tām—all those; *bāḍham*—accepted; *iti*—thus; *upāmantrya*—subsequently informed; *praviśya*—entering; *gajasāhvayam*—the palace of Hastināpura; *striyaḥ ca*—other ladies; *sva-puram*—own residence; *yāsyan*—while starting for; *premṇā*—with love; *rājñā*—by the King; *nivāritaḥ*—stopped.

TRANSLATION

Thus accepting the prayers of Śrīmatī Kuntīdevī, the Lord subsequently informed other ladies of His departure by entering the palace of Hastināpura. But upon preparing to leave, He was stopped by King Yudhiṣṭhira, who implored Him lovingly.

PURPORT

No one could make Lord Kṛṣṇa stay at Hastināpura when He decided to start for Dvārakā, but the simple request of King Yudhiṣṭhira that the Lord remain there for a few days more was immediately effective. This signifies that the power of King Yudhiṣṭhira was loving affection, which the Lord could not deny. The almighty God is thus conquered only by loving service and nothing else. He is fully independent in all His dealings, but He voluntarily accepts obligations by the loving affection of His pure devotees.

TEXT 46

व्यासाद्यैरीश्वरेहाज्ञैः कृष्णेनाद्भुतकर्मणा ।
प्रबोधितोऽपीतिहासैर्नाबुध्यत शुचार्पितः ॥४६॥

vyāsādyair īśvarehājñaiḥ
kṛṣṇenādbhuta-karmaṇā
prabodhito 'pītihāsair
nābudhyata śucārpitaḥ

vyāsa-ādyaiḥ—by great sages headed by Vyāsa; *īśvara*—the almighty God; *īhā*—by the will of; *jñaiḥ*—by the learned; *kṛṣṇena*—by Kṛṣṇa Himself; *adbhuta-karmaṇā*—by one who performs all superhuman work; *prabodhitaḥ*—being solaced; *api*—although; *itihāsaiḥ*—by evidences from the histories; *na*—not; *abudhyata*—satisfied; *śucā arpitaḥ*—distressed.

TRANSLATION

King Yudhiṣṭhira, who was much aggrieved, could not be convinced, despite instructions by great sages headed by Vyāsa and the Lord Kṛṣṇa Himself, the performer of superhuman feats, and despite all historical evidence.

PURPORT

The pious King Yudhiṣṭhira was mortified because of the mass massacre of human beings in the Battle of Kurukṣetra, especially on his account. Duryodhana was there on the throne, and he was doing well in his administration, and in one sense there was no need of fighting. But on the principle of justice Yudhiṣṭhira was to replace him. The whole clique of politics centered around this point, and all the kings and residents of the whole world became involved in this fight between the rival brothers. Lord Kṛṣṇa was also there on the side of King Yudhiṣṭhira. It is said in the *Mahābhārata, Ādi-parva* (20) that 640,000,000 men were killed in the eighteen days of the Battle of Kurukṣetra, and some hundreds of thousands were missing. Practically this was the greatest battle in the world within five thousand years.

This mass killing simply to enthrone Mahārāja Yudhiṣṭhira was too mortifying, so he tried to be convinced with evidences from histories by great sages like Vyāsa and the Lord Himself that the fight was just because the cause was just. But Mahārāja Yudhiṣṭhira would not be satisfied, even though he was instructed by the greatest personalities of the time. Kṛṣṇa is designated herein as the performer of superhuman actions, but in this particular instance neither He nor Vyāsa could convince King Yudhiṣṭhira. Does it mean that He failed to be a superhuman actor? No, certainly not. The interpretation is that the Lord as *īśvara*, or the Supersoul in the hearts of both King Yudhiṣṭhira and Vyāsa, performed still more superhuman action because the Lord desired it. As Supersoul of King Yudhiṣṭhira, He did not allow the King to be convinced by the words of Vyāsa and others, including Himself, because He desired that the King hear instructions from the dying Bhīṣmadeva, who was another great devotee of the Lord. The Lord wanted that at the last stage of his material existence the great warrior Bhīṣmadeva see Him personally and see his beloved grandchildren, King Yudhiṣṭhira, etc., now situated on the throne, and thus pass away very peacefully. Bhīṣmadeva was not at all satisfied to fight against the Pāṇḍavas, who were his beloved fatherless grandchildren. But the *kṣatriyas* are also very stern people, and therefore he was obliged to take the side of Duryodhana because he was maintained at the expense of Duryodhana. Besides this, the Lord also desired that King Yudhiṣṭhira be pacified by the words of Bhīṣmadeva so that the world could see that Bhīṣmadeva excelled all in knowledge, including the Lord Himself.

TEXT 47

आह राजा धर्मसुतश्चिन्तयन् सुहृदां वधम् ।
प्राकृतेनात्मना विप्राः स्नेहमोहवशं गतः ॥४७॥

āha rājā dharma-sutaś
cintayan suhṛdāṁ vadham
prākṛtenātmanā viprāḥ
sneha-moha-vaśaṁ gataḥ

āha—said; *rājā*—King Yudhiṣṭhira; *dharma-sutaḥ*—the son of Dharma (Yamarāja); *cintayan*—thinking of; *suhṛdām*—of the friends; *vadham*—killing; *prākṛtena*—by material conception only; *ātmanā*—by the self; *viprāḥ*—O *brāhmaṇa; sneha*—affection; *moha*—delusion; *vaśam*—being carried away by; *gataḥ*—having gone.

TRANSLATION

King Yudhiṣṭhira, son of Dharma, overwhelmed by the death of his friends, was aggrieved just like a common, materialistic man. O sages, thus deluded by affection, he began to speak.

PURPORT

King Yudhiṣṭhira, though he was not expected to become aggrieved like a common man, became deluded by worldly affection by the will of the Lord (just as Arjuna was apparently deluded). A man who sees knows well that the living entity is neither the body nor the mind, but is transcendental to the material conception of life. The common man thinks of violence and nonviolence in terms of the body, but that is a kind of delusion. Everyone is duty-bound according to one's occupational duties. A *kṣatriya* is bound to fight for the right cause, regardless of the opposite party. In such discharge of duty, one should not be disturbed by annihilation of the material body, which is only an external dress of the living soul. All this was perfectly known to Mahārāja Yudhiṣṭhira, but by the will of the Lord he became just like a common man because there was another great idea behind this delusion: the King would be instructed by Bhīṣma as Arjuna was instructed by the Lord Himself.

TEXT 48

अहो मे पश्यताज्ञानं हृदि रूढं दुरात्मनः ।
पारक्यस्यैव देहस्य बह्व्यो मेऽक्षौहिणीर्हताः ॥४८॥

aho me paśyatājñānaṁ
hṛdi rūḍhaṁ durātmanaḥ
pārakyasyaiva dehasya
bahvyo me 'kṣauhiṇīr hatāḥ

aho—O; *me*—my; *paśyata*—just see; *ajñānam*—ignorance; *hṛdi*—in the heart; *rūḍham*—situated in; *durātmanaḥ*—of the sinful; *pārakyasya*—meant for others; *eva*—certainly; *dehasya*—of the body; *bahvyaḥ*—many, many; *me*—by me; *akṣauhiṇīḥ*—combination of military phalanxes; *hatāḥ*—killed.

TRANSLATION

King Yudhiṣṭhira said: O my lot! I am the most sinful man! Just see my heart, which is full of ignorance! This body, which is ultimately meant for others, has killed many, many phalanxes of men.

PURPORT

A solid phalanx of 21,870 chariots, 21,870 elephants, 109,650 infantry and 65,600 cavalry is called an *akṣauhiṇī*. And many *akṣauhiṇīs* were killed on the Battlefield of Kurukṣetra. Mahārāja Yudhiṣṭhira, as the most pious king of the world, takes for himself the responsibility for killing such a huge number of living beings because the battle was fought to reinstate him on the throne. This body is, after all, meant for others. While there is life in the body, it is meant for the service of others, and when it is dead it is meant to be eaten by dogs and jackals or maggots. He is sorry because for such a temporary body such a huge massacre was committed.

TEXT 49

बालद्विजसुहृन्मित्रपितृभ्रातृगुरुद्रुहः ।
न मे स्यान्निरयान्मोक्षो ह्यपि वर्षायुतायुतैः ॥४९॥

bāla-dvija-suhṛn-mitra-
pitṛ-bhrātṛ-guru-druhaḥ
na me syān nirayān mokṣo
hy api varṣāyutāyutaiḥ

bāla—boys; *dvi-ja*—the twice-born; *suhṛt*—well-wishers; *mitra*—friends; *pitṛ*—parents; *bhrātṛ*—brothers; *guru*—preceptors; *druhaḥ*—one who has killed; *na*—never; *me*—my; *syāt*—there shall be; *nirayāt*—from hell; *mokṣaḥ*—liberation; *hi*—certainly; *api*—although; *varṣa*—years; *ayuta*—millions; *āyutaiḥ*—being added.

TRANSLATION

I have killed many boys, brāhmaṇas, well-wishers, friends, parents, preceptors and brothers. Though I live millions of years, I will not be relieved from the hell that awaits me for all these sins.

PURPORT

Whenever there is a war, there is certainly a massacre of many innocent living beings, such as boys, *brāhmaṇas* and women, whose killing is considered to be the greatest of sins. They are all innocent creatures, and in all circumstances killing of them is forbidden in the scriptures. Mahārāja Yudhiṣṭhira was aware of these mass killings. Similarly, there were friends, parents and preceptors also on both sides, and all of them were killed. It was simply horrible for him to think of such killing, and therefore he was thinking of residing in hell for millions and billions of years.

TEXT 50

नैनो राज्ञः प्रजाभर्तुर्धर्मयुद्धे वधो द्विषाम् ।
इति मे न तु बोधाय कल्पते शासनं वचः ॥५०॥

naino rājñaḥ prajā-bhartur
dharma-yuddhe vadho dviṣām
iti me na tu bodhāya
kalpate śāsanaṁ vacaḥ

na—never; *enaḥ*—sins; *rājñaḥ*—of the king; *prajā-bhartuḥ*—of one who is engaged in the maintenance of the citizens; *dharma*—for the right cause; *yuddhe*—in the fight; *vadhaḥ*—killing; *dviṣām*—of the enemies; *iti*—all these; *me*—for me; *na*—never; *tu*—but; *bodhāya*—for satisfaction; *kalpate*—they are meant for administration; *śāsanam*—injunction; *vacaḥ*—words of.

TRANSLATION

There is no sin for a king who kills for the right cause, who is engaged in maintaining his citizens. But this injunction is not applicable to me.

PURPORT

Mahārāja Yudhiṣṭhira thought that although he was not actually involved in the administration of the kingdom, which was being carried on well by Duryodhana without harm to the citizens, he caused the killing of so many living beings only for his personal gain of the kingdom from the hands of Duryodhana. The killing was committed not in the course of administration but for the sake of self-aggrandizement, and as such he thought himself responsible for all the sins.

TEXT 51

स्त्रीणां मद्धतबन्धूनां द्रोहो योऽसाविहोत्थितः ।
कर्मभिर्गृहमेधीयैर्नाहं कल्पो व्यपोहितुम् ॥५१॥

strīṇāṁ mad-dhata-bandhūnāṁ
droho yo 'sāv ihotthitaḥ
karmabhir gṛhamedhīyair
nāhaṁ kalpo vyapohitum

strīṇām—of the women; *mat*—by me; *hata-bandhūnām*—of the friends who are killed; *drohaḥ*—enmity; *yaḥ*—that; *asau*—all those; *iha*—herewith; *utthitaḥ*—has accrued; *karmabhiḥ*—by dint of work; *gṛhamedhīyaiḥ*—by persons engaged in material welfare; *na*—never; *aham*—I; *kalpaḥ*—can expect; *vyapohitum*—undoing the same.

TRANSLATION

I have killed many friends of women, and I have thus caused enmity to such an extent that it is not possible to undo it by material welfare work.

PURPORT

The *gṛhamedhīs* are those whose only business is to perform welfare work for the sake of material prosperity. Such material prosperity is sometimes hampered by sinful activities, for the materialist is sure to commit sins, even unintentionally, in the course of discharging material duties. To get relief from such sinful reactions, the *Vedas* prescribe several kinds of sacrifices. It is said in the *Vedas* that by performing the *aśvamedha-yajña* (horse sacrifice) one can get relief from even *brahma-hatyā* (killing of a *brāhmaṇa*).

Yudhiṣṭhira Mahārāja performed this *aśvamedha-yajña*, but he thinks that even by performing such *yajñas* it is not possible to get relief from the great sins committed. In war either the husband or the brother or even the father or sons go to fight. And when they are killed, a fresh enmity is created, and thus a chain of actions and reactions increases which is not possible to be counteracted even by thousands of *aśvamedha yajñas.*

The way of work (*karma*) is like that. It creates one action and another reaction simultaneously and thus increases the chain of material activities, binding the performer in material bondage. In the *Bhagavad-gītā* (Bg. 9.27–28) the remedy is suggested that such actions and reactions of the path of work can be checked only when work is done on behalf of the Supreme Lord. The Battle of Kurukṣetra was actually fought by the will of the Supreme Lord Śrī Kṛṣṇa, as it is evident from His version, and only by His will was Yudhiṣṭhira placed on the throne of Hastināpura. Therefore, factually no sin whatsoever touched the Pāṇḍavas, who were only the order carriers of the Lord. For others, who declare war out of personal interest, the whole responsibility lies on them.

TEXT 52

यथा पङ्केन पङ्काम्भः सुरया वा सुराकृतम् ।
भूतहत्यां तथैवैकां न यज्ञैर्मार्ष्टुमर्हति ॥५२॥

yathā paṅkena paṅkāmbhaḥ
surayā vā surākṛtam
bhūta-hatyāṁ tathaivaikāṁ
na yajñair mārṣṭum arhati

yathā—as much as; *paṅkena*—by the mud; *paṅka-ambhaḥ*—water mixed with mud; *surayā*—by wine; *vā*—either; *surākṛtam*—impurity caused by the slight touch of wine; *bhūta-hatyām*—killing of animals; *tathā*—like that; *eva*—certainly; *ekām*—one; *na*—never; *yajñaiḥ*—by the prescribed sacrifices; *mārṣṭum*—to counteract; *arhati*—is worthwhile.

TRANSLATION

As it is not possible to filter muddy water through mud, or purify a wine-stained pot with wine, it is not possible to counteract the killing of men by sacrificing animals.

PURPORT

Aśvamedha-yajñas or *gomedha-yajñas*, sacrifices in which a horse or a bull is sacrificed, were not, of course, for the purpose of killing the animals. Lord Caitanya said that such animals sacrificed on the altar of *yajña* were rejuvenated and a new life was given to them. It was just to prove the efficacy of the hymns of the *Vedas*. By recitation of the hymns of the *Vedas* in the proper way, certainly the performer gets relief from the reactions of sins, but in case of such sacrifices improperly done under inexpert management, surely one has to become responsible for animal sacrifice. In this age of quarrel and hypocrisy there is no possibility of performing the *yajñas* perfectly for want of expert *brāhmaṇas* who are able to conduct such *yajñas*. Mahārāja Yudhiṣṭhira therefore gives a hint to performing sacrifices in the age of Kali. In the Kali-yuga the only sacrifice recommended is the performance of *hari-nāma-yajña* inaugurated by Lord Śrī Caitanya Mahāprabhu. But one should not indulge in animal killing and counteract it by performing the *hari-nāma-yajña*. Those who are devotees of the Lord never kill an animal for self-interest, and (as the Lord ordered Arjuna) they do not refrain from performing the duty of a *kṣatriya*. The whole purpose, therefore, is served when everything is done for the will of the Lord. This is possible only for the devotees.

Thus end the Bhaktivedanta purports of the First Canto, Eighth Chapter, of the Śrīmad-Bhāgavatam, *entitled "Prayers by Queen Kuntī and Parīkṣit Saved."*

CHAPTER NINE

The Passing Away of Bhīṣmadeva in the Presence of Lord Kṛṣṇa

TEXT 1

सूत उवाच
इति भीतः प्रजाद्रोहात्सर्वधर्मविवित्सया ।
ततो विनशनं प्रागाद् यत्र देवव्रतोऽपतत् ॥ १ ॥

sūta uvāca
iti bhītaḥ prajā-drohāt
sarva-dharma-vivitsayā
tato vinaśanaṁ prāgād
yatra deva-vrato 'patat

sūtaḥ uvāca—Śrī Sūta Gosvāmī said; *iti*—thus; *bhītaḥ*—being afraid of; *prajā-drohāt*—because of killing the subjects; *sarva*—all; *dharma*—acts of religion; *vivitsayā*—for understanding; *tataḥ*—thereafter; *vinaśanam*—the place where the fight was held; *prāgāt*—he went; *yatra*—where; *deva-vrataḥ*—Bhīṣmadeva; *apatat*—lay down for passing away.

TRANSLATION

Sūta Gosvāmī said: Being afraid for having killed so many subjects on the Battlefield of Kurukṣetra, Mahārāja Yudhiṣṭhira went to the scene of the massacre. There, Bhīṣmadeva was lying on a bed of arrows, about to pass away.

PURPORT

In this Ninth Chapter, as it is willed by Lord Śrī Kṛṣṇa, Bhīṣmadeva will impart instructions to King Yudhiṣṭhira on the subject of occupational duties. Bhīṣmadeva will also offer his last prayer to the Lord on the verge of passing away from this mortal world and thus become liberated from the bondage of further material engagements. Bhīṣmadeva was endowed with the power of leaving his material body at will, and his lying down on the bed of arrows was his own choice. This passing away of the great warrior attracted the attention of all the contemporary elites, and all of them assembled there to show their feelings of love, respect and affection for the great soul.

TEXT 2

तदा ते भ्रातरः सर्वे सदश्वैः स्वर्णभूषितैः ।
अन्वगच्छन् रथैर्विप्रा व्यासधौम्यादयस्तथा ॥ २ ॥

tadā te bhrātaraḥ sarve
sadaśvaiḥ svarṇa-bhūṣitaiḥ
anvagacchan rathair viprā
vyāsa-dhaumyādayas tathā

tadā—at that time; *te*—all of them; *bhrātaraḥ*—the brothers; *sarve*—all together; *sat-aśvaiḥ*—drawn by first-class horses; *svarṇa*—gold; *bhūṣitaiḥ*—being decorated with; *anvagacchan*—followed one after another; *rathaiḥ*—on the chariots; *viprāḥ*—O *brāhmaṇas;* *vyāsa*—the sage Vyāsa; *dhaumya*—Dhaumya; *ādayaḥ*—and others; *tathā*—also.

TRANSLATION

At that time all his brothers followed him on beautiful chariots drawn by first-class horses decorated with gold ornaments. With them were Vyāsa and ṛṣis like Dhaumya [the learned priest of the Pāṇḍavas] and others.

TEXT 3

भगवानपि विप्रर्षे रथेन सधनञ्जयः ।
स तैर्व्यरोचत नृपः कुबेर इव गुह्यकैः ॥ ३ ॥

bhagavān api viprarṣe
rathena sa-dhanañjayaḥ
sa tair vyarocata nṛpaḥ
kuvera iva guhyakaiḥ

bhagavān—the Personality of Godhead (Śrī Kṛṣṇa); *api*—also; *vipra-ṛṣe*—O sage among the *brāhmaṇas; rathena*—on the chariot; *sa-dhanañjayaḥ*—with Dhanañjaya (Arjuna); *saḥ*—He; *taiḥ*—by them; *vyarocata*—appeared to be highly aristocratic; *nṛpaḥ*—the King (Yudhiṣṭhira); *kuvera*—Kuvera, the treasurer of the demigods; *iva*—as; *guhyakaiḥ*—companions known as Guhyakas.

TRANSLATION

O sage amongst the brāhmaṇas, Lord Śrī Kṛṣṇa, the Personality of Godhead, also followed, seated on a chariot with Arjuna. Thus King Yudhiṣṭhira appeared very aristocratic, like Kuvera surrounded by his companions [the Guhyakas].

PURPORT

Lord Śrī Kṛṣṇa wanted the Pāṇḍavas to be present before Bhīṣmadeva in the most aristocratic order so that he might be pleased to see them happy at the time of his death. Kuvera is the richest of all the demigods, and herein King Yudhiṣṭhira appeared like him (Kuvera), for the procession along with Śrī Kṛṣṇa was quite appropriate to the royalty of King Yudhiṣṭhira.

TEXT 4

दृष्ट्वा निपतितं भूमौ दिवश्च्युतमिवामरम् ।
प्रणेमुः पाण्डवा भीष्मं सानुगाः सह चक्रिणा ॥ ४ ॥

dṛṣṭvā nipatitaṁ bhūmau
divaś cyutam ivāmaram
praṇemuḥ pāṇḍavā bhīṣmaṁ
sānugāḥ saha cakriṇā

dṛṣṭvā—thus seeing; *nipatitam*—lying down; *bhūmau*—on the ground; *divaḥ*—from the sky; *cyutam*—fallen; *iva*—like; *amaram*—demigod; *praṇemuḥ*—bowed down; *pāṇḍavāḥ*—the sons of Pāṇḍu; *bhīṣmam*—unto Bhīṣma; *sa-anugāḥ*—with the younger brothers; *saha*—also with; *cakriṇā*—the Lord (carrying the disc).

TRANSLATION

Seeing him [Bhīṣma] lying on the ground, like a demigod fallen from the sky, the Pāṇḍava King Yudhiṣṭhira, along with his younger brothers and Lord Kṛṣṇa, bowed down before him.

PURPORT

Lord Kṛṣṇa was also a younger cousin of Mahārāja Yudhiṣṭhira as well as the intimate friend of Arjuna. But all the family members of the Pāṇḍavas knew Lord Kṛṣṇa as the Supreme Personality of Godhead. The Lord, although conscious of His supreme position, always behaved in a humanly custom, and so He also bowed down before the dying Bhīṣmadeva as if He were one of the younger brothers of King Yudhiṣṭhira.

TEXT 5

तत्र ब्रह्मर्षयः सर्वे देवर्षयश्च सत्तम ।
राजर्षयश्च तत्रासन् द्रष्टुं भरतपुङ्गवम् ॥ ५ ॥

tatra brahmarṣayaḥ sarve
devarṣayaś ca sattama
rājarṣayaś ca tatrāsan
draṣṭuṁ bharata-puṅgavam

tatra—there; *brahma-ṛṣayaḥ*—*ṛṣis* among the *brāhmaṇas; sarve*—all; *deva-ṛṣayaḥ*—*ṛṣis* among the demigods; *ca*—and; *sattama*—situated in the quality of goodness; *rāja-ṛṣayaḥ*—*ṛṣis* among the kings; *ca*—and; *tatra*—in that place; *āsan*—were present; *draṣṭum*—just to see; *bharata*—the descendants of King Bharata; *puṅgavam*—the chief of.

TRANSLATION

Just to see the chief of the descendants of King Bharata [Bhīṣma], all the great souls in the universe, namely the ṛṣis amongst the demigods, brāhmaṇas and kings, all situated in the quality of goodness, were assembled there.

PURPORT

The *ṛṣis* are those who have attained perfection by spiritual achievements. Such spiritual achievements can be earned by all, whether one is a king or a mendicant. Bhīṣmadeva himself was also one of the *brahmarṣis* and the chief of the descendants of King Bharata. All *ṛṣis* are situated in the quality of goodness. All of them assembled there on hearing the news of the great warrior's impending death.

TEXTS 6–7

पर्वतो नारदो धौम्यो भगवान् बादरायणः ।
बृहदश्वो भरद्वाजः सशिष्यो रेणुकासुतः ॥ ६ ॥
वसिष्ठ इन्द्रप्रमदस्त्रितो गृत्समदोऽसितः ।
कक्षीवान् गौतमोऽत्रिश्च कौशिकोऽथ सुदर्शनः॥ ७॥

parvato nārado dhaumyo
bhagavān bādarāyaṇaḥ
bṛhadaśvo bharadvājaḥ
saśiṣyo reṇukā-sutaḥ

vasiṣṭha indrapramadas
trito gṛtsamado 'sitaḥ
kakṣīvān gautamo 'triś ca
kauśiko 'tha sudarśanaḥ

parvataḥ—Parvata Muni; *nāradaḥ*—Nārada Muni; *dhaumyaḥ*—Dhaumya; *bhagavān*—incarnation of Godhead; *bādarāyaṇaḥ*—Vyāsadeva; *bṛhadaśvaḥ*—Bṛhadaśva; *bharadvājaḥ*—Bharadvāja; *saśiṣyaḥ*—along with disciples; *reṇukā-sutaḥ*—Paraśurāma; *vasiṣṭhaḥ*—

Vasiṣṭha; *indrapramadaḥ*—Indrapramada; *tritaḥ*—Trita; *gṛtsamadaḥ*—Gṛtsamada; *asitaḥ*—Asita; *kakṣīvān*—Kakṣīvān; *gautamaḥ*—Gautama; *atriḥ*—Atri; *ca*—and; *kauśikaḥ*—Kauśika; *atha*—as well as; *sudarśanaḥ*—Sudarśana.

TRANSLATION

All the sages like Parvata Muni, Nārada, Dhaumya, Vyāsa the incarnation of God, Bṛhadaśva, Bharadvāja and Paraśurāma and disciples, Vasiṣṭha, Indrapramada, Trita, Gṛtsamada, Asita, Kakṣīvān, Gautama, Atri, Kauśika and Sudarśana were present.

PURPORT

Parvata Muni is considered to be one of the oldest sages. He is almost always a constant companion of Nārada Muni. They are also spacemen competent to travel in the air without the help of any material vehicle. Parvata Muni is also a *devarṣi*, or a great sage amongst the demigods, like Nārada. He was present along with Nārada at the sacrificial ceremony of Mahārāja Janamejaya, son of Mahārāja Parīkṣit. In this sacrifice all the snakes of the world were to be killed. Parvata Muni and Nārada Muni are called Gandharvas also because they can travel in the air singing the glories of the Lord. Since they can travel in the air, they observed Draupadī's *svayaṁvara* ceremony (selecting of her own husband) from the air. Like Nārada Muni, Parvata Muni also used to visit the royal assembly in the heaven of King Indra. As a Gandharva, sometimes he visited the royal assembly of Kuvera, one of the important demigods. Both Nārada and Parvata were once in trouble with the daughter of Mahārāja Sṛñjaya. Mahārāja Sṛñjaya got the benediction of a son by Parvata Muni.

Nārada Muni is inevitably associated with the narrations of the *Purāṇas*. He is described in the *Bhāgavatam*. In his previous life he was the son of a maidservant, but by good association with pure devotees he became enlightened in devotional service, and in the next life he became a perfect man comparable with himself only. In the *Mahābhārata* his name is mentioned in many places. He is the principle *devarṣi*, or the chief sage amongst the demigods. He is the son and disciple of Brahmājī, and from him the disciplic succession in the line of Brahmā has been spread. He initiated Prahlāda Mahārāja, Dhruva Mahārāja and many celebrated devotees of the Lord. He initiated even Vyāsadeva, the author of the Vedic literatures, and from Vyāsadeva, Madhvācārya was initiated, and thus the Madhva-sampradāya, in which the Gauḍīya-sampradāya is also included, has spread all over the universe. Śrī Caitanya Mahāprabhu belonged to this Madhva-sampradāya; therefore, Brahmājī, Nārada, Vyāsa, down to Madhva, Caitanya and the Gosvāmīs all belonged to the same line of disciplic succession. Nāradajī has instructed many kings from time immemorial. In the *Bhāgavatam* we can see that he instructed Prahlāda Mahārāja while he was in the womb of his mother, and he instructed Vasudeva, father of Kṛṣṇa, as well as Mahārāja Yudhiṣṭhira.

Dhaumya: A great sage who practiced severe penances at Utkocaka Tīrtha and was appointed royal priest of the Pāṇḍava kings. He acted as the priest in many religious functions of the Pāṇḍavas (*saṁskāra*), and also each of the Pāṇḍavas was attended by him at the betrothal of Draupadī. He was present even during the exile of the Pāṇḍavas and used to advise them in circumstances when they were perplexed. He instructed them how to live incognito for one year, and his instructions were strictly followed by the Pāṇḍavas during that time. His name is mentioned also when the general funeral ceremony was performed after the Battle of Kurukṣetra. In the *Anuśāsana-parva* of *Mahābhārata* (127.15-16), he gave religious instructions very elaborately to Mahārāja Yudhiṣṭhira. He was actually the right type of priest of a householder, for he could guide the Pāṇḍavas on the right path of religion. A priest is meant for guiding the householder progressively in the right path of *āśrama-dharma*, or the occupational duty of a particular caste. There is practically no difference between the family priest and the spiritual master. The sages, saints and *brāhmaṇas* were especially meant for such functions.

Bādarāyaṇa (*Vyāsadeva*): He is known as Kṛṣṇa, Kṛṣṇa-dvaipāyana, Dvaipāyana, Satyavatī-suta, Pārāśarya, Parāśarātmaja, Bādarāyaṇa, Vedavyāsa, etc. He was the son of Mahāmuni Parāśara in the womb of Satyavatī prior to her betrothal with Mahārāja Śantanu, the father of the great general Grandfather Bhīṣmadeva. He is a powerful incarnation of Nārāyaṇa, and he broadcasts the Vedic wisdom to the world. As such, Vyāsadeva is offered respects before one chants the Vedic literature, especially the *Purāṇas*. Śukadeva Gosvāmī was his son, and *ṛṣis* like

Vaiśampāyana were his disciples for different branches of the *Vedas.* He is the author of the great epic *Mahābhārata* and the great transcendental literature *Bhāgavatam.* The *Brahma-sūtras*—the *Vedānta-sūtras,* or *Bādarāyaṇa-sūtras*—were compiled by him. Amongst sages he is the most respected author by dint of severe penances. When he wanted to record the great epic *Mahābhārata* for the welfare of all people in the age of Kali, he was feeling the necessity of a powerful writer who could take up his dictation. By the order of Brahmājī, Śrī Gaṇeśajī took up the charge of noting down the dictation on the condition that Vyāsadeva would not stop dictation for a moment. The *Mahābhārata* was thus compiled by the joint endeavor of Vyāsa and Gaṇeśa.

By the order of his mother, Satyavatī, who was later married to Mahārāja Śantanu, and by the request of Bhīṣmadeva, the eldest son of Mahārāja Śantanu by his first wife, the Ganges, he begot three brilliant sons, whose names are Dhṛtarāṣṭra, Pāṇḍu and Vidura. The *Mahābhārata* was compiled by Vyāsadeva after the Battle of Kurukṣetra and after the death of all the heroes of *Mahābhārata.* It was first spoken in the royal assembly of Mahārāja Janamejaya, the son of Mahārāja Parīkṣit.

Bṛhadaśva: An ancient sage who used to meet Mahārāja Yudhiṣṭhira now and then. First of all he met Mahārāja Yudhiṣṭhira at Kāmyavana. This sage narrated the history of Mahārāja Nala. There is another Bṛhadaśva, who is the son of the Ikṣvāku dynasty (*Mahābhārata, Vana-parva* 209.4–5)

Bharadvāja: He is one of the seven great *ṛṣis* and was present at the time of the birth ceremony of Arjuna. The powerful *ṛṣi* sometimes undertook severe penances on the shore of the Ganges, and his *āśrama* is still celebrated at Prayāgadhāma. It is learned that this *ṛṣi,* while taking bath in the Ganges, happened to meet Ghṛtacī, one of the beautiful society girls of heaven, and thus he discharged semen, which was kept and preserved in an earthen pot and from which Droṇa was born. So Droṇācārya is the son of Bharadvāja Muni. Others say that Bharadvāja the father of Droṇa is a different person from Maharṣi Bharadvāja. He was a great devotee of Brahmā. Once he approached Droṇācārya and requested him to stop the Battle of Kurukṣetra.

Paraśurāma, or *Reṇukāsuta:* He is the son of Maharṣi Jamadagni and Śrīmatī Reṇukā. Thus he is also known as Reṇukāsuta. He is one of the powerful incarnations of God, and he killed the *kṣatriya* community as a whole twenty-one times. With the blood of the *kṣatriyas* he pleased the souls of his forefathers. Later on he underwent severe penances at the Mahendra Parvata. After taking the whole earth from the *kṣatriyas*, he gave it in charity to Kaśyapa Muni. Paraśurāma instructed the *Dhanur-veda*, or the science of fighting, to Droṇācārya because he happened to be a *brāhmaṇa*. He was present during the coronation of Mahārāja Yudhiṣṭhira, and he celebrated the function along with other great *ṛṣis*.

Paraśurāma is so old that he met both Rāma and Kṛṣṇa at different times. He fought with Rāma, but he accepted Kṛṣṇa as the Supreme Personality of Godhead. He also praised Arjuna when he saw him with Kṛṣṇa. When Bhīṣma refused to marry Ambā, who wanted him to become her husband, Ambā met Paraśurāma, and by her request only, he asked Bhīṣmadeva to accept her as his wife. Bhīṣma refused to obey his order, although he was one of the spiritual masters of Bhīṣmadeva. Paraśurāma fought with Bhīṣmadeva when Bhīṣma neglected his warning. Both of them fought very severely, and at last Paraśurāma was pleased with Bhīṣma and gave him the benediction of becoming the greatest fighter in the world.

Vasiṣṭha: The great celebrated sage among the *brāhmaṇas*, well known as the Brahmarṣi Vasiṣṭhadeva. He is a prominent figure in both the *Rāmāyaṇa* and *Mahābhārata* periods. He celebrated the coronation ceremony of the Personality of Godhead Śrī Rāma. He was present also on the Battlefield of Kurukṣetra. He could approach all the higher and lower planets, and his name is also connected with the history of Hiraṇyakaśipu. There was a great tension between him and Viśvāmitra, who wanted his *kāmadhenu*, wish-fulfilling cow. Vasiṣṭha Muni refused to spare his *kāmadhenu*, and for this Viśvāmitra killed his one hundred sons. As a perfect *brāhmaṇa* he tolerated all the taunts of Viśvāmitra. Once he tried to commit suicide on account of Viśvāmitra's torture, but all his attempts were unsuccessful. He jumped from a hill, but the stones on which he fell became a stack of cotton, and thus he was saved. He jumped into the ocean, but the waves washed him ashore. He jumped into the river, but the river also washed him ashore. Thus all his suicide attempts were unsuccessful. He is also one of the seven *ṛṣis* and husband of Arundhatī, the famous star.

Indrapramada: Another celebrated *ṛṣi*.

Trita: One of the three sons of Prajāpati Gautama. He was the third son, and his other two brothers were known as Ekat and Dvita. All the brothers were great sages and strict followers of the principles of religion. By dint of severe penances they were promoted to Brahmaloka (the planet where Brahmājī lives). Once Trita Muni fell into a well. He was an organizing worker of many sacrifices, and as one of the great sages he also came to show respect to Bhīṣmajī at his deathbed. He was one of the seven sages in the Varuṇaloka. He hailed from the Western countries of the world. As such, most probably he belonged to the European countries. At that time the whole world was under one Vedic culture.

Gṛtsamada: One of the sages of the heavenly kingdom. He was a close friend of Indra, the King of heaven, and was as great as Bṛhaspati. He used to visit the royal assembly of Mahārāja Yudhiṣṭhira, and he also visited the place where Bhīṣmadeva breathed his last. Sometimes he explained the glories of Lord Śiva before Mahārāja Yudhiṣṭhira. He was the son of Vitahavya, and he resembled in features the body of Indra. Sometimes the enemies of Indra mistook him to be Indra and arrested him. He was a great scholar of the *Ṛg-veda*, and thus he was highly respected by the *brāhmaṇa* community. He lived a life of celibacy and was powerful in every respect.

Asita: There was a king of the same name, but herein the Asita mentioned is the Asita Devala Ṛṣi, a great powerful sage of the time. He explained to his father 1,500,000 verses from the *Mahābhārata.* He was one of the members in the snake sacrifice of Mahārāja Janamejaya. He was also present during the coronation ceremony of Mahārāja Yudhiṣṭhira along with other great *ṛṣis.* He also gave Mahārāja Yudhiṣṭhira instructions while he was on the Añjana Hill. He was also one of the devotees of Lord Śiva.

Kakṣīvān: One of the sons of Gautama Muni and the father of the great sage Candakausika. He was one of the members of Parliament of Mahārāja Yudhiṣṭhira.

Atri: Atri Muni was a great *brāhmaṇa* sage and was one of the mental sons of Brahmājī. Brahmājī is so powerful that simply by thinking of a son he can have it. These sons are known as *mānasa-putras.* Out of seven *mānasa-putras* of Brahmājī and out of the seven great *brāhmaṇa* sages,

Atri was one. In his family the great Pracetās were also born. Atri Muni had two *kṣatriya* sons who became kings. King Arthama is one of them. He is counted as one of the twenty-one *prajāpatis*. His wife's name was Anasūyā, and he helped Mahārāja Parīkṣit in his great sacrifices.

Kauśika: One of the permanent *ṛṣi* members in the royal assembly of Mahārāja Yudhiṣṭhira. He sometimes met Lord Kṛṣṇa. There are several other sages of the same name.

Sudarśana: This wheel which is accepted by the Personality of Godhead (Viṣṇu or Kṛṣṇa) as His personal weapon is the most powerful weapon, greater than the *brahmāstras* or similar other disastrous weapons. In some of the Vedic literatures it is said that Agnideva, the fire-god, presented this weapon to Lord Śrī Kṛṣṇa, but factually this weapon is eternally carried by the Lord. Agnideva presented this weapon to Kṛṣṇa in the same way that Rukmiṇī was given by Mahārāja Rukma to the Lord. The Lord accepts such presentations from His devotees, even though such presentations are eternally His property. There is an elaborate description of this weapon in the *Ādi-parva* of the *Mahābhārata*. Lord Śrī Kṛṣṇa used this weapon to kill Śiśupāla, a rival of the Lord. He also killed Śālva by this weapon, and sometimes He wanted His friend Arjuna to use it to kill his enemies (*Mahābhārata, Virāṭa-parva* 56.3).

TEXT 8

अन्ये च मुनयो ब्रह्मन् ब्रह्मरातादयोऽमलाः ।
शिष्यैरुपेता आजग्मुः कश्यपाङ्गिरसादयः ॥ ८ ॥

anye ca munayo brahman
brahmarātādayo 'malāḥ
śiṣyair upetā ājagmuḥ
kaśyapāṅgirasādayaḥ

anye—many others; *ca*—also; *munayaḥ*—sages; *brahman*—O *brāhmaṇas; brahmarāta*—Śukadeva Gosvāmī; *ādayaḥ*—and such others; *amalāḥ*—completely purified; *śiṣyaiḥ*—by the disciples; *upetāḥ*—accompanied; *ājagmuḥ*—arrived; *kaśyapa*—Kaśyapa; *āṅgirasa*—Āṅgirasa; *ādayaḥ*—others.

TRANSLATION

And many others like Śukadeva Gosvāmī and other purified souls, Kaśyapa and Āṅgirasa and others, all accompanied by their respective disciples, arrived there.

PURPORT

Śukadeva Gosvāmī (*Brahmarāta*): The famous son and disciple of Śrī Vyāsadeva, who taught him first the *Mahābhārata* and then *Śrīmad-Bhāgavatam*. Śukadeva Gosvāmī recited 1,400,000 verses of the *Mahābhārata* in the councils of the Gandharvas, Yakṣas and Rākṣasas, and he recited *Śrīmad-Bhāgavatam* for the first time in the presence of Mahārāja Parīkṣit. He thoroughly studied all the Vedic literatures from his great father. Thus he was a completely purified soul by dint of his extensive knowledge in the principles of religion. From *Mahābhārata*, *Sabhā-parva* (4.11) it is understood that he was also present in the royal assembly of Mahārāja Yudhiṣṭhira and at the fasting of Mahārāja Parīkṣit. As a bona fide disciple of Śrī Vyāsadeva, he inquired from his father very extensively about religious principles and spiritual values, and his great father also satisfied him by teaching him the *yoga* system by which one can attain the spiritual kingdom, the difference between fruitive work and empiric knowledge, the ways and means of attaining spiritual realization, the four *āśramas* (namely the student life, the householder's life, the retired life and the renounced life), the sublime position of the Supreme Personality of Godhead, the process of seeing Him eye to eye, the bona fide candidate for receiving knowledge, the consideration of the five elements, the unique position of intelligence, the consciousness of the material nature and the living entity, the symptoms of the self-realized soul, the working principles of the material body, the symptoms of the influential modes of nature, the tree of perpetual desire, and psychic activities. Sometimes he went to the sun planet with the permission of his father and Nāradajī. Descriptions of his travel in space are given in the *Śānti-parva* of the *Mahābhārata* (332). At last he attained the transcendental realm. He is known by different names like Araṇeya, Aruṇisuta, Vaiyāsaki and Vyāsātmaja.

Kaśyapa: One of the *prajāpatis*, the son of Marīci and one of the sons-in-law of Prajāpati Dakṣa. He is the father of the gigantic bird Garuḍa, who was given elephants and tortoises as eatables. He married thirteen daughters of Prajāpati Dakṣa, and their names are Aditi, Diti, Danu, Kāṣṭhā, Ariṣṭā, Surasā, Ilā, Muni, Krodhavaśā, Tāmrā, Surabhi, Saramā and Timi. He begot many children, both demigods and demons, by those wives. From his first wife, Aditi, all the twelve Ādityas were born; one of them is Vāmana, the incarnation of Godhead. This great sage, Kaśyapa, was also present at the time of Arjuna's birth. He received a presentation of the whole world from Paraśurāma, and later on he asked Paraśurāma to go out of the world. His other name is Ariṣṭanemi. He lives on the northern side of the universe.

Āṅgirasa: He is the son of Maharṣi Aṅgirā and is known as Bṛhaspati, the priest of the demigods. It is said that Droṇācārya was his partial incarnation. Śukrācārya was the spiritual master of the demons, and Bṛhaspati challenged him. His son is Kaca, and he delivered the fire weapon first to Bharadvāja Muni. He begot six sons (like the fire-god) by his wife Candramāsī, one of the reputed stars. He could travel in space, and therefore he could present himself even in the planets of Brahmaloka and Indraloka. He advised the King of heaven, Indra, about conquering the demons. Once he cursed Indra, who thus had to become a hog on the earth and was unwilling to return to heaven. Such is the power of the attraction of the illusory energy. Even a hog does not wish to part with its earthly possessions in exchange for a heavenly kingdom. He was the religious preceptor of the natives of different planets.

TEXT 9

तान् समेतान् महाभागानुपलभ्य वसूत्तमः ।
पूजयामास धर्मज्ञो देशकालविभागवित् ॥ ९ ॥

tān sametān mahā-bhāgān
upalabhya vasūttamaḥ
pūjayām āsa dharma-jño
deśa-kāla-vibhāgavit

tān—all of them; *sametān*—assembled together; *mahā-bhāgān*—all greatly powerful; *upalabhya*—having received; *vasu-uttamaḥ*—the best among the Vasus (Bhīṣmadeva); *pūjayām āsa*—welcomed; *dharma-jñaḥ*—one who knows religious principles; *deśa*—place; *kāla*—time; *vibhāga-vit*—one who knows the adjustment of place and time.

TRANSLATION

Bhīṣmadeva, who was the best amongst the eight Vasus, received and welcomed all the great and powerful ṛṣis who were assembled there, for he knew perfectly all the religious principles according to time and place.

PURPORT

Expert religionists know perfectly well how to adjust religious principles in terms of time and place. All the great *ācāryas* or religious preachers or reformers of the world executed their mission by adjustment of religious principles in terms of time and place. There are different climates and situations in different parts of the world, and if one has to discharge his duties to preach the message of the Lord, he must be expert in adjusting things in terms of the time and place. Bhīṣmadeva was one of the twelve great authorities in preaching this cult of devotional service, and therefore he could receive and welcome all the powerful sages assembled there at his deathbed from all parts of the universe. He was certainly unable at that time to welcome and receive them physically because he was neither at his home nor in a normal healthy condition. But he was quite fit by the activities of his sound mind, and therefore he could utter sweet words with hearty expressions, and all of them were well received. One can perform one's duty by physical work, by mind and by words. And he knew well how to utilize them in the proper place, and therefore there was no difficulty for him to receive them, although physically unfit.

TEXT 10

कृष्णं च तत्प्रभावज्ञ आसीनं जगदीश्वरम् ।
हृदिस्थं पूजयामास माययोपात्तविग्रहम् ॥१०॥

kṛṣṇaṁ ca tat-prabhāva-jña
āsīnaṁ jagad-īśvaram
hṛdi-sthaṁ pūjayām āsa
māyayopātta-vigraham

kṛṣṇam—unto Lord Śrī Kṛṣṇa; *ca*—also; *tat*—of Him; *prabhāva-jñaḥ*—the knower of the glories (Bhīṣma); *āsīnam*—sitting;

jagat-īśvaram—the Lord of the universe; *hṛdi-stham*—situated in the heart; *pūjayām āsa*—worshiped; *māyayā*—by internal potency; *upātta*—manifested; *vigraham*—a form.

TRANSLATION

Lord Śrī Kṛṣṇa is situated in everyone's heart, yet He manifests His transcendental form by His internal potency. This very Lord was sitting before Bhīṣmadeva, and since Bhīṣmadeva knew of His glories, he worshiped Him duly.

PURPORT

The Lord's omnipotency is displayed by His simultaneous presence in every place. He is present always in His eternal abode Goloka Vṛndāvana, and still He is present in everyone's heart and even within every invisible atom. When He manifests His eternal transcendental form in the material world, He does so by His internal potency. The external potency, or the material energy, has nothing to do with His eternal form. All these truths were known to Śrī Bhīṣmadeva, who worshiped Him accordingly.

TEXT 11

पाण्डुपुत्रानुपासीनान् प्रश्रयप्रेमसङ्गतान् ।
अभ्याचष्टानुरागाश्रैरन्धीभूतेन चक्षुषा ॥११॥

pāṇḍu-putrān upāsīnān
praśraya-prema-saṅgatān
abhyācaṣṭānurāgāśrair
andhībhūtena cakṣuṣā

pāṇḍu—the late father of Mahārāja Yudhiṣṭhira and his brothers; *putrān*—the sons of; *upāsīnān*—sitting silently nearby; *praśraya*—being overtaken; *prema*—in feelings of love; *saṅgatān*—having gathered; *abhyācaṣṭa*—congratulated; *anurāga*—feelingly; *aśraiḥ*—by tears of ecstasy; *andhībhūtena*—overwhelmed; *cakṣuṣā*—with his eyes.

TRANSLATION

The sons of Mahārāja Pāṇḍu were sitting silently nearby, overtaken with affection for their dying grandfather. Seeing this, Bhīṣmadeva congratulated them with feeling. There were tears of ecstasy in his eyes, for he was overwhelmed by love and affection.

PURPORT

When Mahārāja Pāṇḍu died, his sons were all small children, and naturally they were brought up under the affection of elderly members of the royal family, specifically by Bhīṣmadeva. Later on, when the Pāṇḍavas were grown up, they were cheated by cunning Duryodhana and company, and Bhīṣmadeva, although he knew that the Pāṇḍavas were innocent and were unnecessarily put into trouble, could not take the side of the Pāṇḍavas for political reasons. At the last stage of his life, when Bhīṣmadeva saw his most exalted grandsons, headed by Mahārāja Yudhiṣṭhira, sitting very gently at his side, the great warrior-grandfather could not check his loving tears, which were automatically flowing from his eyes. He remembered the great tribulations suffered by his most pious grandsons. Certainly he was the most satisfied man because of Yudhiṣṭhira's being enthroned in place of Duryodhana, and thus he began to congratulate them.

TEXT 12

अहो कष्टमहोऽन्याय्यं यद्यूयं धर्मनन्दनाः ।
जीवितुं नार्हथ क्लिष्टं विप्रधर्माच्युताश्रयाः ॥१२॥

aho kaṣṭam aho 'nyāyyaṁ
yad yūyaṁ dharma-nandanāḥ
jīvituṁ nārhatha kliṣṭaṁ
vipra-dharmācyutāśrayāḥ

aho—oh; *kaṣṭam*—what terrible sufferings; *aho*—oh; *anyāyyam*—what terrible injustice; *yat*—because; *yūyam*—all of you good souls; *dharma-nandanāḥ*—sons of religion personified; *jīvitum*—to remain alive; *na*—never; *arhatha*—deserve; *kliṣṭam*—suffering; *vipra*—*brāhmaṇas; dharma*—piety; *acyuta*—God; *āśrayāḥ*—being protected by.

TRANSLATION

Bhīṣmadeva said: Oh, what terrible sufferings and what terrible injustices you good souls suffer for being the sons of religion personified. You did not deserve to remain alive under those tribulations, yet you were protected by the brāhmaṇas, God and religion.

PURPORT

Mahārāja Yudhiṣṭhira was disturbed due to the great massacre in the Battle of Kurukṣetra. Bhīṣmadeva could understand this, and therefore he spoke first of the terrible sufferings of Mahārāja Yudhiṣṭhira. He was put into difficulty by injustice only, and the Battle of Kurukṣetra was fought just to counteract this injustice. Therefore, he should not regret the great massacre. He wanted to point out particularly that they were always protected by the *brāhmaṇas*, the Lord and religious principles. As long as they were protected by these three important items, there was no cause of disappointment. Thus Bhīṣmadeva encouraged Mahārāja Yudhiṣṭhira to dissipate his despondency. As long as a person is fully in cooperation with the wishes of the Lord, guided by the bona fide *brāhmaṇas* and Vaiṣṇavas and strictly following religious principles, one has no cause for despondency, however trying the circumstances of life. Bhīṣmadeva, as one of the authorities in the line, wanted to impress this point upon the Pāṇḍavas.

TEXT 13

संस्थितेऽतिरथे पाण्डौ पृथा बालप्रजा वधूः ।
युष्मत्कृते बहून् क्लेशान् प्राप्ता तोकवती मुहुः ॥१३॥

saṁsthite 'tirathe pāṇḍau
pṛthā bāla-prajā vadhūḥ
yuṣmat-kṛte bahūn kleśān
prāptā tokavatī muhuḥ

saṁsthite—after the demise; *ati-rathe*—of the great general; *pāṇḍau*—Pāṇḍu; *pṛthā*—Kuntī; *bāla-prajā*—having young children; *vadhūḥ*—my daughter-in-law; *yuṣmat-kṛte*—on your account; *bahūn*—multifarious; *kleśān*—afflictions; *prāptā*—underwent; *toka-vatī*—in spite of having grown-up boys; *muhuḥ*—constantly.

TRANSLATION

As far as my daughter-in-law Kuntī is concerned, upon the great General Pāṇḍu's death, she became a widow with many children, and therefore she suffered greatly. And when you were grown up she suffered a great deal also because of your actions.

PURPORT

The sufferings of Kuntīdevī are doubly lamented. She suffered greatly because of early widowhood and to get her minor children brought up in the royal family. And when her children were grown up, she continued to suffer because of her sons' actions. So her sufferings continued. This means that she was destined to suffer by providence, and this one has to tolerate without being disturbed.

TEXT 14

सर्वं कालकृतं मन्ये भवतां च यदप्रियम् ।
सपालो यद्वशे लोको वायोरिव घनावलिः ॥१४॥

sarvaṁ kāla-kṛtaṁ manye
bhavatāṁ ca yad-apriyam
sapālo yad-vaśe loko
vāyor iva ghanāvaliḥ

sarvam—all this; *kāla-kṛtam*—done by inevitable time; *manye*—I think; *bhavatām ca*—for you also; *yat*—whatever; *apriyam*—detestable; *sa-pālaḥ*—with the rulers; *yat-vaśe*—under the control of that time; *lokaḥ*—everyone in every planet; *vayoḥ*—the wind carries; *iva*—as; *ghana-āvaliḥ*—a line of clouds.

TRANSLATION

In my opinion, this is all due to inevitable time, under whose control everyone in every planet is carried, just as the clouds are carried by the wind.

PURPORT

There is control by time all over the space within the universe, as there is control by time all over the planets. All the big gigantic planets, including the sun, are being controlled by the force of air, as the clouds are carried by the force of air. Similarly, the inevitable *kāla*, or time, controls even the action of the air and other elements. Everything, therefore, is controlled by the supreme *kāla*, a forceful representative of the Lord within the material world. Thus Yudhiṣṭhira should not be sorry for the inconceivable action of time. Everyone has to bear the actions and reactions of time as long as one is within the conditions of the material world. Yudhiṣṭhira should not think that he had committed sins in his previous birth and is suffering the consequence. Even the most pious has to suffer the condition of material nature. But a pious man is faithful to the Lord, for he is guided by the bona fide *brāhmaṇa* and Vaiṣṇava following the religious principles. These three guiding principles should be the aim of life. One should not be disturbed by the tricks of eternal time. Even the great controller of the universe, Brahmājī, is also under the control of that time; therefore, one should not grudge being thus controlled by time despite being a true follower of religious principles.

TEXT 15

यत्र धर्मसुतो राजा गदापाणिर्वृकोदरः ।
कृष्णोऽस्त्री गाण्डिवं चापं सुहृत्कृष्णस्ततो विपत् ॥१५॥

yatra dharma-suto rājā
gadā-pāṇir vṛkodaraḥ
kṛṣṇo 'strī gāṇḍivaṁ cāpaṁ
suhṛt kṛṣṇas tato vipat

yatra—where there is; *dharma-sutaḥ*—the son of Dharmarāja; *rājā*—the King; *gadā-pāṇiḥ*—with his mighty club in hand; *vṛkodaraḥ*—Bhīma; *kṛṣṇaḥ*—Arjuna; *astrī*—carrier of the weapon; *gāṇḍivam*—Gāṇḍīva; *cāpam*—bow; *suhṛt*—well-wisher; *kṛṣṇaḥ*—Lord Kṛṣṇa, the Personality of Godhead; *tataḥ*—thereof; *vipat*—reverse.

TRANSLATION

O how wonderful is the influence of inevitable time. It is irreversible—otherwise, how can there be reverses in the presence of King Yudhiṣṭhira, the son of the demigod controlling religion;

Bhīma, the great fighter with a club; the great bowman Arjuna with his mighty weapon Gāṇḍīva; and above all, the Lord, the direct well-wisher of the Pāṇḍavas?

PURPORT

As far as the material or spiritual resources were required, there was no scarcity in the case of the Pāṇḍavas. Materially they were well equipped because two great warriors, namely Bhīma and Arjuna, were there. Spiritually the King himself was the symbol of religion, and above all of them the Personality of Godhead, Lord Śrī Kṛṣṇa, was personally concerned with their affairs as the well-wisher. And yet there were so many reverses on the side of the Pāṇḍavas. Despite the power of pious acts, the power of personalities, the power of expert management and the power of weapons under the direct supervision of Lord Kṛṣṇa, the Pāṇḍavas suffered so many practical reverses, which can only be explained as due to the influence of *kāla*, inevitable time. *Kāla* is identical with the Lord Himself, and therefore the influence of *kāla* indicates the inexplicable wish of the Lord Himself. There is nothing to be lamented when a matter is beyond the control of any human being.

TEXT 16

न ह्यस्य कर्हिचिद्राजन् पुमान् वेद विधित्सितम् ।
यद्विजिज्ञासया युक्ता मुह्यन्ति कवयोऽपि हि ॥१६॥

na hy asya karhicid rājan
pumān veda vidhitsitam
yad vijijñāsayā yuktā
muhyanti kavayo 'pi hi

na—never; *hi*—certainly; *asya*—His; *karhicit*—whatsoever; *rājan*—O King; *pumān*—anyone; *veda*—knows; *vidhitsitam*—plan; *yat*—which; *vijijñāsayā*—with exhaustive inquiries; *yuktāḥ*—being engaged; *muhyanti*—bewildered; *kavayaḥ*—great philosophers; *api*—even; *hi*—certainly.

TRANSLATION

O King, no one can know the plan of the Lord [Śrī Kṛṣṇa]. Even though great philosophers inquire exhaustively, they are bewildered.

PURPORT

The bewilderment of Mahārāja Yudhiṣṭhira over his past sinful acts and the resultant sufferings, etc., is completely negated by the great authority Bhīṣma (one of the twelve authorized persons). Bhīṣma wanted to impress upon Mahārāja Yudhiṣṭhira that since time immemorial no one, including such demigods as Śiva and Brahmā, could ascertain the real plan of the Lord. So what can we understand about it? It is useless also to inquire about it. Even the exhaustive philosophical inquiries of sages cannot ascertain the plan of the Lord. The best policy is simply to abide by the orders of the Lord without argument. The sufferings of the Pāṇḍavas were never due to their past deeds. The Lord had to execute the plan of establishing the kingdom of virtue, and therefore His own devotees suffered temporarily in order to establish the conquest of virtue. Bhīṣmadeva was certainly satisfied by seeing the triumph of virtue, and he was glad to see King Yudhiṣṭhira on the throne, although he himself fought against him. Even a great fighter like Bhīṣma could not win the Battle of Kurukṣetra because the Lord wanted to show that vice cannot conquer virtue, regardless of who tries to execute it. Bhīṣmadeva was a great devotee of the Lord, but he chose to fight against the Pāṇḍavas by the will of the Lord because the Lord wanted to show that a fighter like Bhīṣma cannot win on the wrong side.

TEXT 17

तस्मादिदं दैवतन्त्रं व्यवस्य भरतर्षभ ।
तस्यानुविहितोऽनाथा नाथ पाहि प्रजाः प्रभो ॥१७॥

tasmād idaṁ daiva-tantraṁ
vyavasya bharatarṣabha
tasyānuvihito 'nāthā
nātha pāhi prajāḥ prabho

tasmāt—therefore; *idam*—this; *daiva-tantram*—enchantment of providence only; *vyavasya*—ascertaining; *bharata-ṛṣabha*—O best among the descendants of Bharata; *tasya*—by Him; *anuvihitaḥ*—as desired; *anāthāḥ*—helpless; *nātha*—O master; *pāhi*—just take care of; *prajāḥ*—of the subjects; *prabho*—O Lord.

TRANSLATION

O best among the descendants of Bharata [Yudhiṣṭhira], I maintain, therefore, that all this is within the plan of the Lord. Accepting the inconceivable plan of the Lord, you must follow it. You are now the appointed administrative head, and, my lord, you should now take care of those subjects who are now rendered helpless.

PURPORT

The popular saying is that a housewife teaches the daughter-in-law by teaching the daughter. Similarly, the Lord teaches the world by teaching the devotee. The devotee does not have to learn anything new from the Lord because the Lord teaches the sincere devotee always from within. Whenever, therefore, a show is made to teach the devotee, as in the case of the teachings of *Bhagavad-gītā*, it is for teaching the less intelligent men. A devotee's duty, therefore, is to ungrudgingly accept tribulations from the Lord as a benediction. The Pāṇḍavas were advised by Bhīṣmadeva to accept the responsibility of administration without hesitation. The poor subjects were without protection due to the Battle of Kurukṣetra, and they were awaiting the assumption of power by Mahārāja Yudhiṣṭhira. A pure devotee of the Lord accepts tribulations as favors from the Lord. Since the Lord is absolute, there is no mundane difference between the two.

TEXT 18

एष वै भगवान् साक्षादाद्यो नारायणः पुमान् ।
मोहयन्मायया लोकं गूढश्चरति वृष्णिषु ॥१८॥

eṣa vai bhagavān sākṣād
ādyo nārāyaṇaḥ pumān
mohayan māyayā lokaṁ
gūḍhaś carati vṛṣṇiṣu

eṣaḥ—this; *vai*—positively; *bhagavān*—the Personality of Godhead; *sākṣāt*—original; *ādyaḥ*—the first; *nārāyaṇaḥ*—the Supreme Lord (who lies down on the water); *pumān*—the supreme enjoyer; *mohayan*—bewildering; *māyayā*—by His self-created energy; *lokam*—the planets; *gūḍhaḥ*—who is inconceivable; *carati*—moves; *vṛṣṇiṣu*—among the Vṛṣṇi family.

TRANSLATION

This Śrī Kṛṣṇa is no other than the inconceivable, original Personality of Godhead. He is the first Nārāyaṇa, the supreme enjoyer. But He is moving amongst the descendants of King Vṛṣṇi just like one of us and He is bewildering us with His self-created energy.

PURPORT

The Vedic system of acquiring knowledge is the deductive process. The Vedic knowledge is received perfectly by disciplic succession from authorities. Such knowledge is never dogmatic, as ill conceived by less intelligent persons. The mother is the authority to verify the identity of the father. She is the authority for such confidential knowledge. Therefore, authority is not dogmatic. In the *Bhagavad-gītā* this truth is confirmed in the Fourth Chapter (Bg. 4.2), and the perfect system of learning is to receive it from authority. The very same system is accepted universally as truth, but only the false arguer speaks against it. For example, modern spacecraft fly in the sky, and when scientists say that they travel to the other side of the moon, men believe these stories blindly because they have accepted the modern scientists as authorities. The authorities speak, and the people in general believe them. But in the case of Vedic truths, they have been taught not to believe. Even if they accept them they give a different interpretation. Each and every man wants a direct perception of Vedic knowledge, but foolishly they deny it. This means that the misguided man can believe one authority, the scientist, but will reject the authority of the *Vedas*. The result is that people have degenerated.

Here is an authority speaking about Śrī Kṛṣṇa as the original Personality of Godhead and the first Nārāyaṇa. Even such an impersonalist as Ācārya Śaṅkara has said in the beginning of his commentation on the *Bhagavad-gītā* that Nārāyaṇa, the Personality of Godhead, is beyond the material creation.* The universe is one of the material creations, but Nārāyaṇa is transcendental to such material paraphernalia.

Bhīṣmadeva is one of the twelve *mahājanas* who know the principles of transcendental knowledge. His confirmation of Lord Śrī Kṛṣṇa's being the original Personality of Godhead is also corroborated by the impersonalist Śaṅkara. All other *ācāryas* have also confirmed this statement, and thus there is no chance of not accepting Lord Śrī Kṛṣṇa as the original Personality of Godhead. Bhīṣmadeva says that He is the first Nārāyaṇa. This is also confirmed by Brahmājī in the *Bhāgavatam* (10.14.14). Kṛṣṇa is the first Nārāyaṇa. In the spiritual world (Vaikuṇṭha) there are unlimited numbers of Nārāyaṇas, who are all the same Personality of Godhead and are considered to be the plenary expansions of the original Personality of Godhead, Śrī Kṛṣṇa. The first form of the Lord Śrī Kṛṣṇa first expands Himself as the form of Baladeva, and Baladeva expands in so many other forms, such as Saṅkarṣaṇa, Pradyumna, Aniruddha, Vāsudeva, Nārāyaṇa, Puruṣa, Rāma and Nṛsiṁha. All these expansions are one and the same *viṣṇu-tattva*, and Śrī Kṛṣṇa is the original source of all the plenary expansions. He is therefore the direct Personality of Godhead. He is the creator of the material world, and He is the predominating Deity known as Nārāyaṇa in all the Vaikuṇṭha planets. Therefore, His movements amongst human beings is another sort of bewilderment. The Lord therefore says in the *Bhagavad-gītā* that foolish persons consider Him to be one of the human beings without knowing the intricacies of His movements.

The bewilderment regarding Śrī Kṛṣṇa is due to the action of His two-fold internal and external energies upon the third one, called marginal energy. The living entities are expansions of His marginal energy, and thus they are sometimes bewildered by the internal energy and sometimes by the external energy. By internal energetic bewilderment, Śrī Kṛṣṇa expands Himself into unlimited numbers of Nārāyaṇas and exchanges or accepts transcendental loving service from the living entities in the transcendental world. And by His external energetic expansions, He incarnates Himself in the material world amongst the men, animals

---

* *nārāyaṇaḥ paro 'vyaktād*
aṇḍam avyakta-sambhavam
aṇḍasyāntas tv ime lokāḥ
sapta dvīpā ca medinī
(Bg. *Bhāṣya* of Śaṅkara)

or demigods to reestablish His forgotten relation with the living entities in different species of life. Great authorities like Bhīṣma, however, escape His bewilderment by the mercy of the Lord.

TEXT 19

अस्यानुभावं भगवान् वेद गुह्यतमं शिवः ।
देवर्षिर्नारदः साक्षाद्भगवान् कपिलो नृप ॥१९॥

asyānubhāvaṁ bhagavān
veda guhyatamaṁ śivaḥ
devarṣir nāradaḥ sākṣād
bhagavān kapilo nṛpa

asya—of Him; *anubhāvam*—glories; *bhagavān*—the most powerful; *veda*—knows; *guhya-tamam*—very confidentially; *śivaḥ*—Lord Śiva; *deva-ṛṣiḥ*—the great sage among the demigods; *nāradaḥ*—Nārada; *sākṣāt*—directly; *bhagavān*—the Personality of Godhead; *kapilaḥ*—Kapila; *nṛpa*—O King.

TRANSLATION

O King, Lord Śiva, Nārada the sage amongst the demigods, and Kapila, the incarnation of Godhead, all know very confidentially about His glories through direct contact.

PURPORT

Pure devotees of the Lord are all *bhāvas*, or persons who know the glories of the Lord in different transcendental loving services. As the Lord has innumerable expansions of His plenary form, there are innumerable pure devotees of the Lord, who are engaged in the exchange of service of different humors. Ordinarily there are twelve great devotees of the Lord, namely Brahmā, Nārada, Śiva, Kumāra, Kapila, Manu, Prahlāda, Bhīṣma, Janaka, Śukadeva Gosvāmī, Bali Mahārāja and Yamarāja. Bhīṣmadeva, although one of them, has mentioned only three important names of the twelve who know the glories of the Lord. Śrīla Viśvanātha Cakravartī Ṭhākura, one of the great *ācāryas* in the modern age, explains that *anubhāva*, or the glory of the Lord, is first appreciated by the devotee in ecstasy manifesting the symptoms of perspiring, trembling, weeping, bodily eruptions, etc., which are further enhanced by steady understanding of the glories of the Lord. Such different understandings of *bhāvas* are exchanged between Yaśodā and the Lord (binding the Lord by ropes) and in the chariot driving by the Lord in the exchange of love with Arjuna. These glories of the Lord are exhibited in His being subordinated before His devotees, and that is another feature of the glories of the Lord. Śukadeva Gosvāmī and the Kumāras, although situated in the transcendental position, became converted by another feature of *bhāva* and turned into pure devotees of the Lord. Tribulations imposed upon the devotees by the Lord constitute another exchange of transcendental *bhāva* between the Lord and the devotees. The Lord says "I put My devotee into difficulty, and thus the devotee becomes more purified in exchanging transcendental *bhāva* with Me." Placing the devotee into material troubles necessitates delivering him from the illusory material relations. The material relations are based on reciprocation of material enjoyment, which depends mainly on material resources. Therefore, when material resources are withdrawn by the Lord, the devotee is cent percent attracted toward the transcendental loving service of the Lord. Thus the Lord snatches the fallen soul from the mire of material existence. Tribulations offered by the Lord to His devotee are different from the tribulations resulting from vicious action. All these glories of the Lord are especially known to the great *mahājanas* like Brahmā, Śiva, Nārada, Kapila, Kumāra and Bhīṣma, as mentioned above, and one is able to grasp it by their grace.

TEXT 20

यं मन्यसे मातुलेयं प्रियं मित्रं सुहृत्तमम् ।
अकरोः सचिवं दूतं सौहृदादथ सारथिम् ॥२०॥

yaṁ manyase mātuleyaṁ
priyaṁ mitraṁ suhṛttamam
akaroḥ sacivaṁ dūtaṁ
sauhṛdād atha sārathim

yam—the person; *manyase*—you think; *mātuleyam*—maternal cousin; *priyam*—very dear; *mitram*—friend; *suhṛt-tamam*—ardent well-wisher; *akaroḥ*—executed; *sacivam*—counsel; *dūtam*—

messenger; *sauhṛdāt*—by good will; *atha*—thereupon; *sārathim*—charioteer.

TRANSLATION

O King, that personality whom, out of ignorance only, you thought to be your maternal cousin, your very dear friend, well-wisher, counselor, messenger, benefactor, etc., is that very Personality of Godhead, Śrī Kṛṣṇa.

PURPORT

Lord Śrī Kṛṣṇa, although acting as the cousin, brother, friend, well-wisher, counselor, messenger, benefactor, etc., of the Pāṇḍavas, was still the Supreme Personality of Godhead. Out of His causeless mercy and favor upon His unalloyed devotees, He performs all kinds of service, but that does not mean that He has changed His position as the Absolute Person. To think of Him as an ordinary man is the grossest type of ignorance.

TEXT 21

सर्वात्मनः समदृशो ह्यद्वयस्यानहङ्कृतेः ।
तत्कृतं मतिवैषम्यं निरवद्यस्य न क्वचित् ॥२१॥

sarvātmanaḥ sama-dṛśo
hy advayasyānahaṅkṛteḥ
tat-kṛtaṁ mati-vaiṣamyaṁ
niravadyasya na kvacit

sarva-ātmanaḥ—of one who is present in everyone's heart; *sama-dṛśaḥ*—of one who is equally kind to one and all; *hi*—certainly; *advayasya*—of the Absolute; *anahaṅkṛteḥ*—free from all material identity of false ego; *tat-kṛtam*—everything done by Him; *mati*—consciousness; *vaiṣamyam*—differentiation; *niravadyasya*—freed from all attachment; *na*—never; *kvacit*—at any stage.

TRANSLATION

Being the Absolute Personality of Godhead, He is present in everyone's heart. He is equally kind to everyone, and He is free

from the false ego of differentiation. Therefore whatever He does is free from material inebriety. He is equibalanced.

PURPORT

Because He is absolute, there is nothing different from Him. He is *kaivalya;* there is nothing except Himself. Everything and everyone is the manifestation of His energy, and thus He is present everywhere by His energy, being nondifferent from it. The sun is identified with every inch of the sun rays and every molecular particle of the rays. Similarly, the Lord is distributed by His different energies. He is Paramātmā, or the Supersoul, present in everyone as the supreme guidance, and therefore He is already the chariot driver and counsel of all living beings. When He, therefore, exhibits Himself as chariot driver of Arjuna, there is no change in His exalted position. It is the power of devotional service only that demonstrates Him as the chariot driver or the messenger. Since He has nothing to do with the material conception of life because He is absolute spiritual identity, there is for Him no superior or inferior action. Being the Absolute Personality of Godhead, He has no false ego, and so He does not identify Himself with anything different from Him. The material conception of ego is equibalanced in Him. He does not feel, therefore, inferior by becoming the chariot driver of His pure devotee. It is the glory of the pure devotee that only he can bring about service from the affectionate Lord.

TEXT 22

तथाप्येकान्तभक्तेषु पश्य भूपानुकम्पितम् ।
यन्मेऽसूंस्त्यजतः साक्षात्कृष्णो दर्शनमागतः ॥२२॥

tathāpy ekānta-bhakteṣu
paśya bhūpānukampitam
yan me 'sūṁs tyajataḥ sākṣāt
kṛṣṇo darśanam āgataḥ

tathāpi—still; *ekānta*—unflinching; *bhakteṣu*—unto the devotees; *paśya*—see here; *bhū-pa*—O King; *anukampitam*—how sympathetic; *yat*—for which; *me*—my; *asūn*—life; *tyajataḥ*—ending; *sākṣāt*—

directly; *kṛṣṇaḥ*—the Personality of Godhead; *darśanam*—in my view; *āgataḥ*—has kindly come.

TRANSLATION

Yet, despite His being equally kind to everyone, He has graciously come before me while I am ending my life, for I am His unflinching servitor.

PURPORT

The Supreme Lord, the Absolute Personality of Godhead, Śrī Kṛṣṇa, although equal to everyone, is still more inclined to His unflinching devotee who is completely surrendered and knows no one else as his protector and master. Having unflinching faith in the Supreme Lord as one's protector, friend and master is the natural condition of eternal life. A living entity is so made by the will of the Almighty that he is most happy when placing himself in a condition of absolute dependence.

The opposite tendency is the cause of falldown. The living entity has this tendency of falling down by dint of misidentifying himself as fully independent to lord it over the material world. The root cause of all troubles is there in false egotism. One must draw towards the Lord in all circumstances.

The appearance of Lord Kṛṣṇa at the deathbed of Bhīṣmajī is due to his being an unflinching devotee of the Lord. Arjuna had some bodily relation with Kṛṣṇa because the Lord happened to be his maternal cousin. But Bhīṣma had no such bodily relation. Therefore the cause of attraction was due to the intimate relation of the soul. Yet because the relation of the body is very pleasing and natural, the Lord is more pleased when He is addressed as the son of Mahārāja Nanda, the son of Yaśodā, the lover of Rādhārāṇī. This affinity by bodily relation with the Lord is another feature of reciprocating loving service with the Lord. Bhīṣmadeva is conscious of this sweetness of transcendental humor, and therefore he likes to address the Lord as Vijaya-sakhe, Pārtha-sakhe, etc., exactly like Nanda-nandana or Yaśodā-nandana. The best way to establish our relation in transcendental sweetness is to approach Him through His recognized devotees. One should not try to establish the relation directly; there must be a via medium which is transparent and competent to lead us to the right path.

TEXT 23

भक्त्यावेश्य मनो यस्मिन् वाचा यन्नाम कीर्तयन् ।
त्यजन् कलेवरं योगी मुच्यते कामकर्मभिः ॥२३॥

bhaktyāveśya mano yasmin
vācā yan-nāma kīrtayan
tyajan kalevaraṁ yogī
mucyate kāma-karmabhiḥ

bhaktyā—with devout attention; *āveśya*—meditating; *manaḥ*—mind; *yasmin*—in whose; *vācā*—by words; *yat*—Kṛṣṇa; *nāma*—holy name; *kīrtayan*—by chanting; *tyajan*—quitting; *kalevaram*—this material body; *yogī*—the devotee; *mucyate*—gets release; *kāma-karmabhiḥ*—from fruitive activities.

TRANSLATION

The Personality of Godhead, who appears in the mind of the devotee by attentive devotion and meditation and by chanting of the holy name, releases the devotee from the bondage of fruitive activities at the time of his quitting the material body.

PURPORT

Yoga means concentration of the mind detached from all other subject matter. And actually such concentration is *samādhi*, or cent percent engagement in the service of the Lord. And one who concentrates his attention in that manner is called a *yogī*. Such a *yogī* devotee of the Lord engages himself twenty-four hours daily in the service of the Lord so that his whole attention is engrossed with the thoughts of the Lord in ninefold devotional service, namely hearing, chanting, remembering, worshiping, praying, becoming a voluntary servant, carrying out orders, establishing a friendly relationship, or offering all that one may possess, in the service of the Lord. By such practice of *yoga*, or linking up in the service of the Lord, one is recognized by the Lord Himself, as it is explained in the *Bhagavad-gītā* concerning the highest perfectional stage of *samādhi*. The Lord calls such a rare devotee the best amongst all the *yogīs*. Such a perfect *yogī* is enabled by the divine grace of the Lord to concentrate his mind upon the Lord with a perfect sense of consciousness, and thus by chanting His holy name before quitting the body the *yogī* is at once transferred by the internal energy of the Lord to one of the eternal planets where there is no question of material life and its concomitant factors. In material existence a living being has to endure the material conditions of threefold miseries, life after life, according to his fruitive work. Such material life is produced by material desires only. Devotional service to the Lord does not kill the natural desires of the living being, but they are applied in the right cause of devotional service. This qualifies the desire to be transferred to the spiritual sky. General Bhīṣmadeva is referring to a particular type of *yoga* called *bhakti-yoga*, and he was fortunate enough to have the Lord directly in his presence before he quitted his material body. He therefore desired that the Lord stay before his view in the following verses.

TEXT 24

स देवदेवो भगवान् प्रतीक्षतां
कलेवरं यावदिदं हिनोम्यहम् ।
प्रसन्नहासारुणलोचनोल्लस-
न्मुखाम्बुजो ध्यानपथश्चतुर्भुजः ॥२४॥

sa deva-devo bhagavān pratīkṣatāṁ
kalevaraṁ yāvad idaṁ hinomy aham
prasanna-hāsāruṇa-locanollasan-
mukhāmbujo dhyāna-pathaś catur-bhujaḥ

saḥ—He; *deva-devaḥ*—the Supreme Lord of the lords; *bhagavān*—the Personality of Godhead; *pratīkṣatām*—may kindly wait; *kalevaram*—body; *yāvat*—as long as; *idam*—this (material body); *hinomi*—may quit; *aham*—I; *prasanna*—cheerful; *hāsa*—smiling; *aruṇa-locana*—eyes red like the morning sun; *ullasat*—beautifully decorated; *mukha-ambujaḥ*—the lotus flower of His face; *dhyāna-pathaḥ*—in the path of my meditation; *catur-bhujaḥ*—the four-handed form of Nārāyaṇa (the worshipable Deity of Bhīṣmadeva).

TRANSLATION

May my Lord, who is four-handed and whose beautifully decorated lotus face, with eyes as red as the rising sun, is smiling, kindly await me at that moment when I quit this material body.

PURPORT

Bhīṣmadeva knew well that Lord Kṛṣṇa is the original Nārāyaṇa. His worshipable Deity was four-handed Nārāyaṇa, but he knew that four-handed Nārāyaṇa is a plenary expansion of Lord Kṛṣṇa. Indirectly he desired Lord Śrī Kṛṣṇa to manifest Himself in His four-handed feature of Nārāyaṇa. A Vaiṣṇava is always humble in his behavior. Although it was cent percent certain that Bhīṣmadeva was approaching *Vaikuṇṭha-dhāma* just after leaving his material body, still as a humble Vaiṣṇava he desired to see the beautiful face of the Lord, for after quitting the present body he might not be in a position to see the Lord any more. A Vaiṣṇava is not puffed up, although the Lord guarantees His pure devotee entrance into His abode. Here Bhīṣmadeva says, "as long as I do not quit this body." This means that the great General would quit the body by his own will; he was not being forced by the laws of nature. He was so powerful that he could stay in his body as long as he desired. He got this benediction from his father. He desired that the Lord stay before him in His four-handed Nārāyaṇa feature so that he might concentrate upon Him and thus be in trance in that meditation. Then his mind might be sanctified with thinking of the Lord. Thus he did not mind wherever he might go. A pure devotee is never very anxious to go back to the kingdom of God. He entirely depends on the good will of the Lord. He is equally satisfied even if the Lord desires him to go to hell. The only desire that a pure devotee entertains is that he may always be in rapt attention with thinking of the lotus feet of the Lord, regardless. Bhīṣmadeva wanted this much only: that his mind be absorbed in thinking of the Lord and that he pass away thus. That is the highest ambition of a pure devotee.

TEXT 25

सूत उवाच

युधिष्ठिरस्तदाकर्ण्य शयानं शरपञ्जरे ।
अपृच्छद्विविधान्धर्मानृषीणां चानुशृण्वताम् ॥२५॥

sūta uvāca
yudhiṣṭhiras tad ākarṇya
śayānaṁ śara-pañjare
apṛcchad vividhān dharmān
ṛṣīṇāṁ cānuśṛṇvatām

sūtaḥ uvāca—Śrī Sūta Gosvāmī said; *yudhiṣṭhiraḥ*—King Yudhiṣṭhira; *tat*—that; *ākarṇya*—hearing; *śayānam*—lying down; *śara-pañjare*—on the bed of arrows; *apṛcchat*—asked; *vividhān*—multifarious; *dharmān*—duties; *ṛṣīṇām*—of the *ṛṣis; ca*—and; *anuśṛṇvatām*—hearing after.

TRANSLATION

Sūta Gosvāmī said: Mahārāja Yudhiṣṭhira, after hearing Bhīṣmadeva speak in that appealing tone, asked him, in the presence of all the great ṛṣis, about the essential principles of various religious duties.

PURPORT

Bhīṣmadeva, speaking in that appealing tone, convinced Mahārāja Yudhiṣṭhira that he was very soon passing away. And Mahārāja Yudhiṣṭhira was inspired by Lord Śrī Kṛṣṇa to ask him of the principles of religion. Lord Śrī Kṛṣṇa inspired Mahārāja Yudhiṣṭhira to ask Bhīṣmadeva in the presence of many great sages, indicating thereby that the Lord's devotee like Bhīṣmadeva, although apparently living as a worldly man, is far superior to many great sages, even Vyāsadeva. Another point is that Bhīṣmadeva at that time was not only lying on a deathbed of arrows, but was greatly aggrieved because of that state. One should not have asked him any question at that time, but Lord Śrī Kṛṣṇa wanted to prove that His pure devotees are always sound in body and mind by dint of spiritual enlightenment, and thus in any circumstances a devotee of the Lord is in perfect order to speak of the right way of life. Yudhiṣṭhira also preferred to solve his problematic questions by asking Bhīṣmadeva rather than ask anyone else present there who was seemingly more learned than Bhīṣmadeva. This is all due to the arrangement of the great wheel-carrier Lord Śrī Kṛṣṇa, who establishes the glories of His devotee. The father likes to see the son become more famous than himself. The Lord declares very emphatically that worship of His devotee is more valuable than the worship of the Lord Himself.

TEXT 26

पुरुषस्वभावविहितान् यथावर्णं यथाश्रमम् ।
वैराग्यरागोपाधिभ्यामाम्नातोभयलक्षणान् ॥२६॥

puruṣa-sva-bhāva-vihitān
yathā-varṇaṁ yathāśramam
vairāgya-rāgopādhibhyām
āmnātobhaya-lakṣaṇān

puruṣa—the human being; *sva-bhāva*—by his own acquired qualities; *vihitān*—prescribed; *yathā*—according to; *varṇam*—classification of castes; *yathā*—according to; *āśramam*—orders of life; *vairāgya*—detachment; *rāga*—attachment; *upādhibhyām*—out of such designations; *āmnāta*—systematically; *ubhaya*—both; *lakṣaṇān*—symptoms.

TRANSLATION

At Mahārāja Yudhiṣṭhira's inquiry, Bhīṣmadeva first defined all the classifications of castes and orders of life in terms of the individual's qualifications. Then he systematically, in twofold divisions, described counteraction by detachment and interaction by attachment.

PURPORT

The conception of four castes and four orders of life, as planned by the Lord Himself (Bg. 4.13), is to accelerate transcendental qualities of the individual person so that he may gradually realize his spiritual identity and thus act accordingly to get free from material bondage, or conditional life. In almost all the *Purāṇas* the subject matter is described in the same spirit, and so also in the *Mahābhārata* it is more elaborately described by Bhīṣmadeva in the *Śānti-parva*, beginning from the sixtieth chapter.

The *varṇāśrama-dharma* is prescribed for the civilized human being just to train him to successfully terminate human life. Self-realization is distinguished from the life of the lower animals engaged in eating, sleeping, fearing and mating. Bhīṣmadeva advised for all human beings nine qualifications: (1) not to become angry, (2) not to lie, (3) to equally distribute wealth, (4) to forgive, (5) to beget children only by one's legitimate wife, (6) to be pure in mind and hygienic in body, (7) not to be inimical toward anyone, (8) to be simple, and (9) to support servants or subordinates. One cannot be called a civilized person without acquiring the above-mentioned preliminary qualities. Besides these, the *brāhmaṇas* (the intelligent men), the administrative men, the mercantile community and the laborer class must acquire special qualities in terms of occupational duties mentioned in all the Vedic scriptures. For the intelligent men, controlling the senses is the most essential qualification. It is the basis of morality. Sex indulgence even with a legitimate wife must also be controlled, and thereby family control will automatically follow. An intelligent man abuses his great qualifications if he does not follow the Vedic way of life. This means he must seriously make a study of the Vedic literatures, especially of the *Śrīmad-Bhāgavatam* and the *Bhagavad-gītā*. For learning Vedic knowledge, one must approach a person who is cent percent engaged in devotional service. He must not do things which are forbidden in the *śāstras*. A person cannot be a teacher if he drinks or smokes. In the modern system of education the teacher's academic qualification is taken into consideration without evaluation of his moral life. Therefore, the result of education is misuse of high intelligence in so many ways.

The *kṣatriya*, the member of the administrative class, is especially advised to give charity *and not to accept charity in any circumstances.* Modern administrators raise subscriptions for some political functions, but never give charity to the citizens in any state function. It is just the reverse in the injunctions of the *śāstras*. The administrative class must be well versed in the *śāstras*, but must not take to the profession of teachers. *The administrators should never pretend to become nonviolent* and thereby go to hell. When Arjuna wanted to become a nonviolent coward on the Battlefield of Kurukṣetra, he was severely chastised by Lord Kṛṣṇa. The Lord degraded Arjuna at that time to the status of an uncivilized man for his avowed acceptance of the cult of nonviolence. The administrative class must be personally trained in military education. Cowards should not be elevated to the presidential throne by dint of numerical votes only. The monarchs were all chivalrous personalities, and therefore monarchy should be maintained provided the monarch is regularly trained in the occupational duties of a king. *In fighting, the king or the president should never return home without being hurt by the enemy.* The so-called king of today never visits the warfield. He is very much expert in artificially encouraging the fighting strength in the hope of false national prestige. As soon as the administrative class is turned into a gang of mercantile and laborer men, the whole machinery of government becomes polluted.

The *vaiśyas*, the members of the mercantile communities, are especially advised to protect the cows. Cow protection means increasing the milk productions, namely curd and butter. Agriculture and distribution of the foodstuff are the primary duties of the mercantile community backed by education in Vedic knowledge and trained to give in charity. As the *kṣatriyas* were given charge of the protection of the citizens, *vaiśyas* were given the charge of the protection of animals. Animals are never meant to be killed. Killing of animals is a symptom of barbarian society. For a human being, agricultural produce, fruits and milk are sufficient and compatible foodstuffs. The human society should give more attention to animal protection. The productive energy of the laborer is misused when he is occupied by industrial enterprises. Industry of various types cannot produce the essential needs of man, namely rice, wheat, grains, milk, fruits and vegetables. The production of machines and machine tools increases the artificial living fashion of a class of vested interests and keeps thousands of men in starvation and unrest. This should not be the standard of civilization.

The *śūdra* class is less intelligent and should have no independence. They are meant for rendering sincere service to the three higher sections of the society. The *śūdra* class can attain all comforts of life simply by rendering service to the higher classes. It is especially enjoined that a *śūdra* should never bank money. As soon as the *śūdras* accumulate wealth, it will be misused for sinful activities in wine, women and gambling. *Wine, women and gambling indicate that the population is degraded to less than śūdra quality.* The higher castes should always look after the maintenance of the *śūdras*, and they should provide them with old and used garments. A *śūdra* should not leave his master when the master is old and invalid, and the master should keep the servants satisfied in all respects. The *śūdras* must first of all be satisfied by sumptuous food and clothing before any sacrifice is performed. In this age so many functions are held by spending millions, *but the poor laborer is not sumptuously fed or given charity, clothing, etc.* The laborers are thus dissatisfied, and so they make agitation.

The *varṇas* are, so to speak, classifications of different occupations, and *āśrama-dharma* is gradual progress on the path of self-realization. Both are interrelated, and one is dependent on the other. The main purpose of *āśrama-dharma* is to awaken knowledge and detachment. The *brahmacārī āśrama* is the training ground for the prospective candidates. In this *āśrama* it is instructed that this material world is not actually the home of the living being. The conditioned souls under material bondage are prisoners of matter, and therefore self-realization is the ultimate aim of life. The whole system of *āśrama-dharma* is a means to detachment. One who fails to assimilate this spirit of detachment is allowed to enter into family life with the same spirit of detachment. Therefore, one who attains detachment may at once adopt the fourth order, namely, renounced, and thus live on charity only, not to accumulate wealth, but just to keep body and soul together for ultimate realization. Household life is for *one who is attached*, and the *vānaprastha* and *sannyāsa* orders of life are for *those who are detached* from material life. The *brahmacārī-āśrama* is especially meant for training both the attached and detached.

TEXT 27

दानधर्मान् राजधर्मान् मोक्षधर्मान् विभागशः ।
स्त्रीधर्मान् भगवद्धर्मान् समासव्यासयोगतः ॥२७॥

dāna-dharmān rāja-dharmān
mokṣa-dharmān vibhāgaśaḥ
strī-dharmān bhagavad-dharmān
samāsa-vyāsa-yogataḥ

dāna-dharmān—the acts of charity; *rāja-dharmān*—pragmatic activities of the kings; *mokṣa-dharmān*—the acts for salvation; *vibhāgaśaḥ*—by divisions; *strī-dharmān*—duties of women; *bhagavat-*

dharmān—the acts of the devotees; *samāsa*—generally; *vyāsa*—explicitly; *yogataḥ*—by means of.

TRANSLATION

He then explained, by divisions, acts of charity, the pragmatic activities of a king and activities for salvation. Then he described the duties of women and devotees, both briefly and extensively.

PURPORT

To give charity is one of the householder's main functions, and he should be prepared to give in charity at least fifty percent of his hard-earned money. A *brahmacārī,* or student, should perform sacrifices, a householder should give charity, and a person in the retired life or in the renounced order should practice penances and austerities. Those are the general functions of all the *āśramas*, or orders of life on the path of self-realization. In the *brahmacārī* life the training is sufficiently imparted so that one may understand that the world as property belongs to the Supreme Lord, the Personality of Godhead. No one, therefore, can claim to be the proprietor of anything in the world. Therefore, in the life of a householder, which is a sort of license for sex enjoyment, one must give in charity for the service of the Lord. Everyone's energy is generated or borrowed from the reservoir of energy of the Lord; therefore, the resultant actions of such energy must be given to the Lord in the shape of transcendental loving service for Him. As the rivers draw water from the sea through the clouds and again go down to the sea, similarly our energy is borrowed from the supreme source, the Lord's energy, and it must return to the Lord. That is the perfection of our energy. The Lord, therefore, in the *Bhagavad-gītā* (9.27) says that whatever we do, whatever we undergo as penance, whatever we sacrifice, whatever we eat or whatever we give in charity must be offered to Him (the Lord). That is the way of utilizing our borrowed energy. When our energy is utilized in that way, our energy is purified from the contamination of material inebrieties, and thus we become fit for our original natural life of service to the Lord.

Rāja-dharma is a great science, unlike modern diplomacy for political supremacy. The kings were trained systematically to become munificent and not merely be tax collectors. They were trained to perform different sacrifices only for the prosperity of the subjects. To lead the *prajās* to the attainment of salvation was a great duty of the king. The father, the spiritual master and the king are not to become irresponsible in the matter of leading their subjects to the path of ultimate liberation from birth, death, diseases and old age. When these primary duties are properly discharged, there is no need of government of the people, by the people. In modern days the people in general occupy the administration by the strength of manipulated votes, but they are never trained in the primary duties of the king, and that is also not possible for everyone. Under the circumstances the untrained administrators play havoc to make the subjects happy in all respects. On the other hand, these untrained administrators gradually become rogues and thieves and increase the taxation to finance a top-heavy administration that is useless for all purposes. Actually the qualified *brāhmaṇas* are meant to give direction to the kings for proper administration in terms of the scriptures like the *Manu-saṁhitā* and *Dharma-śāstras* of Parāśara. A typical king is the ideal of the people in general, and if the king is pious, religious, chivalrous and munificent, the citizens generally follow him. Such a king is not a lazy sensuous person living at the cost of the subjects, but alert always to kill thieves and dacoits. The pious kings were not merciful to dacoits and thieves in the name of nonsensical *ahiṁsā* (nonviolence). The thieves and dacoits were punished in an exemplary way so that in the future no one would dare commit such nuisances in an organized form. Such thieves and dacoits were never meant for administration as they are now.

The taxation law was simple. There was no force, no encroachment. The king had a right to take one fourth of the production made by the subject. The king had a right to claim a fourth of one's allotted wealth. One would never grudge parting with it because due to the pious king and religious harmony there was enough natural wealth, namely grains, fruits, flowers, silk, cotton, milk, jewels, minerals, etc., and therefore no one was materially unhappy. The citizens were rich in agriculture and animal husbandry, and therefore they had enough grains, fruits and milk without any artificial needs of soaps and toilets, cinemas and bars.

The king had to see that the reserved energy of humanity was properly utilized. Human energy is meant not exactly for fulfilling animal propensities, but for self-realization. The whole government was specifically designed to fulfill this particular purpose. As such, the king had to select properly the cabinet ministers, but not on the strength of voting background. The ministers, the military commanders and even the ordinary soldiers were all selected by personal qualification, and the king had to supervise them properly before they were appointed to their respective posts. The king was especially vigilant to see that the *tapasvīs*, or persons who sacrificed everything for disseminating spiritual knowledge, were never disregarded. *The king knew well that the Supreme Personality of Godhead never tolerates any insult to His unalloyed devotees.* Such *tapasvīs* were trusted leaders even of the rogues and thieves, who would never disobey the orders of *tapasvīs*. The king would give special protection to illiterates, the helpless and widows of the state. Defense measures were arranged previous to any attack by the enemies. The taxing process was easy, and it was not meant for squandering, but was for strengthening the reserve fund. The soldiers were recruited from all parts of the world, and they were trained for special duties.

As far as salvation is concerned, one has to conquer the principles of lust, anger, unlawful desires, avarice and bewilderment. To get freedom from anger, one should learn how to forgive. To be free from unlawful desires one should not make plans. By spiritual culture one is able to conquer sleep. By tolerance only can one conquer desires and avarice. Disturbances from various diseases can be avoided by regulated diets. By self-control one can be free from false hopes, and money can be saved by avoiding undesirable association. By practice of *yoga* one can control hunger, and worldliness can be avoided by culturing the knowledge of impermanence. Dizziness can be conquered by rising up, and false arguments can be conquered by factual ascertainment. Talkativeness can be avoided by gravity and silence, and by prowess one can avoid fearfulness. Perfect knowledge can be obtained by self-cultivation. One must be free from lust, avarice, anger, dreaming, etc., to actually attain the path of salvation.

As far as the women class are concerned, they are accepted as a power of inspiration for men. As such, women are more powerful than men. Mighty Julius Caesar was controlled by a Cleopatra. Such powerful women are controlled by shyness. Therefore, shyness is important for women. Once this control valve is loosened, women can create havoc in society by adultery. Adultery means production of unwanted children known as *varṇa-saṅkara*, who disturb the world.

The last item taught by Bhīṣmadeva was the process of pleasing the Lord. We are all eternal servants of the Lord, and when we forget this essential part of our nature we are put into material conditions of life. The simple process of pleasing the Lord (for the householders especially) is to install the Deity of the Lord at home. By concentrating on the Deity, one may progressively go on with the daily routine work. Worshiping the Deity at home, serving the devotee, hearing the *Śrīmad-Bhāgavatam*, residing in a holy place and chanting the holy name of the Lord are all inexpensive items by which one can please the Lord. Thus the subject matter was explained by the grandfather to his grandchildren.

TEXT 28

धर्मार्थकाममोक्षांश्च सहोपायान् यथा मुने ।
नानाख्यानेतिहासेषु वर्णयामास तत्त्ववित् ॥२८॥

dharmārtha-kāma-mokṣāṁś ca
sahopāyān yathā mune
nānākhyānetihāseṣu
varṇayām āsa tattvavit

dharma—occupational duties; *artha*—economic development; *kāma*—fulfillment of desires; *mokṣān*—ultimate salvation; *ca*—and; *saha*—along with; *upāyān*—means; *yathā*—as it is; *mune*—O sage; *nānā*—various; *ākhyāna*—by recitation of historical narrations; *itihāseṣu*—in the histories; *varṇayām āsa*—described; *tatta-vit*—one who knows the truth.

TRANSLATION

Then he described the occupational duties of different orders and statuses of life, citing instances from history, for he was himself well acquainted with the truth.

PURPORT

Incidents mentioned in the Vedic literatures, such as the *Purāṇas*, *Mahābhārata* and *Rāmāyaṇa* are factual historical narrations that took place sometime in the past, although not in any chronological order. Such historical facts, being instructive for ordinary men, were assorted without chronological reference. Besides that, they happen on different planets, nay, in different universes, and thus the description of the narrations is sometimes measured by three dimensions. We are simply concerned with the instructive lessons of such incidents, even though they are not in order by our limited range of understanding. Bhīṣmadeva described such narrations before Mahārāja Yudhiṣṭhira in reply to his different questions.

TEXT 29

धर्मं प्रवदतस्तस्य स कालः प्रत्युपस्थितः ।
यो योगिनश्छन्दमृत्योर्वाञ्छितस्तूत्तरायणः ॥२९॥

dharmaṁ pravadatas tasya
sa kālaḥ pratyupasthitaḥ
yo yoginaś chanda-mṛtyor
vāñchitas tūttarāyaṇaḥ

dharmam—occupational duties; *pravadataḥ*—while describing; *tasya*—his; *saḥ*—that; *kālaḥ*—time; *pratyupasthitaḥ*—exactly appeared; *yaḥ*—that is; *yoginaḥ*—for the mystics; *chanda-mṛtyoḥ*—of one who dies according to one's own selection of time; *vāñchitaḥ*—is desired by; *tu*—but; *uttarāyaṇaḥ*—the period when the sun runs on the northern horizon.

TRANSLATION

While Bhīṣmadeva was describing occupational duties, the sun's course ran into the northern hemisphere. This period is desired by mystics who die at their will.

PURPORT

The perfect *yogīs* or mystics can leave the material body at their own sweet will at a suitable time and go to a suitable planet desired by them. In the *Bhagavad-gītā* (8.24) it is said that self-realized souls who have exactly identified themselves with the interest of the Supreme Lord can generally leave the material body during the time of the fire-god's effulgence and when the sun is in the northern horizon, and thus achieve the transcendental sky. In the *Vedas* these times are considered auspicious for quitting the body, and they are taken advantage of by the expert mystics who have perfected the system. Perfection of *yoga* means attainment of such supermental states as to be able to leave the material body as desired. *Yogīs* can also reach any planet within no time without a material vehicle. The *yogīs* can reach the highest planetary system within a very short time, and this is impossible for the materialist. Even attempting to reach the highest planet will take millions of years at a speed of millions of miles per hour. This is a different science, and Bhīṣmadeva knew well how to utilize it. He was just waiting for the suitable moment to quit his material body, and the golden opportunity arrived when he was instructing his noble grandsons, the Pāṇḍavas. He thus prepared himself to quit his body before the exalted Lord Śrī Kṛṣṇa, the pious Pāṇḍavas and the great sages headed by Bhagavān Vyāsa, etc., all great souls.

TEXT 30

तदोपसंहृत्य गिरः सहस्रणी-
विमुक्तसङ्गं मन आदिपूरुषे ।
कृष्णे लसत्पीतपटे चतुर्भुजे
पुरःस्थितेऽमीलितदृग्व्यधारयत् ॥३०॥

tadopasaṁhṛtya giraḥ sahasraṇīr
vimukta-saṅgaṁ mana ādi-pūruṣe
kṛṣṇe lasat-pīta-paṭe catur-bhuje
puraḥ sthite 'mīlita-dṛg vyadhārayat

tadā—at that time; *upasaṁhṛtya*—withdrawing; *giraḥ*—speech; *sahasraṇīḥ*—Bhīṣmadeva (who was expert in thousands of sciences and arts); *vimukta-saṅgam*—completely freed from everything else; *manaḥ*—mind; *ādi-pūruṣe*—unto the original Personality of Godhead; *kṛṣṇe*—unto Kṛṣṇa; *lasat-pīta-paṭe*—decorated with yellow garments; *catur-bhuje*—unto the four-handed original Nārāyaṇa; *puraḥ*—just before; *sthite*—standing; *amīlita*—widespread; *dṛk*—vision; *vyadhārayat*—fixed.

TRANSLATION

Thereupon that man who spoke on different subjects with thousands of meanings and who fought on thousands of battlefields

and protected thousands of men, stopped speaking and, being completely freed from all bondage, withdrew his mind from everything else and fixed his wide-open eyes upon the original Personality of Godhead, Śrī Kṛṣṇa, who stood before him, four-handed, dressed in yellow garments that glittered and shined.

PURPORT

In the momentous hour of leaving his material body, Bhīṣmadeva set the glorious example concerning the important function of the human form of life. *The subject matter which attracts the dying man becomes the beginning of his next life.* Therefore, if one is absorbed in thoughts of the Supreme Lord Śrī Kṛṣṇa, he is sure to go back to Godhead without any doubt. This is confirmed in the *Bhagavad-gītā* (8.5–15):

5: And whoever, at the time of death, quits his body remembering Me alone, at once attains My nature. Of this there is no doubt.

6: Whatever state of being one remembers when he quits his body, that state he will attain without fail.

7: Therefore, Arjuna, you should always think of Me in the form of Kṛṣṇa and at the same time carry out your prescribed duty of fighting. With your activities dedicated to Me and your mind and intelligence fixed on Me, you will attain Me without doubt.

8: He who meditates on the Supreme Personality of Godhead, his mind constantly engaged in remembering Me, undeviated from the path, he, O Pārtha [Arjuna], is sure to reach Me.

9: One should meditate upon the Supreme Person as the one who knows everything, as He who is the oldest, who is the controller, who is smaller than the smallest, who is the maintainer of everything, who is beyond all material conception, who is inconceivable, and who is always a person. He is luminous like the sun and, being transcendental, is beyond this material nature.

10: One who, at the time of death, fixes his life air between the eyebrows and in full devotion engages himself in remembering the Supreme Lord will certainly attain to the Supreme Personality of Godhead.

11: Persons learned in the *Vedas*, who utter *oṁkāra* and who are great sages in the renounced order, enter into Brahman. Desiring such perfection, one practices celibacy. I shall now explain to you this process by which one may attain salvation.

12: The yogic situation is that of detachment from all sensual engagements. Closing all the doors of the senses and fixing the mind on the heart and the life air at the top of the head, one establishes himself in *yoga*.

13: After being situated in this *yoga* practice and vibrating the sacred syllable *oṁ*, the supreme combination of letters, if one thinks of the Supreme Personality of Godhead and quits his body, he will certainly reach the spiritual planets.

14: For one who remembers Me without deviation, I am easy to obtain, O son of Pṛthā, because of his constant engagement in devotional service.

15: After attaining Me, the great souls, who are *yogīs* in devotion, never return to this temporary world, which is full of miseries, because they have attained the highest perfection.

Śrī Bhīṣmadeva attained the perfection of quitting his body at will and was fortunate enough to have Lord Kṛṣṇa, the object of his attention, personally present at the time of death. He therefore fixed his open eyes upon Him. He wanted to see Śrī Kṛṣṇa for a long time out of his spontaneous love for Him. Because he was a pure devotee, he had very little to do with the detailed performance of yogic principles. Simple *bhakti-yoga* is enough to bring about perfection. Therefore, the ardent desire of Bhīṣmadeva was to see the *person* of Lord Kṛṣṇa, the most lovable object, and by the grace of the Lord, Śrī Bhīṣmadeva had this opportunity at the last stage of his breathing.

TEXT 31

विशुद्धया धारणया हताशुभ-
स्तदीक्षयैवाशु गतायुधश्रमः ।
निवृत्तसर्वेन्द्रियवृत्तिविभ्रम-
स्तुष्टाव जन्यं विसृजञ्जनार्दनम् ॥३१॥

viśuddhayā dhāraṇayā hatāśubhas
tad-īkṣayaivāśu gatā-yudha-śramaḥ
nivṛtta-sarvendriya-vṛtti-vibhramas
tuṣṭāva janyaṁ visṛjañ janārdanam

viśuddhayā—by purified; *dhāraṇayā*—meditation; *hata-aśubhaḥ*—one who has minimized the inauspicious qualities of material existence; *tat*—Him; *īkṣayā*—by looking on; *eva*—simply; *āśu*—immediately; *gatā*—having gone away; *yudha*—from the arrows; *śramaḥ*—fatigue; *nivṛtta*—being stopped; *sarva*—all; *indriya*—senses; *vṛtti*—activities; *vibhramaḥ*—being widely engaged; *tuṣṭāva*—he prayed; *janyam*—the material tabernacle; *visṛjan*—while quitting; *janārdanam*—to the controller of the living beings.

TRANSLATION

By pure meditation, looking at Lord Śrī Kṛṣṇa, he at once was freed from all material inauspiciousness and was relieved of all bodily pains caused by the arrow wounds. Thus all the external activities of his senses at once stopped, and he prayed transcendentally to the controller of all living beings while quitting his material body.

PURPORT

The material body is a gift of the material energy, technically called illusion. Identification with the material body is due to forgetfulness of our eternal relationship with the Lord. For a pure devotee of the Lord like Bhīṣmadeva, this illusion was at once removed as soon as the Lord arrived. Lord Kṛṣṇa is like the sun, and the illusory, external material energy is like darkness. In the presence of the sun there is no possibility that darkness can stand. Therefore, just on the arrival of Lord Kṛṣṇa, all material contamination was completely removed, and Bhīṣmadeva was thus able to be transcendentally situated by stopping the activities of the impure senses in collaboration with matter. The soul is originally pure and so also the senses. By material contamination the senses assume the role of imperfection and impurity. By revival of contact with the Supreme Pure, Lord Kṛṣṇa, the senses again become freed from material contaminations. Bhīṣmadeva attained all these transcendental conditions prior to his leaving the material body because of presence of the Lord. The Lord is the controller and benefactor of all living beings. That is the verdict of all *Vedas*. He is the supreme eternity and living entity amongst all the eternal living beings.* And He alone provides all necessities for all kinds of living beings. Thus He provided all facilities to fulfill the transcendental desires of His great devotee Śrī Bhiṣmadeva, who began to pray as follows.

TEXT 32

श्रीभीष्म उवाच
इति मतिरुपकल्पिता वितृष्णा
भगवति सात्वतपुङ्गवे विभूम्नि ।
स्वसुखमुपगते क्वचिद्विहर्तुं
प्रकृतिमुपेयुषि यद्भवप्रवाहः ॥३२॥

śrī-bhīṣma uvāca
iti matir upakalpitā vitṛṣṇā
bhagavati sātvata-puṅgave vibhūmni
sva-sukham upagate kvacid vihartuṁ
prakṛtim upeyuṣi yad-bhava-pravāhaḥ

śrī-bhīṣmaḥ uvāca—Śrī Bhīṣmadeva said; *iti*—thus; *matiḥ*—thinking, feeling and willing; *upakalpitā*—invested; *vitṛṣṇā*—freed from all sense desires; *bhagavati*—unto the Personality of Godhead; *sātvata-puṅgave*—unto the leader of the devotees; *vibhūmni*—unto the great; *sva-sukham*—self-satisfaction; *upagate*—unto He who has attained it; *kvacit*—sometimes; *vihartum*—out of transcendental pleasure; *prakṛtim*—in the material world; *upeyuṣi*—do accept it; *yat-bhava*—from whom the creation; *pravāhaḥ*—is made and annihilated.

TRANSLATION

Bhiṣmadeva said: Let me now invest my thinking, feeling and willing, which were so long engaged in different subjects and

---

**nityo nityānāṁ cetanaś cetanānām*
eko bahūnāṁ yo vidadhāti kāmān
(*Kaṭha Upaniṣad*)

occupational duties, in the all-powerful Lord Śrī Kṛṣṇa. He is always self-satisfied, but sometimes, being the leader of the devotees, He enjoys transcendental pleasure by descending on the material world, although from Him only the material world is created.

PURPORT

Because Bhīṣmadeva was a statesman, the head of the Kuru dynasty, a great general and a leader of *kṣatriyas*, his mind was strewn over so many subjects, and his thinking, feeling and willing were engaged in different matters. Now, in order to achieve pure devotional service, he wanted to invest all powers of thinking, feeling and willing entirely in the Supreme Being, Lord Kṛṣṇa. He is described herein as the leader of the devotees and all-powerful. Although Lord Kṛṣṇa is the original Personality of Godhead, He Himself descends on earth to bestow upon His pure devotees the boon of devotional service. He descends sometimes as Lord Kṛṣṇa as He is, and sometimes as Lord Caitanya. Both are leaders of the pure devotees. Pure devotees of the Lord have no desire other than the service of the Lord, and therefore they are called *sātvata*. The Lord is the chief amongst such *sātvatas*. Bhīṣmadeva, therefore, had no other desires. Unless one is purified from all sorts of material desires, the Lord does not become one's leader. Desires cannot be wiped out, but they have only to be purified. It is confirmed in the *Bhagavad-gītā* by the Lord Himself that He gives His instruction from within the heart of a pure devotee who is constantly engaged in the service of the Lord. Such instruction is given not for any material purpose but only for going back home, back to Godhead (Bg. 10.10). For the ordinary man who wants to lord it over material nature, the Lord not only sanctions and becomes a witness of activities, but He never gives the nondevotee instructions for going back to Godhead. That is the difference in dealings by the Lord with different living beings, both the devotee and the nondevotee. He is leader of all the living beings, as the king of the state rules both the prisoners and the free citizens. But His dealings are different in terms of devotee and nondevotee. Nondevotees never care to take any instruction from the Lord, and therefore the Lord is silent in their case, although He witnesses all their activities and awards them the necessary results, good or bad. The devotees are above this material goodness and badness. They are progressive on the path of transcendence, and therefore they have no desire for anything material. The devotee also knows Śrī Kṛṣṇa as the original Nārāyaṇa because Lord Śrī Kṛṣṇa, by His plenary portion, appears as the Kāraṇodakaśāyī Viṣṇu, the original source of all material creation. The Lord also desires the association of His pure devotees, and for them only the Lord descends on the earth and enlivens them. The Lord appears out of His own will. He is not forced by the conditions of material nature. He is therefore described here as the *vibhu,* or the almighty, for He is never conditioned by the laws of material nature.

TEXT 33

त्रिभुवनकमनं तमालवर्णं
रविकरगौरवराम्बरं दधाने ।
वपुरलककुलावृताननाब्जं
विजयसखे रतिरस्तु मेऽनवद्या ॥३३॥

tri-bhuvana-kamanaṁ tamāla-varṇaṁ
ravi-kara-gaura-vara-ambaraṁ dadhāne
vapur alaka-kulāvṛtānanābjaṁ
vijaya-sakhe ratir astu me 'navadyā

tri-bhuvana—three statuses of planetary systems; *kamanam*—the most desirable; *tamāla-varṇam*—bluish like the *tamāla* tree; *ravi-kara*—sun rays; *gaura*—golden color; *varāmbaram*—glittering dress; *dadhāne*—one who wears; *vapuḥ*—body; *alaka-kula-āvṛta*—covered with paintings of sandalwood pulp; *anana-abjam*—face like a lotus; *vijaya-sakhe*—unto the friend of Arjuna; *ratiḥ astu*—may attraction be reposed upon Him; *me*—my; *anavadyā*—without desire for fruitive results.

TRANSLATION

Śrī Kṛṣṇa is the intimate friend of Arjuna. He has appeared on this earth in His transcendental body, which resembles the bluish color of the tamāla tree. His body attracts everyone in the three planetary systems [upper, middle and lower]. May His glittering yellow dress and His lotus face, covered with paintings of

sandalwood pulp, be the object of my attraction, and may I not desire fruitive results.

PURPORT

When Śrī Kṛṣṇa by His own internal pleasure appears on earth, He does so by the agency of His internal potency. The attractive features of His transcendental body are desired in all the three worlds, namely the upper, middle and lower planetary systems. Nowhere in the universe are there such beautiful bodily features as those of Lord Kṛṣṇa. Therefore His transcendental body has nothing to do with anything materially created. Arjuna is described here as the conqueror, and Kṛṣṇa is described as his intimate friend. Bhīṣmadeva, on his bed of arrows after the Battle of Kurukṣetra, is remembering the particular dress of Lord Kṛṣṇa which He put on as the driver of Arjuna's chariot. While fighting was going on between Arjuna and Bhīṣma, Bhīṣma's attraction was drawn by the glittering dress of Kṛṣṇa, and indirectly he admired his so-called enemy Arjuna for possessing the Lord as his friend. Arjuna was always a conqueror because the Lord was his friend. Bhīṣmadeva takes this opportunity to address the Lord as *vijaya-sakhe* (friend of Arjuna) because the Lord is pleased when He is addressed conjointly with His devotees, who are related with Him in different transcendental humors. While Kṛṣṇa was the charioteer of Arjuna, sun rays glittered on the dress of the Lord, and the beautiful hue created by the reflection of such rays was never forgotten by Bhīṣmadeva. As a great fighter he was relishing the relation of Kṛṣṇa in the chivalrous humor. Transcendental relation with the Lord in any one of the different *rasas* (humors) is relishable by the respective devotees in the highest ecstasy. Less intelligent mundaners who want to make a show of being transcendentally related with the Lord artificially jump at once to the relation of conjugal love, imitating the damsels of Vrajadhāma. Such a cheap relation with the Lord exhibits only the base mentality of the mundaner because one who has relished conjugal humor with the Lord cannot be attached to worldly conjugal *rasa*, which is condemned even by mundane ethics. The eternal relation of a particular soul with the Lord is evolved. A genuine relation of the living being with the Supreme Lord can take any form out of the five principal *rasas*, and it does not make any difference in transcendental degree to the genuine devotee. Bhīṣmadeva is a concrete example of this, and it should be carefully observed how the great general is transcendentally related with the Lord.

TEXT 34

युधि तुरगरजोविधूम्रविष्वक्-
कचलुलितश्रमवार्यलङ्कृतास्ये ।
मम निशितशरैर्विभिद्यमान-
त्वचि विलसत्कवचेऽस्तु कृष्ण आत्मा ॥३४॥

yudhi turaga-rajo-vidhūmra-viṣvak-
kaca-lulita-śramavāry-alaṅkṛtāsye
mama niśita-śarair vibhidyamāna-
tvaci vilasat-kavace 'stu kṛṣṇa ātmā

yudhi—on the battlefield; *turaga*—horses; *rajaḥ*—dust; *vidhūmra*—turned an ashen color; *viṣvak*—waving; *kaca*—hair; *lulita*—scattered; *śramavāri*—perspiration; *alaṅkṛta*—decorated with; *āsye*—unto the face; *mama*—my; *niśita*—sharp; *śaraiḥ*—by the arrows; *vibhidyamāna*—pierced by; *tvaci*—in the skin; *vilasat*—enjoying pleasure; *kavace*—protecting armor; *astu*—let there be; *kṛṣṇe*—unto Śrī Kṛṣṇa; *ātmā*—mind.

TRANSLATION

On the battlefield [where Śrī Kṛṣṇa attended Arjuna out of friendship], the flowing hair of Lord Kṛṣṇa turned ashen due to the dust raised by the hoofs of the horses. And because of His labor, beads of sweat wetted His face. All these decorations, intensified by the wounds dealt by my sharp arrows, were enjoyed by Him. Let my mind thus go unto Śrī Kṛṣṇa.

PURPORT

The Lord is the absolute form of eternity, bliss and knowledge. As such, transcendental loving service to the Lord in one of the five principal relations, namely *śānta, dāsya, sakhya, vātsalya* and *mādhurya,* i.e., neutrality, servitorship, fraternity, filial affection and conjugal love, is graciously accepted by the Lord when offered to the Lord in genuine love and affection. Śrī Bhīṣmadeva is a great devotee of the Lord in the relation of servitorship. Thus his throwing of sharp arrows at the transcendental body of the Lord is as good as the worship of another devotee who throws soft roses upon Him.

It appears that Bhīṣmadeva is repenting the actions he committed against the person of the Lord. But factually the Lord's body was not at all pained, due to His transcendental existence. His body is not matter. Both He Himself and His body are complete spiritual identity. Spirit is never pierced, burnt, dried, moistened, etc. This is vividly explained in the *Bhagavad-gītā.* So also it is stated in the *Skanda Purāṇa.* It is said there that spirit is always uncontaminated and indestructible. It cannot be distressed, nor can it be dried up. When Lord Viṣṇu in His incarnation appears before us, He seems to be like one of the conditioned souls, materially encaged, just to bewilder the *asuras*, or the nonbelievers, who are always alert to kill the Lord, even from the very beginning of His appearance. Kaṁsa wanted to kill Kṛṣṇa, and Rāvaṇa wanted to kill Rāma, because foolishly they were unaware of the fact that the Lord is never killed, for the spirit is never annihilated.

Therefore Bhīṣmadeva's piercing of the body of Lord Kṛṣṇa is a sort of bewildering problem for the nondevotee atheist, but those who are devotees, or liberated souls, are not bewildered.

Bhīṣmadeva appreciated the all-merciful attitude of the Lord because He did not leave Arjuna alone, although He was disturbed by the sharpened arrows of Bhīṣmadeva, nor was He reluctant to come before Bhīṣma's deathbed, even though He was ill-treated by him on the battlefield. Bhīṣma's repentance and the Lord's merciful attitude are both unique in this picture.

Śrī Viśvanātha Cakravartī Ṭhākura, a great *ācārya* and devotee in the humor of conjugal love with the Lord, remarks very saliently in this regard. He says that the wounds created on the body of the Lord by the sharpened arrows of Bhīṣmadeva were as pleasing to the Lord as the biting of a fiancee who bites the body of the Lord directed by a strong sense of sex desire. Such biting by the opposite sex is never taken as a sign of enmity, even if there is a wound on the body. Therefore, the fighting as an exchange of transcendental pleasure between the Lord and His pure devotee, Śrī Bhīṣmadeva, was not at all mundane. Besides that, since the Lord's body and the Lord are identical, there was no possibility of wounds in the absolute body. The apparent wounds caused by the sharpened arrows are misleading to the common man, but one who has a little absolute knowledge can understand the transcendental exchange in the chivalrous relation. The Lord was perfectly happy with the wounds caused by the sharpened arrows of Bhīṣmadeva. The word *vibhidyamāna* is significant because the Lord's skin is not different from the Lord. Because our skin is different from our soul, in our case the word *vibhidyamāna,* or being bruised and cut, would have been quite suitable. Transcendental bliss is of different varieties, and the variety of activities in the mundane world is but a perverted reflection of transcendental bliss. Because everything in the mundane world is qualitatively mundane, it is full of inebrieties, whereas in the absolute realm, because everything is of the same absolute nature, there are varieties of enjoyment without inebriety. The Lord enjoyed the wounds created by His great devotee Bhīṣmadeva, and because Bhīṣmadeva is a devotee in the chivalrous relation, he fixes up his mind on Kṛṣṇa in that wounded condition.

TEXT 35

सपदि सखिवचो निशम्य मध्ये
निजपरयोर्बलयो रथं निवेश्य ।
स्थितवति परसैनिकायुरक्ष्णा
हृतवति पार्थसखे रतिर्ममास्तु ॥३५॥

sapadi sakhi-vaco niśamya madhye
nija-parayor balayo rathaṁ niveśya
sthitavati para-sainikāyur akṣṇā
hṛtavati pārtha-sakhe ratir mamāstu

sapadi—on the battlefield; *sakhi-vacaḥ*—command of the friend; *niśamya*—after hearing; *madhye*—in the midst; *nija*—His own; *parayoḥ*—and the opposite party; *balayoḥ*—strength; *ratham*—chariot; *niveśya*—having entered; *sthitavati*—while staying there; *para-sainika*—of the soldiers on the opposite side; *āyuḥ*—duration of life; *akṣṇā*—by looking over; *hṛtavati*—act of diminishing; *pārtha*—of Arjuna, son of Pṛthā (Kuntī); *sakhe*—unto the friend; *ratiḥ*—intimate relation; *mama*—my; *astu*—let there be.

TRANSLATION

In obedience to the command of His friend, Lord Śrī Kṛṣṇa entered the arena of the Battlefield of Kurukṣetra between the soldiers of Arjuna and Duryodhana, and while there He shortened the life spans of the opposite party by His merciful glance. This was done simply by His looking at the enemy. Let my mind be fixed upon that Kṛṣṇa.

PURPORT

In the *Bhagavad-gītā* (1.21–25) Arjuna ordered the infallible Lord Śrī Kṛṣṇa to place his chariot between the phalanxes of the soldiers. He asked Him to stay there until he had finished observing the enemies he had to face in the battle. When the Lord was so asked, He at once did so, just like an order carrier. And the Lord pointed out all the important men on the opposite side, saying, "Here is Bhīṣma, here is Droṇa," and so on. The Lord, being the supreme living being, is never the order supplier or order carrier of anyone, whoever he may be. But out of His causeless mercy and affection for His pure devotees, sometimes He carries out the order of the devotee like an awaiting servant. By executing the order of a devotee, the Lord becomes pleased, as a father is pleased to carry out the order of his small child. This is possible only out of pure transcendental love between the Lord and His devotees, and Bhīṣmadeva was quite aware of this fact. He therefore addressed the Lord as the friend of Arjuna.

The Lord diminished the duration of life of the opposite party by His merciful glance. It is said that all the fighters who assembled on the Battlefield of Kurukṣetra attained salvation by personally seeing the Lord at the time of death. Therefore, His diminishing the duration of life of Arjuna's enemy does not mean that He was partial to the cause of Arjuna. Factually He was merciful to the opposite party because they would not have attained salvation by dying at home in the ordinary course of life. Here was a chance to see the Lord at the time of death and thus attain salvation from material life. Therefore, the Lord is all good, and whatever He does is for everyone's good. Apparently it was for the victory of

Arjuna, His intimate friend, but factually it was for the good of Arjuna's enemies. Such are the transcendental activities of the Lord, and whoever understands this also gets salvation after quitting this material body. The Lord does no wrong in any circumstance because He is absolute, all good at all times.

TEXT 36

व्यवहितपृतनामुखं निरीक्ष्य
स्वजनवधाद्विमुखस्य दोषबुद्ध्या ।
कुमतिमहरदात्मविद्यया य-
श्चरणरतिः परमस्य तस्य मेऽस्तु ॥३६॥

vyavahita-pṛtanā-mukhaṁ nirīkṣya
sva-jana-vadhād vimukhasya doṣa-buddhyā
kumatim aharad ātma-vidyayā yaś
caraṇa-ratiḥ paramasya tasya me 'stu

vyavahita—standing at a distance; *pṛtanā*—soldiers; *mukham*—faces; *nirīkṣya*—by looking upon; *sva-jana*—kinsmen; *vadhāt*—from the act of killing; *vimukhasya*—one who is reluctant; *doṣa-buddhyā*—by polluted intelligence; *kumatim*—poor fund of knowledge; *aharat*—eradicated; *ātma-vidyayā*—by transcendental knowledge; *yaḥ*—He who; *caraṇa*—to the feet; *ratiḥ*—attraction; *paramasya*—of the Supreme; *tasya*—for Him; *me*—my; *astu*—let there be.

TRANSLATION

When Arjuna was seemingly polluted by ignorance upon observing the soldiers and commanders before him on the battlefield, the Lord eradicated his ignorance by delivering transcendental knowledge. May His lotus feet always remain the object of my attraction.

PURPORT

The kings and the commanders were to stand in the front of the fighting soldiers. That was the system of actual fighting. The kings and commanders were not so-called presidents or ministers of defense as they are today. They would not stay home while the poor soldiers or mercenaries were fighting face to face. This may be the regulation of modern democracy, but when actual monarchy was prevailing, the monarchs were not cowards elected without consideration of qualification. As it was evident from the Battlefield of Kurukṣetra, all the executive heads of both parties, like Droṇa, Bhīṣma, Arjuna and Duryodhana, were not sleeping; all of them were actual participants in the fighting, which was selected to be executed at a place away from the civil residential quarters. This means that the innocent citizens were immune from all effects of fighting between the rival royal parties. The citizens had no business in seeing what was going to happen during such fighting. They were to pay one fourth of their income to the ruler, whether he be Arjuna or Duryodhana. All the commanders of the parties on the Battlefield of Kurukṣetra were standing face to face, and Arjuna saw them with great compassion and lamented that he was to kill his kinsmen on the battlefield for the sake of the empire. He was not at all afraid of the giant military phalanx presented by Duryodhana, but as a merciful devotee of the Lord, renunciation of worldly things was natural for him, and thus he decided not to fight for worldly possessions. But this was due to a poor fund of knowledge, and therefore it is said here that his intelligence became polluted. His intelligence could not be polluted at any time because he was a devotee and constant companion of the Lord, as is clear in the Fourth Chapter of the *Bhagavad-gītā*. Apparently Arjuna's intelligence became polluted because otherwise there would not have been a chance to deliver the teachings of *Bhagavad-gītā* for the good of all polluted conditioned souls engaged in material bondage by the conception of the false material body. The *Bhagavad-gītā* was delivered to the conditioned souls of the world to deliver them from the wrong conception of identifying the body with the soul and to reestablish the soul's eternal relation with the Supreme Lord. *Ātma-vidyā*, or transcendental knowledge of Himself, was primarily spoken by the Lord for the benefit of all concerned in all parts of the universe.

TEXT 37

स्वनिगममपहाय मत्प्रतिज्ञा-
मृतमधिकर्तुमवप्लुतो रथस्थः ।

धृतरथचरणोऽभ्ययाच्चलद्गु-
र्हरिरिव हन्तुमिभं गतोत्तरीयः ॥३७॥

sva-nigamam apahāya mat-pratijñām
ṛtam adhikartum avapluto rathasthaḥ
dhṛta-ratha-caraṇo 'bhyayāc caladgur
harir iva hantum ibhaṁ gatottarīyaḥ

sva-nigamam—own truthfulness; *apahāya*—for nullifying; *mat-pratijñām*—my own promise; *ṛtam*—factual; *adhi*—more; *kartum*—for doing it; *avaplutaḥ*—getting down; *ratha-sthaḥ*—from the chariot; *dhṛta*—taking up; *ratha*—chariot; *caraṇaḥ*—wheel; *abhyayāt*—went hurriedly; *caladguḥ*—trampling the earth; *hariḥ*—lion; *iva*—like; *hantum*—to kill; *ibham*—elephant; *gata*—leaving aside; *uttarīyaḥ*—covering cloth.

TRANSLATION

Fulfilling my desire and sacrificing His own promise, He got down from the chariot, took up its wheel, and ran towards me hurriedly, just as a lion goes to kill an elephant. He even dropped His outer garment on the way.

PURPORT

The Battle of Kurukṣetra was fought on military principles but at the same time in a sporting spirit, like a friend's fight with another friend. Duryodhana criticized Bhīṣmadeva, alleging that he was reluctant to kill Arjuna because of paternal affection. A *kṣatriya* cannot tolerate insults on the principle of fighting. Bhīṣmadeva therefore promised that the next day he would kill all five Pāṇḍavas with special weapons made for the purpose. Duryodhana was satisfied, and he kept the arrows with him to be delivered the next day during the fight. By tricks Arjuna took the arrows from Duryodhana, and Bhīṣmadeva could understand that this was the trick of Lord Kṛṣṇa. So he took a vow that the next day Kṛṣṇa would have to take up weapons Himself, otherwise His friend Arjuna would die. In the next day's fighting Bhīṣmadeva fought so violently that both Arjuna and Kṛṣṇa were in trouble. Arjuna was almost defeated; the situation was so tense that he was about to be killed by Bhīṣmadeva the very next moment. At that time Lord Kṛṣṇa wanted to please His devotee, Bhīṣma, by keeping Bhīṣma's promise, which was more important than His own. Seemingly He broke His own promise. He promised before the beginning of the Battle of Kurukṣetra that He would remain without weapons and would not use His strength for either of the parties. But to protect Arjuna He got down from the chariot, took up the wheel of the chariot and hurriedly rushed at Bhīṣmadeva in an angry mood, as a lion goes to kill an elephant. He dropped His covering cloth on the way, and out of great anger He did not know that He had dropped it. Bhīṣmadeva at once gave up his weapons and stood to be killed by Kṛṣṇa, his beloved Lord. The fighting of the day was thus ended at that very moment, and Arjuna was saved. Of course there was no possibility of Arjuna's death because the Lord Himself was on the chariot, but because Bhīṣmadeva wanted to see Lord Kṛṣṇa take up some weapon to save His friend, the Lord created this situation, making Arjuna's death imminent. He stood before Bhīṣmadeva to show him that his promise was fulfilled and that He had taken up the wheel.

TEXT 38

शितविशिखहतो विशीर्णदंशः
क्षतजपरिप्लुत आततायिनो मे ।
प्रसभमभिससार मद्वधार्थं
स भवतु मे भगवान् गतिर्मुकुन्दः ॥३८॥

śita-viśikha-hato viśīrṇa-daṁśaḥ
kṣataja-paripluta ātatāyino me
prasabham abhisasāra mad-vadhārthaṁ
sa bhavatu me bhagavān gatir mukundaḥ

śita—sharp; *viśikha*—arrows; *hataḥ*—wounded by; *viśīrṇa-daṁśaḥ*—scattered shield; *kṣataja*—by wounds; *pariplutaḥ*—smeared with blood; *ātatāyinaḥ*—the great aggressor; *me*—my; *prasabham*—in an angry mood; *abhisasāra*—began to move on; *mat-vadha-artham*—for the purpose of killing me; *saḥ*—He; *bhavatu*—may become; *me*—my; *bhagavān*—the Personality of Godhead; *gatiḥ*—destination; *mukundaḥ*—who awards salvation.

TRANSLATION

May He, Lord Śrī Kṛṣṇa, the Personality of Godhead, who awards salvation, be my ultimate destination. On the battlefield He charged me, as if angry because of the wounds dealt by my sharp arrows. His shield was scattered, and His body was smeared with blood due to the wounds.

PURPORT

The dealings of Lord Kṛṣṇa and Bhīṣmadeva on the Battlefield of Kurukṣetra are interesting because the activities of Lord Śrī Kṛṣṇa appeared to be partial to Arjuna and at enmity with Bhīṣmadeva; but factually all this was especially meant to show special favor to Bhīṣmadeva, a great devotee of the Lord. *The astounding feature of such dealings is that a devotee can please the Lord by playing the part of an enemy.* The Lord, being absolute, can accept service from His pure devotee even in the garb of an enemy. The Supreme Lord cannot have any enemy, nor can a so-called enemy harm Him because He is *ajita*, or unconquerable. But still He takes pleasure when His pure devotee beats Him like an enemy or rebukes Him from a superior position, although no one can be superior to the Lord. These are some of the transcendental reciprocatory dealings of the devotee with the Lord. And those who have no information of pure devotional service cannot penetrate into the mystery of such dealings. Bhīṣmadeva played the part of a valiant warrior, and he purposely pierced the body of the Lord so that to the common eyes it appeared that the Lord was wounded, but factually all this was to bewilder the nondevotees. The all-spiritual body cannot be wounded, and a devotee cannot become the enemy of the Lord. Had it been so, Bhīṣmadeva would not have desired to have the very same Lord as the ultimate destination of his life. Had Bhīṣmadeva been an enemy of the Lord, Lord Kṛṣṇa could have annihilated him without even moving. There was no need to come before Bhīṣmadeva with blood and wounds. But He did so because the warrior devotee wanted to see the transcendental beauty of the Lord decorated with wounds created by a pure devotee. This is the way of exchanging transcendental *rasa*, or relations between the Lord and the servitor. By such dealings both the Lord and the devotee become glorified in their respective positions. The Lord was so angry that Arjuna checked Him when He was moving towards Bhīṣmadeva, but in spite of

Arjuna's checking, He proceeded towards Bhīṣmadeva as a lover goes to a lover, without caring for hindrances. Apparently His determination was to kill Bhīṣmadeva, but factually it was to please him as a great devotee of the Lord. The Lord is undoubtedly the deliverer of all conditioned souls. The impersonalists desire salvation from Him, and He always awards them according to their aspiration, but here Bhīṣmadeva aspires to see the Lord in His personal feature. All pure devotees aspire for this.

TEXT 39

विजयरथकुटुम्ब आत्ततोत्रे
धृतहयरश्मिनि तच्छ्रियेक्षणीये ।
भगवति रतिरस्तु मे मुमूर्षो-
र्यमिह निरीक्ष्य हता गताः स्वरूपम् ॥३९॥

vijaya-ratha-kuṭumbha ātta-totre
dhṛta-haya-raśmini tac-chriyekṣaṇīye
bhagavati ratir astu me mumūrṣor
yam iha nirīkṣya hatā gatāḥ sva-rūpam

vijaya—Arjuna; *ratha*—chariot; *kuṭumbe*—the object of protection at all risk; *ātta-totre*—with a whip in the right hand; *dhṛta-haya*—controlling the horses; *raśmini*—ropes; *tat-śriyā*—beautifully standing; *īkṣaṇīye*—to look at; *bhagavati*—unto the Personality of Godhead; *ratiḥ astu*—let my attraction be; *mumūrṣoḥ*—one who is about to die; *yam*—upon whom; *iha*—in this world; *nirīkṣya*—by looking; *hatāḥ*—those who died; *gatāḥ*—attained; *sva-rūpam*—original form.

TRANSLATION

At the moment of death, let my ultimate attraction be to Śrī Kṛṣṇa, the Personality of Godhead. I concentrate my mind upon the chariot driver of Arjuna who stood with a whip in His right hand and a bridle rope in His left, who was very careful to give protection to Arjuna's chariot by all means. Those who saw Him on the Battlefield of Kurukṣetra attained their original forms after death.

PURPORT

A pure devotee of the Lord constantly sees the presence of the Lord within himself because of being transcendentally related by loving service. Such a pure devotee cannot forget the Lord for a moment. This is called trance. The mystic (*yogī*) tries to concentrate upon the Supersoul by controlling the senses from all other engagements, and thus he ultimately attains *samādhi.* A devotee more easily attains *samādhi,* or trance, by constantly remembering the Lord's personal feature along with His holy name, fame, pastimes, etc. Therefore, the concentration of the mystic *yogī* and that of the devotee are not on the same level. The concentration of the mystic is mechanical, whereas that of the pure devotee is natural in pure love and spontaneous affection. Bhīṣmadeva was a pure devotee, and as a military marshal he constantly remembered the battlefield feature of the Lord as Pārtha-sārathi, the chariot driver of Arjuna. Therefore, the Lord's pastime as Pārtha-sārathi is also eternal. The pastimes of the Lord, beginning from His birth at the prison house of Kaṁsa up to the *mauśala-līlā* at the end, all move one after another in all the universes, just as the clock hand moves from one point to another. And in such pastimes His associates like the Pāṇḍavas and Bhīṣma are constant eternal companions. So Bhīṣmadeva never forgot the beautiful feature of the Lord as Pārtha-sārathi, which even Arjuna could not see. Arjuna was behind the beautiful Pārtha-sārathi while Bhīṣmadeva was just in front of the Lord. As far as the military feature of the Lord is concerned, Bhīṣmadeva observed this with more relish than Arjuna.

All the soldiers and persons on the Battlefield of Kurukṣetra attained their original spiritual form like the Lord after their death because by the causeless mercy of the Lord they were able to see Him face to face on that occasion. The conditioned souls rotating in the evolutionary cycle from the aquatics up to the form of Brahmā are all in the form of *māyā,* or the form obtained by one's own actions and awarded by material nature. The material forms of the conditioned souls are all foreign dresses, and when the conditioned soul becomes liberated from the clutches of material energy, he attains his original form. The impersonalist wants to attain the impersonal Brahman effulgence of the Lord, but that is not at all congenial to the living sparks, parts and parcels of the Lord. Therefore, the impersonalists again fall down and get material forms, which are all false to the spirit soul. A spiritual form like the Lord's, either two-handed or four-handed, is attained by the devotees of the Lord either in the Vaikuṇṭhas or in the Goloka planet, according to the original nature of the soul. This form, which is cent percent spiritual, is the *svarūpa* of the living being, and all the living beings who participated on the Battlefield of Kurukṣetra, on both sides, attained their *svarūpa*, as confirmed by Bhīṣmadeva. So Lord Śrī Kṛṣṇa was not merciful only to the Pāṇḍavas; He was also merciful to the other parties because all of them attained the same result. Bhīṣmadeva wanted the same facility also, and that was his prayer to the Lord, although his position as an associate of the Lord is assured in all circumstances. The conclusion is that whoever dies looking on the Personality of Godhead within or without attains his *svarūpa*, which is the highest perfection of life.

TEXT 40

ललितगतिविलासवल्गुहास-
प्रणयनिरीक्षणकल्पितोरुमानाः ।
कृतमनुकृतवत्य उन्मदान्धाः
प्रकृतिमगन् किल यस्य गोपवध्वः ॥४०॥

lalita-gati-vilāsa-valguhāsa-
praṇaya-nirīkṣaṇa-kalpitorumānāḥ
kṛta-manu-kṛta-vatya unmadāndhāḥ
prakṛtim agan kila yasya gopa-vadhvaḥ

lalita—attractive; *gati*—movements; *vilāsa*—fascinating acts; *valguhāsa*—sweet smiling; *praṇaya*—loving; *nirīkṣaṇa*—looking upon; *kalpita*—mentality; *urumānāḥ*—highly glorified; *kṛta-manu-kṛtavatyaḥ*—in the act of copying the movements; *unmada-andhāḥ*—gone mad in ecstasy; *prakṛtim*—characteristics; *agan*—underwent; *kila*—certainly; *yasya*—whose; *gopa-vadhvaḥ*—the cowherd damsels.

TRANSLATION

Let my mind be fixed upon Lord Śrī Kṛṣṇa, whose motions and smiles of love attracted the damsels of Vrajadhāma [the gopīs]. The

damsels imitated the characteristic movements of the Lord [after His disappearance from the rāsa dance].

PURPORT

By intense ecstasy in loving service, the damsels of Vrajabhūmi attained qualitative oneness with the Lord by dancing with Him on an equal level, embracing Him in nuptial love, smiling at Him in joke, and looking at Him with a loving attitude. The relation of the Lord with Arjuna is undoubtedly praiseworthy for devotees like Bhīṣmadeva, but the relation of the *gopīs* with the Lord is still more praiseworthy because of their still more purified loving service. By the grace of the Lord, Arjuna was fortunate enough to have the fraternal service of the Lord as chariot driver, but the Lord did not award Arjuna with equal strength. The *gopīs*, however, practically became one with the Lord by attainment of equal footing with the Lord. Bhīṣma's aspiration to remember the *gopīs* is a prayer to have their mercy also at the last stage of his life. The Lord is satisfied more when His pure devotees are glorified, and therefore Bhīṣmadeva has not only glorified the acts of Arjuna, his immediate object of attraction, but has also remembered the *gopīs*, who were endowed with unrivalled opportunities by rendering loving service to the Lord. The *gopīs'* equality with the Lord should never be misunderstood to be like the *sāyujya* liberation of the impersonalist. The equality is one of perfect ecstasy where the differential conception is completely eradicated, for the interests of the lover and the beloved become identical.

TEXT 41

मुनिगणनृपवर्यसंकुलेऽन्तः-
सदसि युधिष्ठिरराजसूय एषाम् ।
अर्हणमुपपेद ईक्षणीयो
मम दृशिगोचर एष आविरात्मा ॥४१॥

muni-gaṇa-nṛpa-varya-saṅkule 'ntaḥ-
sadasi yudhiṣṭhira-rājasūya eṣām
arhaṇam upapeda īkṣaṇīyo
mama dṛśi-gocara eṣa āvir ātmā

muni-gaṇa—the great learned sages; *nṛpa-varya*—the great ruling kings; *saṅkule*—in the great assembly of; *antaḥ-sadasi*—conference; *yudhiṣṭhira*—of Emperor Yudhiṣṭhira; *rāja-sūye*—a royal performance of sacrifice; *eṣām*—of all the great elites; *arhaṇam*—respectful worship; *upapeda*—received; *īkṣaṇīyaḥ*—the object of attraction; *mama*—my; *dṛśi*—sight; *gocaraḥ*—within the view of; *eṣaḥ āviḥ*—personally present; *ātmā*—the soul.

TRANSLATION

At the Rājasūya-yajña [sacrifice] performed by Mahārāja Yudhiṣṭhira, there was the greatest assembly of all the elite men of the world, the royal and learned orders, and in that great assembly Lord Śrī Kṛṣṇa was worshiped by one and all as the most exalted Personality of Godhead. This happened during my presence, and I remembered the incident in order to keep my mind upon the Lord.

PURPORT

After gaining victory in the Battle of Kurukṣetra, Mahārāja Yudhiṣṭhira, the Emperor of the world, performed the Rājasūya sacrificial ceremony. The emperor, in those days, upon his ascendance to the throne, would send a challenge horse all over the world to declare his supremacy, and any ruling prince or king was at liberty to accept the challenge and express his tacit willingness either to obey or to disobey the supremacy of the particular emperor. One who accepted the challenge had to fight with the emperor and establish his own supremacy by victory. The defeated challenger would have to sacrifice his life, making a place for another king or ruler. So Mahārāja Yudhiṣṭhira also dispatched such challenging horses all over the world, and every ruling prince and king all over the world accepted Mahārāja Yudhiṣṭhira's leadership as the Emperor of the world. After this, all rulers of the world under the regime of Mahārāja Yudhiṣṭhira were invited to participate in the great sacrificial ceremony of Rājasūya. Such performances required hundreds of millions of dollars, and it was not an easy job for a petty king. Such a sacrificial ceremony, being too expensive and also difficult to perform under present circumstances, is now impossible in this age of Kali. Nor can anyone secure the required expert priesthood to take charge of the ceremony.

So, after being invited, all the kings and great learned sages of the world assembled in the capital of Mahārāja Yudhiṣṭhira. The learned society, including the great philosophers, religionists, physicians, scientists and all great sages, was invited. That is to say, the *brāhmaṇas* and the *kṣatriyas* were the topmost leading men in society, and they were all invited to participate in the assembly. The *vaiśyas* and *śūdras* were unimportant elements in society, and they are not mentioned herein. Due to the change of social activities in the modern age, the importance of men has also changed in terms of occupational positions.

So in that great assembly, Lord Śrī Kṛṣṇa was the cynosure of neighboring eyes. Everyone wanted to see Lord Kṛṣṇa, and everyone wanted to pay his humble respects to the Lord. Bhīṣmadeva remembered all this and was glad that his worshipful Lord, the Personality of Godhead, was present before him in His actual formal presence. So to meditate on the Supreme Lord is to meditate on the activities, form, pastimes, name and fame of the Lord. That is easier than what is imagined as meditation on the impersonal feature of the Supreme. In the *Bhagavad-gītā* (12.5) it is clearly stated that to meditate upon the impersonal feature of the Supreme is very difficult. It is practically no meditation or simply a waste of time because very seldom is the desired result obtained. The devotees, however, meditate upon the Lord's factual form and pastimes, and therefore the Lord is easily approachable by the devotees. This is also stated in the *Bhagavad-gītā* (12.9). The Lord is nondifferent from His transcendental activities. It is indicated also in this *śloka* that Lord Śrī Kṛṣṇa, while actually present before human society, especially in connection with the Battle of Kurukṣetra, was accepted as the greatest personality of the time, although He might not have been recognized as the Supreme Personality of Godhead. The propaganda that a very great man is worshiped as God after his death is misleading because a man after his death cannot be made into God. Nor can the Personality of Godhead be a human being, even when He is personally present. Both ideas are misconceptions. The idea of anthropomorphism cannot be applicable in the case of Lord Kṛṣṇa.

TEXT 42

तमिममहमजं शरीरभाजां
हृदि हृदि धिष्ठितमात्मकल्पितानाम् ।

प्रतिदृशमिव नैकधार्कमेकं
समधिगतोऽस्मि विधूतभेदमोहः ॥४२॥

tam imam aham ajaṁ śarīra-bhājāṁ
hṛdi hṛdi dhiṣṭhitam ātma-kalpitānām
pratidṛśam iva naikadhārkam ekaṁ
samadhi-gato 'smi vidhūta-bheda-mohaḥ

tam—that Personality of Godhead; *imam*—now present before me; *aham*—I; *ajam*—the unborn; *śarīra-bhājām*—of the conditioned soul; *hṛdi*—in the heart; *hṛdi*—in the heart; *dhiṣṭhitam*—situated; *ātma*—the Supersoul; *kalpitānām*—of the speculators; *pratidṛśam*—in every direction; *iva*—like; *na ekadhā*—not one; *arkam*—the sun; *ekam*—one only; *samadhi-gataḥ asmi*—I have undergone trance in meditation; *vidhūta*—being freed from; *bheda-mohaḥ*—misconception of duality.

TRANSLATION

Now I can meditate with full concentration upon that one Lord, Śrī Kṛṣṇa, now present before me because now I have transcended the misconceptions of duality in regard to His presence in everyone's heart, even in the hearts of the mental speculators. He is in everyone's heart. The sun may be perceived differently, but the sun is one.

PURPORT

Lord Śrī Kṛṣṇa is the one Absolute Supreme Personality of Godhead, but He has expanded Himself into His multiplenary portions by His inconceivable energy. The conception of duality is due to ignorance of His inconceivable energy. In the *Bhagavad-gītā* (9.11) the Lord says that only the foolish take Him to be a mere human being. Such foolish men are not aware of His inconceivable energies. By His inconceivable energy He is present in everyone's heart, as the sun is present before everyone all over the world. The Paramātmā feature of the Lord is an expansion of His plenary portions. He expands Himself as Paramātmā in everyone's heart by His inconceivable energy, and He also expands Himself as the glowing effulgence of *brahmajyoti* by expansion of His personal glow. It is stated in the *Brahma-saṁhitā* that the *brahmajyoti* is His personal glow. Therefore, there is no difference between Him and His personal glow, *brahmajyoti,* or His plenary portions as Paramātmā. Less intelligent persons who are not aware of this fact consider *brahmajyoti* and Paramātmā to be different from Śrī Kṛṣṇa. This misconception of duality is completely removed from the mind of Bhīṣmadeva, and he is now satisfied that it is Lord Śrī Kṛṣṇa only who is all in all in everything. This enlightenment is attained by the great *mahātmās* or devotees, as it is stated in *Bhagavad-gītā* (7.19) that Vāsudeva is all in all in everything and that there is no existence of anything without Vāsudeva. Vāsudeva, or Lord Śrī Kṛṣṇa, is the original Supreme Person, as now confirmed by a *mahājana,* and therefore both the neophytes and the pure devotees must try to follow in his footsteps. That is the way of the devotional line.

The worshipable object of Bhīṣmadeva is Lord Śrī Kṛṣṇa as Pārthasārathi, and that of the *gopīs* is the same Kṛṣṇa in Vṛndāvana as the most attractive Śyāmasundara. Sometimes less intelligent scholars make a mistake and think that the Kṛṣṇa of Vṛndāvana and that of the Battle of Kurukṣetra are different personalities. But for Bhīṣmadeva this misconception is completely removed. Even the impersonalist's object of destination is Kṛṣṇa as the impersonal *jyoti,* and the *yogī's* destination of Paramātmā is also Kṛṣṇa. Kṛṣṇa is both *brahmajyoti* and localized Paramātmā, but in *brahmajyoti* or Paramātmā there is no Kṛṣṇa or sweet relations with Kṛṣṇa. In His personal feature Kṛṣṇa is both Pārthasārathi and Śyāmasundara of Vṛndāvana, but in His impersonal feature He is neither in the *brahmajyoti* nor in the Paramātmā. Great *mahātmās* like Bhīṣmadeva realize all these different features of Lord Śrī Kṛṣṇa, and therefore they worship Lord Kṛṣṇa, knowing Him as the origin of all features.

TEXT 43

सूत उवाच
कृष्ण एवं भगवति मनोवाग्दृष्टिवृत्तिभिः ।
आत्मन्यात्मानमावेश्य सोऽन्तःश्वास उपारमत्॥४३॥

sūta uvāca
kṛṣṇa evaṁ bhagavati
mano-vāg-dṛṣṭi-vṛttibhiḥ

ātmany ātmānam āveśya
so 'ntaḥśvāsa upāramat

sūtaḥ uvāca—Sūta Gosvāmī said; *kṛṣṇe*—Lord Kṛṣṇa, the Supreme Personality of Godhead; *evam*—only; *bhagavati*—unto Him; *manaḥ*—with mind; *vāk*—speech; *dṛṣṭi*—sight; *vṛttibhiḥ*—activities; *ātmani*—unto the Supersoul; *ātmānam*—the living being; *āveśya*—having merged in; *saḥ*—he; *antaḥ-śvāsaḥ*—inhaling; *upāramat*—became silent.

TRANSLATION

Sūta Gosvāmī said: Thus Bhīṣmadeva merged himself in the Supersoul, Lord Śrī Kṛṣṇa, the Supreme Personality of Godhead, with his mind, speech, sight and actions, and thus he became silent, and his breathing stopped.

PURPORT

The stage attained by Bhīṣmadeva while quitting his material body is called *nirvikalpa-samādhi* because he merged his self into thinking of the Lord and his mind into remembering His different activities. He chanted the glories of the Lord, and by his sight he began to see the Lord personally present before him, and thus all his activities became concentrated upon the Lord without deviation. This is the highest stage of perfection, and it is possible for everyone to attain this stage by practice of devotional service. The devotional service of the Lord consists of nine principles of service activities, and they are (1) hearing, (2) chanting, (3) remembering, (4) serving the lotus feet, (5) worshiping, (6) praying, (7) executing the orders, (8) fraternizing, and (9) fully surrendering. Any one of them or all of them are equally competent to award the desired result, but they require to be practiced persistently under the guidance of an expert devotee of the Lord. The first item, hearing, is the most important item of all, and therefore hearing of the *Bhagavad-gītā* and, later on, *Śrīmad-Bhāgavatam* is essential for the serious candidate who wants to attain the stage of Bhīṣmadeva at the end. The unique situation at Bhīṣmadeva's time of death can be attained, even though Lord Kṛṣṇa may not be personally present. His words of the

Bhagavad-gītā or those of *Śrīmad-Bhāgavatam* are identical with the Lord. They are sound incarnations of the Lord, and one can fully utilize them to be entitled to attain the stage of Śrī Bhīṣmadeva, who was one of the eight Vasus. Every man or animal must die at a certain stage of life, but one who dies like Bhīṣmadeva attains perfection, and one who dies forced by the laws of nature dies like an animal. That is the difference between a man and an animal. The human form of life is especially meant for dying like Bhīṣmadeva.

TEXT 44

सम्पद्यमानमाज्ञाय भीष्मं ब्रह्मणि निष्कले ।
सर्वे बभूवुस्ते तूष्णीं वयांसीव दिनात्यये ॥४४॥

sampadyamānam ājñāya
bhīṣmaṁ brahmaṇi niṣkale
sarve babhūvus te tūṣṇīṁ
vayāṁsīva dinātyaye

sampadyamānam—having merged into; *ājñāya*—after knowing this; *bhīṣmam*—about Śrī Bhīṣmadeva; *brahmaṇi*—into the Supreme Absolute; *niṣkale*—unlimited; *sarve*—all present; *babhūvuḥ te*—all of them became; *tūṣṇīm*—silent; *vayāṁsi iva*—like birds; *dina-atyaye*—at the end of the day.

TRANSLATION

Knowing that Bhīṣmadeva had merged into the unlimited eternity of the Supreme Absolute, all present there became silent like birds at the end of the day.

PURPORT

To enter into or to become merged into the unlimited eternity of the Supreme Absolute means to enter the original home of the living being. The living beings are all component parts and parcels of the Absolute Personality of Godhead, and therefore they are eternally related with Him as the servitor and the served. The Lord is served by all His parts and parcels, as the complete machine is served by its parts and parcels.

Any part of the machine removed from the whole is no longer important. Similarly, any part and parcel of the Absolute detached from the service of the Lord is useless. The living beings who are in the material world are all disintegrated parts and parcels of the supreme whole, and they are no longer as important as the original parts and parcels. There are, however, more integrated living beings who are eternally liberated. The material energy of the Lord, called Durgā-śakti, or the superintendent of the prison house, takes charge of the disintegrated parts and parcels, and thus they undergo a conditioned life under the laws of material nature. When the living being becomes conscious of this fact, he tries to go back home, back to Godhead, and thus the spiritual urge of the living being begins. This spiritual urge is called *brahma-jijñāsā*, or inquiry about Brahman. Principally this *brahma-jijñāsā* is successful by knowledge, renunciation and devotional service to the Lord. *Jñāna*, or knowledge, means knowledge of everything of Brahman, the Supreme; renunciation means detachment of material affection, and devotional service is the revival by practice of the original position of the living being. The successful living beings who are eligible to enter into the realm of the Absolute are called the *jñānīs*, the *yogīs* and the *bhaktas*. The *jñānīs* and *yogīs* enter into the impersonal rays of the Supreme, but the *bhaktas* enter into the spiritual planets known as the Vaikuṇṭhas. In these spiritual planets the Supreme Lord as Nārāyaṇa predominates, and the healthy, unconditioned living beings live there by rendering loving service to the Lord in the capacity of servant, friend, parents and fiancée. There the unconditioned living beings enjoy life in full freedom with the Lord, whereas the impersonalist *jñānīs* and *yogīs* enter into the impersonal glowing effulgence of the Vaikuṇṭha planets. The Vaikuṇṭha planets are all self-illuminating like the sun, and the rays of the Vaikuṇṭha planets are called the *brahmajyoti*. The *brahmajyoti* is spread unlimitedly, and the material world is but a covered portion of an insignificant part of the same *brahmajyoti*. This covering is temporary, and therefore it is a sort of illusion.

Bhīṣmadeva, as a pure devotee of the Lord, entered the spiritual realm in one of the Vaikuṇṭha planets where the Lord in His eternal form of *Pārtha-sārathi* predominates over the unconditioned living beings who are constantly engaged in the service of the Lord. The love and affection which bind the Lord and devotee are exhibited in the case of

Bhīṣmadeva. Bhīṣmadeva never forgot the Lord in His transcendental feature as the *Pārtha-sārathi*, and the Lord was present personally before Bhīṣmadeva while he was passing to the transcendental world. That is the highest perfection of life.

TEXT 45

तत्र दुन्दुभयो नेदुर्देवमानववादिताः ।
शशंसुः साधवो राज्ञां खात्पेतुः पुष्पवृष्टयः ॥४५॥

tatra dundubhayo nedur
deva-mānava-vāditāḥ
śaśaṁsuḥ sādhavo rājñāṁ
khāt petuḥ puṣpa-vṛṣṭayaḥ

tatra—thereafter; *dundubhayaḥ*—drums; *neduḥ*—were sounded; *deva*—the demigods from other planets; *mānava*—men from all countries; *vāditāḥ*—beaten by; *śaśaṁsuḥ*—praised; *sādhavaḥ*—honest; *rājñām*—by the royal order; *khāt*—from the sky; *petuḥ*—began to fall; *puṣpa-vṛṣṭayaḥ*—showers of flowers.

TRANSLATION

Thereafter, both men and demigods sounded drums in honor, and the honest royal order commenced demonstrations of honor and respect. And from the sky fell showers of flowers.

PURPORT

Bhīṣmadeva was respected both by the human beings and by the demigods. The human beings live on earth and similar other planets in the Bhūr and Bhuvar group of planets, but the demigods live in the Svar, or heavenly planets, and all of them knew Bhīṣmadeva as a great warrior and devotee of the Lord. As a *mahājana* (or authority) he was on the level of Brahmā, Nārada and Śiva, although he was a human being. Qualification on a par with the great demigods is possible only on attainment of spiritual perfection. Thus Bhīṣmadeva was known all over the universes, and during his time interplanetary travel was effected by finer methods than the futile endeavors of mechanical spacecraft. When the distant planets were informed of the passing away of Bhīṣmadeva, all the inhabitants of the upper planets as well as of the earth dropped showers of flowers to show due respect to the departed great personality. This showering of flowers from heaven is a sign of recognition by great demigods, and it should never be compared to the decoration of a dead body. The body of Bhīṣmadeva lost its material effects due to being surcharged with spiritual realization, and thus the body was spiritualized as when iron becomes red-hot when in contact with fire. The body of a fully self-realized soul is not, therefore, accepted as material. Special ceremonies are observed for such spiritual bodies. The respect and recognition of Bhīṣmadeva are never to be imitated by artificial means, as it has become a fashion to observe the so-called *jayanti* ceremony for any and every common man. According to authorized *śāstras*, such a *jayanti* ceremony for an ordinary man, however exalted he may be materially, is an offense to the Lord because *jayanti* is reserved for the day when the Lord appears on the earth. Bhīṣmadeva was unique in his activities, and his passing away to the kingdom of God is also unique.

TEXT 46

तस्य निर्हरणादीनि सम्परेतस्य भार्गव ।
युधिष्ठिरः कारयित्वा मुहूर्तं दुःखितोऽभवत् ॥४६॥

tasya nirharaṇādīni
samparetasya bhārgava
yudhiṣṭhiraḥ kārayitvā
muhūrtaṁ duḥkhito 'bhavat

tasya—his; *nirharaṇa-ādīni*—funeral ceremony; *samparetasya*—of the dead body; *bhārgava*—O descendant of Bhṛgu; *yudhiṣṭhiraḥ*—Mahārāja Yudhiṣṭhira; *kārayitvā*—having performed it; *muhūrtam*—for a moment; *duḥkhitaḥ*—sorry; *abhavat*—became.

TRANSLATION

O descendant of Bhṛgu [Śaunaka], after performing funeral rituals for the dead body of Bhīṣmadeva, Mahārāja Yudhiṣṭhira was momentarily overtaken with grief.

PURPORT

Bhīṣmadeva was not only a great family head of Mahārāja Yudhiṣṭhira, but also he was a great philosopher and friend to him, his brothers and his mother. Since Mahārāja Pāṇḍu, the father of the five brothers headed by Mahārāja Yudhiṣṭhira, had died, Bhīṣmadeva was the most affectionate grandfather of the Pāṇḍavas and caretaker of the widow daughter-in-law Kuntīdevī. Although Mahārāja Dhṛtarāṣṭra, the elder uncle of Mahārāja Yudhiṣṭhira, was there to look after them, his affection was more on the side of his hundred sons, headed by Duryodhana. Ultimately a colossal clique was fabricated to deprive the five fatherless brothers of the rightful claim of the kingdom of Hastināpura. There was great intrigue, common in imperial palaces, and the five brothers were exiled to the wilderness. But Bhīṣmadeva was always a sincerely sympathetic well-wisher, grandfather, friend and philosopher to Mahārāja Yudhiṣṭhira, even up to the last moment of his life. He died very happily by seeing Mahārāja Yudhiṣṭhira to the throne, otherwise he would have long ago quitted his material body, instead of suffering agony over the undue sufferings of the Pāṇḍavas. He was simply waiting for the opportune moment because he was sure and certain that the sons of Pāṇḍu would come out victorious in the Battlefield of Kurukṣetra, as His Lordship Śrī Kṛṣṇa was their protector. As a devotee of the Lord, he knew that the Lord's devotee cannot be vanquished at any time. Mahārāja Yudhiṣṭhira was quite aware of all these good wishes of Bhīṣmadeva, and therefore he must have been feeling the great separation. He was sorry for the separation of a great soul, and not for the material body which Bhīṣmadeva relinquished. The funeral ceremony was a necessary duty, although Bhīṣmadeva was a liberated soul. Since Bhīṣmadeva was without issue, the eldest grandson, namely Mahārāja Yudhiṣṭhira, was the rightful person to perform this ceremony. It was a great boon to Bhīṣmadeva that an equally great son of the family undertook the last rites of a great man.

TEXT 47

तुष्टुवुर्मुनयो हृष्टाः कृष्णं तद्गुह्यनामभिः ।
ततस्ते कृष्णहृदयाः स्वाश्रमान् प्रययुः पुनः ॥४७॥

tuṣṭuvur munayo hṛṣṭāḥ
kṛṣṇaṁ tad-guhya-nāmabhiḥ
tatas te kṛṣṇa-hṛdayāḥ
svāśramān prayayuḥ punaḥ

tuṣṭuvuḥ—satisfied; *munayaḥ*—the great sages, headed by Vyāsadeva, etc.; *hṛṣṭāḥ*—all in a happy mood; *kṛṣṇam*—unto Lord Kṛṣṇa, the Personality of Godhead; *tat*—His; *guhya*—confidential; *nāmabhiḥ*—by His holy name, etc.; *tataḥ*—thereafter; *te*—they; *kṛṣṇa-hṛdayāḥ*—persons who always bear Lord Kṛṣṇa in their hearts; *sva-āśramān*—to their respective hermitages; *prayayuḥ*—returned; *punaḥ*—again.

TRANSLATION

All the great sages then glorified Lord Śrī Kṛṣṇa, who was present there, by confidential Vedic hymns. Then all of them returned to their respective hermitages, bearing always Lord Kṛṣṇa within their hearts.

PURPORT

The devotees of the Lord are always in the heart of the Lord, and the Lord is always in the hearts of the devotees. That is the sweet relation between the Lord and His devotees. Due to unalloyed love and devotion for the Lord, the devotees always see Him within themselves, and the Lord also, although He has nothing to do and nothing to aspire to, is always busy in attending to the welfare of His devotees. For the ordinary living beings the law of nature is there for all actions and reactions, but He is always anxious to put His devotees on the right path. The devotees, therefore, are under the direct care of the Lord. And the Lord also voluntarily puts Himself under the care of His devotees only. So all the sages, headed by Vyāsadeva, were devotees of the Lord, and therefore they chanted the Vedic hymns after the funeral ceremony just to please the Lord, who was present there personally. All the Vedic hymns are chanted to please Lord Kṛṣṇa. This is confirmed in the *Bhagavad-gītā* (15.15). All the *Vedas, Upaniṣads, Vedānta*, etc., are seeking Him only, and all hymns are for glorifying Him only. The sages, therefore, performed the exact acts suitable for the purpose, and they happily departed for their respective hermitages.

TEXT 48

ततो युधिष्ठिरो गत्वा सहकृष्णो गजाह्वयम् ।
पितरं सान्त्वयामास गान्धारीं च तपस्विनीम् ॥४८॥

tato yudhiṣṭhiro gatvā
saha-kṛṣṇo gajāhvayam
pitaraṁ sāntvayām āsa
gāndhārīṁ ca tapasvinīm

tataḥ—thereafter; *yudhiṣṭhiraḥ*—Mahārāja Yudhiṣṭhira; *gatvā*—going there; *saha*—with; *kṛṣṇaḥ*—the Lord; *gajāhvayam*—in the capital named Gajāhvaya Hastināpura; *pitaram*—unto his uncle (Dhṛtarāṣṭra); *sāntvayām āsa*—consoled; *gāndhārīm*—the wife of Dhṛtarāṣṭra; *ca*—and; *tapasvinīm*—an ascetic lady.

TRANSLATION

Thereafter, Mahārāja Yudhiṣṭhira at once went to his capital, Hastināpura, accompanied by Lord Śrī Kṛṣṇa, and there he consoled his uncle and aunt Gāndhārī, who was an ascetic.

PURPORT

Dhṛtarāṣṭra and Gāndhārī, the father and the mother of Duryodhana and his brothers, were the elder uncle and aunt of Mahārāja Yudhiṣṭhira. After the Battle of Kurukṣetra, the celebrated couple, having lost all their sons and grandsons, were under the care of Mahārāja Yudhiṣṭhira. They were passing their days in great agony over such a heavy loss of life and were practically living the life of ascetics. The death news of Bhīṣmadeva, uncle of Dhṛtarāṣṭra, was another great shock for the King and the Queen, and therefore they required solace from Mahārāja Yudhiṣṭhira. Mahārāja Yudhiṣṭhira was conscious of his duty, and he at once hurried to the spot with Lord Kṛṣṇa and satisfied the bereaved Dhṛtarāṣṭra with kind words, from both himself and the Lord also.

Gāndhārī was a powerful ascetic, although she was living the life of a faithful wife and a kind mother. It is said that Gāndhārī also voluntarily closed her eyes because of the blindness of her husband. A wife's duty is to follow the husband cent percent. And Gāndhārī was so true to her husband that she followed him even in his perpetual blindness. Therefore in her actions she was a great ascetic. Besides that, the shock she suffered because of the wholesale killing of her one hundred sons and her grandsons also was certainly too much for a woman. But she suffered all this just like an ascetic. Gāndhārī, although a woman, is no less than Bhīṣmadeva in character. They are both remarkable personalities in the *Mahābhārata.*

TEXT 49

पित्रा चानुमतो राजा वासुदेवानुमोदितः ।
चकार राज्यं धर्मेण पितृपैतामहं विभुः ॥४९॥

pitrā cānumato rājā
vāsudevānumoditaḥ
cakāra rājyaṁ dharmeṇa
pitṛ-paitāmahaṁ vibhuḥ

pitrā—by his uncle, Dhṛtarāṣṭra; *ca*—and; *anumataḥ*—with his approval; *rājā*—King Yudhiṣṭhira; *vāsudeva-anumoditaḥ*—confirmed by Lord Śrī Kṛṣṇa; *cakāra*—executed; *rājyam*—the kingdom; *dharmeṇa*—in compliance with the codes of royal principles; *pitṛ*—father; *paitāmaham*—forefather; *vibhuḥ*—as great as.

TRANSLATION

After this, the great religious King, Mahārāja Yudhiṣṭhira, executed the royal power in the kingdom strictly according to the codes and royal principles approved by his uncle and confirmed by Lord Śrī Kṛṣṇa.

PURPORT

Mahārāja Yudhiṣṭhira was not a mere tax collector. He was always conscious of his duty as a king, which is no less than that of a father or spiritual master. The king is to see to the welfare of the citizens from all angles of social, political, economic and spiritual upliftment. The king must know that human life is meant for liberating the encaged soul from the bondage of material conditions, and therefore his duty is to see that the citizens are properly looked after to attain this highest stage of perfection.

Mahārāja Yudhiṣṭhira followed these principles strictly, as will be seen from the next chapter. Not only did he follow the principles, but he also got approval from his old uncle, who was experienced in political affairs, and that was also confirmed by Lord Kṛṣṇa, the speaker of the philosophy of *Bhagavad-gītā*.

Mahārāja Yudhiṣṭhira is the ideal monarch, and monarchy under a trained king like Mahārāja Yudhiṣṭhira is by far the most superior form of government, superior to modern republics or governments of the people, by the people. The mass of people, especially in this age of Kali, are all born *śūdras*, basically lowborn, ill-trained, unfortunate and badly associated. They themselves do not know the highest perfectional aim of life. Therefore, votes cast by them actually have no value, and thus persons elected by such irresponsible votes cannot be responsible representatives like Mahārāja Yudhiṣṭhira.

Thus end the Bhaktivedanta purports of the First Canto, Ninth Chapter, of the Śrīmad-Bhāgavatam, *entitled "The Passing Away of Bhīṣmadeva in the Presence of Lord Kṛṣṇa."*

CHAPTER TEN

Departure of Lord Kṛṣṇa for Dvārakā

TEXT 1

शौनक उवाच
हत्वा स्वरिक्थस्पृध आततायिनो
युधिष्ठिरो धर्मभृतां वरिष्ठः ।
सहानुजैः प्रत्यवरुद्धभोजनः
कथं प्रवृत्तः किमकारषीत्ततः ॥ १ ॥

śaunaka uvāca
hatvā svariktha-spṛdha ātatāyino
yudhiṣṭhiro dharma-bhṛtāṁ variṣṭhaḥ
sahānujaiḥ pratyavaruddha-bhojanaḥ
kathaṁ pravṛttaḥ kim akāraṣīt tataḥ

śaunakaḥ uvāca—Śaunaka inquired; *hatvā*—after killing; *sva-riktha*—the legal inheritance; *spṛdhaḥ*—desiring to usurp; *ātatāyinaḥ*—the aggressor; *yudhiṣṭhiraḥ*—King Yudhiṣṭhira; *dharma-bhṛtām*—of those who strictly follow religious principles; *variṣṭhaḥ*—greatest; *saha-anujaiḥ*—with his younger brothers; *pratyavaruddha*—restricted; *bhojanaḥ*—acceptance of necessities; *katham*—how; *pravṛttaḥ*—engaged; *kim*—what; *akāraṣīt*—executed; *tataḥ*—thereafter.

TRANSLATION

Śaunaka Muni asked: After killing his enemies who desired to usurp his rightful inheritance, how did the greatest of all religious men, Mahārāja Yudhiṣṭhira, assisted by his brothers, rule his subjects? Surely he could not freely enjoy his kingdom with unrestricted consciousness.

PURPORT

Mahārāja Yudhiṣṭhira was the greatest of all men of religion. Thus he was not at all inclined to fight with his cousins for the sake of enjoying the kingdom: he fought for the right cause because the kingdom of Hastināpura was his rightful inheritance and his cousins wanted to usurp it for themselves. He fought, therefore, for the right cause under the guidance of Lord Śrī Kṛṣṇa, but he could not enjoy the results of his victory because his cousins were all killed in the fight. He therefore ruled over the kingdom as a matter of duty, assisted by his younger brothers. The inquiry was important for Śaunaka Ṛṣi, who wanted to know about the behavior of Mahārāja Yudhiṣṭhira when he was at ease to enjoy the kingdom.

TEXT 2

सूत उवाच
वंशं कुरोर्वंशदवाग्निनिर्हृतं
संरोहयित्वा भवभावनो हरिः ।
निवेशयित्वा निजराज्य ईश्वरो
युधिष्ठिरं प्रीतमना बभूव ह ॥ २ ॥

sūta uvāca
vaṁśaṁ kuror vaṁśa-davāgni-nirhṛtaṁ
saṁrohayitvā bhava-bhāvano hariḥ
niveśayitvā nija-rājya īśvaro
yudhiṣṭhiraṁ prīta-manā babhūva ha

sūtaḥ uvāca—Sūta Gosvāmī replied; *vaṁśam*—dynasty; *kuroḥ*—of King Kuru; *vaṁśa-dava-agni*—a forest fire set by the bamboos; *nirhṛtam*—exhausted; *saṁrohayitvā*—seedling of the dynasty; *bhava-bhāvanaḥ*—the maintainer of creation; *hariḥ*—the Personality of Godhead, Śrī Kṛṣṇa; *niveśayitvā*—having reestablished; *nija-rājye*—in his own kingdom; *īśvaraḥ*—the Supreme Lord; *yudhiṣṭhiram*—unto Mahārāja Yudhiṣṭhira; *prīta-manāḥ*—pleased in His mind; *babhūva ha*—became.

TRANSLATION

Sūta Gosvāmī said: Lord Śrī Kṛṣṇa, the Supreme Personality of Godhead, who is the maintainer of the world, became pleased after reestablishing Mahārāja Yudhiṣṭhira in his own kingdom and after restoring the Kuru dynasty, which had been exhausted by the bamboo fire of anger.

PURPORT

This world is compared to a forest fire caused by the cohesion of bamboo bushes. Such a forest fire takes place automatically, for bamboo cohesion occurs without external cause. Similarly, in the material world the wrath of those who want to lord it over material nature interacts, and the fire of war takes place, exhausting the unwanted population. Such fires or wars take place, and the Lord has nothing to do with them. But because He wants to maintain the creation, He desires the mass of people to follow the right path of self-realization, which enables the living beings to enter into the kingdom of God. The Lord wants the suffering human beings to come back home, back to Him, and cease to suffer the threefold material pangs. The whole plan of creation is made in that way, and one who does not come to his senses suffers in the material world by pangs inflicted by the illusory energy of the Lord. The Lord therefore wants His bona fide representative to rule the world. Lord Śrī Kṛṣṇa descended to establish this sort of regime and to kill the unwanted persons who have nothing to do with His plan. The Battle of Kurukṣetra was fought according to the plan of the Lord so that undesirable persons could get out of the world and a peaceful kingdom under His devotee could be established. The Lord was therefore fully satisfied when King Yudhiṣṭhira was on the throne and the seedling of the dynasty of Kuru, in the person of Mahārāja Parīkṣit, was saved.

TEXT 3

निशम्य भीष्मोक्तमथाच्युतोक्तं
प्रवृत्तविज्ञानविधूतविभ्रमः ।
शशास गामिन्द्र इवाजिताश्रयः
परिध्युपान्तामनुजानुवर्तितः ॥ ३ ॥

niśamya bhīṣmoktam athācyutoktaṁ
pravṛtta-vijñāna-vidhūta-vibhramaḥ
śaśāsa gām indra ivājitāśrayaḥ
paridhyupāntām anujānuvartitaḥ

niśamya—after listening; *bhīṣma-uktam*—what was spoken by Bhīṣmadeva; *atha*—as also; *acyuta-uktam*—what was spoken by the infallible Lord Kṛṣṇa; *pravṛtta*—being engaged in; *vijñāna*—perfect knowledge; *vidhūta*—completely washed; *vibhramaḥ*—all misgivings; *śaśāsa*—ruled over; *gām*—the earth; *indra*—the king of the heavenly planet; *iva*—like; *ajita-āśrayaḥ*—protected by the invincible Lord; *paridhi-upāntām*—including the seas; *anuja*—the younger brothers; *anuvartitaḥ*—being followed by them.

TRANSLATION

Mahārāja Yudhiṣṭhira, after being enlightened by what was spoken by Bhīṣmadeva and Lord Śrī Kṛṣṇa, the infallible, engaged himself in matters of perfect knowledge because all his misgivings were eradicated. Thus he ruled over the earth and seas and was followed by his younger brothers.

PURPORT

The modern English law of primogeniture, or the law of inheritance by the firstborn, was also prevalent in those days when Mahārāja Yudhiṣṭhira ruled the earth and seas. In those days the King of Hastināpura (now part of New Delhi) was the emperor of the world, including the seas, up to the time of Mahārāja Parīkṣit, the grandson of Mahārāja Yudhiṣṭhira. Mahārāja Yudhiṣṭhira's younger brothers were acting as his ministers and commanders of state, and there was full cooperation between the perfectly religious brothers of the King. Mahārāja Yudhiṣṭhira was the ideal king or representative of Lord Śrī Kṛṣṇa to rule over the kingdom of earth and was comparable to King Indra, the representative ruler of the heavenly planets. The demigods like Indra, Candra, Sūrya, Varuṇa and Vāyu are representative kings of different planets of the universe, and similarly Mahārāja Yudhiṣṭhira was also one of them, ruling over the kingdom of the earth. Mahārāja Yudhiṣṭhira was not a typically unenlightened political leader of modern democracy. Mahārāja Yudhiṣṭhira was instructed by Bhīṣmadeva and the infallible Lord also, and therefore he had full knowledge of everything in perfection.

The modern elected executive head of a state is just like a puppet because he has no kingly power. Even if he is enlightened like Mahārāja Yudhiṣṭhira, he cannot do anything out of his own good will due to his constitutional position. Therefore, there are so many states over the earth quarreling because of ideological differences or other selfish motives. But a king like Mahārāja Yudhiṣṭhira had no ideology of his own. He had but to follow the instructions of the infallible Lord and the Lord's representative and the authorized agent, Bhīṣmadeva. It is instructed in the *śāstras* that one should follow the great authority and the infallible Lord without any personal motive and manufactured ideology. Therefore, it was possible for Mahārāja Yudhiṣṭhira to rule the whole world, including the seas, because the principles were infallible and universally applicable to everyone. The conception of one world state can only be fulfilled if we can follow the infallible authority. An imperfect human being cannot create an ideology acceptable to everyone. Only the perfect and the infallible can create a program which is applicable at every place and can be followed by all in the world. It is the person who rules, and not the impersonal government. If the person is perfect, the government is perfect. If the person is a fool, the government is a fool's paradise. That is the law of nature. There are so many stories of imperfect kings or executive heads. Therefore, the executive head must be a trained person like Mahārāja Yudhiṣṭhira, and he must have the full autocratic power to rule over the world. The conception of a world state can take shape only under the regime of a perfect king like Mahārāja Yudhiṣṭhira. The world was happy in those days because there were kings like Mahārāja Yudhiṣṭhira to rule over the world.

TEXT 4

कामं ववर्ष पर्जन्यः सर्वकामदुघा मही ।
सिषिचुः स्म व्रजान् गावः पयसोधस्वतीर्मुदा ॥ ४ ॥

kāmaṁ vavarṣa parjanyaḥ
sarva-kāma-dughā mahī

siṣicuḥ sma vrajān gāvaḥ
payasodhasvatīr mudā

kāmam—everything needed; *vavarṣa*—was showered; *parjanyaḥ*—rains; *sarva*—everything; *kāma*—necessities; *dughā*—producer; *mahī*—the land; *siṣicuḥ sma*—moisten; *vrajān*—pasturing grounds; *gāvaḥ*—the cow; *payasā udhasvatīḥ*—due to swollen milk bags; *mudā*—because of a joyful attitude.

TRANSLATION

During the reign of Mahārāja Yudhiṣṭhira, the clouds showered all the water that people needed, and the earth produced all the necessities of man in profusion. Due to its fatty milk bag and cheerful attitude, the cow used to moisten the grazing ground with milk.

PURPORT

The basic principle of economic development is centered on *land* and *cows.* The necessities of human society are food grains, fruits, milk, minerals, clothing, wood, etc. One requires all these items to fulfill the material needs of the body. Certainly one does not require flesh and fish or iron tools and machinery. During the regime of Mahārāja Yudhiṣṭhira, all over the world there were regulated rainfalls. Rainfalls are not in the control of the human being. The heavenly King Indradeva is the controller of rains, and he is the servant of the Lord. When the Lord is obeyed by the king and the people under the king's administration, there are regulated rains from the horizon, and these rains are the causes of all varieties of production on the land. Not only do regulated rains help ample production of grains and fruits, but when they combine with astronomical influences there is ample production of valuable stones and pearls. Grains and vegetables can sumptuously feed a man and animals, and a fatty cow delivers enough milk to supply a man sumptuously with vigor and vitality. If there is enough milk, enough grains, enough fruit, enough cotton, enough silk and enough jewels, then why do the people need cinemas, houses of prostitution, slaughterhouses, etc.? What is the need of an artificial luxurious life of cinema, cars, radio, flesh and hotels? Has this civilization produced anything but quarreling individually and nationally? Has this civilization enhanced the cause of equality and fraternity by sending thousands of men into a hellish factory and the war fields at the whims of a particular man?

It is said here that the cows used to moisten the pasturing land with milk because their milk bags were fatty and the animals were joyful. Do they not require, therefore, proper protection for a joyful life by being fed with a sufficient quantity of grass in the field? Why should men kill cows for their selfish purposes? Why should man not be satisfied with grains, fruits and milk, which, combined together, can produce hundreds and thousands of palatable dishes. Why are there slaughterhouses all over the world to kill innocent animals? Mahārāja Parīkṣit, grandson of Mahārāja Yudhiṣṭhira, while touring his vast kingdom, saw a black man attempting to kill a cow. The King at once arrested the butcher and chastised him sufficiently. Should not a king or executive head protect the lives of the poor animals who are unable to defend themselves? Is this humanity? Are not the animals of a country citizens also? Then why are they allowed to be butchered in organized slaughterhouses? Are these the signs of equality, fraternity and nonviolence?

Therefore, in contrast with the modern, advanced, civilized form of government, an autocracy like Mahārāja Yudhiṣṭhira's is by far superior to a so-called democracy in which animals are killed and a man less than an animal is allowed to cast votes for another less-than-animal man.

We are all creatures of material nature. In the *Bhagavad-gītā* it is said that the Lord Himself is the seed-giving father and material nature is the mother of *all living beings in all shapes.* Thus mother material nature has enough foodstuff both for animals and for men, by the grace of the Father Almighty, Śrī Kṛṣṇa. The human being is the elder brother of all other living beings. He is endowed with intelligence more powerful than animals for realizing the course of nature and the indications of the Almighty Father. Human civilizations should depend on the production of material nature without artificially attempting economic development to turn the world into a chaos of artificial greed and power only for the purpose of artificial luxuries and sense gratification. This is but the life of dogs and hogs.

TEXT 5

नद्यः समुद्रा गिरयः सवनस्पतिवीरुधः ।
फलन्त्योषधयः सर्वाः काममन्वृतु तस्य वै ॥ ५ ॥

nadyaḥ samudrā girayaḥ
savanaspati-vīrudhaḥ
phalanty oṣadhayaḥ sarvāḥ
kāmam anvṛtu tasya vai

nadyaḥ—rivers; *samudrāḥ*—oceans; *girayaḥ*—hills and mountains; *savanaspati*—vegetables; *vīrudhaḥ*—creepers; *phalanti*—active; *oṣadhayaḥ*—drugs; *sarvāḥ*—all; *kāmam*—necessities; *anvṛtu*—seasonal; *tasya*—for the King; *vai*—certainly.

TRANSLATION

The rivers, oceans, hills, mountains, forests, creepers and active drugs, in every season, paid their tax quota to the King in profusion.

PURPORT

Since Mahārāja Yudhiṣṭhira was under the protection of the *ajita,* the infallible Lord, as above mentioned, the properties of the Lord, namely the rivers, oceans, hills, forests, etc., were all pleased, and they used to supply their respective quota of taxes to the King. The secret to success *is to take refuge under the protection of the Supreme Lord.* Without His sanction, nothing can be possible. To make economic development by our own endeavors on the strength of tools and machinery is not all. The sanction of the Supreme Lord must be there, otherwise despite all instrumental arrangements everything will be unsuccessful. The ultimate cause of success is the *daiva,* the Supreme. Kings like Mahārāja Yudhiṣṭhira knew perfectly well that the king is the agent of the Supreme Lord to look after the welfare of the mass of people. Actually the state belongs to the Supreme Lord. The rivers, oceans, forests, hills, drugs, etc., are not creations of man. They are all creations of the Supreme Lord, and the living being is allowed to make use of the property of the Lord for the service of the Lord. Today's slogan is that everything is for the people, and therefore the government is for the people and by the people. But to produce a new species of humanity at the present moment on the basis of God consciousness and perfection of human life, the ideology of godly communism, the world has to again follow in the footsteps of kings like Mahārāja Yudhiṣṭhira or Parīkṣit. There is enough of everything by the will of the Lord, and we can make proper use of things to live comfortably without enmity between men, or animal and man or nature. The control of the Lord is everywhere, and if the Lord is pleased, every part of nature will be pleased. The river will flow profusely to fertilize the land; the oceans will supply sufficient quantities of minerals, pearls and jewels; the forest will supply sufficient wood, drugs and vegetables, and the seasonal changes will effectively help produce fruits and flowers in profuse quantity. The artificial way of living depending on factories and tools can render so-called happiness only to a limited number at the cost of millions. Since the energy of the mass of people is engaged in factory production, the natural products are being hampered, and for this the mass is unhappy. Without being educated properly, the mass of people are following in the footsteps of the vested interests by exploiting natural reserves, and therefore there is acute competition between individual and individual and nation and nation. There is no control by the trained agent of the Lord. We must look into the defects of modern civilization by comparison here, and should follow in the footsteps of Mahārāja Yudhiṣṭhira to cleanse man and wipe out anachronisms.

TEXT 6

नाधयो व्याधयः क्लेशा दैवभूतात्महेतवः ।
अजातशत्रावभवन् जन्तूनां राज्ञि कर्हिचित् ॥ ६ ॥

nādhayo vyādhayaḥ kleśā
daiva-bhūtātma-hetavaḥ
ajāta-śatrāv abhavan
jantūnāṁ rājñi karhicit

na—never; *ādhayaḥ*—anxieties; *vyādhayaḥ*—diseases; *kleśāḥ*—trouble due to excessive heat and cold; *daiva-bhūta-ātma*—all due to the body, supernatural power and other living beings; *hetavaḥ*—due to the cause of; *ajāta-śatrau*—unto one who has no enemy; *abhavan*—happened; *jantūnām*—of the living beings; *rājñi*—unto the King; *karhicit*—at any time.

TRANSLATION

Because of the King's having no enemy, the living beings were not at any time disturbed by mental agonies, diseases, or excessive heat or cold.

PURPORT

To be nonviolent to human beings and to be a killer or enemy of the poor animals is Satan's philosophy. In this age there is enmity toward poor animals, and therefore the poor creatures are always anxious. The reaction of the poor animals is being forced on human society, and therefore there is always the strain of cold or hot war between men, individually, collectively or nationally. At the time of Mahārāja Yudhiṣṭhira, there were no different nations, although there were different subordinate states. The whole world was united, and the supreme head, being a trained king like Yudhiṣṭhira, kept all the inhabitants free from anxiety, diseases and excessive heat and cold. They were not only economically well-to-do, but also physically fit and undisturbed by supernatural power, by enmity from other living beings and by disturbance of bodily and mental agonies. There is a proverb in Bengali that a bad king spoils the kingdom and a bad housewife spoils the family. This truth is applicable here also. Because the King was pious and obedient to the Lord and sages, because he was no one's enemy and because he was a recognized agent of the Lord and therefore protected by Him, all the citizens under the King's protection were, so to speak, directly protected by the Lord and His authorized agents. Unless one is pious and recognized by the Lord, he cannot make others happy who are under his care. There is full cooperation between man and God and man and nature, and this conscious cooperation between man and God and man and nature, as exemplified by King Yudhiṣṭhira, can bring about happiness, peace and prosperity in the world. The attitude of exploiting one another, the custom of the day, will only bring misery.

TEXT 7

उषित्वा हास्तिनपुरे मासान् कतिपयान् हरिः ।
सुहृदां च विशोकाय स्वसुश्च प्रियकाम्यया ॥ ७ ॥

uṣitvā hāstinapure
māsān katipayān hariḥ
suhṛdāṁ ca viśokāya
svasuś ca priya-kāmyayā

uṣitvā—staying; *hāstinapure*—in the city of Hastināpura; *māsān*—months; *katipayān*—a few; *hariḥ*—Lord Śrī Kṛṣṇa; *suhṛdām*—relatives; *ca*—also; *viśokāya*—for pacifying them; *svasuḥ*—the sister; *ca*—and; *priya-kāmyayā*—for pleasing.

TRANSLATION

Śrī Hari, Lord Śrī Kṛṣṇa, resided at Hastināpura for a few months to pacify His relatives and please His own sister [Subhadrā].

PURPORT

Kṛṣṇa was to start for Dvārakā, His own kingdom, after the Battle of Kurukṣetra and Yudhiṣṭhira's being enthroned, but to oblige the request of Mahārāja Yudhiṣṭhira and to show special mercy to Bhīṣmadeva, Lord Kṛṣṇa stopped at Hastināpura, the capital of the Pāṇḍavas. The Lord decided to stay especially to pacify the aggrieved King as well as to please Subhadrā, sister of Lord Śrī Kṛṣṇa. Subhadrā was especially to be pacified because she lost her only son, Abhimanyu, who was just married. The boy left his wife, Uttarā, mother of Mahārāja Parīkṣit. The Lord is always pleased to satisfy His devotees in any capacity. Only His devotees can play the parts of His relatives. The Lord is absolute.

TEXT 8

आमन्त्र्य चाभ्यनुज्ञातः परिष्वज्याभिवाद्य तम् ।
आरुरोह रथं कैश्चित्परिष्वक्तोऽभिवादितः ॥ ८ ॥

āmantrya cābhyanujñātaḥ
pariṣvajyābhivādya tam
āruroha rathaṁ kaiścit
pariṣvakto 'bhivāditaḥ

āmantrya—taking permission; *ca*—and; *abhyanujñātaḥ*—being permitted; *pariṣvajya*—embracing; *abhivādya*—bowing down at the feet; *tam*—unto Mahārāja Yudhiṣṭhira; *āruroha*—ascended; *ratham*—the chariot; *kaiścit*—by someone; *pariṣvaktaḥ*—being embraced; *abhivāditaḥ*—being offered obeisances.

TRANSLATION

Afterwards, when the Lord asked permission to depart and the King gave it, the Lord offered His respects to Mahārāja Yudhiṣṭhira by bowing down at his feet, and the King embraced Him. After this the Lord, being embraced by others and receiving their obeisances, got into His chariot.

PURPORT

Mahārāja Yudhiṣṭhira was the elder cousin of Lord Kṛṣṇa, and therefore while departing from him the Lord bowed down at the King's feet. The King embraced Him as a younger brother, although the King knew perfectly well that Kṛṣṇa is the Supreme Personality of Godhead. The Lord takes pleasure when some of His devotees accept Him as less important in terms of love. No one is greater than or equal to the Lord, but He takes pleasure in being treated as younger than His devotees. These are all transcendental pastimes of the Lord. The impersonalist cannot enter into the supernatural roles played by the devotee of the Lord. Thereafter Bhīma and Arjuna embraced the Lord because they were of the same age, but Nakula and Sahadeva bowed down before the Lord because they were younger than He.

TEXTS 9-10

सुभद्रा द्रौपदी कुन्ती विराटतनया तथा ।
गान्धारी धृतराष्ट्रश्च युयुत्सुर्गौतमो यमौ ॥ ९ ॥
वृकोदरश्च धौम्यश्च स्त्रियो मत्स्यसुतादयः ।
न सेहिरे विमुह्यन्तो विरहं शार्ङ्गधन्वनः ॥१०॥

subhadrā draupadī kuntī
virāṭa-tanayā tathā
gāndhārī dhṛtarāṣṭraś ca
yuyutsur gautamo yamau

vṛkodaraś ca dhaumyaś ca
striyo matsya-sutādayaḥ

na sehire vimuhyanto
virahaṁ śārṅga-dhanvanaḥ

subhadrā—the sister of Kṛṣṇa; *draupadī*—the wife of the Pāṇḍavas; *kuntī*—the mother of the Pāṇḍavas; *virāṭa-tanayā*—the daughter of Virāṭa (Uttarā); *tathā*—also; *gāndhārī*—the mother of Duryodhana; *dhṛtarāṣṭraḥ*—the father of Duryodhana; *ca*—and; *yuyutsuḥ*—the son of Dhṛtarāṣṭra by his *vaiśya* wife; *gautamaḥ*—Kṛpācārya; *yamau*—the twin brothers Nakula and Sahadeva; *vṛkodaraḥ*—Bhīma; *ca*—and; *dhaumyaḥ*—Dhaumya; *ca*—and; *striyaḥ*—also other ladies of the palace; *matsya-sutā-ādayaḥ*—the daughter of a fisherman (Satyavatī, Bhīṣma's stepmother); *na*—could not; *sehire*—tolerate; *vimuhyantaḥ*—almost fainting; *viraham*—separation; *śārṅga-dhanvanaḥ*—of Śrī Kṛṣṇa, who bears a conch in His hand.

TRANSLATION

At that time Subhadrā, Draupadī, Kuntī, Uttarā, Gāndhārī, Dhṛtarāṣṭra, Yuyutsu, Kṛpācārya, Nakula, Sahadeva, Bhīmasena, Dhaumya and Satyavatī all nearly fainted because it was impossible for them to bear separation from Lord Kṛṣṇa.

PURPORT

Lord Śrī Kṛṣṇa is so attractive for the living beings, especially for the devotees, that it is impossible for them to tolerate separation. The conditioned soul under the spell of illusory energy forgets the Lord, otherwise he cannot. The feeling of such separation cannot be described, but it can simply be imagined by devotees only. After His separation from Vṛndāvana and the innocent rural cowherd boys, girls, ladies and others, they all felt shock throughout their lives, and the separation of Rādhārāṇī, the most beloved cowherd girl, is beyond expression. Once they met at Kurukṣetra during a solar eclipse, and the feeling which was expressed by them is heartrending. There is, of course, a difference in the qualities of the transcendental devotees of the Lord, but none of them who have ever contacted the Lord by direct communion or otherwise can leave Him for a moment. That is the attitude of the pure devotee.

TEXTS 11-12

सत्सङ्गान्मुक्तदुःसङ्गो हातुं नोत्सहते बुधः ।
कीर्त्यमानं यशो यस्य सकृदाकर्ण्य रोचनम् ॥११॥
तस्मिन्न्यस्तधियः पार्थाः सहेरन् विरहं कथम् ।
दर्शनस्पर्शसंलापशयनासनभोजनैः ॥१२॥

sat-saṅgān mukta-duḥsaṅgo
hātuṁ notsahate budhaḥ
kīrtyamānaṁ yaśo yasya
sakṛd ākarṇya rocanam

tasmin nyasta-dhiyaḥ pārthāḥ
saheran virahaṁ katham
darśana-sparśa-saṁlāpa-
śayanāsana-bhojanaiḥ

sat-saṅgāt—by the association of pure devotees; *mukta-duḥsaṅgaḥ*—freed from bad materialistic association; *hātum*—to give up; *na utsahate*—never attempts; *budhaḥ*—one who has understood the Lord; *kīrtyamānam*—glorifying; *yaśaḥ*—fame; *yasya*—whose; *sakṛt*—once only; *ākarṇya*—hearing only; *rocanam*—pleasing; *tasmin*—unto Him; *nyasta-dhiyaḥ*—one who has given his mind unto Him; *pārthāḥ*—the sons of Pṛthā; *saheran*—can tolerate; *viraham*—separation; *katham*—how; *darśana*—seeing face to face; *sparśa*—touching; *saṁlāpa*—conversing; *śayana*—sleeping; *āsana*—sitting; *bhojanaiḥ*—dining together.

TRANSLATION

The intelligent, who have understood the Supreme Lord in association with pure devotees and have become freed from bad materialistic association, can never avoid hearing the glories of the Lord, even though they have heard them only once. How, then, could the Pāṇḍavas tolerate His separation, for they had been intimately associated with His person, seeing Him face to face, touching Him, conversing with Him, and sleeping, sitting and dining with Him?

PURPORT

The living being's constitutional position is one of serving a superior. He is obliged to serve by force the dictates of illusory material energy in different phases of sense gratification. And in serving the senses he is never tired. Even though he may be tired, the illusory energy perpetually forces him to do so without being satisfied. There is no end to such sense gratificatory business, and the conditioned soul becomes entangled in such servitude without hope of release. The release is only effected by association with pure devotees. By such association one is gradually promoted to his transcendental consciousness. Thus he can know that his eternal position is to render service unto the Lord and not to the perverted senses in the capacity of lust, anger, desire to lord it over, etc. Material society, friendship and love are all different phases of lust. Home, country, family, society, wealth and all sorts of corollaries are all causes of bondage in the material world, where the threefold miseries of life are concomitant factors. By associating with pure devotees and by hearing them submissively, attachment for material enjoyment becomes slackened, and attraction for hearing about the transcendental activities of the Lord becomes prominent. Once they are, they will go on progressively without stoppage, like fire in gunpowder. It is said that Hari, the Personality of Godhead, is so transcendentally attractive that even those who are self-satisfied by self-realization and are factually liberated from all material bondage also become devotees of the Lord. Under the circumstances it is easily understood what must have been the position of the Pāṇḍavas, who were constant companions of the Lord. They could not even think of separation from Śrī Kṛṣṇa, since the attraction was more intense for them because of continuous personal contact. His remembrance by His form, quality, name, fame, pastimes, etc., is also attractive for the pure devotee, so much so that he forgets all forms, quality, name, fame and activities of the mundane world, and due to his mature association with pure devotees he is not out of contact with the Lord for a moment.

TEXT 13

सर्वे तेऽनिमिषैरक्षैस्तमनुद्रुतचेतसः ।
वीक्षन्तः स्नेहसम्बद्धा विचेलुस्तत्र तत्र ह ॥१३॥

sarve te 'nimiṣair akṣais
tam anu druta-cetasaḥ
vīkṣantaḥ sneha-sambaddhā
vicelus tatra tatra ha

sarve—all; *te*—they; *animiṣaiḥ*—without twinkling of the eyes; *akṣaiḥ*—by the eye; *tam anu*—after Him; *druta-cetasaḥ*—melted heart; *vīkṣantaḥ*—looking upon Him; *sneha-sambaddhāḥ*—bound by pure affection; *viceluḥ*—began to move; *tatra tatra*—here and there; *ha*—so they did.

TRANSLATION

All their hearts were melting for Him on the pot of attraction. They looked at Him without blinking their eyes, and they moved hither and thither in perplexity.

PURPORT

Kṛṣṇa is naturally attractive for all living beings because He is the chief eternal amongst all eternals. He alone is the maintainer of the many eternals. This is stated in the *Kaṭha Upaniṣad,* and thus one can obtain permanent peace and prosperity by revival of one's eternal relation with Him, now forgotten under the spell of *māyā,* the illusory energy of the Lord. Once this relation is slightly revived, the conditioned soul at once becomes freed from the illusion of material energy and becomes mad after the association of the Lord. This association is made possible not only by personal contact with the Lord, but also by association with His name, fame, form and quality. *Śrīmad-Bhāgavatam* trains the conditioned soul to this stage of perfection by submissive hearing from the pure devotee.

TEXT 14

न्यरुन्धन्नुद्गलद्बाष्पमौत्कण्ठ्याद्देवकीसुते ।
निर्यात्यगारान्नोऽभद्रमिति स्याद्बान्धवस्त्रियः ॥१४॥

nyarundhann udgalad bāṣpam
autkaṇṭhyād devakī-sute
niryāty agārān no 'bhadram
iti syād bāndhava-striyaḥ

nyarundhan—checking with great difficulty; *udgalat*—overflowing; *bāṣpam*—tears; *autkaṇṭhyāt*—because of great anxiety; *devakī-sute*—unto the son of Devakī; *niryāti*—having come out; *agārāt*—from the palace; *naḥ*—not; *abhadram*—inauspiciousness; *iti*—thus; *syāt*—may happen; *bāndhava*—relative; *striyaḥ*—ladies.

TRANSLATION

The female relatives, whose eyes were flooded with tears out of anxiety for Kṛṣṇa, came out of the palace. They could stop their tears only with great difficulty. They feared that tears would cause misfortune at the time of departure.

PURPORT

There were hundreds of ladies in the palace of Hastināpura. All of them were affectionate to Kṛṣṇa. All of them were relatives also. When they saw that Kṛṣṇa was going away from the palace for His native place, they were very anxious for Him, and as usual tears began to roll down their cheeks. They thought, at the same time, that tears at that moment might be a cause of misfortune for Kṛṣṇa; therefore they wanted to check them. This was very difficult for them because the tears could not be checked. Therefore, they smeared their tears in their eyes, and their hearts throbbed. Therefore ladies who were the wives and daughters-in-law of those who died in the battlefield never came in direct contact with Kṛṣṇa. But all of them heard of Him and His great activities, and thus they thought of Him, talked of Him, His name, fame, etc., and became affectionate also, like those who were in direct contact. Therefore directly or indirectly anyone who thinks of Kṛṣṇa, talks of Kṛṣṇa or worships Kṛṣṇa becomes attached to Him. Because Kṛṣṇa is absolute, there is no difference between His name, form, quality, etc. Our intimate relation with Kṛṣṇa can be confidentially revived by our talking of, hearing of, or remembering Him. It is so done due to spiritual potency.

TEXT 15

मृदङ्गशङ्खभेर्यश्च वीणापणवगोमुखाः ।
धुन्धुर्यानकघण्टाद्या नेदुर्दुन्दुभयस्तथा ॥१५॥

mṛdaṅga-śaṅkha-bheryaś ca
vīṇā-paṇava-gomukhāḥ
dhundhury-ānaka-ghaṇṭādyā
nedur dundubhayas tathā

mṛdaṅga—sweet sounding drum; *śaṅkha*—conchshell; *bheryaḥ*—brass band; *ca*—and; *vīṇā*—string band; *paṇava*—a kind of flute; *gomukhāḥ*—another flute; *dhundhurī*—another drum; *ānaka*—kettle; *ghaṇṭā*—bell; *ādyāḥ*—others; *neduḥ*—sounded; *dundubhayaḥ*—other different types of drums; *tathā*—at that time.

TRANSLATION

While the Lord was departing from the palace of Hastināpura, different types of drums—like the mṛdaṅga, dhola, nagra, dhundhurī and dundubhi—and flutes of different types, the viṇā, gomukha and bherī, all sounded together to show Him honor.

TEXT 16

प्रासादशिखरारूढाः कुरुनार्यो दिदृक्षया ।
ववृषुः कुसुमैः कृष्णं प्रेमव्रीडास्मितेक्षणाः ॥१६॥

prāsāda-śikharārūḍhāḥ
kuru-nāryo didṛkṣayā
vavṛṣuḥ kusumaiḥ kṛṣṇaṁ
prema-vrīḍā-smitekṣaṇāḥ

prāsāda—palace; *śikhara*—the roof; *ārūḍhāḥ*—ascending; *kuru-nāryaḥ*—the ladies of the Kuru royalty; *didṛkṣayā*—seeing; *vavṛṣuḥ*—showered; *kusumaiḥ*—by flowers; *kṛṣṇam*—upon Lord Kṛṣṇa; *prema*—out of affection and love; *vrīḍā-smita-īkṣaṇāḥ*—glancing with shy smiles.

TRANSLATION

Out of a loving desire to see the Lord, the royal ladies of the Kurus got up on top of the palace, and smiling with affection and shyness, they showered flowers upon the Lord.

PURPORT

Shyness is a particular extra-natural beauty of the fair sex, and it commands respect from the opposite sex. This custom was observed even during the days of the *Mahābhārata*, i.e., more than five thousand years ago. It is only the less intelligent persons not well versed in the history of the world who say that observance of separation of female from male is an introduction of the Mohammedan period in India. This incident from the *Mahābhārata* period proves definitely that the ladies of the palace observed strict *pardā* (restricted association with men), and instead of coming down in the open air where Lord Kṛṣṇa and others were assembled, the ladies of the palace went up on the top of the palace and from there paid their respects to Lord Kṛṣṇa by showers of flowers. It is definitely stated here that the ladies were smiling there on the top of the palace, checked by shyness. This shyness is a gift of nature to the fair sex, and it enhances their beauty and prestige, even if they are of a less important family or even if they are less attractive. We have practical experience of this fact. A sweeper woman commanded the respect of many respectable gentlemen simply by manifesting a lady's shyness. Half-naked ladies in the street do not command any respect, but a shy sweeper's wife commands respect from all.

Human civilization, as conceived of by the sages of India, is to help one free himself from the clutches of illusion. The material beauty of a woman is an illusion because actually the body is made of earth, water, fire, air, etc. But because there is the association of the living spark with matter, it appears to be beautiful. No one is attracted by an earthen doll, even if it is most perfectly prepared to attract the attention of others. The dead body has no beauty because no one will accept the dead body of a so-called beautiful woman. Therefore, the conclusion is that the spirit spark is beautiful, and because of the soul's beauty one is attracted by the beauty of the outward body. The Vedic wisdom, therefore, forbids us to be attracted by false beauty. But because we are now in the darkness of ignorance, the Vedic civilization allows very restricted mixing of woman and man. They say that the woman is considered to be the fire, and the man is considered to be the butter. The butter must melt in association with fire, and therefore they may be brought together only when it is necessary. And shyness is a check to the unrestricted mixing. It is nature's gift, and it must be utilized.

TEXT 17

सितातपत्रं जग्राह मुक्तादामविभूषितम् ।
रत्नदण्डं गुडाकेशः प्रियः प्रियतमस्य ह ॥१७॥

sitātapatraṁ jagrāha
muktādāma-vibhūṣitam
ratna-daṇḍaṁ guḍākeśaḥ
priyaḥ priyatamasya ha

sita-ātapatram—soothing umbrella; *jagrāha*—took up; *muktā-dāma*—decorated with laces and pearls; *vibhūṣitam*—embroidered; *ratna-daṇḍam*—with a handle of jewels; *guḍākeśaḥ*—Arjuna, the expert warrior, or one who has conquered sleep; *priyaḥ*—most beloved; *priyatamasya*—of the most beloved; *ha*—so he did.

TRANSLATION

At that time Arjuna, the great warrior and conqueror of sleep, who is the intimate friend of the most beloved Supreme Lord, took up an umbrella which had a handle of jewels and was embroidered with lace and pearls.

PURPORT

Gold, jewels, pearls and valuable stones were used in the luxurious royal ceremonies. They are all nature's gifts and are produced by the hills, oceans, etc., by the order of the Lord, when man does not waste his valuable time in producing unwanted things in the name of necessities. By so-called development of industrial enterprises, they are now using pots of gutta-percha instead of metals like gold, silver, brass and copper. They are using margarine instead of purified butter, and one fourth of the city population has no shelter.

TEXT 18

उद्धवः सात्यकिश्चैव व्यजने परमाद्भुते ।
विकीर्यमाणः कुसुमै रेजे मधुपतिः पथि ॥१८॥

uddhavaḥ sātyakiś caiva
vyajane paramādbhute
vikīryamāṇaḥ kusumai
reje madhu-patiḥ pathi

uddhavaḥ—a cousin-brother of Kṛṣṇa's; *sātyakiḥ*—His driver; *ca*—and; *eva*—certainly; *vyajane*—engaged in fanning; *parama-adbhute*—decorative; *vikīryamāṇaḥ*—seated on scattered; *kusumaiḥ*—flowers all around; *reje*—commanded; *madhu-patiḥ*—the master of Madhu (Kṛṣṇa); *pathi*—on the road.

TRANSLATION

Uddhava and Sātyaki began to fan the Lord with decorated fans, and the Lord, as the master of Madhu, seated on scattered flowers, commanded them along the road.

TEXT 19

अश्रूयन्ताशिषः सत्यास्तत्र तत्र द्विजेरिताः ।
नानुरूपानुरूपाश्च निर्गुणस्य गुणात्मनः ॥१९॥

aśrūyantāśiṣaḥ satyās
tatra tatra dvijeritāḥ
nānurūpānurūpāś ca
nirguṇasya guṇātmanaḥ

aśrūyanta—being heard; *āśiṣaḥ*—benediction; *satyāḥ*—all truths; *tatra*—here; *tatra*—there; *dvija-īritāḥ*—sounded by learned *brāhmaṇas; na*—not; *anurūpa*—befitting; *anurūpāḥ*—fitting; *ca*—also; *nirguṇasya*—of the Absolute; *guṇa-ātmanaḥ*—playing the role of a human being.

TRANSLATION

It was being heard here and there that the benedictions being paid to Kṛṣṇa were neither befitting nor unbefitting because they were all for the Absolute, who was now playing the part of a human being.

PURPORT

At places there were sounds of Vedic benediction aiming at the Personality of Godhead Śrī Kṛṣṇa. The benedictions were fitting in the sense that the Lord was playing the part of a human being, as if a cousin of Mahārāja Yudhiṣṭhira, but they were also unfitting because the Lord is absolute and has nothing to do with any kind of material relativities. He is *nirguṇa*, or there are no material qualities in Him, but He is full of transcendental qualities. In the transcendental world there is nothing contradictory, whereas in the relative world everything has its opposite. In the relative world white is the opposite conception of black, but in the transcendental world there is no distinction between white and black. Therefore the sounds of benedictions uttered by the learned *brāhmaṇas* here and there appear to be contradictory in relation with the Absolute Person, but when they are applied to the Absolute Person they lose all contradiction and become transcendental. One example may clear this idea. Lord Śrī Kṛṣṇa is sometimes described as a thief. He is very famous amongst His pure devotees as the Mākhana-cora. He used to steal butter from the houses of neighbors at Vṛndāvana in His early age. Since then He is famous as a thief. But in spite of His being famous as a thief, He is worshiped as a thief, whereas in the mundane world a thief is punished and is never praised. Since He is the Absolute Personality of Godhead, everything is applicable to Him, and still in spite of all contradictions He is the Supreme Personality of Godhead.

TEXT 20

अन्योन्यमासीत्संजल्प उत्तमश्लोकचेतसाम् ।
कौरवेन्द्रपुरस्त्रीणां सर्वश्रुतिमनोहरः ॥२०॥

anyonyam āsīt sañjalpa
uttama-śloka-cetasām
kauravendra-pura-strīṇāṁ
sarva-śruti-mano-haraḥ

anyonyam—among each other; *āsīt*—there was; *sañjalpaḥ*—talking; *uttama-śloka*—the Supreme, who is praised by selected poetry; *cetasām*—of those whose hearts are absorbed in that way; *kaurava-in-*

dra—the king of the Kurus; *pura*—capital; *strīṇām*—all the ladies; *sarva*—all; *śruti*—the *Vedas; manaḥ-haraḥ*—attractive to the mind.

TRANSLATION

Absorbed in the thought of the transcendental qualities of the Lord, who is sung in select poetry, the ladies on the roofs of all the houses of Hastināpura began to talk of Him. This talk was more attractive than the hymns of the Vedas.

PURPORT

In the *Bhagavad-gītā* it is said that in all the Vedic literatures the goal is the Personality of Godhead Śrī Kṛṣṇa. Factually the glories of the Lord are depicted in such literature as the *Vedas, Rāmāyaṇa* and *Mahābhārata.* And in the *Bhāgavatam* they are specifically mentioned in respect to the Supreme Lord. Therefore, while the ladies on the tops of the houses in the capital of the kings of the Kuru dynasty were talking about the Lord, their talk was more pleasing than the Vedic hymns. Anything sung in the praise of the Lord is *Śruti-mantra.* There are songs of Ṭhākura Narottama dāsa, one of the *ācāryas* in the Gauḍīya-sampradāya, composed in simple Bengali language. But Ṭhākura Viśvanātha Cakravartī, another very learned *ācārya* of the same *sampradāya,* has approved the songs by Ṭhākura Narottama dāsa to be as good as Vedic *mantras.* And this is so because of the subject matter. The language is immaterial, but the subject matter is important. The ladies, who were all absorbed in the thought and actions of the Lord, developed the consciousness of Vedic wisdom by the grace of the Lord. And therefore although such ladies might not have been very learned scholars in Sanskrit or otherwise, still whatever they spoke was more attractive than the Vedic hymns. The Vedic hymns in the *Upaniṣads* are sometimes indirectly directed to the Supreme Lord. But the talks of the ladies were directly spoken of the Lord, and thus they were more pleasing to the heart. The ladies' talks appeared to be more valuable than the learned *brāhmaṇas'* benedictions.

TEXT 21

स वै किलायं पुरुषः पुरातनो
य एक आसीदविशेष आत्मनि ।

अग्रे गुणेभ्यो जगदात्मनीश्वरे
निमीलितात्मन्निशि सुप्तशक्तिषु ॥२१॥

sa vai kilāyaṁ puruṣaḥ purātano
ya eka āsīd aviśeṣa ātmani
agre guṇebhyo jagad-ātmanīśvare
nimīlitātman niśi supta-śaktiṣu

saḥ—He (Kṛṣṇa); *vai*—as I remember; *kila*—definitely; *ayam*—this; *puruṣaḥ*—Personality of Godhead; *purātanaḥ*—the original; *yaḥ*—who; *ekaḥ*—only one; *āsīt*—existed; *aviśeṣaḥ*—materially unmanifested; *ātmani*—own self; *agre*—before creation; *guṇebhyaḥ*—of the modes of nature; *jagat-ātmani*—unto the Supersoul; *īśvare*—unto the Supreme Lord; *nimīlita*—merged into; *ātman*—the living entity; *niśi supta*—inactive at night; *śaktiṣu*—of the energies.

TRANSLATION

They said: Here He is, the original Personality of Godhead as we definitely remember Him. He alone existed before the manifested creation of the modes of nature, and in Him only, because He is the Supreme Lord, all living beings merge, as if sleeping at night, their energy suspended.

PURPORT

There are two types of dissolution of the manifested cosmos. At the end of every 4,320,000,000 solar years, when Brahmā, the lord of one particular universe, goes to sleep, there is one annihilation. And at the end of Lord Brahmā's life, which takes place at the end of Brahmā's one hundred years of age, in our calculation at the end of 8,640,000,000 *x* 30 *x* 12 *x* 100 solar years, there is complete annihilation of the entire universe, and in both the periods both the material energy called the *mahat-tattva* and the marginal energy called *jīva-tattva* merge in the person of the Supreme Lord. The living beings remain asleep within the body of the Lord until there is another creation of the material world, and that is the way of the creation, maintenance and annihilation of the material manifestation.

The material creation is effected by the interaction of the three modes of material nature set in action by the Lord, and therefore it is said here that the Lord existed before the modes of material nature were set in motion. In the *Śruti-mantra* it is said that only Viṣṇu, the Supreme Lord, existed before the creation, and there was no Brahmā, Śiva or other demigods. Viṣṇu means the Mahā-Viṣṇu, who is lying on the Causal Ocean. By His breathing only all the universes are generated in seeds and gradually develop into gigantic forms with innumerable planets within each and every universe. The seeds of universes develop into gigantic forms in the way seeds of a banyan tree develop into numberless banyan trees.

This Mahā-Viṣṇu is the plenary portion of the Lord Śrī Kṛṣṇa, who is mentioned in the *Brahma-saṁhitā* as follows:

"Let me offer my respectful obeisances unto the original Personality of Godhead, Govinda, whose plenary portion is the Mahā-Viṣṇu. All the Brahmās, the heads of the universes, live only for the period of His exhaling, after the universes are generated from the pores of His transcendental body." (*Brahma-saṁhitā* 5.58)

Thus Govinda, or Lord Kṛṣṇa, is the cause of Mahā-Viṣṇu also. The ladies talking about this Vedic truth must have heard it from authoritative sources. An authoritative source is the only means of knowing about transcendental subject matter definitely. There is no alternative.

The merging of the living beings into the body of Mahā-Viṣṇu takes place automatically at the end of Brahmā's one hundred years. But that does not mean that the individual living being loses his identity. The identity is there, and as soon as there is another creation by the supreme will of the Lord, all the sleeping, inactive living beings are again let loose to begin their activities in the continuation of past different spheres of life. It is called *suptotthita-nyāya*, or awakening from sleep and again engaging in one's respective continuous duty. When a man is asleep at night, he forgets himself, what he is, what his duty is and everything of his waking state. But as soon as he awakens from slumber, he remembers all that he has to do and thus engages himself again in his prescribed activities. The living beings also remain merged in the body of Mahā-Viṣṇu during the period of annihilation, but as soon as there is another creation they arise to take up their unfinished work. This is also confirmed in the *Bhagavad-gītā* (8.18–20).

The Lord existed before the creative energy was set in action. The

Lord is not a product of the material energy. His body is completely spiritual, and there is no difference between His body and Himself. Before creation the Lord remained in His abode, which is absolute and one.

TEXT 22

स एव भूयो निजवीर्यचोदितां
स्वजीवमायां प्रकृतिं सिसृक्षतीम् ।
अनामरूपात्मनि रूपनामनी
विधित्समानोऽनुससार शास्त्रकृत ॥२२॥

sa eva bhūyo nija-vīrya-coditāṁ
sva-jīva-māyāṁ prakṛtiṁ sisṛkṣatīm
anāma-rūpātmani rūpa-nāmanī
vidhitsamāno 'nusasāra śāstra-kṛt

saḥ—He; *eva*—thus; *bhūyaḥ*—again; *nija*—own personal; *vīrya*—potency; *coditām*—performance of; *sva*—own; *jīva*—living being; *māyām*—external energy; *prakṛtim*—unto material nature; *sisṛkṣatīm*—while re-creating; *anāma*—without mundane designation; *rūpa-ātmani*—forms of the soul; *rūpa-nāmanī*—forms and names; *vidhitsamānaḥ*—desiring to award; *anusasāra*—entrusted; *śāstra-kṛt*—the compiler of revealed scripture.

TRANSLATION

The Personality of Godhead, again desiring to give names and forms to His parts and parcels, the living entities, placed them under the guidance of material nature. By His own potency, material nature is empowered to re-create.

PURPORT

The living entities are parts and parcels of the Lord. They are of two varieties, namely *nitya-mukta* and *nitya-baddha.* The *nitya-muktas* are eternally liberated souls, and they are eternally engaged in the reciprocation of transcendental loving service with the Lord in His eternal abode beyond the manifested mundane creations. But the *nitya-baddha,* or eternally conditioned souls, are entrusted to His external energy, *māyā,* for rectification of their rebellious attitude toward the Supreme Father. *Nitya-baddhas* are eternally forgetful of their relation with the Lord as parts and parcels. They are bewildered by the illusory energy as products of matter, and thus they are very busy in making plans in the material world for becoming happy. They go on merrily with plans, but by the will of the Lord both the planmakers and the plans are annihilated at the end of a certain period, as above mentioned. This is confirmed in the *Bhagavad-gītā* as follows: "O son of Kuntī, at the end of the millennium all the living entities merge into My nature, and again when the time of creation is ripe, I begin creation by the agency of My external energy." (Bg. 9.7)

The word *bhūyaḥ* indicates again and again, that is to say the process of creation, maintenance and annihilation is going on perpetually by the external energy of the Lord. He is the cause of everything. But the living beings, who are constitutionally the parts and parcels of the Lord and are forgetful of the sweet relation, are given a chance again to get rid of the clutches of the external energy. And to revive his (the living being's) consciousness, the revealed scriptures are also created by the Lord. Vedic literatures are the guiding directions for the conditioned souls so they can get free from the repetition of creation and annihilation of the material world and the material body.

The Lord says in the *Bhagavad-gītā*, "This created world and material energy are under My control. Under the influence of *prakṛti*, automatically they are created again and again, and this is done by Me through the agency of My external energy."

Actually the spiritual spark living entities have no material names or forms. But in order to fulfill their desire to lord it over the material energy of material forms and names, they are given a chance for such false enjoyment, and at the same time they are given a chance to understand the real position through the revealed scriptures. The foolish and forgetful living being is always busy with false forms and false names. Modern nationalism is the culmination of such false names and false forms. Men are mad after false name and form. The form of body obtained under certain conditions is taken up as factual, and the name also taken bewilders the conditioned soul into misusing the energy in the name of so many "isms." The scriptures, however, supply the clue for understanding the real position, but men are reluctant to take lessons from the scriptures created by the Lord for different places and times. For example, the *Bhagavad-gītā* is the guiding principle for every human being, but by the spell of material energy they do not take care to carry out the programs of life in terms of the *Bhagavad-gītā*. *Śrīmad-Bhāgavatam* is the post-graduate study of knowledge for one who has thoroughly understood the principles of the *Bhagavad-gītā*. Unfortunately people have no taste for them, and therefore they are under the clutches of *māyā* for repetition of birth and death.

TEXT 23

स वा अयं यत्पदमत्र सूरयो
जितेन्द्रिया निर्जितमातरिश्वनः ।
पश्यन्ति भक्त्युत्कलितामलात्मना
नन्वेष सत्त्वं परिमार्ष्टुमर्हति ॥२३॥

sa vā ayaṁ yat padam atra sūrayo
jitendriyā nirjita-mātariśvanaḥ
paśyanti bhakty-utkalitāmalātmanā
nanv eṣa sattvaṁ parimārṣṭum arhati

saḥ—He; *vai*—by providence; *ayam*—this; *yat*—that which; *padam atra*—here is the same Personality of Godhead, Śrī Kṛṣṇa; *sūrayaḥ*—great devotees; *jita-indriyāḥ*—who have overcome the influence of the senses; *nirjita*—thoroughly controlled; *mātariśvanaḥ*—life; *paśyanti*—can see; *bhakti*—by dint of devotional service; *utkalita*—developed; *amala-ātmanā*—those whose minds are thoroughly cleansed; *nanu eṣaḥ*—certainly by this only; *sattvam*—existence; *parimārṣṭum*—for purifying the mind completely; *arhati*—deserve.

TRANSLATION

Here is the same Supreme Personality of Godhead whose transcendental form is experienced by the great devotees who are completely cleansed of material consciousness by dint of rigid devotional service and full control of life and the senses. And that is the only way to purify existence.

PURPORT

As it is stated in *Bhagavad-gītā*, the Lord can be known in His real nature by dint of pure devotional service only. So it is stated here that only the great devotees of the Lord who are able to clear the mind of all material dust by rigid devotional service can experience the Lord as He is. *Jitendriya* means one who has full control over the senses. The senses are active parts of the body, and their activities cannot be stopped. The artificial means of the yogic processes to make the senses inactive has proved to be abject failure, even in the case of great *yogīs* like Viśvāmitra Muni. Viśvāmitra Muni controlled the senses by yogic trance, but when he happened to meet Menakā (a heavenly society woman), he became a victim of sex, and the artificial way of controlling the senses failed. But in the case of a pure devotee, the senses are not at all artificially stopped from doing anything, but they are given different good engagements. When the senses are engaged in more attractive activities, there is no chance of their being attracted by any inferior engagements. In the *Bhagavad-gītā* it is said that *the senses can be controlled only by better engagements.* Devotional service necessitates purifying the senses or engaging them in the activities of devotional service. Devotional service is not inaction. Anything done in the service of the Lord becomes at once purified of its material nature. The material conception is due to ignorance only. There is nothing beyond Vāsudeva. The Vāsudeva conception gradually develops in the heart of the learned after a prolonged acceleration of the receptive organs. But the process ends in the knowledge of accepting Vāsudeva as all in all. In the case of devotional service, this very same method is accepted from the very beginning, and by the grace of the Lord all factual knowledge becomes revealed in the heart of a devotee due to dictation by the Lord from within. Therefore controlling the senses by devotional service is the only and easiest means.

TEXT 24

स वा अयं सख्यनुगीतसत्कथो
वेदेषु गुह्येषु च गुह्यवादिभिः ।
य एक ईशो जगदात्मलीलया
सृजत्यवत्यत्ति न तत्र सज्जते ॥२४॥

sa vā ayaṁ sakhy anugīta-sat-katho
vedeṣu guhyeṣu ca guhya-vādibhiḥ
ya eka īśo jagad-ātma-līlayā
sṛjaty avaty atti na tatra sajjate

saḥ—He; *vai*—also; *ayam*—this; *sakhi*—O my friend; *anugīta*—described; *sat-kathaḥ*—the excellent pastimes; *vedeṣu*—in the Vedic literatures; *guhyeṣu*—confidentially; *ca*—as also; *guhya-vādibhiḥ*—by the confidential devotees; *yaḥ*—one who; *ekaḥ*—one only; *īśaḥ*—the supreme controller; *jagat*—of the complete creation; *ātma*—Supersoul; *līlayā*—by manifestation of pastimes; *sṛjati*—creates; *avati atti*—also maintains and annihilates; *na*—never; *tatra*—there; *sajjate*—becomes attached to it.

TRANSLATION

O dear friends, here is that very Personality of Godhead whose attractive and confidential pastimes are described in the confidential parts of Vedic literature by His great devotees. It is He only who creates, maintains and annihilates the material world and yet remains unaffected.

PURPORT

As it is stated in the *Bhagavad-gītā*, all the Vedic literatures are glorifying the greatness of Lord Śrī Kṛṣṇa. Here it is confirmed in the *Bhāgavatam* also. The *Vedas* are expanded by many branches and subbranches by great devotees and empowered incarnations of the Lord like Vyāsa, Nārada, Śukadeva Gosvāmī, the Kumāras, Kapila, Prahlāda, Janaka, Bali and Yamarāja, but in the *Śrīmad-Bhāgavatam* especially, the confidential parts of His activities are described by the confidential devotee Śukadeva Gosvāmī. In the *Vedānta-sūtras* or *Upaniṣads* there is only a hint of the confidential parts of His pastimes. In such Vedic literatures as the *Upaniṣads*, the Lord has expressively been distinguished from the mundane conception of His existence. His identity being fully spiritual, His form, name, quality, and paraphernalia, etc., have been elaborately distinguished from matter, and therefore He is sometimes misunderstood by less intelligent persons as impersonal. But factually He is the Supreme Person, Bhagavān, and He is partially represented as Paramātmā or impersonal Brahman.

TEXT 25

यदा ह्यधर्मेण तमोधियो नृपा
जीवन्ति तत्रैष हि सत्त्वतः किल ।
धत्ते भगं सत्यमृतं दयां यशो
भवाय रूपाणि दधद्युगे युगे ॥२५॥

yadā hy adharmeṇa tamo-dhiyo nṛpā
jīvanti tatraiṣa hi sattvataḥ kila
dhatte bhagaṁ satyam ṛtaṁ dayāṁ yaśo
bhavāya rūpāṇi dadhad yuge yuge

yadā—whenever; *hi*—assuredly; *adharmeṇa*—against the principles of God's will; *tamaḥ-dhiyaḥ*—persons in the lowest material modes; *nṛpāḥ*—kings and administrators; *jīvanti*—live like animals; *tatra*—thereupon; *eṣaḥ*—He; *hi*—only; *sattvataḥ*—transcendental; *kila*—certainly; *dhatte*—is manifested; *bhagam*—supreme power; *satyam*—truth; *ṛtam*—positiveness; *dayām*—mercy; *yaśaḥ*—wonderful activities; *bhavāya*—for the maintenance; *rūpāṇi*—in various forms; *dadhat*—manifested; *yuge*—different periods; *yuge*—and ages.

TRANSLATION

Whenever there are kings and administrators living like animals in the lowest modes of existence, the Lord in His transcendental form manifests His supreme power, the Truth Positive, shows special mercy to the faithful, performs wonderful activities and manifests various transcendental forms as is necessary in different periods and ages.

PURPORT

As mentioned above, the cosmic creation is the property of the Supreme Lord. This is the basic philosophy of *Īśopaniṣad:* everything is the property of the Supreme Being. No one should encroach upon the property of the Supreme Lord. One should accept only what is kindly awarded by Him. Therefore, the earth or any other planet or universe is the absolute property of the Lord. The living beings are certainly His parts and parcels, or sons, and thus every one of them has a right to live at the mercy of the Lord to execute his prescribed work. No one, therefore, can encroach upon the right of another individual man or animal without being so sanctioned by the Lord. The king or the administrator is the representative of the Lord to look after the management of the Lord's will. He must therefore be a recognized person like Mahārāja Yudhiṣṭhira or Parīkṣit. Such kings have full responsibility and knowledge from authorities about the administration of the world. But at times, due to the influence of the ignorance mode of material nature (*tamo-guṇa*), the lowest of the material modes, kings and administrators come into power without knowledge and responsibility, and such foolish administrators live like animals for the sake of their own personal interest. The result is that the whole atmosphere becomes surcharged with anarchy and vicious elements. Nepotism, bribery, cheating, aggression and, therefore, famine, epidemic, war and similar other disturbing features become prominent in human society. And the devotees of the Lord or the faithful are persecuted by all means. All these symptoms indicate the time of an incarnation of the Lord to reestablish the principles of religion and to vanquish the maladministrators. This is also confirmed in the *Bhagavad-gītā*.

The Lord then appears in His transcendental form without any tinge of material qualities. He descends just to keep the state of His creation in a normal condition. The normal condition is that the Lord has provided each and every planet with all the needs of the native living beings. They can happily live and execute their predestined occupations to attain salvation at the end, following the rules and regulations mentioned in the revealed scriptures. The material world is created to satisfy the whims of the *nitya-baddha*, or everlasting conditioned souls, just as naughty boys are provided with playing cradles. Otherwise, there was no need of the material world. But when they become intoxicated with the power of material science to exploit the resources unlawfully without the sanction of the Lord, and that also only for sense gratification, there is necessity of the Lord's incarnation to chastise the rebellious and to protect the faithful.

When He descends, He exhibits superhuman acts just to prove His supreme right, and materialists like Rāvaṇa, Hiraṇyakaśipu and Kaṁsa are sufficiently punished. He acts in a manner which no one can imitate.

For example, the Lord, when He appeared as Rāma, bridged the Indian Ocean. When He appeared as Kṛṣṇa, from His very childhood He showed superhuman activities by killing Pūtanā, Aghāsura, Śakaṭāsura, Kāliya, etc., and then His maternal uncle Kaṁsa. When He was at Dvārakā He married 16,108 queens, and all of them were blessed with a sufficient number of children. The sum total of His personal family members amounted to about 100,000, popularly known as the Yadu-vaṁśa. And again, during His lifetime, He managed to vanquish them all. He is famous as the Govardhana-dhārī Hari because He lifted at the age of only seven the hill known as Govardhana. The Lord killed many undesirable kings in His time, and as *kṣatriya* He fought chivalrously. He is famous as the *asamordhva*, unparalleled. No one is equal to or greater than Him.

TEXT 26

अहो अलं श्लाघ्यतमं यदोः कुल-
महो अलं पुण्यतमं मधोर्वनम् ।
यदेष पुंसामृषभः श्रियः पतिः
स्वजन्मना चङ्क्रमणेन चाञ्चति ॥२६॥

aho alaṁ ślāghyatamaṁ yadoḥ kulam
aho alaṁ puṇyatamaṁ madhor vanam
yad eṣa puṁsām ṛṣabhaḥ śriyaḥ patiḥ
sva-janmanā caṅkramaṇena cāñcati

aho—oh; *alam*—verily; *ślāghya-tamam*—supremely glorified; *yadoḥ*—of King Yadu; *kulam*—dynasty; *aho*—oh; *alam*—verily; *puṇya-tamam*—supremely virtuous; *madhoḥ vanam*—the land of Mathurā; *yat*—because; *eṣaḥ*—this; *puṁsām*—of all the living beings; *ṛṣabhaḥ*—supreme leader; *śriyaḥ*—of the goddess of fortune; *patiḥ*—husband; *sva-janmanā*—by His appearance; *caṅkramaṇena*—by crawling; *ca añcati*—glories.

TRANSLATION

Oh, how supremely glorified is the dynasty of King Yadu, and how virtuous is the land of Mathurā, where the supreme leader of

all living beings, the husband of the goddess of fortune, has taken His birth and wandered in His childhood.

PURPORT

In the *Bhagavad-gītā* the Personality of Godhead Śrī Kṛṣṇa has expressively given a description of His transcendental appearance, disappearance and activities. The Lord appears in a particular family or place by His inconceivable potency. He does not take His birth as a conditioned soul quits his body and accepts another body. His birth is like the appearance and disappearance of the sun. The sun arises on the eastern horizon, but that does not mean that the eastern horizon is the parent of the sun. The sun is existent in every part of the solar system, but he becomes visible at a scheduled time and so also becomes invisible at another scheduled time. Similarly, the Lord appears in this universe like the sun and again leaves our sight at another time. He exists at all times and at every place, but by His causeless mercy when He appears before us we take it for granted that He has taken His birth. Anyone who can understand this truth, in terms of the statements of revealed scriptures, certainly becomes liberated just after quitting the present body. Liberation is obtainable after many births and after great endeavor in patience and perseverance, in knowledge and renunciation. But simply by knowing in truth about the Lord's transcendental births and activities, one can get liberation at once. That is the verdict of the *Bhagavad-gītā*. But those who are in the darkness of ignorance conclude that the Lord's birth and activities in the material world are similar to those of the ordinary living being. Such imperfect conclusions cannot give anyone liberation. His birth, therefore, in the family of King Yadu as the son of King Vasudeva and His transfer into the family of Nanda Mahārāja in the land of Mathurā are all transcendental arrangements made by the internal potency of the Lord. The fortunes of the Yadu dynasty and that of the inhabitants of the land of Mathurā cannot be materially estimated. If simply by knowing the transcendental nature of the birth and activities of the Lord one can get liberation easily, we can just imagine what is in store for those who actually enjoyed the company of the Lord in person as a family member or as a neighbor. All those who were fortunate enough to associate with the Lord, the husband of the goddess of fortune, certainly obtained something *more than what is known as liberation.*

Therefore, rightly, the dynasty and the land are both ever glorious by the grace of the Lord.

TEXT 27

अहो बत स्वर्यशसस्तिरस्करी
कुशस्थली पुण्ययशस्करी भुवः ।
पश्यन्ति नित्यं यदनुग्रहेषितं
स्मितावलोकं स्वपतिं स्म यत्प्रजाः ॥२७॥

aho bata svar-yaśasas tiraskarī
kuśasthalī puṇya-yaśaskarī bhuvaḥ
paśyanti nityaṁ yad anugraheṣitaṁ
smitāvalokaṁ sva-patiṁ sma yat-prajāḥ

aho bata—how wonderful this is; *svaḥ-yaśasaḥ*—the glories of the heavenly planets; *tiraskarī*—that which defeats; *kuśasthalī*—Dvārakā; *puṇya*—virtue; *yaśaskarī*—famous; *bhuvaḥ*—the planet earth; *paśyanti*—see; *nityam*—constantly; *yat*—that which; *anugraha-iṣitam*—to bestow benediction; *smita-avalokam*—glance with the favor of sweet smiling; *sva-patim*—unto the soul of the living being (Kṛṣṇa); *sma*—used to; *yat-prajāḥ*—the inhabitants of the place.

TRANSLATION

Undoubtedly it is wonderful that Dvārakā has defeated the glories of the heavenly planets and has enhanced the celebrity of the earth. The inhabitants of Dvārakā are always seeing the soul of all living beings [Kṛṣṇa] in His loving feature. He glances at them and favors them with sweet smiles.

PURPORT

The heavenly planets are inhabited by demigods like Indra, Candra, Varuṇa and Vāyu and the pious souls reach there after performance of many virtuous acts on earth. Modern scientists agree that the timing arrangement in higher planetary systems is different from that of the earth. Thus it is understood from the revealed scriptures that the duration of life there is ten thousand years (by our calculation). Six months on earth is equal to one day on the heavenly planets. Facilities of enjoyment are also similarly enhanced, and the beauty of the inhabitants is legendary. Common men on the earth are very much fond of reaching the heavenly planets because they have heard that comforts of life are far greater there than on the earth. They are now trying to reach the moon by spacecraft. Considering all this, the heavenly planets are more celebrated than the earth. But the celebrity of earth has defeated that of the heavenly planets because of Dvārakā, where Lord Śrī Kṛṣṇa reigned as King. Three places, namely Vṛndāvana, Mathurā and Dvārakā, are more important than the famous planets within the universe. These places are perpetually sanctified because whenever the Lord descends on earth He displays His transcendental activities particularly in these three places. They are perpetually the holy lands of the Lord, and the inhabitants still take advantage of the holy places, even though the Lord is now out of their sight. The Lord is the soul of all living beings, and He desires always to have all the living beings, in their *svarūpa*, in their constitutional position, to participate in transcendental life in His association. His attractive features and sweet smiles go deep into the heart of everyone, and once it is so done the living being is admitted into the kingdom of God, from which no one returns. This is confirmed in the *Bhagavad-gītā.*

The heavenly planets may be very famous for offering better facilities of material enjoyment, but as we learn from the *Bhagavad-gītā* (9.20–21), one has to come back again to the earth planet as soon as the acquired virtue is finished. Dvārakā is certainly more important than the heavenly planets because whoever has been favored with the smiling glance of the Lord shall never come back again to this rotten earth, which is certified by the Lord Himself as a place of misery. Not only this earth but also all the planets of the universes are places of misery because in none of the planets within the universe is there eternal life, eternal bliss and eternal knowledge. Any person engaged in the devotional service of the Lord is recommended to live in one of the above-mentioned three places, namely Dvārakā, Mathurā or Vṛndāvana. Because devotional service in these three places is magnified, those who go there to follow the principles in terms of instructions imparted in the revealed scriptures surely achieve the same result as obtained during the presence of Lord

Śrī Kṛṣṇa. His abode and He Himself are identical, and a pure devotee under the guidance of another experienced devotee can obtain all the results, even at present.

TEXT 28

नूनं व्रतस्नानहुतादिनेश्वरः
समर्चितो ह्यस्य गृहीतपाणिभिः ।
पिबन्ति याः सख्यधरामृतं मुहु-
र्व्रजस्त्रियः सम्मुमुहुर्यदाशयाः ॥२८॥

nūnaṁ vrata-snāna-hutādineśvaraḥ
samarcito hy asya gṛhīta-pāṇibhiḥ
pibanti yāḥ sakhy adharāmṛtaṁ muhur
vraja-striyaḥ sammumuhur yad-āśayāḥ

nūnam—certainly in the previous birth; *vrata*—vow; *snāna*—bath; *huta*—sacrifice in the fire; *ādinā*—by all these; *īśvaraḥ*—the Personality of Godhead; *samarcitaḥ*—perfectly worshiped; *hi*—certainly; *asya*—His; *gṛhīta-pāṇibhiḥ*—by the married wives; *pibanti*—relishes; *yāḥ*—those who; *sakhi*—O friend; *adhara-amṛtam*—the nectar from His lips; *muhuḥ*—again and again; *vraja-striyaḥ*—the damsels of Vrajabhūmi; *sammumuhuḥ*—often fainted; *yat-āśayāḥ*—expecting to be favored in that way.

TRANSLATION

O friends, just think of His wives, whose hands He has accepted. How they must have undergone vows, baths, fire sacrifices and perfect worship of the Lord of the universe to constantly relish now the nectar from His lips [by kissing]. The damsels of Vrajabhūmi would often faint just by expecting such favors.

PURPORT

Religious rites prescribed in the scriptures are meant to purify the mundane qualities of the conditioned souls to enable them to be gradually promoted to the stage of rendering transcendental service unto the

Supreme Lord. Attainment of this stage of pure spiritual life is the highest perfection, and this stage is called *svarūpa,* or the factual identity of the living being. Liberation means renovation of this stage of *svarūpa.* In that perfect stage of *svarūpa,* the living being is established in five phases of loving service, one of which is the stage of *mādhurya-rasa,* or the humor of conjugal love. The Lord is always perfect in Himself, and thus He has no hankering for Himself. He, however, becomes a master, a friend, a son or a husband to fulfill the intense love of the devotee concerned. Herein two classes of devotees of the Lord are mentioned in the stage of conjugal love. One is *svakīya,* and the other is *parakīya.* Both of them are in conjugal love with the Personality of Godhead Kṛṣṇa. The queens at Dvārakā were *svakīya,* or duly married wives, but the damsels of Vraja were young friends of the Lord while He was unmarried. The Lord stayed at Vṛndāvana till the age of sixteen, and His friendly relations with the neighboring girls were in terms of *parakīya.* These girls, as well as the queens, underwent severe penances by taking vows, bathing and offering sacrifices in the fire, as prescribed in the scriptures. The rites, as they are, are not an end in themselves, nor are fruitive action, culture of knowledge or perfection in mystic powers ends in themselves. They are all means to attain to the highest stage of *svarūpa,* to render constitutional transcendental service to the Lord. Each and every living being has his individual position in one of the above-mentioned five different kinds of reciprocating means with the Lord, and in one's pure spiritual form of *svarūpa* the relation becomes manifest without mundane affinity. The kissing of the Lord, either by His wives or His young girl friends who aspired to have the Lord as their fiancé, is not of any mundane perverted quality. Had such things been mundane, a liberated soul like Śukadeva would not have taken the trouble to relish them, nor would Lord Śrī Caitanya Mahāprabhu have been inclined to participate in those subjects after renouncing worldly life. The stage is earned after many lives of penance.

TEXT 29

या वीर्यशुल्केन हृताः स्वयंवरे
प्रमथ्य चैद्यप्रमुखान् हि शुष्मिणः ।

प्रद्युम्नसाम्बाम्बसुतादयोऽपरा
याश्चाहृता भौमवधे सहस्रशः ॥२९॥

ya vīrya-śulkena hṛtāḥ svayaṁvare
pramathya caidya-pramukhān hi śuṣmiṇaḥ
pradyumna-sāmbāmba-sutādayo 'parā
yāś cāhṛtā bhauma-vadhe sahasraśaḥ

yā—the lady; *vīrya*—prowess; *śulkena*—by payment of the price; *hṛtāḥ*—taken away by force; *svayaṁvare*—in the open selection of the bridegroom; *pramathya*—harassing; *caidya*—King Śiśupāla; *pramukhān*—headed by; *hi*—positively; *śuṣmiṇaḥ*—all very powerful; *pradyumna*—Pradyumna (Kṛṣṇa's son); *sāmba*—Sāmba; *amba*—Amba; *suta-ādayaḥ*—children; *aparāḥ*—other ladies; *yāḥ*—those; *ca*—also; *āhṛtāḥ*—similarly brought; *bhauma-vadhe*—after killing kings; *sahasraśaḥ*—by the thousands.

TRANSLATION

The children of these ladies are Pradyumna, Sāmba, Amba, etc. Ladies like Rukmiṇī, Satyabhāmā and Jāmbavatī were forcibly taken away by Him from their svayaṁvara ceremonies after He defeated many powerful kings, headed by Śiśupāla. And other ladies were also forcibly taken away by Him after He killed Bhaumāsura and thousands of his assistants. All of these ladies are glorious.

PURPORT

Exceptionally qualified daughters of powerful kings were allowed to make a choice of their own bridegrooms in open competition, and such ceremonies were called *svayaṁvara*, or selection of the bridegroom. Because the *svayaṁvara* was an open competition between the rival and valiant princes, such princes were invited by the father of the princess, and usually there were regular fights between the invited princely order in a sporting spirit. But it so happened that sometimes the belligerent princes were killed in such marriage-fighting, and the victorious prince was offered the trophy princess for whom so many princes died. Rukmiṇī, the principal queen of Lord Kṛṣṇa, was the daughter of the King of

Vidarbha, who wished that his qualified and beautiful daughter be given away to Lord Kṛṣṇa. But her eldest brother wanted her to be given away to King Śiśupāla, who happened to be a cousin of Kṛṣṇa. So there was open competition, and as usual Lord Kṛṣṇa emerged successful, after harassing Śiśupāla and other princes by His unrivalled prowess. Rukmiṇī had ten sons, like Pradyumna. There were other queens also taken away by Lord Kṛṣṇa in a similar way. Full description of this beautiful booty of Lord Kṛṣṇa will be given in the Tenth Canto. There were 16,100 beautiful girls who were daughters of many kings and were forcibly stolen by Bhaumāsura, who kept them captive for his carnal desire. These girls prayed piteously to Lord Kṛṣṇa for their deliverance, and the merciful Lord, called by their fervent prayer, released them all by fighting and killing Bhaumāsura. All these captive princesses were then accepted by the Lord as His wives, although in the estimation of society they were all fallen girls. The all-powerful Lord Kṛṣṇa accepted the humble prayers of these girls and married them with the adoration of queens. So altogether Lord Kṛṣṇa had 16,108 queens at Dvārakā, and in each of them He begot ten children. All these children grew up, and each had as many children as the father. The aggregate of the family numbered 10,000,000.

TEXT 30

एताः परं स्त्रीत्वमपास्तपेशलं
निरस्तशौचं बत साधु कुर्वते ।
यासां गृहात्पुष्करलोचनः पति-
र्न जात्वपैत्याहृतिभिर्हृदि स्पृशन् ॥३०॥

etāḥ paraṁ strītvam apāstapeśalaṁ
nirasta-śaucaṁ bata sādhu kurvate
yāsāṁ gṛhāt puṣkara-locanaḥ patir
na jātv apaity āhṛtibhir hṛdi spṛśan

etāḥ—all these women; *param*—highest; *strītvam*—womanhood; *apāstapeśalam*—without individuality; *nirasta*—without; *śaucam*—purity; *bata sādhu*—auspiciously glorified; *kurvate*—do they make;

yāsām—from whose; *gṛhāt*—homes; *puṣkara-locanaḥ*—the lotus-eyed; *patiḥ*—husband; *na jātu*—never at any time; *apaiti*—goes away; *āhṛtibhiḥ*—by presentation; *hṛdi*—in the heart; *spṛśan*—endeared.

TRANSLATION

All these women auspiciously glorified their lives despite their being without individuality and without purity. Their husband, the lotus-eyed Personality of Godhead, never left them alone at home. He always pleased their hearts by making valuable presentations.

PURPORT

The devotees of the Lord are purified souls. As soon as the devotees surrender unto the lotus feet of the Lord sincerely, the Lord accepts them, and thus the devotees at once become free from all material contaminations. Such devotees are above the three modes of material nature. There is no bodily disqualification of a devotee, just as there is no qualitative difference between the Ganges water and the unfilthy drain water when they are amalgamated. Women, merchants and laborers are not very intelligent, and thus it is very difficult for them to understand the science of God or to be engaged in the devotional service of the Lord. They are more materialistic, and less than them are the Kirātas, Hūṇas, Āndhras, Pulindas, Pulkaśas, Ābhīras, Kaṅkas, Yavanas, Khasas, etc., but all of them can be delivered if they are properly engaged in the devotional service of the Lord. By engagement in the service of the Lord, the designative disqualifications are removed, and as pure souls they become eligible to enter into the kingdom of God.

The fallen girls under the clutches of Bhaumāsura sincerely prayed to Lord Śrī Kṛṣṇa for their deliverance, and their sincerity of purpose made them at once pure by virtue of devotion. The Lord therefore accepted them as His wives, and thus their lives became glorified. Such auspicious glorification was still more glorified when the Lord played with them as the most devoted husband.

The Lord used to live with His 16,108 wives constantly. He expanded Himself into 16,108 plenary portions, and each and every one of them was the Lord Himself without deviation from the Original Personality.

The *Śruti-mantra* affirms that the Lord can expand Himself into many. As husband of so many wives, He pleased them all with presentations, even at a costly endeavor. He brought the *pārijāta* plant from heaven and implanted it at the palace of Satyabhāmā, one of the principal queens. If, therefore, anyone desires the Lord to become one's husband, the Lord fulfills such desires in full.

TEXT 31

एवंविधा गदन्तीनां स गिरः पुरयोषिताम् ।
निरीक्षणेनाभिनन्दन् सस्मितेन ययौ हरिः ॥३१॥

evaṁvidhā gadantīnāṁ
sa giraḥ pura-yoṣitām
nirīkṣaṇenābhinandan
sasmitena yayau hariḥ

evaṁvidhāḥ—in this way; *gadantīnām*—thus praying and talking about Him; *saḥ*—He (the Lord); *giraḥ*—of words; *pura-yoṣitām*—of the ladies of the capital; *nirīkṣaṇena*—by His grace of glancing over them; *abhinandan*—and greeting them; *sa-smitena*—with a smiling face; *yayau*—departed; *hariḥ*—the Personality of Godhead.

TRANSLATION

While the ladies of the capital of Hastināpura were greeting Him and talking in this way, the Lord, smiling, accepted their good greetings, and casting the grace of His glance over them, He departed from the city.

TEXT 32

अजातशत्रुः पृतनां गोपीथाय मधुद्विषः ।
परेभ्यः शङ्कितः स्नेहात्प्रायुङ्क्त चतुरङ्गिणीम् ॥३२॥

ajāta-śatruḥ pṛtanāṁ
gopīthāya madhu-dviṣaḥ
parebhyaḥ śaṅkitaḥ snehāt
prāyuṅkta catur-aṅgiṇīm

ajāta-śatruḥ—Mahārāja Yudhiṣṭhira, who was no one's enemy; *pṛtanām*—defensive forces; *gopīthāya*—for giving protection; *madhu-dviṣaḥ*—of the enemy of Madhu (Śrī Kṛṣṇa); *parebhyaḥ*—from others (enemies); *śaṅkitaḥ*—being afraid of; *snehāt*—out of affection; *prāyuṅkta*—engaged; *catuḥ-aṅginīm*—four defensive divisions.

TRANSLATION

Mahārāja Yudhiṣṭhira, although no one's enemy, engaged four divisions of defense [horse, elephant, chariot and army] to accompany Lord Kṛṣṇa, the enemy of the asuras [demons]. The Mahārāja did this because of the enemy, and also out of affection for the Lord.

PURPORT

Natural defensive measures are horses and elephants combined with chariots and men. Horses and elephants are trained to move to any part of the hills or forests and plains. The charioteers could fight with many horses and elephants by the strength of powerful arrows, even up to the standard of the *brahmāstra* (similar to modern atomic weapons). Mahārāja Yudhiṣṭhira knew well that Kṛṣṇa is everyone's friend and well-wisher, and yet there were *asuras* who were by nature envious of the Lord. So out of fear of attack from others and out of affection also, he engaged all varieties of defensive forces as bodyguards of Lord Kṛṣṇa. If required, Lord Kṛṣṇa Himself was sufficient to defend Himself from the attack of others who counted the Lord as their enemy, but still He accepted all the arrangements made by Mahārāja Yudhiṣṭhira because He could not disobey the King, who was His elder cousin. The Lord plays the part of a subordinate in His transcendental sporting, and thus sometimes He puts Himself in the care of Yaśodāmātā for His protection in His so-called helplessness of childhood. That is the transcendental *līlā*, or pastime of the Lord. The basic principle for all transcendental exchanges between the Lord and His devotees is exhibited to enjoy a transcendental bliss for which there is no comparison, even up to the level of *brahmānanda*.

TEXT 33

अथ दूरागतान् शौरिः कौरवान् विरहातुरान् ।
संनिवर्त्य दृढं स्निग्धान् प्रायात्स्वनगरीं प्रियैः ॥३३॥

atha dūrāgatān śauriḥ
kauravān virahāturān
sannivartya dṛḍhaṁ snigdhān
prāyāt sva-nagarīṁ priyaiḥ

atha—thus; *dūrāgatān*—having accompanied Him for a long distance; *śauriḥ*—Lord Kṛṣṇa; *kauravān*—the Pāṇḍavas; *virahāturān*—overwhelmed by a sense of separation; *sannivartya*—politely persuaded; *dṛḍham*—determined; *snigdhān*—full of affection; *prāyāt*—proceeded; *sva-nagarīm*—towards His own city (Dvārakā); *priyaiḥ*—with dear companions.

TRANSLATION

Out of profound affection for Lord Kṛṣṇa, the Pāṇḍavas, who were of the Kuru dynasty, accompanied Him a considerable distance to see Him off. They were overwhelmed with the thought of future separation. The Lord, however, persuaded them to return home, and He proceeded towards Dvārakā with His dear companions.

TEXTS 34-35

कुरुजाङ्गलपाञ्चालान् शूरसेनान् सयामुनान् ।
ब्रह्मावर्तं कुरुक्षेत्रं मत्स्यान् सारस्वतानथ ॥३४॥
मरुधन्वमतिक्रम्य सौवीराभीरयोः परान् ।
आनर्तान् भार्गवोपागाच्छ्रान्तवाहो मनाग्विभुः॥३५॥

kuru-jāṅgala-pāñcālān
śūrasenān sayāmunān
brahmāvartaṁ kurukṣetraṁ
matsyān sārasvatān atha

maru-dhanvam atikramya
sauvīrābhīrayoḥ parān
ānartān bhārgavopāgāc
chrāntavāho manāg vibhuḥ

kuru-jāṅgala—the province of Delhi; *pāñcālān*—part of the province Pānjab; *śūrasenān*—part of the province of Uttar Pradesh; *sa*—with; *yāmunān*—the districts on the bank of the Yamunā; *brahmāvartam*—part of northern Uttar Pradesh; *kurukṣetram*—the place where the battle was fought; *matsyān*—the province Matsyā; *sārasvatān*—part of Punjab; *atha*—and so on; *maru*—Rajasthan, the land of deserts; *dhanvam*—Madhya Pradesh, where water is very scanty; *ati-kramya*—after passing; *sauvīra*—Saurastra; *ābhīrayoḥ*—part of Gujurat; *parān*—western side; *ānartān*—the province of Dvārakā; *bhārgava*—O Śaunaka; *upāgāt*—overtaken by; *śrānta*—fatigue; *vāhaḥ*—the horses; *manāk vibhuḥ*—slightly, because of the long journey.

TRANSLATION

O Śaunaka, the Lord then proceeded towards Kurujāṅgala, Pāñcālā, Śūrasenā, the land on the bank of the River Yamunā, Brahmāvarta, Kurukṣetra, Matsyā, Sārasvatā, the province of the desert and the land of scanty water. After crossing these provinces He gradually reached the Sauvīra and Ābhīra provinces, then west of these, reached Dvārakā at last.

PURPORT

The provinces passed over by the Lord in those days were differently named, but the direction given is sufficient to indicate that He traveled through Delhi, Punjab, Rajasthan, Madhya Pradesh, Saurastra and Gujarat and at last reached His home province at Dvārakā. We do not gain any profit simply by researching the analogous provinces of those days up to now, but it appears that the desert of Rajasthan and the provinces of scanty water like Madhya Pradesh were present even five thousand years ago. The theory of soil experts that the desert developed in recent years is not supported by the statements of *Bhāgavatam.* We may leave the matter for expert geologists to research because the changing universe has different phases of geological development. We are satisfied that the Lord has now reached His own province, Dvārakādhāma, from the Kuru provinces. Kurukṣetra continues to exist since the Vedic age, and it is sheer foolishness when interpreters ignore or deny the existence of Kurukṣetra.

TEXT 36

तत्र तत्र ह तत्रत्यैर्हरिः प्रत्युद्यतार्हणः ।
सायं भेजे दिशं पश्चाद्गविष्ठो गां गतस्तदा ॥३६॥

tatra tatra ha tatratyair
hariḥ pratyudyatārhaṇaḥ
sāyaṁ bheje diśaṁ paścād
gaviṣṭho gāṁ gatas tadā

tatra tatra—at different places; *ha*—it so happened; *tatratyaiḥ*—by local inhabitants; *hariḥ*—the Personality of Godhead; *pratyudyata-arhaṇaḥ*—being offered presentations and worshipful regards; *sāyam*—the evening; *bheje*—having overtaken; *diśam*—direction; *paścāt*—eastern; *gaviṣṭhaḥ*—the sun in the sky; *gām*—to the ocean; *gataḥ*—having gone; *tadā*—at that time.

TRANSLATION

On His journey through these provinces He was welcomed, worshiped and given various presentations. In the evening, in all places, the Lord suspended His journey to perform evening rites. This was regularly observed after sunset.

PURPORT

It is said here that the Lord observed the religious principles regularly while He was on the journey. There are certain philosophical speculations that even the Lord is under the obligations of fruitive action. But actually this is not the case. He does not depend on the action of any good or bad work. *Since the Lord is absolute, everything done by Him is good for everyone.* But when He descends on earth, He acts for the protection of the devotees and for the annihilation of the impious nondevotees. Although He has no obligatory duty, still He does everything so that others may follow. That is the way of factual teaching; one must act properly himself and teach the same to others, otherwise no one will accept one's blind teaching. He is Himself the awarder of fruitive results. He is self-sufficient, and yet He acts according to the rulings of the revealed scripture in order to teach us the process. If He does not do so, the common man may go wrong. But in the advanced stage, when one can understand the transcendental nature of the Lord, one does not try to imitate Him. This is not possible.

The Lord in human society does what is the duty of everyone, but sometimes He does something extraordinary and not to be imitated by the living being. His acts of evening prayer as stated herein must be followed by the living being, but it is not possible to follow His mountain-lifting or dancing with the *gopīs.* One cannot imitate the sun, which can exhaust water even from a filthy place; the most powerful can do something which is all-good, but our imitation of such acts will put us into endless difficulty. Therefore, in all actions, the experienced guide, the spiritual master, who is the manifested mercy of the Lord, should always be consulted, and the path of progress will be assured.

Thus end the Bhaktivedanta purports of the First Canto, Tenth Chapter, of the Śrīmad-Bhāgavatam, *entitled "Departure of Lord Kṛṣṇa for Dvārakā."*

CHAPTER ELEVEN

Lord Kṛṣṇa's Entrance into Dvārakā

TEXT 1

सूत उवाच
आनर्तान् स उपव्रज्य स्वृद्धाञ्जनपदान् स्वकान् ।
दध्मौ दरवरं तेषां विषादं शमयन्निव ॥ १ ॥

sūta uvāca
ānartān sa upavrajya
svṛddhāñ jana-padān svakān
dadhmau daravaraṁ teṣāṁ
viṣādaṁ śamayann iva

sūtaḥ uvāca—Sūta Gosvāmī said; *ānartān*—the country known as Ānartān (Dvārakā); *saḥ*—He; *upavrajya*—reaching the border of; *svṛddhān*—most prosperous; *jana-padān*—city; *svakān*—His own; *dadhmau*—sounded; *daravaram*—the auspicious conchshell (Pāñcajanya); *teṣām*—of them; *viṣādam*—dejection; *śamayan*—pacifying; *iva*—seemingly.

TRANSLATION

Sūta Gosvāmī said: Upon reaching the border of His most prosperous metropolis, known as the country of the Ānartas [Dvārakā], the Lord sounded His auspicious conchshell, heralding His arrival and apparently pacifying the dejection of the inhabitants.

PURPORT

The beloved Lord was away from His own prosperous metropolis of Dvārakā for a considerably long period because of the Battle of Kurukṣetra, and thus all the inhabitants were overcome with melancholia due to the separation. When the Lord descends on the earth, His eternal associates also come with Him, just as the entourage of a king accompanies him. Such associates of the Lord are eternally liberated souls, and they cannot bear the separation of the Lord even for a moment because of intense affection for the Lord. Thus the inhabitants of the city of Dvārakā were in a mood of dejection and expected the arrival of the Lord at any moment. So the heralding sound of the auspicious conchshell was very encouraging, and apparently the sound pacified their dejection. They were still more aspirant to see the Lord amongst themselves, and all of them became alert to receive Him in the befitting manner. These are the signs of spontaneous love of Godhead.

TEXT 2

स उच्चकाशे धवलोदरो दरो-
ऽप्युरुक्रमस्याधरशोणशोणिमा ।
दाध्मायमानः करकञ्जसम्पुटे
यथाब्जखण्डे कलहंस उत्स्वनः ॥ २ ॥

sa uccakāśe dhavalodaro daro
'py urukramasyādharaśoṇa-śoṇimā
dādhmāyamānaḥ kara-kañja-sampuṭe
yathābja-khaṇḍe kala-haṁsa utsvanaḥ

saḥ—that; *uccakāśe*—became brilliant; *dhavala-udaraḥ*—white and fat-boweled; *daraḥ*—conchshell; *api*—although it is so; *urukramasya*—of the great adventurer; *adharaśoṇa*—by the transcendental quality of His lips; *śoṇimā*—reddened; *dādhmāyamānaḥ*—being sounded; *kara-kañja-sampuṭe*—being caught by the grip of the lotus hand; *yathā*—as it is; *abja-khaṇḍe*—by the stems of lotus flowers; *kala-haṁsaḥ*—ducking swan; *utsvanaḥ*—loudly sounding.

TRANSLATION

The white and fat-boweled conchshell, being gripped by the hand of Lord Kṛṣṇa and sounded by Him, appeared to be reddened by the touch of His transcendental lips. It seemed that a white swan was playing in the stems of red lotus flowers.

PURPORT

The redness of the white conchshell due to the lip-touch of the Lord is a symbol of spiritual significance. The Lord is all spirit, and matter is ignorance of this spiritual existence. Factually there is nothing like matter in spiritual enlightenment, and this spiritual enlightenment takes place at once by the contact of the Supreme Lord Śrī Kṛṣṇa. The Lord is present in every particle of all existence, and He can manifest His presence in anyone. By ardent love and devotional service to the Lord, or in other words by spiritual contact with the Lord, everything becomes spiritually reddened like the conchshell in the grip of the Lord, and the *paramahaṁsa*, or the supremely intelligent person, plays the part of the ducking swan in the water of spiritual bliss, eternally decorated by the lotus flower of the Lord's feet.

TEXT 3

तमुपश्रुत्य निनदं जगद्भयभयावहम् ।
प्रत्युद्ययुः प्रजाः सर्वा भर्तृदर्शनलालसाः ॥ ३ ॥

tam upaśrutya ninadaṁ
jagad-bhaya-bhayāvaham
pratyudyayuḥ prajāḥ sarvā
bhartṛ-darśana-lālasāḥ

tam—that; *upaśrutya*—having overheard; *ninadam*—sound; *jagat-bhaya*—the fear of material existence; *bhaya-āvaham*—the threatening principle; *prati*—towards; *udyayuḥ*—rapidly proceeded; *prajāḥ*—the citizens; *sarvāḥ*—all; *bhartṛ*—the protector; *darśana*—audience; *lālasāḥ*—having so desired.

TRANSLATION

The citizens of Dvārakā, having heard that sound which threatens fear personified in the material world, began to run towards Him fast, just to have a long desired audience with the Lord, who is the protector of all devotees.

PURPORT

As already explained, the citizens of Dvārakā who lived at the time of Lord Kṛṣṇa's presence there were all liberated souls who descended there along with the Lord as entourage. All were very anxious to have an audience with the Lord, although because of spiritual contact they were never separated from the Lord. Just as the *gopīs* at Vṛndāvana used to think of Kṛṣṇa while He was away from the village for cowherding engagements, the citizens of Dvārakā were all immersed in thought of the Lord while He was away from Dvārakā to attend the Battle of Kurukṣetra. Some distinguished fiction writer in Bengal concluded that the Kṛṣṇa of Vṛndāvana, that of Mathurā and that of Dvārakā were different personalities. Historically there is no truth in this conclusion. The Kṛṣṇa of Kurukṣetra and the Kṛṣṇa of Dvārakā are one and the same personality.

The citizens of Dvārakā were thus in a state of melancholy due to the Lord's absence from the transcendental city, as much as we are put in a state of melancholy at night because of the absence of the sun. The sound heralded by Lord Kṛṣṇa was something like the heralding of the sunrise in the morning. So all the citizens of Dvārakā awoke from a state of slumber because of the sunrise of Kṛṣṇa, and they all hastened towards Him just to have an audience. The devotees of the Lord know no one else as protector.

This sound of the Lord is identical with the Lord, as we have tried to explain by the nondual position of the Lord. The material existence of our present status is full of fear. Out of the four problems of material existence, namely the food problem, the shelter problem, the fear problem and the mating problem, the fear problem gives us more trouble than the others. We are always fearful due to our ignorance of the next problem. The whole material existence is full of problems, and thus the fear problem is always prominent. This is due to our association with the illusory energy of the Lord, known as *māyā* or external energy, yet all fear is vanished as soon as there is the sound of the Lord, represented by His holy name, as it was sounded by Lord Śrī Caitanya Mahāprabhu in the following sixteen words:

Hare Kṛṣṇa, Hare Kṛṣṇa, Kṛṣṇa Kṛṣṇa, Hare Hare
Hare Rāma, Hare Rāma, Rāma Rāma, Hare Hare

We can take advantage of these sounds and be free from all threatening problems of material existence.

TEXTS 4-5

तत्रोपनीतबलयो रवेर्दीपमिवादृताः ।
आत्मारामं पूर्णकामं निजलाभेन नित्यदा ॥ ४ ॥
प्रीत्युत्फुल्लमुखाः प्रोचुर्हर्षगद्गदया गिरा ।
पितरं सर्वसुहृदमवितारमिवार्भकाः ॥ ५ ॥

tatropanīta-balayo
raver dīpam ivādṛtāḥ
ātmārāmaṁ pūrṇa-kāmaṁ
nija-lābhena nityadā

prīty-utphulla-mukhāḥ procur
harṣa-gadgadayā girā
pitaraṁ sarva-suhṛdam
avitāram ivārbhakāḥ

tatra—thereupon; *upanīta*—having offered; *balayaḥ*—presentations; *raveḥ*—up to the sun; *dīpam*—lamp; *iva*—like; *ādṛtāḥ*—being evaluated; *ātma-ārāmam*—unto the self-sufficient; *pūrṇa-kāmam*—fully satisfied; *nija-lābhena*—by His own potencies; *nitya-dā*—one who supplies incessantly; *prīti*—affection; *utphulla-mukhāḥ*—cheerful faces; *procuḥ*—said; *harṣa*—gladdened; *gadgadayā*—ecstatic; *girā*—speeches; *pitaram*—unto the father; *sarva*—all; *suhṛdam*—friends; *avitāram*—the guardian; *iva*—like; *arbhakāḥ*—wards.

TRANSLATION

The citizens arrived before the Lord with their respective presentations, offering them to the fully satisfied and self-sufficient one, who, by His own potency, incessantly supplies others. These presentations were like the offering of a lamp to the sun. Yet the citizens began to speak in ecstatic language to receive the Lord, just as wards welcome their guardian and father.

PURPORT

The Supreme Lord Kṛṣṇa is described herein as *ātmārāma.* He is self-sufficient, and there is no need for Him to seek happiness from anything beyond Himself. He is self-sufficient because His very transcendental existence is total bliss. He is eternally existent; He is all-cognizant and all-blissful. Therefore, any presentation, however valuable it may be, is not needed by Him. But still, because He is the well-wisher for one and all, He accepts from everyone everything that is offered to Him in pure devotional service. It is not that He is in want for such things, because the things are themselves generated from His energy. The comparison is made herein that making offerings to the Lord is something like offering a lamp in the worship of the sun-god. Anything fiery and illuminating is but an emanation of the energy of the sun, and yet to worship the sun-god it is necessary to offer him a lamp. In the worship of the sun, there is some sort of demand made by the worshiper, but in the case of devotional service to the Lord, there is no question of demand from either side. It is all a sign of pure love and affection between the Lord and the devotee.

The Lord is the Supreme Father of all living beings, and therefore those who are conscious of this *vital* relation with God can make filial demands from the Father, and the Father is pleased to supply the demands of such obedient sons without bargaining. The Lord is just like the *desire tree*, and from Him everyone can have everything by the causeless mercy of the Lord. As the Supreme Father, the Lord, however, does not supply to a pure devotee what is considered to be a barrier to the discharge of devotional service. Those who are engaged in the devotional service of the Lord can rise to the position of unalloyed devotional service by His transcendental attraction.

TEXT 6

नताः स्म ते नाथ सदाङ्घ्रिपङ्कजं
विरिञ्चवैरिञ्च्यसुरेन्द्रवन्दितम् ।
परायणं क्षेममिहेच्छतां परं
न यत्र कालः प्रभवेत् परः प्रभुः ॥ ६ ॥

natāḥ sma te nātha sadāṅghri-paṅkajaṁ
viriñca-vairiñcya-surendra-vanditam
parāyaṇaṁ kṣemam ihecchatāṁ paraṁ
na yatra kālaḥ prabhavet paraḥ prabhuḥ

natāḥ—bowed down; *sma*—we had done so; *te*—unto You; *nātha*—O Lord; *sadā*—always; *aṅghri-paṅkajam*—the lotus feet; *viriñca*—Brahmā, the first living being; *vairiñcya*—sons of Brahmā like Sanaka and Sanātana; *sura-indra*—the King of heaven; *vanditam*—worshiped by; *parāyaṇam*—the supreme; *kṣemam*—welfare; *iha*—in this life; *icchatām*—one who so desires; *param*—the highest; *na*—never; *yatra*—wherein; *kālaḥ*—inevitable time; *prabhavet*—can exert its influence; *paraḥ*—transcendental; *prabhuḥ*—the Supreme Lord.

TRANSLATION

The citizens said: O Lord, You are worshiped by all demigods like Brahmā, the four Sanas and even the King of heaven. You are the ultimate rest for those who are really aspiring to achieve the highest benefit of life. You are the supreme transcendental Lord, and inevitable time cannot exert its influence upon You.

PURPORT

The Supreme Lord is Śrī Kṛṣṇa, as confirmed in *Bhagavad-gītā*, *Brahma-saṁhitā* and other authorized Vedic literatures. No one is equal to or greater than Him, and that is the verdict of all scriptures. The influence of time and space is exerted upon the dependent living entities, who are all parts and parcels of the Supreme Lord. The living entities are predominated Brahman, whereas the Supreme Lord is the predominating Absolute. As soon as we forget this clear fact, we are at once in illusion, and thus we are put into threefold miseries, as one is put into dense darkness. The clear consciousness of the cognizant living being is God consciousness, in which one bows down unto Him in all circumstances.

TEXT 7

भवाय नस्त्वं भव विश्वभावन
त्वमेव माताथ सुहृत्पतिः पिता ।
त्वं सद्गुरुर्नः परमं च दैवतं
यस्यानुवृत्त्या कृतिनो बभूविम ॥ ७ ॥

bhavāya nas tvaṁ bhava viśva-bhāvana
tvam eva mātātha suhṛt-patiḥ pitā

tvaṁ sad-gurur naḥ paramaṁ ca daivataṁ
yasyānuvṛttyā kṛtino babhūvima

bhavāya—for welfare; *naḥ*—for us; *tvam*—Your Lordship; *bhava*—just become; *viśva-bhāvana*—the creator of the universe; *tvam*—Your Lordship; *eva*—certainly; *mātā*—mother; *atha*—as also; *suhṛt*—well-wisher; *patiḥ*—husband; *pitā*—father; *tvam*—Your Lordship; *sat-guruḥ*—spiritual master; *naḥ*—our; *paramam*—the supreme; *ca*—and; *daivatam*—worshipable Deity; *yasya*—whose; *anuvṛttyā*—following in the footsteps; *kṛtinaḥ*—successful; *babhūvima*—we have become.

TRANSLATION

O creator of the universe, You are our mother, well-wisher, Lord, father, spiritual master and worshipable Deity. By following in Your footsteps we have become successful in every respect. We pray, therefore, that You continue to bless us with Your mercy.

PURPORT

The all-good Personality of Godhead, being the creator of the universe, also plans for the good of all good living beings. The good living beings are advised by the Lord to follow His good advice, and by doing so they become successful in all spheres of life. There is no need to worship any deity but the Lord. The Lord is all-powerful, and if He is satisfied by our obedience unto His lotus feet, He is competent to bestow upon us all kinds of blessings for the successful execution of both our material and spiritual lives. For attaining spiritual existence, the human form is a chance for all to understand our eternal relation with God. Our relation with Him is eternal; it can neither be broken nor vanquished. It may be forgotten for the time being, but it can be revived also by the grace of the Lord, if we follow His injunctions, which are revealed in the scriptures of all times and all places.

TEXT 8

अहो सनाथा भवता स्म यद्वयं
त्रैविष्टपानामपि दूरदर्शनम् ।

प्रेमस्मितस्निग्धनिरीक्षणाननं
पश्येम रूपं तव सर्वसौभगम् ॥ ८ ॥

aho sanāthā bhavatā sma yad vayaṁ
traiviṣṭapānām api dūra-darśanam
prema-smita-snigdha-nirīkṣaṇānanaṁ
paśyema rūpaṁ tava sarva-saubhagam

aho—oh, it is our good luck; *sa-nāthāḥ*—to be under the protection of the master; *bhavatā*—by Your good self; *sma*—as we have become; *yat vayam*—as we are; *traiviṣṭa-pānām*—of the demigods; *api*—also; *dūra-darśanam*—very rarely seen; *prema-smita*—smiling with love; *snigdha*—affectionate; *nirīkṣaṇa-ānanam*—face looking in that mode; *paśyema*—let us look; *rūpam*—beauty; *tava*—Your; *sarva*—all; *saubhagam*—auspiciousness.

TRANSLATION

Oh, it is our good luck that we have come again today under Your protection by Your presence, for Your Lordship rarely visits even the denizens of heaven. Now it is possible for us to look into Your smiling face, which is full of affectionate glances. We can now see Your transcendental form, full of all auspiciousness.

PURPORT

The Lord in His eternal personal form can be seen only by the pure devotees. The Lord is never impersonal, but He is the Supreme Absolute Personality of Godhead, possible to be visited by devotional service face to face, which is impossible to be done even by the denizens of higher planets. When Brahmājī and other demigods want to consult Lord Viṣṇu, the plenary portion of Lord Kṛṣṇa, they have to wait on the shore of the ocean of milk where Lord Viṣṇu is lying on White Land (Śvetadvīpa). This ocean of milk and the Śvetadvīpa planet are the replica of Vaikuṇṭhaloka within the universe. Neither Brahmājī nor the demigods like Indra can enter into this island of Śvetadvīpa, but they can stand on the shore of the ocean of milk and transmit their message to Lord Viṣṇu, known as Kṣīrodakaśāyī Viṣṇu. Therefore, the Lord is rarely seen by them, but the inhabitants of Dvārakā, because of their being pure devotees without any tinge of the material contamination of fruitive activities and empiric philosophical speculation, can see Him face to face by the grace of the Lord. This is the original state of the living entities and can be attained by reviving our natural and constitutional state of life, which is discovered by devotional service only.

TEXT 9

यर्ह्यम्बुजाक्षापससार भो भवान्
कुरून् मधून् वाथ सुहृद्दिदृक्षया ।
तत्राब्दकोटिप्रतिमः क्षणो भवेद्
रविं विनाक्ष्णोरिव नस्तवाच्युत ॥ ९ ॥

yarhy ambujākṣāpasasāra bho bhavān
kurūn madhūn vātha suhṛd-didṛkṣayā
tatrābda-koṭi-pratimaḥ kṣaṇo bhaved
raviṁ vinākṣṇor iva nas tavācyuta

yarhi—whenever; *ambuja-akṣa*—O lotus-eyed one; *apasasāra*—You go away; *bho*—oh; *bhavān*—Yourself; *kurūn*—the descendants of King Kuru; *madhūn*—the inhabitants of Mathurā (Vrajabhūmi); *vā*—either; *atha*—therefore; *suhṛt-didṛkṣayā*—for meeting them; *tatra*—at that time; *abda-koṭi*—millions of years; *pratimaḥ*—like; *kṣaṇaḥ*—moments; *bhavet*—becomes; *ravim*—the sun; *vinā*—without; *akṣṇoḥ*—of the eyes; *iva*—like that; *naḥ*—ours; *tava*—Your; *acyuta*—O infallible one.

TRANSLATION

O lotus-eyed Lord, whenever You go away to Mathurā, Vṛndāvana or Hastināpura to meet Your friends and relatives, every moment of Your absence seems like a million years. O infallible one, at that time our eyes become useless, as if bereft of sun.

PURPORT

We are all proud of our material senses for making experiments to determine the existence of God. But we forget that our senses are not absolute by themselves. They can only act under certain conditions. For example, our eyes. As long as the sunshine is there, our eyes are useful to a certain extent. But in the absence of sunshine, the eyes are useless. Lord Śrī Kṛṣṇa, being the primeval Lord, the Supreme Truth, is compared to the sun. Without Him all our knowledge is either false or partial. The opposite of the sun is the darkness, and similarly the opposite of Kṛṣṇa is *māyā*, or illusion. The devotees of the Lord can see everything in true perspective due to the light disseminated by Lord Kṛṣṇa. By the grace of the Lord the pure devotee cannot be in the darkness of ignorance. Therefore, it is necessary that we must always be in the sight of Lord Kṛṣṇa so that we can see both ourselves and the Lord with His different energies. As we cannot see anything in the absence of the sun, so also we cannot see anything including our own self, without the factual presence of the Lord. Without Him all our knowledge is covered by illusion.

TEXT 10

कथं वयं नाथ चिरोषिते त्वयि प्रसन्नदृष्ट्याखिलतापशोषणम् ।
जीवेम ते सुन्दरहासशोभितमपश्यमाना वदनं मनोहरम् ।
इति चोदीरिता वाचः प्रजानां भक्तवत्सलः ।
शृण्वानोऽनुग्रहं दृष्ट्या वितन्वन् प्राविशत् पुरम् ॥१०॥

katham vayaṁ nātha ciroṣite tvayi
prasanna-dṛṣṭyākhila-tāpa-śoṣaṇam
jīvema te sundara-hāsa-śobhitam
apaśyamānā vadanaṁ manoharam

iti coditā vācaḥ
prajānāṁ bhakta-vatsalaḥ
śṛṇvāno 'nugrahaṁ dṛṣṭyā
vitanvan prāviśat puram

katham—how; *vayam*—we; *nātha*—O Lord; *ciroṣite*—being abroad almost always; *tvayi*—by You; *prasanna*—satisfaction; *dṛṣṭyā*—by the glance; *akhila*—universal; *tāpa*—miseries; *śoṣaṇam*—vanquishing; *jīvema*—shall be able to live; *te*—Your; *sundara*—beautiful; *hāsa*—

smiling; *śobhitam*—decorated; *apaśyamānāḥ*—without seeing; *vadanam*—face; *manoharam*—attractive; *iti*—thus; *ca*—and; *udīritāḥ*—speaking; *vācaḥ*—words; *prajānām*—of the citizens; *bhakta-vatsalaḥ*—kind to the devotees; *śṛṇvānaḥ*—thus learning; *anugraham*—kindness; *dṛṣṭyā*—by glances; *vitanvan*—distributing; *prāviśat*—entered; *puram*—Dvārakāpurī.

TRANSLATION

O master, if You live abroad all the time, then we cannot look at Your attractive face, whose smiles vanquish all our sufferings. How can we exist without Your presence?

Upon hearing their speeches, the Lord, who is very kind to the citizens and the devotees, entered the city of Dvārakā and acknowledged all their greetings by casting His transcendental glance over them.

PURPORT

Lord Kṛṣṇa's attraction is so powerful that once being attracted by Him one cannot tolerate separation from Him. Why is this so? Because we are all eternally related with Him as the sun rays are eternally related with the sun disc. The sun rays are molecular parts of the solar radiation. Thus the sun rays and the sun cannot be separated. The separation by the cloud is temporary and artificial, and as soon as the cloud is cleared, the sun rays again display their natural effulgence in the presence of the sun. Similarly, the living entities, who are molecular parts of the whole spirit, are separated from the Lord by the artificial covering of *māyā*, illusory energy. This illusory energy, or the curtain of *māyā*, has to be removed, and when it is so done, the living entity can see the Lord face to face, and all his miseries are at once removed. Every one of us wants to remove the miseries of life, but we do not know how to do it. The solution is given here, and it rests on us to assimilate it or not.

TEXT 11

मधुभोजदशार्हार्हकुकुरान्धकवृष्णिभिः ।
आत्मतुल्यबलैर्गुप्तां नागैर्भोगवतीमिव ॥११॥

madhu-bhoja-daśārhārha-
kukurāndhaka-vṛṣṇibhiḥ
ātma-tulya-balair guptāṁ
nāgair bhogavatīm iva

madhu—Madhu; *bhoja*—Bhoja; *daśārha*—Daśārha; *arha*—Arha; *kukura*—Kukura; *andhaka*—Andhaka; *vṛṣṇibhiḥ*—by the descendants of Vṛṣṇi; *ātma-tulya*—as good as Himself; *balaiḥ*—by strength; *guptām*—protected; *nāgaiḥ*—by the Nāgas; *bhogavatīm*—the capital of Nāgaloka; *iva*—like.

TRANSLATION

As Bhogavatī, the capital of Nāgaloka, is protected by the Nāgas, so was Dvārakā protected by the descendants of Vṛṣṇi—Bhoja, Madhu, Daśārha, Arha, Kukura, Andhaka, etc.—who were as strong as Lord Kṛṣṇa.

PURPORT

The Nāgaloka planet is situated below the earth planet, and it is understood that the sun rays are hampered there. The darkness of the planet is, however, removed by the flashes of the jewels set on the heads of the Nāgas (celestial serpents), and it is said that there are beautiful gardens, rivulets, etc., for the enjoyment of the Nāgas. It is understood here also that the place is well protected by the inhabitants. So also the city of Dvārakā was well protected by the descendants of Vṛṣṇi, who were as powerful as the Lord, insofar as He manifested His strength upon this earth.

TEXT 12

सर्वर्तुसर्वविभवपुण्यवृक्षलताश्रमैः ।
उद्यानोपवनारामैर्वृतपद्माकरश्रियम् ॥१२॥

sarvartu-sarva-vibhava-
puṇya-vṛkṣa-latāśramaiḥ
udyānopavanārāmair
vṛta-padmākara-śriyam

sarva—all; *ṛtu*—seasons; *sarva*—all; *vibhava*—opulences; *puṇya*—pious; *vṛkṣa*—trees; *latā*—creepers; *āśramaiḥ*—with hermitages; *udyāna*—orchards; *upavana*—flower gardens; *ārāmaiḥ*—pleasure gardens and beautiful parks; *vṛta*—surrounded by; *padma-ākara*—the birthplaces of lotuses or nice reservoirs of water; *śriyam*—increasing the beauty.

TRANSLATION

The city of Dvārakāpurī was filled with the opulences of all seasons. There were hermitages, orchards, flower gardens, parks and reservoirs of water breeding lotus flowers all over.

PURPORT

Perfection of human civilization is made possible by utilizing the gifts of nature in their own way. As we find herewith in the description of its opulence, Dvārakā was surrounded by flower gardens and fruit orchards along with reservoirs of water and growing lotuses. There is no mention of mills and factories supported by slaughterhouses, which are the necessary paraphernalia of the modern metropolis. The propensity to utilize nature's own gifts is still there, even in the heart of modern civilized man. The leaders of modern civilization select their own residential quarters in a place where there are such naturally beautiful gardens and reservoirs of water, but they leave the common men to reside in congested areas without parks and gardens. Herein of course we find a different description of the city of Dvārakā. It is understood that the whole *dhāma*, or residential quarter, was surrounded by such gardens and parks with reservoirs of water where lotuses grew. It is understood that all the people depended on nature's gifts of fruits and flowers without industrial enterprises promoting filthy huts and slums for residential quarters. Advancement of civilization is estimated not on the growth of mills and factories to deteriorate the finer instincts of the human being, but on developing the potent spiritual instincts of human beings and giving them a chance to go back to Godhead. Development of factories and mills is called *ugra-karma*, or pungent activities, and such activities deteriorate the finer sentiments of the human being and society to form a dungeon of demons.

We find herein the mention of pious trees which produce seasonal flowers and fruits. The impious trees are useless jungles only, and they can only be used to supply fuels. In the modern civilization such impious trees are planted on the sides of roads. Human energy should be properly utilized in developing the finer senses for spiritual understanding, in which lies the solution of life. Fruits, flowers, beautiful gardens, parks and reservoirs of water with ducks and swans playing in the midst of lotus flowers, and cows giving sufficient milk and butter are essential for developing the finer tissues of the human body. As against this, the dungeons of mines, factories and workshops develop demoniac propensities in the working class. The vested interests flourish at the cost of the working class, and consequently there are severe clashes between them in so many ways. The description of Dvārakā-dhāma is the ideal of human civilization.

TEXT 13

गोपुरद्वारमार्गेषु कृतकौतुकतोरणाम् ।
चित्रध्वजपताकाग्रैरन्तः प्रतिहतातपाम् ॥१३॥

gopura-dvāra-mārgeṣu
kṛta-kautuka-toraṇām
citra-dhvaja-patākāgrair
antaḥ pratihatātapām

gopura—the gateway of the city; *dvāra*—door; *mārgeṣu*—on different roads; *kṛta*—undertaken; *kautuka*—because of the festival; *toraṇām*—decorated arch; *citra*—painted; *dhvaja*—flags; *patākā-agraiḥ*—by the foremost signs; *antaḥ*—within; *pratihata*—checked; *ātapām*—sunshine.

TRANSLATION

The city gateway, the household doors and festooned arches along the roads were all nicely decorated with festive signs like plantain trees and mango leaves, all to welcome the Lord. Flags, garlands and painted signs and slogans all combined to shade the sunshine.

PURPORT

Signs of decoration in special festivals were also collected from the gifts of nature, such as the plantain trees, the mango trees, fruits and flowers. Mango trees, coconut palms and plantain trees are still accepted as auspicious signs. The flags mentioned above were all painted with the picture of either Garuḍa or Hanumān, the two great servitors of the Lord. For devotees, such paintings and decorations are still adored, and the servitor of the master is paid more respects for the satisfaction of the Lord.

TEXT 14

सम्मार्जितमहामार्गरथ्यापणकचत्वराम् ।
सिक्तां गन्धजलैरुप्तां फलपुष्पाक्षताङ्कुरैः ॥१४॥

sammārjita-mahā-mārga-
rathyāpaṇaka-catvarām
siktāṁ gandha-jalair uptāṁ
phala-puṣpākṣatāṅkuraiḥ

sammārjita—thoroughly cleansed; *mahā-mārga*—highways; *rathya*—lanes and subways; *āpaṇaka*—shopping marketplaces; *catvarām*—public meeting places; *siktām*—moistened with; *gandha-jalaiḥ*—scented water; *uptām*—was strewn with; *phala*—fruits; *puṣpa*—flowers; *akṣata*—unbroken; *aṅkuraiḥ*—seeds.

TRANSLATION

The highways, subways, lanes, markets and public meeting places were all thoroughly cleansed and then moistened with scented water. And to welcome the Lord, fruits, flowers and unbroken seeds were strewn everywhere.

PURPORT

Scented waters prepared by distilling flowers like rose and *keora* were requisitioned to wet the roads, streets and lanes of Dvārakādhāma. Such places, along with the marketplace and public meeting places, were thoroughly cleansed. From the above description, it appears that the city of Dvārakādhāma was considerably big, containing many highways, streets and public meeting places with parks, gardens and reservoirs of water, all very nicely decorated with flowers and fruits. And to welcome the Lord such flowers and fruits with unbroken seeds of grain were also strewn over the public places. Unbroken seeds of grain or fruits in the seedling stage were considered auspicious, and they are still so used by the Hindus in general on festival days.

TEXT 15

द्वारि द्वारि गृहाणां च दध्यक्षतफलेक्षुभिः ।
अलंकृतां पूर्णकुम्भैर्बलिभिर्धूपदीपकैः ॥१५॥

dvāri dvāri gṛhāṇāṁ ca
dadhy-akṣata-phalekṣubhiḥ
alaṅkṛtāṁ pūrṇa-kumbhair
balibhir dhūpa-dīpakaiḥ

dvāri dvāri—the door of each and every house; *gṛhāṇām*—of all the residential buildings; *ca*—and; *dadhi*—curd; *akṣata*—unbroken; *phala*—fruit; *ikṣubhiḥ*—sugarcane; *alaṅkṛtām*—decorated; *pūrṇa-kumbhaiḥ*—full water pots; *balibhiḥ*—along with articles for worship; *dhūpa*—incense; *dīpakaiḥ*—with lamps and candles.

TRANSLATION

In each and every door of the residential houses, auspicious things like curd, unbroken fruits, sugarcane and full waterpots with articles for worship, incense and candles were all displayed.

PURPORT

The process of reception according to Vedic rites is not at all dry. The reception was made not simply by decorating the roads and streets as above mentioned, but by worshiping the Lord with requisite ingredients like incense, lamps, flowers, sweets, fruits and other palatable eatables, according to one's capacity. All were offered to the Lord, and the remnants of the foodstuff were distributed amongst the gathering citizens. So it was not like a dry reception of these modern days. Each and every house was ready to receive the Lord in a similar way, and thus each and every house on the roads and streets distributed such remnants of food to the citizens, and therefore the festival was successful. Without distribution of food, no function is complete, and that is the way of Vedic culture.

TEXTS 16-17

निशम्य प्रेष्ठमायान्तं वसुदेवो महामनाः ।
अक्रूरश्चोग्रसेनश्च रामश्चाद्भुतविक्रमः ॥१६॥
प्रद्युम्नश्चारुदेष्णश्च साम्बो जाम्बवतीसुतः ।
प्रहर्षवेगोच्छशितशयनासनभोजनाः ॥१७॥

niśamya preṣṭham āyāntaṁ
vasudevo mahā-manāḥ
akrūraś cograsenaś ca
rāmaś cādbhuta-vikramaḥ

pradyumnaś cārudeṣṇaś ca
sāmbo jāmbavatī-sutaḥ
praharṣa-vegocchaśita-
śayanāsana-bhojanāḥ

niśamya—just hearing; *preṣṭham*—the dearmost; *āyāntam*—coming home; *vasudevaḥ*—Vasudeva (the father of Kṛṣṇa); *mahā-manāḥ*—the magnanimous; *akrūraḥ*—Akrūra; *ca*—and; *ugrasenaḥ*—Ugrasena; *ca*—and; *rāmaḥ*—Balarāma (the elder brother of Kṛṣṇa); *ca*—and; *adbhuta*—superhuman; *vikramaḥ*—prowess; *pradyumnaḥ*—Pradyumna; *cārudeṣṇaḥ*—Cārudeṣṇa; *ca*—and; *sāmbaḥ*—Sāmba; *jāmbavatī-sutaḥ*—the son of Jāmbavatī; *praharṣa*—extreme happiness; *vega*—force; *ucchaśita*—being influenced by; *śayana*—lying down; *āsana*—sitting on; *bhojanāḥ*—dining.

TRANSLATION

On hearing that the most dear Kṛṣṇa was approaching Dvārakādhāma, magnanimous Vasudeva, Akrūra, Ugrasena, Balarāma (the superhumanly powerful), Pradyumna, Cārudeṣṇa and Sāmba the

son of Jāmbavatī, all extremely happy, abandoned resting, sitting and dining.

PURPORT

Vasudeva: Son of King Śūrasena, husband of Devakī and father of Lord Śrī Kṛṣṇa. He is the brother of Kuntī and father of Subhadrā. Subhadrā was married with her cousin Arjuna, and this system is still prevalent in some parts of India. Vasudeva was appointed minister of Ugrasena, and later on he married eight daughters of Ugrasena's brother Devaka. Devakī is only one of them. Kaṁsa was his brother-in-law, and Vasudeva accepted voluntary imprisonment by Kaṁsa on mutual agreement to deliver the eighth son of Devakī. This was foiled by the will of Kṛṣṇa. As maternal uncle of the Pāṇḍavas, he took active parts in the purificatory process of the Pāṇḍavas. He sent for the priest Kaśyapa at the Śatasṛṅga Parvata, and he executed the functions. When Kṛṣṇa appeared within the bars of Kaṁsa's prison house, He was transferred by Vasudeva to the house of Nanda Mahārāja, the foster father of Kṛṣṇa, at Gokula. Kṛṣṇa disappeared along with Baladeva prior to the disappearance of Vasudeva, and Arjuna (Vasudeva's nephew) undertook the charge of the funeral ceremony after Vasudeva's disappearance.

Akrūra: The commander in chief of the Vṛṣṇi dynasty and a great devotee of Lord Kṛṣṇa. Akrūra attained success in devotional service to the Lord by the one single process of offering prayers. He was the husband of Sūtanī, daughter of Ahūka. He supported Arjuna when Arjuna took Subhadrā forcibly away by the will of Kṛṣṇa. Both Kṛṣṇa and Akrūra went to see Arjuna after his successful kidnapping of Subhadrā. Both of them presented dowries to Arjuna after this incidence. Akrūra was present also when Abhimanyu, the son of Subhadrā, was married with Uttarā, mother of Mahārāja Parīkṣit. Ahūka, the father-in-law of Akrūra, was not on good terms with Akrūra. But both of them were devotees of the Lord.

Ugrasena: One of the powerful kings of the Vṛṣṇi dynasty and cousin of Mahārāja Kuntibhoja. His other name is Ahūka. His minister was Vasudeva, and his son was the powerful Kaṁsa. This Kaṁsa imprisoned his father and became the King of Mathurā. By the grace of Lord Kṛṣṇa and His brother, Lord Baladeva, Kaṁsa was killed, and Ugrasena was reinstalled on the throne. When Śālva attacked the city of Dvārakā,

Ugrasena fought very valiantly and repulsed the enemy. Ugrasena inquired from Nāradajī about the divinity of Lord Kṛṣṇa. When the Yadu dynasty was to be vanquished, Ugrasena was entrusted with the iron lump produced from the womb of Sāmba. He cut the iron lump into pieces and then pasted it and mixed it up with the sea water on the coast of Dvārakā. After this, he ordered complete prohibition within the city of Dvārakā and the kingdom. He got salvation after his death.

Baladeva: He is the divine son of Vasudeva by his wife Rohiṇī. He is also known as Rohiṇī-nandana, the beloved son of Rohiṇī. He was also entrusted to Nanda Mahārāja along with His mother, Rohiṇī, when Vasudeva embraced imprisonment by mutual agreement with Kaṁsa. So Nanda Mahārāja is also the foster father of Baladeva along with Lord Kṛṣṇa. Lord Kṛṣṇa and Lord Baladeva were constant companions from Their very childhood, although They were stepbrothers. He is the plenary manifestation of the Supreme Personality of Godhead, and therefore He is as good and powerful as Lord Kṛṣṇa. He belongs to the *viṣṇu-tattva* (the principle of Godhead). He attended the *svayaṁvara* ceremony of Draupadī along with Śrī Kṛṣṇa. When Subhadrā was kidnapped by Arjuna by the organized plan of Śrī Kṛṣṇa, Baladeva was very angry with Arjuna and wanted to kill him at once. Śrī Kṛṣṇa, for the sake of His dear friend, fell at the feet of Lord Baladeva and implored Him not to be so angry. Śrī Baladeva was thus satisfied. Similarly, He was once very angry with the Kauravas, and He wanted to throw their whole city into the depths of the Yamunā. But the Kauravas satisfied Him by surrendering unto His divine lotus feet. He was actually the seventh son of Devakī prior to the birth of Lord Kṛṣṇa, but by the will of the Lord He was transferred to the womb of Rohiṇī to escape the wrath of Kaṁsa. His other name is therefore Saṅkarṣaṇa, who is also the plenary portion of Śrī Baladeva. Because He is as powerful as Lord Kṛṣṇa and can bestow spiritual power to the devotees, He is therefore known as Baladeva. In the *Vedas* also it is enjoined that no one can know the Supreme Lord without being favored by Baladeva. *Bala* means spiritual strength not physical. Some less intelligent persons interpret *bala* as the strength of the body. But no one can have spiritual realization by physical strength. Physical strength ends with the end of the physical body, but spiritual strength follows the spirit soul to the next transmigration, and therefore the strength obtained by Baladeva is never wasted. The strength is eternal, and thus Baladeva is the original spiritual master of all devotees.

Śrī Baladeva was also a class friend of Lord Śrī Kṛṣṇa as a student of Sāndīpani Muni. In His childhood He killed many *asuras* along with Śrī Kṛṣṇa, and specifically He killed the Dhenukāsura at Tālavana. During the Kurukṣetra battle, He remained neutral, and He tried His best not to bring about the fight. He was in favor of Duryodhana, but still He remained neutral. When there was a club-fight between Duryodhana and Bhīmasena, He was present on the spot. He was angry at Bhīmasena when the latter struck Duryodhana on the thigh or below the belt, and He wanted to retaliate the unfair action. Lord Śrī Kṛṣṇa saved Bhīma from His wrath. But He left the place at once, being disgusted at Bhīmasena, and after His departure Duryodhana fell to the ground to meet his death. The funeral ceremony of Abhimanyu, the son of Arjuna, was performed by Him, as He was the maternal uncle. It was impossible to be performed by any one of the Pāṇḍavas, who were all overwhelmed with grief. At the last stage, He departed from this world by producing a great white snake from His mouth, and thus He was carried by Śeṣanāga in the shape of a serpent.

Pradyumna: Incarnation of Kāmadeva or, according to others, incarnation of Sanat-kumāra, born as the son of the Personality of Godhead Lord Śrī Kṛṣṇa and Lakṣmīdevī Śrīmatī Rukmiṇī, the principal queen at Dvārakā. He was one of those who went to congratulate Arjuna upon his marrying Subhadrā. He was one of the great generals who fought with Śālva, and while fighting with him he became unconscious on the battlefield. His charioteer brought him back to the camp from the battlefield, and for this action he was very sorry and rebuked his charioteer. However, he fought again with Śālva and was victorious. He heard all about the different demigods from Nāradajī. He is one of the four plenary expansions of Lord Śrī Kṛṣṇa. He is the third one. He inquired from his father, Śrī Kṛṣṇa, about the glories of the *brāhmaṇas.* During the fratricidal war amongst the descendants of Yadu, he died at the hand of Bhoja, another king of the Vṛṣṇis. After his death, he was installed in his original position.

Cārudeṣṇa: Another son of Lord Śrī Kṛṣṇa and Rukmiṇīdevī. He was also present during the *svayaṁvara* ceremony of Draupadī. He was a great warrior like his brothers and father. He fought with Vivinidhaka and killed him in the fight.

Sāmba: One of the great heroes of the Yadu dynasty and the son of Lord Śrī Kṛṣṇa by His wife Jāmbavatī. He learned the military art of throwing arrows from Arjuna, and he became a member of parliament during the time of Mahārāja Yudhiṣṭhira. He was present during the Rājasūya-yajña of Mahārāja Yudhiṣṭhira. When all the Vṛṣṇis were assembled during the time of Prabhāsa-yajña, his glorious activities were narrated by Sātyaki before Lord Baladeva. He was also present along with his father, Lord Śrī Kṛṣṇa, during the *aśvamedha-yajña* performed by Yudhiṣṭhira. He was presented before some *ṛṣis* falsely dressed as a pregnant woman by his brothers, and in fun he asked the *ṛṣis* what he was going to deliver. The *ṛṣis* replied that he would deliver a lump of iron, which would be the cause of fratricidal war in the family of Yadu. The next day, in the morning, Sāmba delivered a large lump of iron, which was entrusted with Ugrasena for necessary action. Actually later on there was the foretold fratricidal war, and Sāmba died in that war.

So all these sons of Lord Kṛṣṇa left their respective palaces and leaving aside all engagements, including lying down, sitting and dining, hastened toward their exalted father.

TEXT 18

वारणेन्द्रं पुरस्कृत्य ब्राह्मणैः ससुमङ्गलैः ।
शङ्खतूर्यनिनादेन ब्रह्मघोषेण चादृताः ।
प्रत्युज्जग्मू रथैर्हृष्टाः प्रणयागतसाध्वसाः ॥१८॥

vāraṇendraṁ puraskṛtya
brāhmaṇaiḥ sasumaṅgalaiḥ
śaṅkha-tūrya-ninādena
brahma-ghoṣeṇa cādṛtāḥ
pratyujjagmū rathair hṛṣṭāḥ
praṇayāgata-sādhvasāḥ

vāraṇa-indram—elephants on the auspicious mission; *puraskṛtya*—putting in the front; *brāhmaṇaiḥ*—by the *brāhmaṇas; sasumaṅgalaiḥ*—with all-auspicious signs; *śaṅkha*—conchshell; *tūrya*—

bugle; *ninādena*—by the sound of; *brahma-ghoṣeṇa*—by chanting the hymns of the *Vedas; ca*—and; *ādṛtāḥ*—glorified; *prati*—towards; *ujjagmuḥ*—proceeded hurriedly; *rathaiḥ*—on the chariots; *hṛṣṭāḥ*—in cheerfulness; *praṇayāgata*—saturated with affection; *sādhvasāḥ*—all-respectful.

TRANSLATION

They hastened toward the Lord on chariots with brāhmaṇas bearing flowers. Before them were elephants, emblems of good fortune. Conchshells and bugles were sounded, and Vedic hymns were chanted. Thus they offered their respects, which were saturated with affection.

PURPORT

The Vedic way of receiving a great personality creates an atmosphere of respect, which is saturated with affection and veneration for the person received. The auspicious atmosphere of such a reception depends on the paraphernalia described above, including conchshells, flowers, incense, decorated elephants, and the qualified *brāhmaṇas* reciting verses from the Vedic literatures. Such a program of reception is full of sincerity, on the part of both the receiver and the received.

TEXT 19

वारमुख्याश्च शतशो यानैस्तद्दर्शनोत्सुकाः ।
लसत्कुण्डलनिर्भातकपोलवदनश्रियः ॥१९॥

vāramukhyāś ca śataśo
yānais tad-darśanotsukāḥ
lasat-kuṇḍala-nirbhāta-
kapola-vadana-śriyaḥ

vāramukhyāḥ—well-known prostitutes; *ca*—and; *śataśaḥ*—hundreds of; *yānaiḥ*—by vehicles; *tat-darśana*—for meeting Him (Lord Śrī Kṛṣṇa); *utsukāḥ*—very much anxious; *lasat*—hanging; *kuṇḍala*—earrings; *nirbhāta*—dazzling; *kapola*—forehead; *vadana*—face; *śriyaḥ*—beauty.

TRANSLATION

At the same time, many hundreds of well-known prostitutes began to proceed on various vehicles. They were all very eager to meet the Lord, and their beautiful faces were decorated with dazzling earrings, which enhanced the beauty of their foreheads.

PURPORT

We may not hate even the prostitutes if they are devotees of the Lord. Even to date there are many prostitutes in great cities of India who are sincere devotees of the Lord. By tricks of chance one may be obliged to adopt a profession which is not very adorable in society, but that does not hamper one in executing devotional service to the Lord. Devotional service to the Lord is uncheckable in all circumstances. It is understood herewith that even in those days, about five thousand years ago, there were prostitutes in a city like Dvārakā, where Lord Kṛṣṇa resided. This means that prostitutes are necessary citizens for the proper upkeep of society. The government opens wine shops, but this does not mean that the government encourages the drinking of wine. The idea is that there is a class of men who will drink at any cost, and it has been experienced that prohibition in great cities encouraged illicit smuggling of wine. Similarly, men who are not satisfied at home require such concessions, and if there is no prostitute, then such low men will induce others into prostitution. It is better that prostitutes be available in the marketplace so that the sanctity of society can be maintained. It is better to maintain a class of prostitutes than to encourage prostitutes within society. The real reformation is to enlighten all people to become devotees of the Lord, and that will check all kinds of deteriorating factors of life.

Śrī Bilvamaṅgala Ṭhākura, a great *ācārya* of the Viṣṇusvāmī Vaiṣṇava sect, in his householder life was overly attached to a prostitute who happened to be a devotee of the Lord. One night when the Ṭhākura came to Cintāmaṇi's house in torrents of rain and thunder, Cintāmaṇi was astonished to see how the Ṭhākura could come on such a dreadful night after crossing a foaming river which was full of waves. She said to Ṭhākura Bilvamaṅgala that his attraction for the flesh and bone of an insignificant woman like her would be properly utilized if it could be diverted to the devotional service of the Lord to achieve attraction for the transcendental beauty of the Lord. It was a momentous hour for the Ṭhākura, and he took a turn towards spiritual realization by the words of a prostitute. Later on the Ṭhākura accepted the prostitute as his spiritual master, and in several places of his literary works he has glorified the name of Cintāmaṇi, who showed him the right path.

In the *Bhagavad-gītā* (9.32) the Lord says, "O son of Pṛthā, even the low-born *caṇḍālas* and those who are born in a family of unbelievers, and even the prostitutes, shall attain perfection of life if they take shelter of unalloyed devotional service to Me, because in the path of devotional service there are no impediments due to degraded birth and occupation. The path is open for everyone who agrees to follow it."

It appears that the prostitutes of Dvārakā, who were so eager to meet the Lord, were all His unalloyed devotees, and thus they were all on the path of salvation according to the above version of the *Bhagavad-gītā.* Therefore, the only reformation that is necessary in society is to make an organized effort to turn the citizens into devotees of the Lord, and thus all good qualities of the denizens of heaven will overtake them in their own way. On the other hand, those who are nondevotees have no good qualifications whatsoever, however they may be materially advanced. The difference is that the devotees of the Lord are on the path of liberation, whereas the nondevotees are on the path of further entanglement in material bondage. The criterion of advancement of civilization is whether the people are educated and advanced on the path of salvation.

TEXT 20

नटनर्तकगन्धर्वाः सूतमागधवन्दिनः ।
गायन्ति चोत्तमश्लोकचरितान्यद्भुतानि च ॥२०॥

naṭa-nartaka-gandharvāḥ
sūta-māgadha-vandinaḥ
gāyanti cottamaśloka-
caritāny adbhutāni ca

naṭa—dramatists; *nartaka*—dancers; *gandharvāḥ*—celestial singers; *sūta*—professional historians; *māgadha*—professional genealogists; *vandinaḥ*—professional learned speakers; *gāyanti*—chant;

ca—respectively; *uttamaśloka*—the Supreme Lord; *caritāni*—activities; *adbhutāni*—all superhuman; *ca*—and.

TRANSLATION

Expert dramatists, artists, dancers, singers, historians, genealogists and learned speakers all gave their respective contributions, being inspired by the superhuman pastimes of the Lord. Thus they proceeded on and on.

PURPORT

It appears that five thousand years ago the society also needed the services of the dramatists, artists, dancers, singers, historians, genealogists, public speakers, etc. Dancers, singers and dramatic artists mostly hailed from the *śūdra* community, whereas the learned historians, genealogists and public speakers hailed from the *brāhmaṇa* community. All of them belonged to a particular caste, and they became so trained in their respective families. Such dramatists, dancers, singers, historians, genealogists and public speakers would dwell on the subject of the Lord's superhuman activities in different ages and millenniums, and not on ordinary events. Nor were they in chronological order. All the *Purāṇas* are historical facts described only in relation with the Supreme Lord in different ages and times as well as on different planets also. Therefore, we do not find any chronological order. The modern historians, therefore, cannot catch up the link, and thus they unauthoritatively remark that the *Purāṇas* are all imaginary stories only.

Even one hundred years ago in India, all dramatic performances were centered around the superhuman activities of the Supreme Lord. The common people would be verily entertained by the performances of dramas, and *yātrā* parties played wonderfully on the superhuman activities of the Lord, and thus even the illiterate agriculturist would be a participant in the knowledge of Vedic literature, despite a considerable lack of academic qualifications. Therefore, expert players in drama, dancers, singers, speakers, etc., are required for the spiritual enlightenment of the common man. The genealogists would give account completely of the descendants of a particular family. Even at the present moment the guides in the pilgrimage sites of India submit a complete account of genealogical tables before a newcomer. This wonderful act sometimes attracts more customers to receive such important information.

TEXT 21

भगवांस्तत्र बन्धूनां पौराणामनुवर्तिनाम् ।
यथाविध्युपसंगम्य सर्वेषां मानमादधे ॥२१॥

bhagavāṁs tatra bandhūnāṁ
paurāṇām anuvartinām
yathā-vidhy upasaṅgamya
sarveṣāṁ mānam ādadhe

bhagavān—Śrī Kṛṣṇa, the Personality of Godhead; *tatra*—in that place; *bandhūnām*—of the friends; *paurāṇām*—of the citizens; *anuvartinām*—those who approached Him to receive and welcome; *yathā-vidhi*—as it behooves; *upasaṅgamya*—going nearer; *sarveṣām*—for each and every one; *mānam*—honor and respects; *ādadhe*—offered.

TRANSLATION

Lord Kṛṣṇa, the Personality of Godhead, approached them and offered due honor and respect to each and every one of the friends, relatives, citizens and all others who came to receive and welcome Him.

PURPORT

The Supreme Lord Personality of Godhead is neither impersonal nor an inert object unable to reciprocate the feelings of His devotees. Here the word *yathā-vidhi*, or "just as it behooves" is significant. He reciprocates "just as it behooves" with His different types of admirers and devotees. Of course, the pure devotees are of one type only because they have no other object for service but the Lord, and therefore the Lord also reciprocates with such pure devotees just as it behooves, namely, He is always attentive to all the matters of His pure devotees. There are others who designate Him as impersonal, and so the Lord also does not take any personal interest. He satisfies everyone in terms of one's development of spiritual consciousness, and a sample of such reciprocation is exhibited here with His different welcomers.

TEXT 22

प्रह्वाभिवादनाश्लेषकरस्पर्शस्मितेक्षणैः ।
आश्वास्य चाश्वपाकेभ्यो वरैश्चाभिमतैर्विभुः ॥२२॥

prahvābhivādanāśleṣa-
kara-sparśa-smitekṣaṇaiḥ
āśvāsya cāśvapākebhyo
varaiś cābhimatair vibhuḥ

prahvā—by bowing His head; *abhivādana*—by greeting with words; *āśleṣa*—embracing; *kara-sparśa*—shaking hands; *smita-īkṣaṇaiḥ*—by a glancing smile; *āśvāsya*—by encouragement; *ca*—and; *āśvapākebhyaḥ*—down to the lowest rank of dog-eaters; *varaiḥ*—by benedictions; *ca*—also; *abhimataiḥ*—as desired by; *vibhuḥ*—the Almighty.

TRANSLATION

The Almighty Lord greeted everyone present by bowing His head, exchanging greetings, embracing, shaking hands, looking and smiling, giving assurances and awarding benedictions, even to the lowest in rank.

PURPORT

To receive the Lord Śrī Kṛṣṇa there were all grades of population, beginning from Vasudeva, Ugrasena and Gargamuni—the father, grandfather and teacher—down to the prostitutes and *caṇḍālas,* who are accustomed to eat dogs. And every one of them was properly greeted by the Lord in terms of rank and position. As pure living entities, all are the separated parts and parcels of the Lord, and thus no one is alien by His eternal relation. Such pure living entities are graded differently in terms of contamination of the modes of material nature, but the Lord is equally affectionate to all His parts and parcels, despite material gradation. He descends only to recall these materialistic living beings back to His kingdom, and intelligent persons take advantage of this facility offered by the Personality of Godhead to all living beings. No one is rejected by the Lord from the kingdom of God, and it remains with the living being to accept this or not.

TEXT 23

स्वयं च गुरुभिर्विप्रैः सदारैः स्थविरैरपि ।
आशीर्भिर्युज्यमानोऽन्यैर्वन्दिभिश्चाविशत्पुरम् ॥२३॥

svayaṁ ca gurubhir vipraiḥ
sadāraiḥ sthavirair api
āśīrbhir yujyamāno 'nyair
vandibhiś cāviśat puram

svayam—Himself; *ca*—also; *gurubhiḥ*—by elderly relatives; *vipraiḥ*—by the *brāhmaṇas; sadāraiḥ*—with their wives; *sthaviraiḥ*—invalid; *api*—also; *āśīrbhiḥ*—by the blessing of; *yujyamānaḥ*—being praised by; *anyaiḥ*—by others; *vandibhiḥ*—admirers; *ca*—and; *aviśat*—entered; *puram*—the city.

TRANSLATION

Then the Lord personally entered the city accompanied by elderly relatives and invalid brāhmaṇas with their wives, all offering benedictions and singing the glories of the Lord. Others also praised the glories of the Lord.

PURPORT

The *brāhmaṇas* in society were never attentive to banking money for future retired life. When they were old invalids, they used to approach the assembly of the kings, and simply by praising the glorious deeds performed by the kings, along with their wives, they would be provided with all necessities of life. Such *brāhmaṇas* were not, so to speak, flatterers of the kings, but the kings were actually glorified by their actions, and they were sincerely still more encouraged in pious acts by such *brāhmaṇas* in a dignified way. Lord Śrī Kṛṣṇa is worthy of all glories, and the praying *brāhmaṇas* and others were glorified themselves by chanting the glories of the Lord.

TEXT 24

राजमार्गं गते कृष्णे द्वारकायाः कुलस्त्रियः ।
हर्म्याण्यारुरुहुर्विप्र तदीक्षणमहोत्सवाः ॥२४॥

rāja-mārgaṁ gate kṛṣṇe
dvārakāyāḥ kula-striyaḥ
harmyāṇy āruruhur vipra
tad-īkṣaṇa-mahotsavāḥ

rāja-mārgam—the public roads; *gate*—while passing over; *kṛṣṇe*—by Lord Kṛṣṇa; *dvārakāyāḥ*—of the city of Dvārakā; *kula-striyaḥ*—ladies of the respectable families; *harmyāṇi*—on the palaces; *āruruhuḥ*—got up; *vipra*—O *brāhmaṇas; tat-īkṣaṇa*—just to look upon Him (Kṛṣṇa); *mahā-utsavāḥ*—accepted as the greatest festival.

TRANSLATION

When Lord Kṛṣṇa passed over the public roads, all the ladies from the respectable families of Dvārakā went up to the roofs of their palaces just to have a look at the Lord. They considered this to be the greatest festival.

PURPORT

To have a look at the Lord is a great festive occasion undoubtedly, as it was considered by the metropolitan ladies of Dvārakā. This is still followed by the devout ladies of India. Especially during the days of the Jhulana and Janmāṣṭamī ceremonies, the ladies of India still throng up in the greatest number at the temple of the Lord, where His transcendental eternal form is worshiped. The transcendental form of the Lord installed in a temple is not different from the Lord personally. Such a form of the Lord is called *arca-vigraha,* or *arcā* incarnation, and is expanded by the Lord by His internal potency just to facilitate the devotional service of His innumerable devotees who are in the material world. The material senses cannot perceive the spiritual nature of the Lord, and therefore the Lord accepts the *arca-vigraha,* which is apparently made of material elements like earth, wood and stone but actually there is no material contamination. The Lord being *kaivalya* (one alone), there is no matter in

His Divine Grace A. C. Bhaktivedanta Swami Prabhupāda
Founder-*Ācārya* of the International Society for Krishna Consciousness

PLATE ONE

After the battle of Kurukṣetra, Lord Kṛṣṇa seated Himself on His chariot to start for Dvārakā. Then He saw Uttarā hurrying toward Him in fear. She cried out, "O Lord of lords, Lord of the universe! O greatest of the mystics! Please protect me, for there is no one else who can save me from the clutches of death in this world of duality. O all-powerful Lord, a fiery iron arrow is coming towards me fast. My Lord, let it burn me personally, if You so desire, but please do not let it burn and abort my embryo." Having patiently heard Uttarā's words, Lord Śrī Kṛṣṇa, who is always very affectionate to His devotees, at once understood that Aśvatthāmā, the son of Droṇācārya, had thrown the nuclear weapon called the *brahmāstra* to finish the last life in the Pāṇḍava family. Being the Lord of supreme mysticism, Lord Śrī Kṛṣṇa, who resides within everyone's heart as the Supersoul, immediately covered the embryo of Uttarā by His personal energy. Thus, although the supreme *brahmāstra* weapon released by Aśvatthāmā was irresistible and without check or counteraction, when confronted by the strength of Lord Kṛṣṇa it was neutralized and foiled. *(pp. 8–15)*

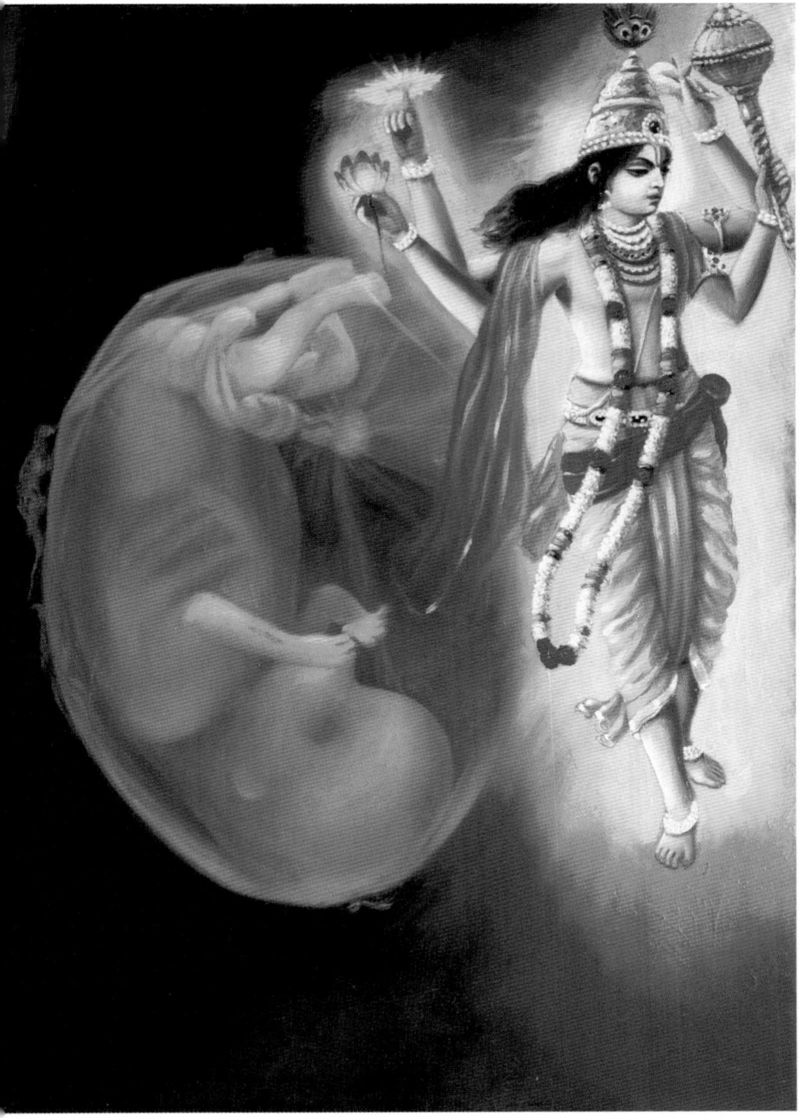

PLATE TWO

Bhīṣmadeva was the valiant grandsire of the Kuru dynasty (in which the Pāṇḍavas appeared), titular grandfather of all the fighters in the Battle of Kurukṣetra, and the chief descendant of King Bharata. At the end of the battle, Bhīṣma lay fatally wounded, on a bed of arrows. Just to pay their respects to him, all the great souls in the universe, namely the *brāhmaṇas* and kings and the *ṛṣis* among the demigods (all situated in the quality of goodness), assembled before him. The Pāṇḍava King Yudhiṣṭhira, along with his younger brothers and Lord Kṛṣṇa, also came before him. Bhīṣmadeva welcomed all the great and powerful *ṛṣis*, for he knew perfectly all the religious principles according to time and place. And when he saw the sons of King Pāṇḍu sitting silently nearby, overcome with affection for their dying grandfather, Bhīṣmadeva congratulated them with feeling. There were tears of ecstasy in his eyes, for he was overwhelmed by love and affection for the Supreme Personality of Godhead, Lord Kṛṣṇa. *(pp. 72–84)*

PLATE THREE

The Battle of Kurukṣetra was fought on military principles but at the same time in a sporting spirit, as a friend fights with another friend. Duryodhana criticized Bhīṣmadeva, alleging that he was reluctant to kill Arjuna because of paternal affection. A *kṣatriya* cannot tolerate insults to his fighting skills, so Bhīṣmadeva promised that the next day he would kill all five Pāṇḍavas with special weapons for the purpose. Duryodhana was satisfied, and he kept the arrows with him to be delivered the next day during the fight.

By tricks Arjuna took the arrows from Duryodhana, but Bhīṣmadeva could understand that this was actually the work of Lord Kṛṣṇa. So, Bhīṣma took a vow that the next day Kṛṣṇa would have to take up weapons Himself; otherwise, His friend Arjuna would die. On the next day, Bhīṣmadeva fought so violently that both Arjuna and Kṛṣṇa seemed to be in trouble. Arjuna appeared almost defeated; so tense was the situation that Bhīṣmadeva was about to kill Arjuna. At that time Lord Kṛṣṇa wanted to please His devotee Bhīṣmadeva by fulfilling his vow. Seemingly, Kṛṣṇa broke His own promise to remain weaponless and refrain from helping either of the parties. But to protect Arjuna, Kṛṣṇa got down from the chariot, took up one of its wheels, and rushed at Bhīṣmadeva in an angry mood, like a lion going to kill an elephant. Kṛṣṇa dropped His covering cloth on the way, and out of great anger He did not know that He dropped it. Bhīṣmadeva at once gave up his weapons and stood to be killed by Kṛṣṇa, his beloved Lord. But by Kṛṣṇa's arrangement the fighting of the day ended at that very moment, and both Arjuna and Bhīṣma were saved. *(p. 125)*

PLATE FOUR

By intense ecstasy of loving service, the damsels of Vrajabhūmi attained qualitative oneness with the Lord by dancing with Him on an equal level, embracing Him in nuptial love, smiling at Him in joke, and looking at Him with a loving attitude. Indeed, when they approached Him for the *rāsa* dance, they said, "Dear Kṛṣṇa, by seeing Your beautiful face decorated with tresses of hair, by seeing the beauty of Your earrings falling on your cheeks, and by seeing the nectar of Your lips, the beauty of Your smiling glances, Your two arms, which assure complete fearlessness, and Your broad chest, whose beauty arouses conjugal attraction, we have simply surrendered ourselves to becoming Your maidservants." *(p. 130)*

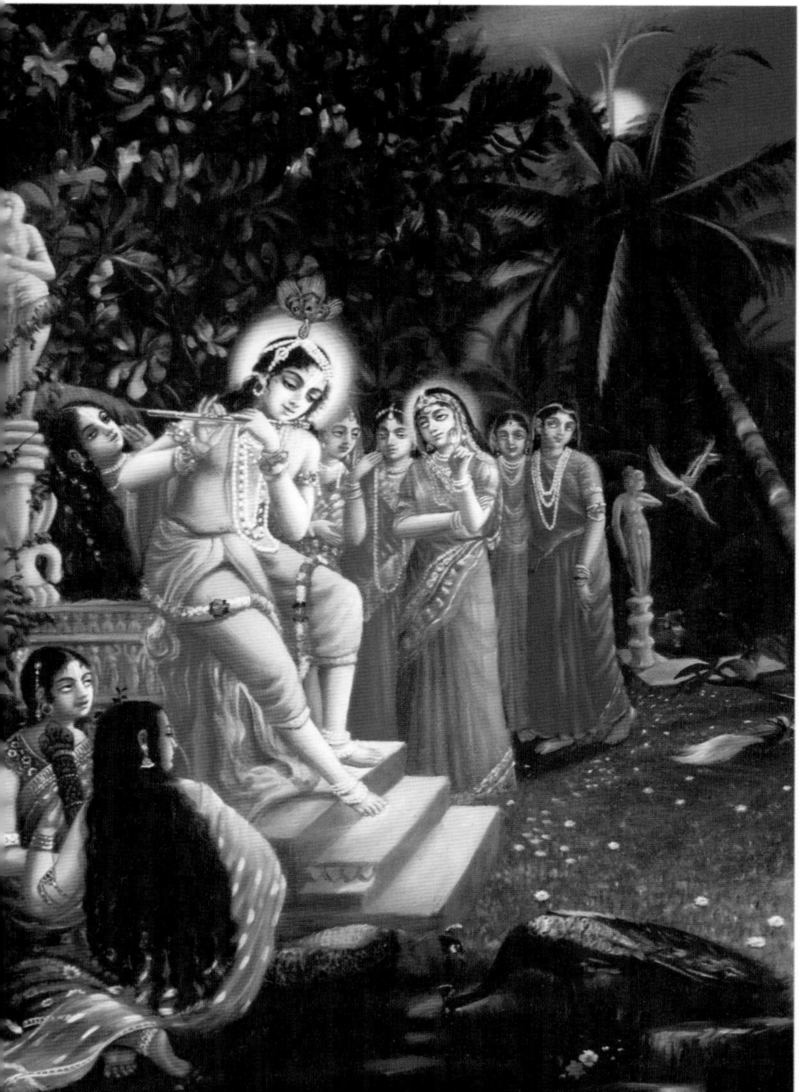

PLATE FIVE

Because of Lord Kṛṣṇa's absence from the transcendental city of Dvārakā, the citizens were in a state of melancholy, just as we are in a state of melancholy at night because of the absence of the sun. Upon reaching the border of Dvārakā, Lord Kṛṣṇa sounded His auspicious conchshell, heralding His arrival and pacifying the dejection of the inhabitants. Having heard that sound, which threatens fear personified, the citizens of Dvārakā began running toward Him fast just to have His long-desired audience. As they approached Him, they saw that the white, fat-bowled conchshell gripped by the Lord's hand appeared reddened by the touch of His transcendental lips. Indeed, it seemed like a white swan playing in the stems of red lotus flowers. *(pp. 195–196)*

PLATE SIX

While entering the city of Dvārakā, Lord Kṛṣṇa acknowledged all the inhabitants' greetings by casting His transcendental glance over them. The city was filled with the opulences of all seasons. There were hermitages, orchards, flower gardens, parks and reservoirs of water filled with lotus flowers. The highways, subways, lanes, markets and public meeting places were all thoroughly cleansed and then moistened with scented water. And to welcome the Lord, the residents of Dvārakā strew flowers, fruits and unbroken seeds everywhere. The residents hastened toward the Lord on chariots, upon which rode *brāhmaṇas* bearing flowers. In front of the chariots were elephants, which are emblems of good fortune. Conchshells and bugles were sounded, and Vedic hymns were chanted. Thus, the residents offered their respects, which were saturated with affection. In return, Lord Kṛṣṇa, the Personality of Godhead, approached them and offered due honor and respect to each and every one of the friends, relatives, citizens and others who came to receive and welcome Him. As the Lord passed along the public road of Dvārakā, His head was protected from sunshine by a white umbrella. White feathered fans moved in semicircles, and showers of flowers fell upon the road. His yellow garments and garlands of flowers made it appear as if a dark cloud were surrounded simultaneously by the sun, the moon, lightning and rainbows. *(pp. 205–229)*

PLATE SEVEN

When Lord Kṛṣṇa entered His palaces, which were perfect to the fullest extent, His 16,108 queens rejoiced within their minds to see their husband home after a long period abroad. The queens got up at once from their meditation seats and, as was socially customary, covered their faces shyly and looked about coyly. The insuperable ecstasy was so strong that they first embraced the Lord in the innermost recesses of their hearts, then they embraced Him visually, then sent their sons to embrace Him, and finally, though they tried to restrain their feelings, they shed tears. *(pp. 232–236)*

Him. He is one without a second, and therefore the Almighty Lord can appear in any form without being contaminated by the material conception. Therefore, festivities in the temple of the Lord, as held generally, are like festivals performed during the manifestive days of the Lord of Dvārakā, about five thousand years ago. The authorized *ācāryas*, who know the science perfectly, install such temples of the Lord under regulative principles just to offer facilities to the common man, but persons who are less intelligent, without being conversant with the science, mistake this great attempt to be *idol worship* and poke their nose into that to which they have no access. Therefore, the ladies or men who observe festivals in the temples of the Lord just to have a look at the transcendental form are a thousand times more glorious than those who are nonbelievers in the transcendental form of the Lord.

It appears from the verse that the inhabitants of Dvārakā were all owners of big palaces. This indicates the prosperity of the city. The ladies got up on the roofs just to have a look at the procession and the Lord. The ladies did not mix with the crowd on the street, and thus their respectability was perfectly observed. There was no artificial equality with the man. Female respectability is preserved more elegantly by keeping the woman separate from the man. The sexes should not mix unrestrictedly.

TEXT 25

नित्यं निरीक्षमाणानां यदपि द्वारकौकसाम् ।
न वितृप्यन्ति हि दृशः श्रियोधामाङ्गमच्युतम् ॥२५॥

nityaṁ nirīkṣamāṇānāṁ
yad api dvārakaukasām
na vitṛpyanti hi dṛśaḥ
śriyo dhāmāṅgam acyutam

nityam—regularly, always; *nirīkṣamāṇānām*—of those who look at Him; *yat*—although; *api*—in spite of; *dvārakā-okasām*—the inhabitants of Dvārakā; *na*—never; *vitṛpyanti*—satisfied; *hi*—exactly; *dṛśaḥ*—sight; *śriyaḥ*—beauties; *dhāma-aṅgam*—the bodily reservoir; *acyutam*—the infallible.

TRANSLATION

The inhabitants of Dvārakā were regularly accustomed to look upon the reservoir of all beauty, the infallible Lord, yet they were never satiated.

PURPORT

When the ladies of the city of Dvārakā got up on the roofs of their palaces, they never thought that they had previously many times seen the beautiful body of the infallible Lord. This indicates that they had no satiation in desiring to see the Lord. Anything material seen for a number of times ultimately becomes unattractive by the law of satiation. The law of satiation acts materially, but there is no scope for it in the spiritual realm. The word infallible is significant here, because although the Lord has mercifully descended on earth, He is still infallible. The living entities are fallible because when they come in contact with the material world they lack their spiritual identity, and thus the body materially obtained becomes subjected to birth, growth, transformation, situation, deterioration and annihilation under the laws of nature. The Lord's body is not like that. He descends as He is and is never under the laws of the material modes. His body is the source of everything that be, the reservoir of all beauties beyond our experience. No one, therefore, is satiated by seeing the transcendental body of the Lord because there are always manifestations of newer and newer beauties. The transcendental name, form, qualities, entourage, etc., are all spiritual manifestations, and there is no satiation in chanting the holy name of the Lord, there is no satiation in discussing the qualities of the Lord, and there is no limitation of the entourage of the Lord. He is the source of all and is limitless.

TEXT 26

श्रियो निवासो यस्योरः पानपात्रं मुखं दृशाम् ।
बाहवो लोकपालानां सारङ्गाणां पदाम्बुजम् ॥२६॥

śriyo nivāso yasyoraḥ
pāna-pātraṁ mukhaṁ dṛśām
bāhavo loka-pālānāṁ
sāraṅgāṇāṁ padāmbujam

śriyaḥ—of the goddess of fortune; *nivāsaḥ*—residential place; *yasya*—one whose; *uraḥ*—chest; *pāna-pātram*—the drinking pot; *mukham*—face; *dṛśām*—of eyes; *bāhavaḥ*—the arms; *loka-pālānām*—of the administrative demigods; *sāraṅgāṇām*—of the devotees who talk and sing of the essence or substance; *pada-ambujam*—the lotus feet.

TRANSLATION

The Lord's chest is the abode of the goddess of fortune. His moonlike face is the drinking vessel for eyes which hanker after all that is beautiful. His arms are the resting places for the administrative demigods. And His lotus feet are the refuge of pure devotees who never talk or sing of any subject except His Lordship.

PURPORT

There are different classes of human beings, all seeking different enjoyments from different objects. There are persons who are seeking after the favor of the goddess of fortune, and for them the Vedic literatures give information that the Lord is always served with all reverence by thousands and thousands of goddesses of fortune at the *cintāmaṇi-dhāma,** the transcendental abode of the Lord where the trees are all desire trees and the buildings are made of touchstone. The Lord Govinda is engaged there in herding the *surabhi* cows as His natural occupation. These goddesses of fortune can be seen automatically if we are attracted by the bodily features of the Lord. The impersonalists cannot observe such goddesses of fortune because of their dry speculative habit. And those who are artists, overtaken by the beautiful creation, should better see to the beautiful face of the Lord for complete satisfaction. The face of the Lord is the embodiment of beauty. What they call beautiful nature is but His smile, and what they call the sweet songs of the birds are but specimens of the whispering voice of the Lord. There are administrative demigods in charge of departmental service of cosmic management, and there are tiny administrative gods in the state service. They are always

---

**cintāmaṇi-prakara-sadmasu kalpa-vṛkṣa-*
lakṣāvṛteṣu surabhīr abhipālayantam
lakṣmī-sahasra-śata-sambhrama-sevyamānaṁ
govindam ādi-puruṣaṁ tam ahaṁ bhajāmi (Bs. 5.29)

afraid of other competitors, but if they take shelter of the arms of the Lord, the Lord can protect them always from the attacks of enemies. A faithful servant of the Lord engaged in the service of administration is the ideal executive head and can well protect the interest of the people in general. Other so-called administrators are symbols of anachronisms leading to the acute distress of the people who are governed by them. The administrators can remain safely under the protection of the arms of the Lord. The essence of everything is the Supreme Lord: He is called the *sāram.* And those who sing and talk about Him are called the *sāraṅgas,* or the pure devotees. The pure devotees are always hankering after the lotus feet of the Lord. The lotus has a kind of honey which is transcendentally relished by the devotees. They are like the bees who are always after the honey. Śrīla Rūpa Gosvāmī, the great devotee *ācārya* of the Gauḍīya-Vaiṣṇava-sampradāya, has sung a song about this lotus honey, comparing himself to the bee: "O my Lord Kṛṣṇa, I beg to offer my prayers unto You. My mind is like the bee, and it is after some honey. Kindly, therefore, give my bee-mind a place at Your lotus feet, which are the resources for all transcendental honey. I know that even big demigods like Brahmā do not see the rays of the nails of Your lotus feet, even though they are engaged in deep meditation for years together. Still, O infallible one, my ambition is such, for You are very merciful to your surrendered devotees. O Mādhava, I know also that I have no genuine devotion for the service of Your lotus feet, but because Your Lordship is inconceivably powerful, You can do what is impossible to be done. Your lotus feet can deride even the nectar of the heavenly kingdom, and therefore I am very much attracted by them. O supreme eternal, please, therefore, let my mind be fixed at Your lotus feet so that eternally I may be able to relish the taste of Your transcendental service." The devotees are satisfied with being placed at the lotus feet of the Lord and have no ambition to see His all-beautiful face or aspire for the protection of the strong arms of the Lord. They are humble by nature, and the Lord is always leaning towards such humble devotees.

TEXT 27

सितातपत्रव्यजनैरुपस्कृतः
प्रसूनवर्षैरभिवर्षितः पथि ।

पिशङ्गवासा वनमालया बभौ
घनो यथार्कोडुपचापवैद्युतैः ॥२७॥

sitātapatra-vyajanair upaskṛtaḥ
prasūna-varṣair abhivarṣitaḥ pathi
piśaṅga-vāsā vana-mālayā babhau
ghano yathārkoḍupa-cāpa-vaidyutaiḥ

sita-ātapatra—white umbrella; *vyajanaiḥ*—with a *cāmara* fan; *upaskṛtaḥ*—being served by; *prasūna*—flowers; *varṣaiḥ*—by the showers; *abhivarṣitaḥ*—thus being covered; *pathi*—on the road; *piśaṅga-vāsāḥ*—by the yellow garments; *vana-mālayā*—by the flower garlands; *babhau*—thus it became; *ghanaḥ*—cloud; *yathā*—as if; *arka*—the sun; *uḍupa*—the moon; *cāpa*—the rainbow; *vaidyutaiḥ*—by the lightning.

TRANSLATION

As the Lord passed along the public road of Dvārakā, His head was protected from the sunshine by a white umbrella. White feathered fans moved in semicircles, and showers of flowers fell upon the road. His yellow garments and garlands of flowers made it appear as if a dark cloud were surrounded simultaneously by sun, moon, lightning and rainbows.

PURPORT

The sun, moon, rainbow and lightning do not appear in the sky simultaneously. When there is sun, the moonlight becomes insignificant, and if there are clouds and a rainbow, there is no manifestation of lightning. The Lord's bodily hue is just like a new monsoon cloud. He is compared herein to the cloud. The white umbrella over His head is compared to the sun. The movement of the bunch-hair fan of flukes is compared to the moon. The showers of flowers are compared to the stars. His yellow garments are compared to the rainbow. So all these activities of the firmament, being impossible simultaneous factors, cannot be adjusted by comparison. The adjustment is possible only when we think of the inconceivable potency of the Lord. The Lord is all-powerful, and in His presence anything impossible can be made possible by His inconceivable energy. But the situation created at the time of His passing on the roads of Dvārakā was beautiful and could not be compared to anything besides the description of natural phenomena.

TEXT 28

प्रविष्टस्तु गृहं पित्रोः परिष्वक्तः स्वमातृभिः ।
ववन्दे शिरसा सप्त देवकीप्रमुखा मुदा ॥२८॥

praviṣṭas tu gṛhaṁ pitroḥ
pariṣvaktaḥ sva-mātṛbhiḥ
vavande śirasā sapta
devakī-pramukhā mudā

praviṣṭaḥ—after entering; *tu*—but; *gṛham*—houses; *pitroḥ*—of the father; *pariṣvaktaḥ*—embraced; *sva-mātṛbhiḥ*—by His own mothers; *vavande*—offered obeisances; *śirasā*—His head; *sapta*—seven; *devakī*—Devakī; *pramukhā*—headed by; *mudā*—gladly.

TRANSLATION

After entering the house of His father, He was embraced by the mothers present, and the Lord offered His obeisances unto them by placing His head at their feet. The mothers were headed by Devakī [His real mother].

PURPORT

It appears that Vasudeva, the father of Lord Kṛṣṇa, had completely separate residential quarters where he lived with his eighteen wives, out of whom Śrīmatī Devakī is the real mother of Lord Kṛṣṇa. But in spite of this, all other stepmothers were equally affectionate to Him, as will be evident from the following verse. Lord Kṛṣṇa also did not distinguish His real mother from His stepmothers, and He equally offered His obeisances unto all the wives of Vasudeva present on the occasion. According to scriptures also, there are seven mothers: (1) the real mother, (2) the wife of the spiritual master, (3) the wife of a *brāhmaṇa*, (4) the wife of the king, (5) the cow, (6) the nurse, and (7) the earth. All of them are mothers. Even by this injunction of the *śāstras*, the stepmother, who is the wife of the father, is also as good as the mother because the father is also one of the spiritual masters. Lord Kṛṣṇa, the Lord of the universe, plays the part of an ideal son just to teach others how to treat their stepmothers.

TEXT 29

ताः पुत्रमङ्कमारोप्य स्नेहस्नुतपयोधराः ।
हर्षविह्वलितात्मानः सिषिचुर्नेत्रजैर्जलैः ॥२९॥

tāḥ putram aṅkam āropya
sneha-snuta-payodharāḥ
harṣa-vihvalitātmānaḥ
siṣicur netrajair jalaiḥ

tāḥ—all of them; *putram*—the son; *aṅkam*—the lap; *āropya*—having placed on; *sneha-snuta*—moistened by affection; *payodharāḥ*—breasts filled up; *harṣa*—delight; *vihvalita-ātmānaḥ*—overwhelmed by; *siṣicuḥ*—wet; *netrajaiḥ*—from the eyes; *jalaiḥ*—water.

TRANSLATION

The mothers, after embracing their son, sat Him on their laps. Due to pure affection, milk sprang from their breasts. They were overwhelmed with delight, and the tears from their eyes wetted the Lord.

PURPORT

When Lord Kṛṣṇa was at Vṛndāvana even the cows would become moistened by affection towards Him, and He would draw milk from the nipples of every affectionate living being, so what to speak of the stepmothers who were already as good as His own mother.

TEXT 30

अथाविशत् स्वभवनं सर्वकाममनुत्तमम् ।
प्रासादा यत्र पत्नीनां सहस्राणि च षोडश ॥३०॥

athāviśat sva-bhavanaṁ
sarva-kāmam anuttamam
prāsādā yatra patnīnāṁ
sahasrāṇi ca ṣoḍaśa

atha—thereafter; *aviśat*—entered; *sva-bhavanam*—personal palaces; *sarva*—all; *kāmam*—desires; *anuttamam*—perfect to the fullest extent; *prāsādāḥ*—palaces; *yatra*—where; *patnīnām*—of the wives numbering; *sahasrāṇi*—thousands; *ca*—over and above; *ṣoḍaśa*—sixteen.

TRANSLATION

Thereafter, the Lord entered His palaces, which were perfect to the fullest extent. His wives lived in them, and they numbered over sixteen thousand.

PURPORT

Lord Kṛṣṇa had 16,108 wives, and for each and every one of them there was a fully equipped palace complete with necessary compounds and gardens. Full description of these palaces is given in the Tenth Canto. All the palaces were made of the best marble stone. They were illuminated by jewels and decorated by curtains and carpets of velvet and silk, nicely bedecked and embroidered with gold lace. The Personality of Godhead means one who is full with all power, all energy, all opulences, all beauties, all knowledge and all renunciation. Therefore, in the palaces of the Lord there was nothing wanting for fulfilling all desires of the Lord. The Lord is unlimited, and therefore His desires are also unlimited, and the supply is also unlimited. Everything being unlimited, it is concisely described here as *sarva-kāmam*, or full with all desirable equipment.

TEXT 31

पत्न्यः पतिं प्रोष्य गृहानुपागतं
विलोक्य संजातमनोमहोत्सवाः ।
उत्तस्थुरारात् सहसासनाशयात्
साकं व्रतैर्व्रीडितलोचनाननाः ॥३१॥

patnyaḥ patiṁ proṣya gṛhānupāgataṁ
vilokya sañjāta-mano-mahotsavāḥ
uttasthur ārāt sahasāsanāśayāt
sākaṁ vratair vrīḍita-locanānanāḥ

patnyaḥ—the ladies (wives of Lord Śrī Kṛṣṇa); *patim*—husband; *proṣya*—who was away from home; *gṛha-anupāgatam*—now returned home; *vilokya*—thus seeing; *sañjāta*—having developed; *manaḥ-mahā-utsavāḥ*—a sense of joyful ceremony within the mind; *uttasthuḥ*—got up; *ārāt*—from a distance; *sahasā*—all of a sudden; *āsanā*—from the seats; *āśayāt*—from the state of meditation; *sākam*—along with; *vrataiḥ*—the vow; *vrīḍita*—looking coyly; *locana*—eyes; *ānanāḥ*—with such faces.

TRANSLATION

The queens of Lord Śrī Kṛṣṇa rejoiced within their minds to see their husband home after a long period abroad. The queens got up at once from their seats and meditations. As was socially customary, they covered their faces shyly and looked about coyly.

PURPORT

As mentioned above, the Lord entered His home palaces occupied by 16,108 queens. This means that the Lord at once expanded Himself in as many plenary expansions as there were queens and palaces and entered in each and every one of them simultaneously and separately. Here is another manifestation of the feature of His internal potency. He can expand Himself in as many forms of spiritual identity as He desires, even though He is one without a second. It is confirmed by the *Śruti-mantra* that the Absolute is one alone, and yet He becomes many as soon as He so desires. These manifold expansions of the Supreme Lord are manifested as plenary and separated portions. The separated portions are representations of His energy, and the plenary portions are manifestations of His Personality. Thus the Personality of Godhead manifested Himself in 16,108 plenary expansions and simultaneously entered into each and every one of the palaces of the queens. This is called *vaibhava,* or the transcendental potency of the Lord. And because He can do so, He is also known as Yogeśvara. Ordinarily, a *yogī* or mystic living being is able to expand himself at utmost to tenfold expansions of his body, but the Lord can do so to the extent of as many thousands or infinitely, as He likes. Unbelievers become astonished to learn that Lord Kṛṣṇa married more than 16,000 queens because they think of Lord Kṛṣṇa as one of them and measure the potency of the Lord by their own limited potency. One should know, therefore, that the Lord is never on the level of the living beings, who are but expansions of His marginal potency, and one should never equalize the potent and the potency, although there is very little difference of quality between the potent and the potency. The queens were also expansions of His internal potency, and thus the potent and potencies are perpetually exchanging transcendental pleasures, known as pastimes of the Lord. One should not, therefore, become astonished to learn that the Lord married so many wives. On the contrary, one should affirm that even if the Lord marries sixteen thousand million wives, He is not completely manifesting His unlimited and inexhaustible potency. He married *only* 16,000 wives and entered in each and every one of the different palaces just to impress in the history of the human beings on the surface of the earth that the Lord is never equal to or less than any human being, however powerful he may be. No one, therefore, is either equal to or greater than the Lord. The Lord is always great in all respects. "God is great" is eternal truth.

Therefore, as soon as the queens saw from a distance their husband, who was away from home for long periods due to the Battle of Kurukṣetra, they all arose from the slumber of meditation and prepared to receive their most beloved. According to Yājñavalkya's religious injunctions, a woman whose husband is away from home should not take part in any social functions, should not decorate her body, should not laugh and should not go to any relative's house in any circumstance. This is the vow of the ladies whose husbands are away from home. At the same time, it is also enjoined that a wife should never present herself before the husband in an unclean state. She must decorate herself with ornaments and good dress and should always be present before the husband in a happy and joyous mood. The queens of Lord Kṛṣṇa were all in meditation, thinking of the Lord's absence, and were always meditating upon Him. The Lord's devotees cannot live for a moment without meditating on the Lord, and what to speak of the queens, who were all goddesses of fortune incarnated as queens in the pastimes of the Lord at

Dvārakā. They can never be separated from the Lord, either by presence or by trance. The *gopīs* at Vṛndāvana could not forget the Lord when the Lord was away in the forest cow herding. When the Lord boy Kṛṣṇa was absent from the village, the *gopīs* at home used to worry about Him traversing the rough ground with His soft lotus feet. By thinking thus, they were sometimes overwhelmed in trance and mortified in the heart. Such is the condition of the pure associates of the Lord. They are always in trance, and so the queens also were in trance during the absence of the Lord. Presently, having seen the Lord from a distance, they at once gave up all their engagements, including the vows of women as described above. According to Śrī Viśvanātha Carkavartī Ṭhākura, there was a regular psychological reaction on the occasion. First of all, rising from their seats, although they wanted to see their husband, they were deterred because of feminine shyness. But due to strong ecstasy, they overcame that stage of weakness and became caught up with the idea of embracing the Lord, and this thought factually made them unconscious of their surrounding environment. This prime state of ecstasy annihilated all other formalities and social conventions, and thus they escaped all stumbling blocks on the path of meeting the Lord. And that is the perfect stage of meeting the Lord of the soul, Śrī Kṛṣṇa.

TEXT 32

तमात्मजैर्दृष्टिभिरन्तरात्मना
दुरन्तभावाः परिरेभिरे पतिम् ।
निरुद्धमप्यास्रवदम्बु नेत्रयो-
र्विलज्जतीनां भृगुवर्य वैक्लवात् ॥३२॥

tam ātmajair dṛṣṭibhir antarātmanā
duranta-bhāvāḥ parirebhire patim
niruddham apy āsravad ambu netrayor
vilajjatīnāṁ bhṛgu-varya vaiklavāt

tam—Him (the Lord); *ātma-jaiḥ*—by the sons; *dṛṣṭibhiḥ*—by the sight; *antara-ātmanā*—by the innermost part of the heart; *duranta-bhāvāḥ*—insuperable ecstasy; *parirebhire*—embraced; *patim*—husband; *niruddham*—choked up; *api*—in spite of; *āsravat*—tears;

ambu—like drops of water; *netrayoḥ*—from the eyes; *vilajjatīnām*—of those situated in shyness; *bhṛgu-varya*—O chief of the Bhṛgus; *vaiklavāt*—inadvertently.

TRANSLATION

The insuperable ecstasy was so strong that the queens, who were shy, first embraced the Lord in the innermost recesses of their hearts. Then they embraced Him visually, and then they sent their sons to embrace Him [which is equal to personal embracing]. But, O chief amongst the Bhṛgus, though they tried to restrain their feelings, they inadvertently shed tears.

PURPORT

Although due to feminine shyness there were many hindrances to embracing the dear husband, Lord Śrī Kṛṣṇa, the queens performed that act by seeing Him, by putting Him in the cores of their hearts, and by sending their sons to embrace Him. Still, the act remained unfinished, and tears rolled down their cheeks despite all endeavors to check them. One indirectly embraces the husband by sending the son to embrace him because the son is developed as part of the mother's body. The embrace of the son is not exactly the embrace of husband and wife from the sexual point of view, but the embrace is satisfaction from the affectionate point of view. The embrace of the eyes is more effective in the conjugal relation, and thus according to Śrīla Jīva Gosvāmī there is nothing wrong in such an exchange of feeling between husband and wife.

TEXT 33

यद्यप्यसौ पार्श्वगतो रहोगत-
स्तथापि तस्याङ्घ्रियुगं नवं नवम् ।
पदे पदे का विरमेत तत्पदा-
चलापि यच्छ्रीर्न जहाति कर्हिचित् ॥३३॥

yadyapy asau pārśva-gato raho-gatas
tathāpi tasyāṅghri-yugaṁ navaṁ navam
pade pade kā virameta tat-padāc
calāpi yac chrīr na jahāti karhicit

yadi—although; *api*—certainly; *asau*—He (Lord Śrī Kṛṣṇa); *pārśva-gataḥ*—just by the side; *rahaḥ-gataḥ*—exclusively alone; *tathāpi*—still; *tasya*—His; *aṅghri-yugam*—the feet of the Lord; *navam navam*—newer and newer; *pade*—step; *pade*—in every step; *kā*—who; *virameta*—can be detached from; *tat-padāt*—from His feet; *calāpi*—moving; *yat*—whom; *śrīḥ*—the goddess of fortune; *na*—never; *jahāti*—quits; *karhicit*—at any time.

TRANSLATION

Although Lord Śrī Kṛṣṇa was constantly by their sides, as well as exclusively alone, His feet appeared to them to be newer and newer. The goddess of fortune, although by nature always restless and moving, could not quit the Lord's feet. So what woman can be detached from those feet, having once taken shelter of them?

PURPORT

Conditioned living beings are always after the favor of the goddess of fortune, although by nature she is moving from one place to another. In the material world no one is permanently fortunate, however clever one may be. There have been so many big empires in different parts of the world, there have been so many powerful kings all over the world, and there have been so many fortunate men, but all of them have been liquidated gradually. This is the law of material nature. But spiritually it is different. According to *Brahma-saṁhitā*, the Lord is served very respectfully by hundreds and thousands of goddesses of fortune. They are always in a lonely place also with the Lord. But still the association of the Lord is so inspiringly newer and newer that they cannot quit the Lord for a moment, even though they are by nature very restless and are moving about. The spiritual relation with the Lord is so enlivening and resourceful that no one can leave the company of the Lord, once having taken shelter of Him.

The living beings are by constitution feminine by nature. The male or enjoyer is the Lord, and all manifestations of His different potencies are feminine by nature. In the *Bhagavad-gītā*, the living beings are designated as *parā prakṛti*, or the superior potency. The material elements are *aparā prakṛti*, or inferior potency. Such potencies are always employed for the satisfaction of the employer, or the enjoyer. The supreme enjoyer is the Lord Himself, as stated in the *Bhagavad-gītā* (5.29). The potencies, therefore, when engaged directly in the service of the Lord, revive the natural color, and thus there is no disparity in the relation of the potent and potency.

Generally people engaged in service are always seeking some post under the government or the supreme enjoyer of the state. Since the Lord is the supreme enjoyer of everything in or outside the universe, it is happiness to be employed by Him. Once engaged in the supreme governmental service of the Lord, no living being wishes to be relieved from the engagement. The highest perfection of human life is to seek some employment under the Lord's supreme service. That will make one extremely happy. One need not seek the moving goddess of fortune without the relation of the Lord.

TEXT 34

एवं नृपाणां क्षितिभारजन्मना-
मक्षौहिणीभिः परिवृत्ततेजसाम् ।
विधाय वैरं श्वसनो यथानलं
मिथो वधेनोपरतो निरायुधः ॥३४॥

evaṁ nṛpāṇāṁ kṣiti-bhāra-janmanām
akṣauhiṇībhiḥ parivṛtta-tejasām
vidhāya vairaṁ śvasano yathānalaṁ
mitho vadhenoparato nirāyudhaḥ

evam—thus; *nṛpāṇām*—of the kings or administrators; *kṣiti-bhāra*—the burden of the earth; *janmanām*—born in that way; *akṣauhiṇībhiḥ*—empowered by a military strength of horses, elephants, chariots and infantry; *parivṛtta*—being puffed up by such surroundings; *tejasām*—prowess; *vidhāya*—having created; *vairam*—hostility; *śvasanaḥ*—interaction of the wind and the pipe plants; *yathā*—as it is; *analam*—fire; *mithaḥ*—with one another; *vadhena*—by killing them; *uparataḥ*—relieved; *nirāyudhaḥ*—by Himself without being a party to such fighting.

TRANSLATION

The Lord was pacified after killing those kings who were burdensome to the earth. They were puffed up with their military

strength, their horses, elephants, chariots, infantry, etc. He Himself was not a party in the fight. He simply created hostility between the powerful administrators, and they fought amongst themselves. He was like the wind which causes friction between bamboos and so sparks a fire.

PURPORT

As stated above, the living beings are not factual enjoyers of things which are manifested as God's creation. The Lord is the genuine proprietor and enjoyer of everything manifested in His creation. Unfortunately, influenced by the deluding energy, the living being becomes *a false enjoyer* under the dictation of the modes of nature. Puffed up by such a false sense of becoming God, the deluded living being increases his material strength by so many activities and thus becomes the burden of the earth, so much so that the earth becomes completely uninhabitable by the sane. This state of affairs is called *dharmasya glāniḥ*, or misuse of the energy of the human being. When such misuse of human energy is prominent, the saner living beings become perturbed by the awkward situation created by the vicious administrators, who are simply burdens of the earth, and the Lord appears by His internal potency just to save the saner section of humanity and to alleviate the burden due to the earthly administrators in different parts of the world. He does not favor either of the unwanted administrators, but by His potential power He creates hostility between such unwanted administrators, as the air creates fire in the forest by the friction of the bamboos. The fire in the forest takes place automatically by the force of the air, and similarly the hostility between different groups of politicians takes place by the unseen design of the Lord. The unwanted administrators, puffed up by false power and military strength, thus become engaged in fighting amongst themselves over ideological conflicts and so exhaust themselves of all powers. The history of the world reflects this factual will of the Lord, and it will continue to be enacted until the living beings are attached to the service of the Lord. In the *Bhagavad-gītā* this fact is very vividly described (Bg. 7.14). It is said, "The deluding energy is My potency, and thus it is not possible for the dependent living beings to supersede the strength of the material modes. But those who take shelter in Me [the Personality of Godhead Śrī Kṛṣṇa] can cross over the gigantic ocean of material energy." This means that no one can establish peace and prosperity in the world by fruitive activities or by speculative philosophy or ideology. The only way is to surrender unto the Supreme Lord and thus become free from the illusion of the deluding energy.

Unfortunately persons who are engaged in destructive work are unable to surrender to the Personality of Godhead. They are all fools of the first order; they are the lowest of the human species of life; they are robbed of their knowledge, although apparently they seem to be academically educated. They are all of the demoniac mentality, always challenging the supreme power of the Lord. Those who are very materialistic, always hankering after material power and strength, are undoubtedly fools of the first order because they have no information of the living energy, and being ignorant of that supreme spiritual science, they are absorbed in material science, which ends with the end of the material body. They are the lowest of human beings because the human life is especially meant for reestablishing the lost relation with the Lord, and they miss this opportunity by being engaged in material activities. They are robbed of their knowledge because even after prolonged speculation they cannot reach to the stage of knowing the Personality of Godhead, the *summum bonum* of everything. And all of them are men of demoniac principle, and they suffer the consequences, as did such materialistic heroes as Rāvaṇa, Hiraṇyakaśipu, Kaṁsa and others.

TEXT 35

स एष नरलोकेऽस्मिन्नवतीर्णः स्वमायया ।
रेमे स्त्रीरत्नकूटस्थो भगवान् प्राकृतो यथा ॥३५॥

sa eṣa nara-loke 'sminn
avatīrṇaḥ sva-māyayā
reme strī-ratna-kūṭastho
bhagavān prākṛto yathā

saḥ—He (the Supreme Personality of Godhead); *eṣaḥ*—all these; *nara-loke*—on this planet of human beings; *asmin*—on this; *avatīrṇaḥ*—having appeared; *sva*—personal, internal; *māyayā*—causeless mercy; *reme*—enjoyed; *strī-ratna*—woman who is competent to become a wife of the Lord; *kūṭasthaḥ*—among; *bhagavān*—the Personality of Godhead; *prākṛtaḥ*—mundane; *yathā*—as if it were.

TRANSLATION

That Supreme Personality of Godhead Śrī Kṛṣṇa, out of His causeless mercy, appeared on this planet by His internal potency and enjoyed Himself amongst competent women as if He were engaging in mundane affairs.

PURPORT

The Lord married and lived like a householder. This is certainly like a mundane affair, but when we learn that He married 16,108 wives and *lived with them separately* in each and every palace, certainly it is not mundane. Therefore, the Lord, living as a householder amongst His competent wives, is never mundane, and His behavior with them is never to be understood as mundane sex relation. The women who became the wives of the Lord are certainly not ordinary women, because to get the Lord as one's husband is the result of many, many millions of births' *tapasya* (austerity). When the Lord appears on different *lokas*, or planets, or on this planet of human beings, He displays His transcendental pastimes just to attract the conditioned souls to become His eternal servitors, friends, parents and lovers respectively in the transcendental world, where the Lord eternally reciprocates such exchanges of service. Service is pervertedly represented in the material world and broken untimely, resulting in sad experience. The illusioned living being conditioned by material nature cannot understand out of ignorance that all our relations here in the mundane world are temporary and full of inebrieties. Such relations cannot help us be happy perpetually, but if the same relation is established with the Lord, then we are transferred to the transcendental world after leaving this material body and become eternally related with Him in the relation we desire. The women amongst whom He lived as their husband are not, therefore, women of this mundane world, but are eternally related with Him as transcendental wives, a position which they attained by perfection of devotional service. That is their competency. The Lord is *paraṁ brahma*, or the Supreme Personality of Godhead. Conditioned souls seek after perpetual happiness in all places—not only on this earth but also on other planets throughout the universe—because constitutionally a spiritual spark, as he is, can travel to any part of God's creation. But being conditioned by the material modes, he tries to travel in space by spacecraft and so fails to reach his destination. The law of gravitation is binding upon him like the shackles of a prisoner. By other processes he can reach anywhere, but even if he reaches the highest planet, he cannot attain that perpetual happiness for which he is searching life after life. When he comes to his senses, however, he seeks after Brahman happiness, knowing it for certain that unlimited happiness, which he is seeking, is never attainable in the material world. As such, the Supreme Being, Parabrahman, certainly does not seek His happiness anywhere in the material world. Nor can His paraphernalia of happiness be found in the material world. He is not impersonal. Because He is the leader and Supreme Being amongst innumerable living beings, He cannot be impersonal. He is exactly like us, and He has all the propensities of an individual living being in fullness. He marries exactly like us, but His marriage is neither mundane nor limited by our experience in the conditioned state. His wives, therefore, appear like mundane women, but factually they are all transcendental liberated souls, perfect manifestations of internal energy.

TEXT 36

उद्दाममावपिशुनामलवल्गुहास-
व्रीडावलोकनिहतो मदनोऽपि यासाम् ।
सम्मुह्य चापमजहात्प्रमदोत्तमास्ता
यस्येन्द्रियं विमथितुं कुहकैर्न शेकुः ॥३६॥

uddāma-bhāva-piśunāmala-valgu-hāsa-
vrīḍāvaloka-nihato madano 'pi yāsām
sammuhya cāpam ajahāt pramadottamās tā
yasyendriyaṁ vimathituṁ kuhakair na śekuḥ

uddāma—very grave; *bhāva*—expression; *piśuna*—exciting; *amala*—spotless; *valgu-hāsa*—beautiful smiling; *vrīḍa*—corner of the eye; *avaloka*—looking; *nihataḥ*—conquered; *madanaḥ*—Cupid (or *amadana*—the greatly tolerant Śiva); *api*—also; *yāsām*—whose;

sammuhya—being overpowered by; *cāpam*—bows; *ajahāt*—gave up; *pramada*—woman, who maddens; *uttamāḥ*—of high grade; *tā*—all; *yasya*—whose; *indriyam*—senses; *vimathitum*—to perturb; *kuhakaiḥ*—by magical feats; *na*—never; *śekuḥ*—was able.

TRANSLATION

Although the queens' beautiful smiles and furtive glances were all spotless and exciting, and although they could conquer Cupid himself by making him give up his bow in frustration, and although even the tolerant Śiva could fall victim to them, still, despite all their magical feats and attractions, they could not agitate the senses of the Lord.

PURPORT

The path of salvation or the path going back to Godhead always forbids the association of women, and the complete *sanātana-dharma* or *varṇāśrama-dharma* scheme forbids or restricts association with women. How, then, can one be accepted as the Supreme Personality of Godhead who is addicted to more than sixteen thousand wives? This question may be relevantly raised by inquisitive persons really anxious to know about the transcendental nature of the Supreme Lord. And to answer such questions, the sages at Naimiṣāraṇya have discussed the transcendental character of the Lord in this and in following verses. It is clear herein that the feminine attractive features which can conquer Cupid or even the supermost tolerant Lord Śiva could not conquer the senses of the Lord. Cupid's business is to invoke mundane lust. The whole universe is moving being agitated by Cupid's arrow. The activities of the world are being carried on by the central attraction of male and female. A male is searching after a mate to his liking, and the female is looking after a suitable male. That is the way of material stimulus. And as soon as a male is combined with a female, the material bondage of the living being is at once tightly interlocked by sex relation, and as a result of this, both the male's and female's attraction for sweet home, motherland, bodily offspring, society and friendship and accumulation of wealth becomes the illusory field of activities, and thus a false but indefatigable attraction for the temporary material existence, which is full of miseries, is manifest. Those who are, therefore, on the path of salvation for going back home back to Godhead, are especially advised by all scriptural instruction to become free from such paraphernalia of material attraction. And that is possible only by the association of the devotees of the Lord, who are called the *mahātmās*. Cupid throws his arrow upon the living beings to make them mad after the opposite sex, whether the party is actually beautiful or not. Cupid's provocations are going on, even among beastly societies who are all ugly-looking in the estimation of the civilized nations. Thus Cupid's influence is exerted even amongst the ugliest forms, and what to speak of the most perfect beauties. Lord Śiva, who is considered to be most tolerant, was also struck by Cupid's arrow because he also became mad after the *Mohinī* incarnation of the Lord and acknowledged himself to be defeated. Cupid, however, was himself captivated by the grave and exciting dealings of the goddesses of fortune, and he voluntarily gave up his bow and arrow in a spirit of frustration. Such was the beauty and attraction of the queens of Lord Kṛṣṇa. Yet they could not disturb the transcendental senses of the Lord. This is because the Lord is all-perfect *ātmārāma*, or self-sufficient. He does not require anyone's extraneous help for His personal satisfaction. Therefore, the queens could not satisfy the Lord by their feminine attractiveness, but *they satisfied Him by their sincere affection and service.* Only by unalloyed transcendental loving service could they satisfy the Lord, and the Lord was pleased to treat them as wives in reciprocation. Thus being satisfied by their unalloyed service only, the Lord reciprocated the service just like a devout husband. Otherwise He had no business becoming the husband of so many wives. He is the husband of everyone, but to one who accepts Him as such, He reciprocates. This unalloyed affection for the Lord is never to be compared to mundane lust. It is purely transcendental. And the grave dealings, which the queens displayed in natural feminine ways, were also transcendental because the feelings were expressed out of transcendental ecstasy. It is already explained in the previous verse that the Lord appeared like a mundane husband, but factually His relation with His wives was transcendental, pure and unconditioned by the modes of material nature.

TEXT 37

तमयं मन्यते लोको ह्यसङ्गमपि सङ्गिनम् ।
आत्मौपम्येन मनुजं व्यापृण्वानं यतोऽबुधः ॥३७॥

tam ayaṁ manyate loko
hy asaṅgam api saṅginam
ātmaupamyena manujaṁ
vyāpṛṇvānaṁ yato 'budhaḥ

tam—unto Lord Kṛṣṇa; *ayam*—all these (common men); *manyate*—do speculate within the mind; *lokaḥ*—the conditioned souls; *hi*—certainly; *asaṅgam*—unattached; *api*—in spite of; *saṅginam*—affected; *ātma*—self; *aupamyena*—by comparison with the self; *manujam*—ordinary man; *vyāpṛṇvānam*—being engaged in; *yataḥ*—because; *abudhaḥ*—foolish because of ignorance.

TRANSLATION

The common materialistic conditioned souls speculate that the Lord is one of them. Out of their ignorance they think that the Lord is affected by matter, although He is unattached.

PURPORT

The word *abudhaḥ* is significant here. Due to ignorance only, the foolish mundane wranglers misunderstand the Supreme Lord and spread their foolish imaginations amongst innocent persons by propaganda. The Supreme Lord Śrī Kṛṣṇa is the original primeval Personality of Godhead, and when He was personally present before the eyes of everyone, He displayed full-fledged divine potency in every field of activities. As we have already explained in the first verse of *Śrīmad-Bhāgavatam*, He is completely independent to act however He likes, but all His actions are full of bliss, knowledge and eternity. Only the foolish mundaners misunderstand Him, unaware of His eternal form of knowledge and bliss, which is confirmed in the *Bhagavad-gītā* and *Upaniṣads*. His different potencies work in a perfect plan of natural sequence, and doing everything by the agency of His different potencies, He remains eternally the supreme independent. When He descends on the material world by His causeless mercy to different living beings, He does so by His own potency. He is not subject to any condition of the material modes of nature, and He descends as He is originally. The mental speculators misunderstand Him as the Supreme Person, and they consider His impersonal features as inexplicable Brahman to be all. Such a conception is also the product of conditioned life because they cannot go beyond their own personal capacity. Therefore, one who considers the Lord on the level of one's limited potency is only a common man. Such a man cannot be convinced that the Personality of Godhead is always unaffected by the modes of material nature. He cannot understand that the sun is always unaffected by infectious matter. The mental speculators compare everything from the standpoint of experimental knowledge of their own selves. Thus when the Lord is found to act like an ordinary person in matrimonial bondage, they consider Him to be like one of them, without considering that the Lord can at once marry sixteen thousand wives or more. Due to a poor fund of knowledge they accept one side of the picture while disbelieving the other. This means that due to ignorance only they always think of Lord Kṛṣṇa as like themselves and make their own conclusions, which are absurd and unauthentic from the version of the *Śrīmad-Bhāgavatam.*

TEXT 38

एतदीशनमीशस्य प्रकृतिस्थोऽपि तद्गुणैः ।
न युज्यते सदात्मस्थैर्यथा बुद्धिस्तदाश्रया ॥३८॥

etad īśanam īśasya
prakṛti-stho 'pi tad-guṇaiḥ
na yujyate sadātma-sthair
yathā buddhis tad-āśrayā

etat—this; *īśanam*—divinity; *īśasya*—of the Personality of Godhead; *prakṛti-sthaḥ*—being in contact with material nature; *api*—in spite of; *tat-guṇaiḥ*—by the qualities; *na*—never; *yujyate*—is affected; *sadā ātma-sthaiḥ*—by those who are situated in eternity; *yathā*—as is; *buddhiḥ*—intelligence; *tat*—the Lord; *āśrayā*—those who are under the shelter of.

TRANSLATION

This is the divinity of the Personality of Godhead: He is not affected by the qualities of material nature, even though He is in contact with them. Similarly, the devotees who have taken shelter of the Lord do not become influenced by the material qualities.

PURPORT

In the *Vedas* and Vedic literatures (*Śruti* and *Smṛti*) it is affirmed that in the Divinity there is nothing material. He is transcendental (*nirguṇa*) only, the supreme cognizant. Hari, or the Personality of Godhead, is the supreme transcendental person situated beyond the range of material affection. These statements are also confirmed even by Ācārya Śaṅkara. One may argue that His relation with the goddesses of fortune may be transcendental, but what about His relation with the Yadu dynasty, being born in that family, or His killing the nonbelievers like Jarāsandha and other *asuras* directly in contact with the modes of material nature. The answer is that the divinity of the Personality of Godhead is never in contact with the qualities of material nature in any circumstances. Actually He is in contact with such qualities because He is the ultimate source of everything, yet He is above the actions of such qualities. He is known, therefore, as Yogeśvara, or the master of mystic power, or in other words the all-powerful. Even His learned devotees are not affected by the influence of the material modes. The great six Gosvāmīs of Vṛndāvana all came from greatly rich and aristocratic families, but when they adopted the life of mendicants at Vṛndāvana, superficially they appeared to be in wretched conditions of life, but factually they were the richest of all in spiritual values. Such *mahā-bhāgavatas*, or first-grade devotees, although moving amongst men, are not contaminated by honor or insult, hunger or satisfaction, sleep or wakefulness, which are all resultant actions of the three modes of material nature. Similarly, some of them are engaged in worldly dealings, yet are unaffected. Unless these neutralities of life are there, one cannot be considered situated in transcendence. The Divinity and His associates are on the same transcendental plane, and their glories are always sanctified by the action of *yogamāyā*, or the internal potency of the Lord. The devotees of the Lord are always transcendental, even if they are sometimes found to have fallen in their behavior. The Lord emphatically declares in the *Bhagavad-gītā* (9.30) that even if an unalloyed devotee is found to be fallen due to a previous material contamination, he is nevertheless to be accepted as fully transcendental because of his being engaged cent percent in the devotional service of the Lord. The Lord protects him always because of his rendering service unto Him, and the fallen conditions are to be considered accidental and temporary. They will vanish in no time.

TEXT 39

तं मेनिरेऽबला मूढाः स्त्रैणं चानुव्रतं रहः ।
अप्रमाणविदो भर्तुरीश्वरं मतयो यथा ॥३९॥

taṁ menire 'balā mūḍhāḥ
straiṇaṁ cānuvrataṁ rahaḥ
apramāṇa-vido bhartur
īśvaraṁ matayo yathā

tam—unto Lord Śrī Kṛṣṇa; *menire*—took it for granted; *abalāḥ*—delicate; *mūḍhāḥ*—because of simplicity; *straiṇam*—one who is dominated by his wife; *ca*—also; *anuvratam*—follower; *rahaḥ*—lonely place; *apramāṇa-vidaḥ*—unaware of the extent of glories; *bhartuḥ*—of their husband; *īśvaram*—the supreme controller; *matayaḥ*—thesis; *yathā*—as it is.

TRANSLATION

The simple and delicate women truly thought that Lord Śrī Kṛṣṇa, their beloved husband, followed them and was dominated by them. They were unaware of the extent of the glories of their husband, as the atheists are unaware of Him as the supreme controller.

PURPORT

Even the transcendental wives of Lord Śrī Kṛṣṇa did not know completely the unfathomable glories of the Lord. This ignorance is not mundane because there is some action of the internal potency of the Lord in the exchange of feelings between Him and His eternal associates. The Lord exchanges transcendental relations in five ways, as proprietor, master, friend, son and lover, and in each of these pastimes He plays fully by the potency of *yogamāyā*, the internal potency. He plays exactly like an equal friend with the cowherd boys or even with friends like Arjuna. He plays exactly like a son in the presence of Yaśodāmātā, He plays exactly like a lover in the presence of the cowherd damsels, and He plays exactly like a husband in the presence of the queens of Dvārakā. Such devotees of the Lord never think of the Lord as the Supreme, but think of Him exactly as a common friend, a pet son, or a lover or husband very much dear to heart and soul. That is the relation between the Lord and His transcendental devotees, who act as His associates in the spiritual sky, where there are innumerable Vaikuṇṭha planets. When the Lord descends, He does so along with His entourage to display a complete picture of the transcendental world, where pure love and devotion for the Lord prevail without any mundane tinge of lording it over the creation of the Lord. Such devotees of the Lord are all liberated souls, perfect representations of the marginal or internal potency in complete negation of the influence of the external potency. The wives of Lord Kṛṣṇa were made to forget the immeasurable glories of the Lord by the internal potency so that there might not be any flaw of exchange, and they took it for granted that the Lord was a henpecked husband, always following them in lonely places. In other words, even the personal associates of the Lord do not know Him perfectly well, so what do the thesis writers or mental speculators know about the transcendental glories of the Lord? The mental speculators present different theses as to His becoming the causes of the creation, the ingredients of the creation, or the material and efficient cause of the creation, etc., but all this is but partial knowledge about the Lord. Factually they are as ignorant as the common man. The Lord can be known by the mercy of the Lord only, and by no other means. But since the dealings of the Lord with His wives are based on pure transcendental love and devotion, the wives are all on the transcendental plane without material contamination.

Thus end the Bhaktivedanta purports of the First Canto, Eleventh Chapter, of the Śrīmad-Bhāgavatam, *entitled "Lord Kṛṣṇa's Entrance into Dvārakā."*

CHAPTER TWELVE

Birth of Emperor Parīkṣit

TEXT 1

श्रीशौनक उवाच
अश्वत्थाम्नोपसृष्टेन ब्रह्मशीर्ष्णोरुतेजसा ।
उत्तराया हतो गर्भ ईशेनाजीवितः पुनः ॥ १ ॥

śaunaka uvāca
aśvatthāmnopasṛṣṭena
brahma-śīrṣṇoru-tejasā
uttarāyā hato garbha
īśenājīvitaḥ punaḥ

śaunakaḥ uvāca—the sage Śaunaka said; *aśvatthāmna*—of Aśvatthāmā (the son of Droṇa); *upasṛṣtena*—by release of; *brahma-śīrṣṇā*—the invincible weapon, *brahmāstra; uru-tejasā*—by high temperature; *uttarāyāḥ*—of Uttarā (mother of Parīkṣit); *hataḥ*—being spoiled; *garbhaḥ*—womb; *īśena*—by the Supreme Lord; *ājīvitaḥ*—brought to life; *punaḥ*—again.

TRANSLATION

The sage Śaunaka said: The womb of Uttarā, mother of Mahārāja Parīkṣit, was spoiled by the dreadful and invincible brahmāstra weapon released by Aśvatthāmā. But Mahārāja Parīkṣit was saved by the Supreme Lord.

PURPORT

The sages assembled in the forest of Naimiṣāraṇya inquired from Sūta Gosvāmī about the birth of Mahārāja Parīkṣit, but in the course of the narration other topics like the release of the *brahmāstra* by the son of Droṇa, his punishment by Arjuna, Queen Kuntīdevī's prayers, the Pāṇḍavas' visit to the place where Bhīṣmadeva was lying, his prayers and thereafter the Lord's departure for Dvārakā were discussed. His arrival at Dvārakā and residing with the sixteen thousand queens, etc., were narrated. The sages were absorbed in hearing such descriptions, but now they wanted to turn to the original topic, and thus the inquiry was made by Śaunaka Ṛṣi. So the subject of the release of the *brahmāstra* weapon by Aśvatthāmā is renewed.

TEXT 2

तस्य जन्म महाबुद्धेः कर्माणि च महात्मनः ।
निधनं च यथैवासीत्स प्रेत्य गतवान् यथा ॥ २ ॥

tasya janma mahā-buddheḥ
karmāṇi ca mahātmanaḥ
nidhanaṁ ca yathaivāsīt
sa pretya gatavān yathā

tasya—his (of Mahārāja Parīkṣit); *janma*—birth; *mahā-buddheḥ*—of great intelligence; *karmāṇi*—activities; *ca*—also; *mahā-ātmanaḥ*—of the great devotee; *nidhanam*—demise; *ca*—also; *yathā*—as it was; *eva*—of course; *āsīt*—happened; *saḥ*—he; *pretya*—destination after death; *gatavān*—achieved; *yathā*—as it were.

TRANSLATION

How was the great emperor Parīkṣit, who was a highly intelligent and great devotee, born in that womb? How did his death take place, and what did he achieve after his death?

PURPORT

The king of Hastināpura (now Delhi) used to be the emperor of the world, at least till the time of the son of Emperor Parīkṣit. Mahārāja Parīkṣit was saved by the Lord in the womb of his mother, so he could certainly be saved from an untimely death due to the ill will of the son of a *brāhmaṇa*. Because the age of Kali began to act just after the assumption of power by Mahārāja Parīkṣit, the first sign of misgivings was exhibited in the cursing of such a greatly intelligent and devoted king as Mahārāja Parīkṣit. The king is the protector of the helpless citizens, and their welfare, peace and prosperity depend on him. Unfortunately, by the instigation of the fallen age of Kali, an unfortunate *brāhmaṇa's* son was employed to condemn the innocent Mahārāja Parīkṣit, and so the

King had to prepare himself for death within seven days. Mahārāja Parīkṣit is especially famous as one who is protected by Viṣṇu, and when he was unduly cursed by a *brāhmaṇa's* son, he could have invoked the mercy of the Lord to save him, but he did not want to because he was a pure devotee. A pure devotee never asks the Lord for any undue favor. Mahārāja Parīkṣit knew that the curse of the *brāhmaṇa's* son upon him was unjustified, as everyone else knew, but he did not want to counteract it because he knew also that the age of Kali had begun and that the first symptom of the age, namely degradation of the highly talented *brāhmaṇa* community, had also begun. He did not want to interfere with the current of the time, but he prepared himself to meet death very cheerfully and very properly. Being fortunate, he got at least seven days to prepare himself to meet death, and so he properly utilized the time in the association of Śukadeva Gosvāmī, the great saint and devotee of the Lord.

TEXT 3

तदिदं श्रोतुमिच्छामो गदितुं यदि मन्यसे ।
ब्रूहि नः श्रद्दधानानां यस्य ज्ञानमदाच्छुकः ॥ ३ ॥

tad idaṁ śrotum icchāmo
gadituṁ yadi manyase
brūhi naḥ śraddadhānānāṁ
yasya jñānam adāc chukaḥ

tat—all; *idam*—this; *śrotum*—to hear; *icchāmaḥ*—all willing; *gaditum*—to narrate; *yadi*—if; *manyase*—you think; *brūhi*—please speak; *naḥ*—we; *śraddadhānānām*—who are very much respectful; *yasya*—whose; *jñānam*—transcendental knowledge; *adāt*—delivered; *śukaḥ*—Śrī Śukadeva Gosvāmī.

TRANSLATION

We all respectfully want to hear about him [Mahārāja Parīkṣit] to whom Śukadeva Gosvāmī imparted transcendental knowledge. Please speak on this matter.

PURPORT

Śukadeva Gosvāmī imparted transcendental knowledge to Mahārāja Parīkṣit during the remaining seven days of his life, and Mahārāja

Parīkṣit heard him properly, just like an ardent student. The effect of such a bona fide hearing and chanting of *Śrīmad-Bhāgavatam* was equally shared by both the hearer and the chanter. Both of them were benefited. Out of the nine different transcendental means of devotional service to the Lord prescribed in the *Bhāgavatam*, either all of them, or some of them or even one of them are equally beneficial if properly discharged. Mahārāja Parīkṣit and Śukadeva Gosvāmī were serious performers of the first two important items, namely the process of chanting and the process of hearing, and therefore both of them were successful in their laudable attempt. Transcendental realization is attained by such serious hearing and chanting and not otherwise. There is a type of spiritual master and disciple much advertised in this age of Kali. It is said that the master injects spiritual force into the disciple by an electrical current generated by the master, and the disciple begins to feel the shock. He becomes unconscious, and the master weeps for his exhausting his store of so-called spiritual assets. Such bogus advertisement is going on in this age, and the poor common man is becoming the victim of such advertisement. We do not find such folk tales in the dealings of Śukadeva Gosvāmī and his great disciple Mahārāja Parīkṣit. The sage recited *Śrīmad-Bhāgavatam* in devotion, and the great King heard him properly. The King did not feel any shock of electrical current from the master, nor did he become unconscious while receiving knowledge from the master. One should not, therefore, become a victim of these unauthorized advertisements made by some bogus representative of Vedic knowledge. The sages of Naimiṣāraṇya were very respectful in hearing about Mahārāja Parīkṣit because of his receiving knowledge from Śukadeva Gosvāmī by means of *ardent hearing*. Ardent hearing from the bona fide master is the only way to receive transcendental knowledge, and there is no need for medical performances or occult mysticism for miraculous effects. The process is simple, but only the sincere party can achieve the desired result.

TEXT 4

सूत उवाच

अपीपलद्धर्मराजः पितृवद् रञ्जयन् प्रजाः ।
निःस्पृहः सर्वकामेभ्यः कृष्णपादानुसेवया ॥ ४ ॥

sūta uvāca
apīpalad dharma-rājaḥ
pitṛvad rañjayan prajāḥ
niḥspṛhaḥ sarva-kāmebhyaḥ
kṛṣṇa-pādānusevayā

sūtaḥ uvāca—Śrī Sūta Gosvāmī said; *apīpalat*—administered prosperity; *dharma-rājaḥ*—King Yudhiṣṭhira; *pitṛ-vat*—exactly like his father; *rañjayan*—pleasing; *prajāḥ*—all those who took birth; *niḥspṛhaḥ*—without personal ambition; *sarva*—all; *kāmebhyaḥ*—from sense gratification; *kṛṣṇa-pāda*—the lotus feet of Lord Śrī Kṛṣṇa; *anusevayā*—by dint of rendering continuous service.

TRANSLATION

Śrī Sūta Gosvāmī said: Emperor Yudhiṣṭhira administered generously to everyone during his reign. He was exactly like his father. He had no personal ambition and was freed from all sorts of sense gratification because of his continuous service unto the lotus feet of the Lord Śrī Kṛṣṇa.

PURPORT

As mentioned in our introduction, "There is a need for the science of Kṛṣṇa in human society for all the suffering humanity of the world, and we simply request the leading personalities of all nations to take to the science of Kṛṣṇa for their own good, for the good of society, and for the good of all the people of the world." So it is confirmed herein by the example of Mahārāja Yudhiṣṭhira, the personality of goodness. In India the people hanker after *Rāma-rājya* because the Personality of Godhead was the ideal king and all other kings or emperors in India controlled the destiny of the world for the prosperity of every living being who took birth on the earth. Herein the word *prajāḥ* is significant. The etymological import of the word is "that which is born." On the earth there are many species of life, from the aquatics up to the perfect human beings, and all are known as *prajās*. Lord Brahmā, the creator of this particular universe, is known as the *prajāpati* because he is the grandfather of all who have taken birth. Thus *prajā* is used in a broader sense than it is now used. The king represents all living beings, the aquatics, plants, trees, reptiles, birds, animals and man. Every one of them is a part and parcel of the Supreme Lord (Bg. 14.4), and the king, being the representative of the Supreme Lord, is duty-bound to give proper protection to every one of them. This is not the case with the presidents and dictators of this demoralized system of administration, where the lower animals are given no protection while the higher animals are given so-called protection. But this is a great science which can be learned only by one who knows the *science of Kṛṣṇa.* By knowing the science of Kṛṣṇa, one can become the most perfect man in the world, and unless one has knowledge in this science, all qualifications and doctorate diplomas acquired by academic education are spoiled and useless. Mahārāja Yudhiṣṭhira knew this science of Kṛṣṇa very well, for it is stated here that by continuous cultivation of this science, or by continuous devotional service to Lord Kṛṣṇa, he acquired the qualification of administering the state. The father is sometimes seemingly cruel to the son, but that does not mean that the father has lost the qualification to be a father. A father is always a father because he always has the good of the son at heart. The father wants every one of his sons to become a better man than himself. Therefore, a king like Mahārāja Yudhiṣṭhira, who was the personality of goodness, wanted everyone under his administration, especially human beings who have better developed consciousness, to become devotees of Lord Kṛṣṇa so that everyone can become free from the trifles of material existence. His motto of administration was all good for the citizens, for as personified goodness he knew perfectly well what is actually good for them. He conducted the administration on that principle, and not on the *rākṣasi,* demonic, principle of sense gratification. As an ideal king, he had no personal ambition, and there was no place for sense gratification because all his senses at all times were engaged in the loving service of the Supreme Lord, which includes the partial service to the living beings, who form the parts and parcels of the complete whole. Those who are busy rendering service to the parts and parcels, leaving aside the whole, only spoil time and energy, as one does when watering the leaves of a tree without watering the root. If water is poured on the root, the leaves are enlivened perfectly and automatically, but if water is poured on the leaves only, the whole energy is spoiled. Mahārāja Yudhiṣṭhira, therefore, was constantly engaged in the service of the Lord, and thus the parts and parcels of the Lord, the living beings under his careful administration, were perfectly attended with all comforts in this life and all progress in the next. That is the way of perfect management of state administration.

TEXT 5

सम्पदः क्रतवो लोका महिषी भ्रातरो मही ।
जम्बुद्वीपाधिपत्यं च यशश्च त्रिदिवं गतम् ॥ ५ ॥

sampadaḥ kratavo lokā
mahiṣī bhrātaro mahī
jambudvīpādhipatyaṁ ca
yaśaś ca tri-divaṁ gatam

sampadaḥ—opulence; *kratavaḥ*—sacrifices; *lokāḥ*—future destination; *mahiṣī*—the queens; *bhrātaraḥ*—the brothers; *mahī*—the earth; *jambu-dvīpa*—the globe or planet of our residence; *ādhipatyam*—sovereignty; *ca*—also; *yaśaḥ*—fame; *ca*—and; *tri-divam*—celestial planets; *gatam*—spread over.

TRANSLATION

News even reached the celestial planets about Mahārāja Yudhiṣṭhira's worldly possessions, the sacrifices by which he would attain a better destination, his queen, his stalwart brothers, his extensive land, his sovereignty over the planet earth, and his fame, etc.

PURPORT

Only a rich and great man's name and fame are known all over the world, and the name and fame of Mahārāja Yudhiṣṭhira reached the higher planets because of his good administration, worldly possessions, glorious wife Draupadī, the strength of his brothers Bhīma and Arjuna, and his solid sovereign power over the world, known as Jambudvīpa. Here the word *lokāḥ* is significant. There are different *lokas* or higher planets scattered all over the sky, both material and spiritual. A person can reach them by dint of his work in the present life, as stated in

Bhagavad-gītā (9.25). No forceful entrance is allowed there. The tiny material scientists and engineers who have discovered vehicles to travel over a few thousand miles in outer space will not be allowed entrance. That is not the way to reach the better planets. One must qualify himself to enter into such happy planets by sacrifice and service. Those who are sinful in every step of life can expect only to be degraded into animal life to suffer more and more the pangs of material existence, and this is also stated in *Bhagavad-gītā* (16.19). Mahārāja Yudhiṣṭhira's good sacrifices and qualifications were so lofty and virtuous that even the residents of the higher celestial planets were already prepared to receive him as one of them.

TEXT 6

किं ते कामाः सुरस्पार्हा मुकुन्दमनसो द्विजाः ।
अधिजहुर्मुदं राज्ञः क्षुधितस्य यथेतरे ॥ ६ ॥

kiṁ te kāmāḥ sura-spārhā
mukunda-manaso dvijāḥ
adhijahrur mudaṁ rājñaḥ
kṣudhitasya yathetare

kim—what for; *te*—all those; *kāmāḥ*—objects of sense enjoyment; *sura*—of the denizens of heaven; *spārhāḥ*—aspirations; *mukunda-manasaḥ*—of one who is already God conscious; *dvijāḥ*—O *brāhmaṇas;* *adhijahruḥ*—could satisfy; *mudam*—pleasure; *rājñaḥ*—of the king; *kṣudhitasya*—of the hungry; *yathā*—as it is; *itare*—in other things.

TRANSLATION

O brāhmaṇas, the opulence of the King was so enchanting that the denizens of heaven aspired for it. But because he was absorbed in the service of the Lord, nothing could satisfy him except the Lord's service.

PURPORT

There are two things in the world which can satisfy living beings. When one is materially engrossed, he is satisfied only by sense gratification, but when one is liberated from the conditions of the material modes, he is satisfied only by rendering loving service for the satisfaction of the Lord. This means that the living being is constitutionally a *servitor,* and not one who is *served.* Being illusioned by the conditions of the external energy, one falsely thinks himself to be the served, but actually he is not served; he is servant of the senses like lust, desire, anger, avarice, pride, madness and intolerance. When one is in his proper senses by attainment of spiritual knowledge, he realizes that he is not the master of the material world, but is only a servant of the senses. At that time he begs for the service of the Lord and thus becomes happy without being illusioned by so-called material happiness. Mahārāja Yudhiṣṭhira was one of the liberated souls, and therefore for him there was no pleasure in a vast kingdom, good wife, obedient brothers, happy subjects and prosperous world. These blessings automatically follow for a pure devotee, even though the devotee does not aspire for them. The example set herein is exactly suitable. It is said that one who is hungry is never satisfied by anything other than food.

The whole material world is full of hungry living beings. The hunger is not for good food, shelter or sense gratification. *The hunger is for the spiritual atmosphere.* Due to ignorance only they think that the world is dissatisfied because there is not sufficient food, shelter, defense and objects of sense gratification. This is called illusion. When the living being is hungry for spiritual satisfaction, he is misrepresented by material hunger. But the foolish leaders cannot see that even the people who are most sumptuously materially satisfied are still hungry. And what is their hunger and poverty? This hunger is actually for spiritual food, spiritual shelter, spiritual defense and spiritual sense gratification. These can be obtained in the association of the Supreme Spirit, Lord Śrī Kṛṣṇa, and therefore one who has them cannot be attracted by the so-called food, shelter, defense and sense gratification of the material world, even if they are relished by the denizens of the heavenly planets. Therefore, in the *Bhagavad-gītā* (8.16) it is said by the Lord that even in the topmost planet of the universe, namely the Brahmaloka, where the duration of life is multiplied by millions of years by earth calculation, one cannot satisfy his hunger. Such hunger can be satisfied only when the living being is situated in immortality, which is attained in the spiritual sky, far, far above the Brahmaloka, in the association of Lord Mukunda, the Lord who awards His devotees the transcendental pleasure of liberation.

TEXT 7

मातुर्गर्भगतो वीरः स तदा भृगुनन्दन ।
ददर्श पुरुषं कञ्चिद्दह्यमानोऽस्त्रतेजसा ॥ ७ ॥

mātur garbha-gato vīraḥ
sa tadā bhṛgu-nandana
dadarśa puruṣaṁ kañcid
dahyamāno 'stra-tejasā

mātuḥ—mother; *garbha*—womb; *gataḥ*—being situated there; *vīraḥ*—the great fighter; *saḥ*—child Parīkṣit; *tadā*—at that time; *bhṛgu-nandana*—O son of Bhṛgu; *dadarśa*—could see; *puruṣam*—the Supreme Lord; *kañcit*—as someone else; *dahyamānaḥ*—suffering from being burned; *astra*—the *brahmāstra; tejasā*—temperature.

TRANSLATION

O son of Bhṛgu [Śaunaka], when the child Parīkṣit, the great fighter, was in the womb of his mother, Uttarā, and was suffering from the burning heat of the brahmāstra [thrown by Aśvatthāmā], he could observe the Supreme Lord coming to him.

PURPORT

Death generally involves remaining in trance for seven months. A living being, according to his own action, is allowed to enter into the womb of a mother by the vehicle of a father's semen, and thus he develops his desired body. This is the law of birth in specific bodies according to one's past actions. When he is awake from trance, he feels the inconvenience of being confined within the womb, and thus he wants to come out of it and sometimes fortunately prays to the Lord for such liberation. Mahārāja Parīkṣit, while in the womb of his mother, was struck by the *brahmāstra* released by Aśvatthāmā, and he was feeling the burning heat. But because he was a devotee of the Lord, the Lord at once appeared Himself within the womb by His all-powerful energy, and the child could see that someone else had come to save him. Even in that helpless condition, the child Parīkṣit endured the unbearable temperature due to his being a great fighter by nature. And for this reason the word *vīraḥ* has been used.

TEXT 8

अङ्गुष्ठमात्रममलं स्फुरत्पुरटमौलिनम् ।
अपीव्यदर्शनं श्यामं तडिद्वाससमच्युतम् ॥ ८ ॥

aṅguṣṭha-mātram amalaṁ
sphurat-puraṭa-maulinam
apīvya-darśanaṁ śyāmaṁ
taḍid vāsasam acyutam

aṅguṣṭha—by the measure of a thumb; *mātram*—only; *amalam*—transcendental; *sphurat*—blazing; *puraṭa*—gold; *maulinam*—helmet; *apīvya*—very beautiful; *darśanam*—to look at; *śyāmam*—blackish; *taḍit*—lightning; *vāsasam*—clothing; *acyutam*—the Infallible (the Lord).

TRANSLATION

He [the Lord] was only thumb high, but He was all transcendental. He had a very beautiful, blackish, infallible body, and He wore a dress of lightning yellow and a helmet of blazing gold. Thus He was seen by the child.

TEXT 9

श्रीमद्दीर्घचतुर्बाहुं तप्तकाञ्चनकुण्डलम् ।
क्षतजाक्षं गदापाणिमात्मनः सर्वतोदिशम् ।
परिभ्रमन्तमुल्काभां भ्रामयन्तं गदां मुहुः ॥ ९ ॥

śrīmad-dīrgha-catur-bāhuṁ
tapta-kāñcana-kuṇḍalam
kṣatajākṣaṁ gadā-pāṇim
ātmanaḥ sarvato diśam
paribhramantam ulkābhāṁ
bhrāmayantaṁ gadāṁ muhuḥ

śrīmat—enriched; *dīrgha*—prolonged; *catuḥ-bāhum*—four-handed; *tapta-kāñcana*—molten gold; *kuṇḍalam*—earrings; *kṣataja-akṣam*—eyes with the redness of blood; *gadā-pāṇim*—hand with a club; *ātmanaḥ*—own; *sarvataḥ*—all; *diśam*—around; *paribhramantam*—loitering; *ulkābhām*—like shooting stars; *bhrāmayantam*—encircling; *gadām*—the club; *muhuḥ*—constantly.

TRANSLATION

The Lord was enriched with four hands, earrings of molten gold and eyes blood red with fury. As He loitered about, His club constantly encircled Him like a shooting star.

PURPORT

It is said in the *Brahma-saṁhitā* (Ch. 5) that the Supreme Lord Govinda, by His one plenary portion, enters into the halo of the universe and distributes himself as Paramātmā, or the Supersoul, not only within the heart of every living being, but also within every atom of the material elements. Thus the Lord is all-pervading by His inconceivable potency, and thus He entered the womb of Uttarā to save His beloved devotee Mahārāja Parīkṣit. In the *Bhagavad-gītā* (9.31) the Lord assured everyone that His devotees are never to be vanquished. No one can kill a devotee of the Lord because he is protected by the Lord, and no one can save a person whom the Lord desires to kill. The Lord is all-powerful, and therefore He can both save and kill as He likes. He became visible to His devotee Mahārāja Parīkṣit even in that awkward position (in the womb of his mother) in a shape just suitable for his vision. The Lord can become bigger than thousands of universes and can become smaller than an atom at the same time. Merciful as He is, He becomes just suitable to the vision of the limited living being. He is unlimited. He is not limited by any measurement of our calculation. He can become bigger than what we can think of, and He can become smaller than what we can conceive. But in all circumstances He is the same all-powerful Lord. There is no difference between the thumblike Viṣṇu in the womb of Uttarā and the full-fledged Nārāyaṇa in the Vaikuṇṭha-dhāma, the kingdom of Godhead. He accepts the form of *arcā-vigraha* (worshipable Deity) just to accept service from His different incapable devotees. By the mercy of the *arcā-vigraha*, the form of the Lord in material elements, the devotees who are in the material world can easily approach the Lord, although He is not conceivable by the material senses. The *arcā-vigraha* is therefore an all-spiritual form of the Lord to be perceived by the material devotees; such an *arcā-vigraha* of the Lord is never to be considered material. There is no difference between matter and spirit for the Lord, although there is a gulf of difference between the two in the case of the conditioned living being. For the Lord there is nothing but spiritual existence, and similarly there is nothing except spiritual existence for the pure devotee of the Lord in his intimate relation with the Lord.

TEXT 10

अस्त्रतेजः स्वगदया नीहारमिव गोपतिः ।
विधमन्तं संनिकर्षे पर्यैक्षत क इत्यसौ ॥१०॥

astra-tejaḥ sva-gadayā
nīhāram iva gopatiḥ
vidhamantaṁ sannikarṣe
paryaikṣata ka ity asau

astra-tejaḥ—radiation of the *brahmāstra; sva-gadayā*—by means of His own club; *nīhāram*—drops of dew; *iva*—like; *gopatiḥ*—the sun; *vidhamantam*—the act of vanishing; *sannikarṣe*—nearby; *paryaikṣata*—observing; *kaḥ*—who; *iti asau*—this body.

TRANSLATION

The Lord was thus engaged in vanquishing the radiation of the brahmāstra, just as the sun evaporates a drop of dew. He was observed by the child, who thought about who He was.

TEXT 11

विधूय तदमेयात्मा भगवान्धर्मगुब् विभुः ।
मिषतो दशमासस्य तत्रैवान्तर्दधे हरिः ॥११॥

vidhūya tad ameyātmā
bhagavān dharma-gub vibhuḥ

miṣato daśamāsasya
tatraivāntardadhe hariḥ

vidhūya—having completely washed off; *tat*—that; *ameyātmā*—the all-pervading Supersoul; *bhagavān*—the Personality of Godhead; *dharma-gup*—the protector of righteousness; *vibhuḥ*—the Supreme; *miṣataḥ*—while observing; *daśamāsasya*—of one who is dressed by all directions; *tatra eva*—then and there; *antaḥ*—out of sight; *dadhe*—became; *hariḥ*—the Lord.

TRANSLATION

While thus being observed by the child, the Supreme Lord Personality of Godhead, the Supersoul of everyone and the protector of the righteous, who stretches in all directions and who is unlimited by time and space, disappeared at once.

PURPORT

Child Parīkṣit was not observing a living being who is limited by time and space. There is a gulf of difference between the Lord and the individual living being. The Lord is mentioned herein as the supreme living being unlimited by time and space. Every living being is limited by time and space. Even though a living being is qualitatively one with the Lord, quantitatively there is a great difference between the Supreme Soul and the common individual soul. In the *Bhagavad-gītā* both the living beings and the Supreme Being are said to be all-pervading (*yena sarvam idaṁ tatam*), yet there is a difference between these two kinds of all-pervasiveness. A common living being or soul can be all-pervading within his own limited body, but the supreme living being is all-pervading in all space and all time. A common living being cannot extend its influence over another common living being by its all-pervasiveness, but the Supreme Supersoul, the Personality of Godhead, is unlimitedly able to exert His influence over all places and all times and over all living beings. And because He is all-pervasive, unlimited by time and space, He can appear even within the womb of the mother of child Parīkṣit. He is mentioned herein as the protector of the righteous. Anyone who is a surrendered soul unto the Supreme is righteous, and he is specifically protected by the Lord in all circumstances. The Lord is the indirect protector of the unrighteous also, for He rectifies their sins through His external potency. The Lord is mentioned herein as one who is dressed in the ten directions. This means dressed with garments on ten sides, up and down. He is present everywhere and can appear and disappear at His will from everywhere and anywhere. His disappearance from the sight of the child Parīkṣit does not mean that He appeared on the spot from any other place. He was present there, and even after His disappearance He was there, although invisible to the eyes of the child. This material covering of the effulgent firmament is also something like a womb of the mother nature, and we are all put into the womb by the Lord, the father of all living beings. He is present everywhere, even in this material womb of mother Durgā, and those who are deserving can see the Lord.

TEXT 12

ततः सर्वगुणोदर्के सानुकूलग्रहोदये ।
जज्ञे वंशधरः पाण्डोर्भूयः पाण्डुरिवौजसा ॥१२॥

tataḥ sarva-guṇodarke
sānukūla-grahodaye
jajñe vaṁśa-dharaḥ pāṇḍor
bhūyaḥ pāṇḍur ivaujasā

tataḥ—thereupon; *sarva*—all; *guṇa*—good signs; *udarke*—having gradually evolved; *sa-anukūla*—all favorable; *grahodaye*—constellation of stellar influence; *jajñe*—took birth; *vaṁśa-dharaḥ*—heir apparent; *pāṇḍoḥ*—of Pāṇḍu; *bhūyaḥ*—being; *pāṇḍuḥ iva*—exactly like Pāṇḍu; *ojasā*—by prowess.

TRANSLATION

Thereupon, when all the good signs of the zodiac gradually evolved, the heir apparent of Pāṇḍu, who would be exactly like him in prowess, took birth.

PURPORT

Astronomical calculations of stellar influences upon a living being are not suppositions, but are factual, as confirmed in *Śrīmad-Bhāgavatam.* Every living being is controlled by the laws of nature at every minute, just as a citizen is controlled by the influence of the state. The state laws are grossly observed, but the laws of material nature, being subtle to our gross understanding, cannot be experienced grossly. As stated in the *Bhagavad-gītā* (3.9), every action of life produces another reaction, which is binding upon us, and only those who are acting on behalf of Yajña (Viṣṇu) are not bound by reactions. Our actions are judged by the higher authorities, the agents of the Lord, and thus we are awarded bodies according to our activities. The law of nature is so subtle that every part of our body is influenced by the respective stars, and a living being obtains his working body to fulfill his terms of imprisonment by the manipulation of such astronomical influence. A man's destiny is therefore ascertained by the birthtime constellation of stars, and a factual horoscope is made by a learned astrologer. It is a great science, and misuse of a science does not make it useless. Mahārāja Parīkṣit or even the Personality of Godhead appear in certain constellations of good stars, and thus the influence is exerted upon the body thus born at an auspicious moment. The most auspicious constellation of stars takes place during the appearance of the Lord in this material world, and it is specifically called *jayantī*, a word not to be abused for any other purposes. Mahārāja Parīkṣit was not only a great *kṣatriya* emperor, but also a great devotee of the Lord. Thus he cannot take his birth at any inauspicious moment. As a proper place and time is selected to receive a respectable personage, so also to receive such a personality as Mahārāja Parīkṣit, who was especially cared for by the Supreme Lord, a suitable moment is chosen when all good stars assembled together to exert their influence upon the King. Thus he took his birth just to be known as the great hero of *Śrīmad-Bhāgavatam.* This suitable arrangement of astral influences is never a creation of man's will, but is the arrangement of the superior management of the agency of the Supreme Lord. Of course, the arrangement is made according to the good or bad deeds of the living being. Herein lies the importance of pious acts performed by the living being. Only by pious acts can one be allowed to get good wealth, good education and beautiful features. The *saṁskāras* of the school of *sanātana-dharma* (man's eternal engagement) are highly suitable for creating an atmosphere for taking advantage of good stellar influences, and therefore *garbhādhāna-saṁskāra,* or the first seedling purificatory process prescribed for the higher castes, is the beginning of all pious acts to receive a good pious and intelligent class of men in human society. There will be peace and prosperity in the world due to good and sane population only; there is hell and disturbance only because of the unwanted, insane populace addicted to sex indulgence.

TEXT 13

तस्य प्रीतमना राजा विप्रैर्धौम्यकृपादिभिः ।
जातकं कारयामास वाचयित्वा च मङ्गलम् ॥१३॥

tasya prīta-manā rājā
viprair dhaumya-kṛpādibhiḥ
jātakaṁ kārayām āsa
vācayitvā ca maṅgalam

tasya—his; *prīta-manāḥ*—satisfied; *rājā*—King Yudhiṣṭhira; *vipraiḥ*—by the learned *brāhmaṇas; dhaumya*—Dhaumya; *kṛpa*—Kṛpa; *ādibhiḥ*—and others also; *jātakam*—one of the purificatory processes performed just after the birth of a child; *kārayām āsa*—had them performed; *vācayitvā*—by recitation; *ca*—also; *maṅgalam*—auspicious.

TRANSLATION

King Yudhiṣṭhira, who was very satisfied with the birth of Mahārāja Parīkṣit, had the purificatory process of birth performed. Learned brāhmaṇas, headed by Dhaumya and Kṛpa, recited auspicious hymns.

PURPORT

There is a need for a good and intelligent class of *brāhmaṇas* who are expert in performing the purificatory processes prescribed in the system of *varṇāśrama-dharma.* Unless such purificatory processes are performed, there is no possibility of good population, and in the age of Kali the population all over the world is of *śūdra* quality or lower for want of this purificatory process. It is not possible, however, to revive the Vedic process of purification in this age, for want of proper facilities and good *brāhmaṇas*, but there is the *Pāñcarātrika* system also recommended for this age. The *Pāñcarātrika* system acts on the *śūdra* class of men, supposedly the population of the Kali-yuga, and it is the prescribed purificatory process suitable to the age and time. Such a purificatory process is allowed only for spiritual upliftment and not for any other purpose. Spiritual upliftment is never conditioned by higher or lower parentage.

After the *garbhādhāna* purificatory process, there are certain other *saṁskāras* like *sīmāntonnayana, sadha-bhakṣaṇam,* etc., during the period of pregnancy, and when the child is born the first purificatory process is *jāta-karma.* This was performed duly by Mahārāja Yudhiṣṭhira with the help of good and learned *brāhmaṇas* like Dhaumya, the royal priest, and Kṛpācārya, who was not only a priest but also a great general. Both these learned and perfect priests, assisted by other good *brāhmaṇas,* were employed by Mahārāja Yudhiṣṭhira to perform the ceremony. Therefore all the *saṁskāras,* purificatory processes, are not mere formalities or social functions only, but they are all for practical purposes and can be successfully performed by expert *brāhmaṇas* like Dhaumya and Kṛpa. Such *brāhmaṇas* are not only rare, but also not available in this age, and therefore, for the purpose of spiritual upliftment in this fallen age, the Gosvāmīs prefer the purificatory processes under *Pāñcarātrika* formulas to the Vedic rites.

Kṛpācārya is the son of the great Ṛṣi Śaradvān and was born in the family of Gautama. The birth is said to be accidental. By chance, the great Ṛṣi Śaradvān met Jānapadī, a famous society girl of heaven, and the Ṛṣi Śaradvān discharged semen in two parts. By one part immediately a male child and by the other part a female child were born as twins. The male child was later on known as Kṛpa, and the female child was known as Kṛpī. Mahārāja Śantanu, while engaged in chase in the jungle, picked up the children and brought them up to the brahminical status by the proper purificatory process. Kṛpācārya later became a great general like Droṇācārya, and his sister was married to Droṇācārya. Kṛpācārya later on took part in the Battle of Kurukṣetra and joined the party of Duryodhana. Kṛpācārya helped kill Abhimanyu, the father of Mahārāja Parīkṣit, but he was still held in esteem by the family of the Pāṇḍavas due to his being as great a *brāhmaṇa* as Droṇācārya. When the Pāṇḍavas were sent to the forest after being defeated in the gambling game with Duryodhana, Dhṛtarāṣṭra entrusted the Pāṇḍavas to Kṛpācārya for guidance. After the end of the battle, Kṛpācārya again became a member of the royal assembly, and he was called during the birth of Mahārāja

Parīkṣit for recitation of auspicious Vedic hymns to make the ceremony successful. Mahārāja Yudhiṣṭhira, while quitting the palace for his great departure to the Himalayas, entrusted Kṛpācārya with Mahārāja Parīkṣit as his disciple, and he left home satisfied because of Kṛpācārya's taking charge of Mahārāja Parīkṣit. The great administrators, kings and emperors were always under the guidance of learned *brāhmaṇas* like Kṛpācārya and thus were able to act properly in the discharge of political responsibilities.

TEXT 14

हिरण्यं गां महीं ग्रामान् हस्त्यश्वान्नृपतिर्वरान् ।
प्रादात्स्वन्नं च विप्रेभ्यः प्रजातीर्थे स तीर्थवित्॥ १४॥

hiraṇyaṁ gāṁ mahīṁ grāmān
hasty-aśvān nṛpatir varān
prādāt svannaṁ ca viprebhyaḥ
prajā-tīrthe sa tīrthavit

hiraṇyam—gold; *gām*—cows; *mahīm*—land; *grāmān*—villages; *hasti*—elephants; *aśvān*—horses; *nṛpatiḥ*—the King; *varān*—rewards; *prādāt*—gave in charity; *su-annam*—good food grains; *ca*—and; *viprebhyaḥ*—unto the *brāhmaṇas; prajā-tīrthe*—on the occasion of giving in charity on the birthday of a son; *saḥ*—he; *tīrtha-vit*—one who knows how, when and where charity is to be given.

TRANSLATION

Upon the birth of a son, the King, who knew how, where and when charity should be given, gave gold, land, villages, elephants, horses and good food grains to the brāhmaṇas.

PURPORT

Only the *brāhmaṇas* and *sannyāsīs* are authorized to accept charity from the householders. In all the different occasions of *saṁskāras*, especially during the time of birth, marriage and death, wealth is distributed to the *brāhmaṇas* because the *brāhmaṇas* give the highest quality of service in regard to the prime necessity of humankind. The charity was substantial in the shape of gold, land, villages, horses, elephants and food grains, with other materials for cooking complete foodstuff. The *brāhmaṇas* were not, therefore, poor in the actual sense of the term. On the contrary, because they possessed gold, land, villages, horses, elephants and sufficient grains, they had nothing to earn for themselves. They would simply devote themselves to the well-being of the entire society.

The word *tīrthavit* is significant because the King knew well where and when charity has to be given. Charity is never unproductive or blind. In the *śāstras* charity was offered to persons who deserve to accept charity by dint of spiritual enlightenment. The so-called *daridra-nārāyaṇa*, a misconception of the Supreme Lord by unauthorized persons, is never to be found in the *śāstras* as the object of charity. Nor can a wretched poor man receive much munificent charity in the way of horses, elephants, land and villages. The conclusion is that the intelligent men, or the *brāhmaṇas* specifically engaged in the service of the Lord, were properly maintained without anxiety for the needs of the body, and the King and other householders gladly looked after all their comforts.

It is enjoined in the *śāstras* that as long as a child is joined with the mother by the navel pipe, the child is considered to be of one body with the mother, but as soon as the pipe is cut and the child is separated from the mother, the purificatory process of *jāta-karma* is performed. The administrative demigods and past forefathers of the family come to see a newly born child, and such an occasion is specifically accepted as the proper time for distributing wealth to the right persons productively for the spiritual advancement of society.

TEXT 15

तमूचुर्ब्राह्मणास्तुष्टा राजानं प्रश्रयान्वितम् ।
एष ह्यस्मिन् प्रजातन्तौ पुरूणां पौरवर्षभ ॥१५॥

tam ūcur brāhmaṇās tuṣṭā
rājānaṁ praśrayānvitam
eṣa hy asmin prajā-tantau
purūṇāṁ pauravarṣabha

tam—unto him; *ūcuḥ*—addressed; *brāhmaṇāḥ*—the learned *brāhmaṇas; tuṣṭāḥ*—very much satisfied; *rājānam*—unto the King;

praśraya-anvitam—very much obliging; *eṣaḥ*—this; *hi*—certainly; *asmin*—in the chain of; *prajā-tantau*—descending line; *purūṇām*—of the Pūrus; *paurava-ṛṣabha*—the chief among the Pūrus.

TRANSLATION

The learned brāhmaṇas, who were very satisfied with the charities of the King, addressed him as the chief amongst the Pūrus and informed him that his son was certainly in the line of descent from the Pūrus.

TEXT 16

दैवेनाप्रतिघातेन शुक्ले संस्थामुपेयुषि ।
रातो वोऽनुग्रहार्थाय विष्णुना प्रभविष्णुना ॥१६॥

daivenāpratighātena
śukle saṁsthām upeyuṣi
rāto vo 'nugrahārthāya
viṣṇunā prabhaviṣṇunā

daivena—by supernatural power; *apratighātena*—by what is irresistible; *śukle*—unto the pure; *saṁsthām*—destruction; *upeyuṣi*—having been enforced; *rātaḥ*—restored; *vaḥ*—for you; *anugraha-arthāya*—for the sake of obliging; *viṣṇunā*—by the all-pervasive Lord; *prabhaviṣṇunā*—by the all-powerful.

TRANSLATION

The brāhmaṇas said: This spotless son has been restored by the all-powerful and all-pervasive Lord Viṣṇu, the Personality of Godhead, in order to oblige you. He was saved when he was doomed to be destroyed by an irresistible supernatural weapon.

PURPORT

The child Parīkṣit was saved by the all-powerful and all-pervasive Viṣṇu (Lord Kṛṣṇa) for two reasons. The first reason is that the child in the womb of his mother was spotless due to his being a pure devotee of the Lord. The second reason is that the child was the only surviving male descendant of Puru, the pious forefather of the virtuous King

Yudhiṣṭhira. The Lord wants to continue the line of pious kings to rule over the earth as His representatives for the actual progress of a peaceful and prosperous life. After the Battle of Kurukṣetra, even up to the next generation of Mahārāja Yudhiṣṭhira was annihilated, and there were none who could generate another son in the great royal family. Mahārāja Parīkṣit, the son of Abhimanyu, was the only surviving heir apparent in the family, and by the irresistible supernatural *brahmāstra* weapon of Aśvatthāmā, he was forced to be annihilated. Lord Kṛṣṇa is described herein as Viṣṇu, and this is also significant. Lord Kṛṣṇa, the original Personality of Godhead, does the work of protection and annihilation in His capacity of Viṣṇu. Lord Viṣṇu is the plenary expansion of Lord Kṛṣṇa. The all-pervasive activities of the Lord are executed by Him in His Viṣṇu feature. Child Parīkṣit is described here as spotlessly white because he is an unalloyed devotee of the Lord. Such unalloyed devotees of the Lord appear on the earth just to execute the mission of the Lord. The Lord desires the conditioned souls hovering in the material creation to be reclaimed to go back home, back to Godhead, and thus He helps them by preparing the transcendental literatures like the *Vedas*, by sending missionaries of saints and sages and by deputing His representative, the spiritual master. Such transcendental literatures, missionaries and representatives of the Lord are spotlessly white because the contamination of the material qualities cannot even touch them. They are always protected by the Lord when they are threatened with annihilation. Such foolish threats are made by the gross materialists. The *brahmāstra*, which was thrown by Aśvatthāmā at the child Parīkṣit, was certainly supernaturally powerful, and nothing of the material world could resist its force of penetration. But the all-powerful Lord, who is present everywhere, within and without, could counteract it by His all-powerful potency just to save a bona fide servant of the Lord and descendant of another devotee, Mahārāja Yudhiṣṭhira, who was always obliged by the Lord by His causeless mercy.

TEXT 17

तस्मान्नाम्ना विष्णुरात इति लोके भविष्यति।
न संदेहो महाभाग महाभागवतो महान् ॥१७॥

tasmān nāmnā viṣṇu-rāta
iti loke bhaviṣyati

na sandeho mahā-bhāga
mahā-bhāgavato mahān

tasmāt—therefore; *nāmnā*—by the name; *viṣṇu-rātaḥ*—protected by Viṣṇu, the Personality of Godhead; *iti*—thus; *loke*—in all the planets; *bhaviṣyati*—shall become well known; *na*—no; *sandehaḥ*—doubts; *mahā-bhāga*—most fortunate; *mahā-bhāgavataḥ*—the first-class devotee of the Lord; *mahān*—qualified by all good qualities.

TRANSLATION

For this reason this child will be well known in the world as one who is protected by the Personality of Godhead. O most fortunate one, there is no doubt that this child will become a first-class devotee and will be qualified with all good qualities.

PURPORT

The Lord gives protection to all living beings because He is their supreme leader. The Vedic hymns confirm that the Lord is the Supreme Person amongst all personalities. The difference between the two living beings is that the one, the Personality of Godhead, provides for all other living beings, and by knowing Him one can achieve eternal peace (*Kaṭha Upaniṣad*). Such protection is given by His different potencies to different grades of living beings. But as far as His unalloyed devotees are concerned, He gives the protection personally. Therefore, Mahārāja Parīkṣit is protected from the very beginning of his appearance in the womb of his mother. And because he is especially given protection by the Lord, the indication must be concluded that the child would be a first-grade devotee of the Lord with all good qualities. There are three grades of devotees, namely the *mahā-bhāgavata*, *madhyama-adhikārī* and the *kaniṣṭha-adhikārī*. Those who go to the temples of the Lord and offer worshipful respect to the Deity without sufficient knowledge in the theological science and therefore without any respect for the devotees of the Lord are called materialistic devotees, or *kaniṣṭha-adhikārī*, the third-grade devotees. Secondly, the devotees who have developed a mentality of genuine service to the Lord and who thus make friendships only with similar devotees, show favor to the neophytes and avoid the atheists are called the second-grade devotees. But those who see everything in the

Lord or everything of the Lord and also see in everything an eternal relation of the Lord, so that there is nothing within their purview of sight except the Lord, are called the *mahā-bhāgavatas*, or the first-grade devotees of the Lord. Such first-grade devotees of the Lord are perfect in all respects. A devotee who may be in any of these categories is automatically qualified by all good qualities, and thus a *mahā-bhāgavata* devotee like Mahārāja Parīkṣit is certainly perfect in all respects. And because Mahārāja Parīkṣit took his birth in the family of Mahārāja Yudhiṣṭhira, he is addressed herein as the *mahā-bhāgavata*, or the greatest of the fortunates. The family in which a *mahā-bhāgavata* takes his birth is fortunate because due to the birth of a first-grade devotee the members of the family, past, present and future up to one hundred generations, become liberated by the grace of the Lord, out of respect for His beloved devotee. Therefore, the highest benefit is done to one's family simply by becoming an unalloyed devotee of the Lord.

TEXT 18

श्रीराजोवाच

अप्येष वंश्यान् राजर्षीन् पुण्यश्लोकान् महात्मनः ।
अनुवर्तिता स्विद्यशसा साधुवादेन सत्तमाः ॥१८॥

śrī-rājovāca
apy eṣa vaṁśyān rājarṣīn
puṇya-ślokān mahātmanaḥ
anuvartitā svid yaśasā
sādhu-vādena sattamāḥ

śrī-rājā—the all-good king (Mahārāja Yudhiṣṭhira); *uvāca*—said; *api*—whether; *eṣaḥ*—this; *vaṁśyān*—family; *rāja-ṛṣīn*—of saintly kings; *puṇya-ślokān*—pious by the very name; *mahā-ātmanaḥ*—all great souls; *anuvartitā*—follower; *svit*—will it be; *yaśasā*—by achievements; *sādhu-vādena*—by glorification; *sat-tamāḥ*—O great souls.

TRANSLATION

The good King [Yudhiṣṭhira] inquired: O great souls, will he become as saintly a king, as pious in his very name and as famous and

glorified in his achievements, as others who appeared in this great royal family?

PURPORT

The forefathers of King Yudhiṣṭhira were all great saintly kings, pious and glorified by their great achievements. They were all saints on the royal throne. And therefore all the members of the state were happy, pious, well behaved, prosperous and spiritually enlightened. Under strict guidance of the great souls and spiritual injunctions, such great saintly kings were trained up, and as a result the kingdom was full of saintly persons and was a happy land of spiritual life. Mahārāja Yudhiṣṭhira was himself a replica of his ancestors, and he desired that the next king after him become exactly like his great forefathers. He was happy to learn from the learned *brāhmaṇas* that by astrological calculations the child would be born a first-grade devotee of the Lord, and more confidentially he wanted to know whether the child was going to follow in the footsteps of his great forefathers. That is the way of the monarchical state. The reigning king should be a pious, chivalrous devotee of the Lord and fear personified for the upstarts. He must also leave an heir apparent equally qualified to rule over the innocent citizens. In the modern setup of the democratic states, the people themselves are fallen to the qualities of the *śūdras* or less, and the government is run by their representative, who is ignorant of the scriptural mode of administrative education. Thus the whole atmosphere is surcharged with *śūdra* qualities, manifested by lust and avarice. Such administrators quarrel every day among themselves. The cabinet of ministers changes often due to party and group selfishness. Everyone wants to exploit the state resources till he dies. No one retires from political life unless forced to do so. How can such low-grade men do good to the people? The result is corruption, intrigue and hypocrisy. They should learn from the *Śrīmad-Bhāgavatam* how ideal the administrators must be before they can be given charge of different posts.

TEXT 19

श्रीब्राह्मणा ऊचुः

पार्थ प्रजाविता साक्षादिक्ष्वाकुरिव मानवः ।
ब्रह्मण्यः सत्यसंधश्च रामो दाशरथिर्यथा ॥१९॥

brāhmaṇā ūcuḥ
pārtha prajāvitā sākṣād
ikṣvākur iva mānavaḥ
brahmaṇyaḥ satya-sandhaś ca
rāmo dāśarathir yathā

brāhmaṇāḥ—the good *brāhmaṇas; ūcuḥ*—said; *pārtha*—O son of Pṛthā (Kuntī); *prajā*—those who are born; *avitā*—maintainer; *sākṣāt*—directly; *ikṣvākuḥ iva*—exactly like King Ikṣvāku; *mānavaḥ*—son of Manu; *brahmaṇyaḥ*—followers and respectful to the *brāhmaṇas; satya-sandhaḥ*—truthful by promise; *ca*—also; *rāmaḥ*—the Personality of Godhead Rāma; *dāśarathiḥ*—the son of Mahārāja Daśaratha; *yathā*—like Him.

TRANSLATION

The learned brāhmaṇas said: O son of Pṛthā, this child shall be exactly like King Ikṣvāku, son of Manu, in maintaining all those who are born. And as for following the brahminical principles, especially in being true to his promise, he shall be exactly like Rāma, the Personality of Godhead, the son of Mahārāja Daśaratha.

PURPORT

Prajā means the living being who has taken his birth in the material world. Actually the living being has no birth and no death, but because of his separation from the service of the Lord and due to his desire to lord it over material nature, he is offered a suitable body to satisfy his material desires. In doing so, one becomes conditioned by the laws of material nature, *and the material body is changed in terms of his own work.* The living entity thus transmigrates from one body to another in 8,400,000 species of life. But due to his being the part and parcel of the Lord, he not only is maintained with all necessaries of life by the Lord, but also is protected by the Lord and His representatives, the saintly kings. These saintly kings give protection to all the *prajās*, or living beings, to live and to fulfill their terms of imprisonment. Mahārāja Parīkṣit was actually an ideal saintly king because while touring his kingdom he happened to see that a poor cow was about to be killed by the personified Kali, whom he at once took to task as a murderer. This means that even the animals were given protection by the saintly administrators, not from any sentimental point of view, but because those who have taken their birth in the material world have the right to live. All the saintly kings, beginning from the King of the sun globe down to the King of the earth, are so inclined by the influence of the Vedic literatures. The Vedic literatures are taught in higher planets also, as there is reference in the *Bhagavad-gītā* (4.1) about the teachings to the sun-god (Vivasvān) by the Lord, and such lessons are transferred by disciplic succession, as it was done by the sun-god to his son Manu, and from Manu to Mahārāja Ikṣvāku. There are fourteen Manus in one day of Brahmā, and the Manu referred to herein is the seventh Manu, who is one of the *prajāpatis* (those who create progeny), and he is the son of the sun-god. He is known as the Vaivasvata Manu. He had ten sons, and Mahārāja Ikṣvāku is one of them. Mahārāja Ikṣvāku also learned *bhakti-yoga* as taught in the *Bhagavad-gītā* from his father, Manu, who got it from his father, the sun-god. Later on the teaching of the *Bhagavad-gītā* came down by disciplic succession from Mahārāja Ikṣvāku, but in course of time the chain was broken by unscrupulous persons, and therefore it again had to be taught to Arjuna on the Battlefield of Kurukṣetra. So all the Vedic literatures are current from the very beginning of creation of the material world, and thus the Vedic literatures are known as *apauruṣeya* (not made by man). The Vedic knowledge was spoken by the Lord and first heard by Brahmā, the first created living being within the universe.

Mahārāja Ikṣvāku: One of the sons of Vaivasvata Manu. He had one hundred sons. He prohibited meat eating. His son Śaśāda became the next king after his death.

Manu: The Manu mentioned in this verse as the father of Ikṣvāku is the seventh Manu, of the name Vaivasvata Manu, the son of sun-god Vivasvān, to whom Lord Kṛṣṇa instructed the teachings of *Bhagavad-gītā* prior to His teaching them to Arjuna. Mankind is the descendant of Manu. This Vaivasvata Manu had ten sons, named Ikṣvāku, Nabhaga, Dhṛṣṭa, Śaryāti, Nariṣyanta, Nābhāga, Diṣṭa, Karūṣa, Pṛṣadhra and Vasumān. The Lord's incarnation Matsya (the gigantic fish) was advented during the beginning of Vaivasvata Manu's reign. He learned the principles of *Bhagavad-gītā* from his father, Vivasvān, the sun-god, and he reinstructed the same to his son Mahārāja Ikṣvāku. In the beginning of the Tretā-yuga the sun-god instructed devotional service to Manu, and

Manu in his turn instructed it to Ikṣvāku for the welfare of the whole human society.

Lord Rāma: The Supreme Personality of Godhead incarnated Himself as Śrī Rāma, accepting the sonhood of His pure devotee Mahārāja Daśaratha, the King of Ayodhyā. Lord Rāma descended along with His plenary portions, and all of them appeared as His younger brothers. In the month of Caitra on the ninth day of the growing moon in the Tretā-yuga, the Lord appeared, as usual, to establish the principles of religion and to annihilate the disturbing elements. When He was just a young boy, He helped the great sage Viśvāmitra by killing Subāhu and striking Mārīcā, the she-demon, who was disturbing the sages in their daily discharge of duties. The *brāhmaṇas* and *kṣatriyas* are meant to cooperate for the welfare of the mass of people. The *brāhmaṇa* sages endeavor to enlighten the people by perfect knowledge, and the *kṣatriyas* are meant for their protection. Lord Rāmacandra is the ideal king for maintaining and protecting the highest culture of humanity, known as *brahmaṇya-dharma.* The Lord is specifically the protector of the cows and the *brāhmaṇas,* and hence He enhances the prosperity of the world. He rewarded the administrative demigods by effective weapons to conquer the demons through the agency of Viśvāmitra. He was present in the bow sacrifice of King Janaka, and by breaking the invincible bow of Śiva, He married Sītādevī, daughter of Mahārāja Janaka.

After His marriage He accepted exile in the forest for fourteen years by the order of His father, Mahārāja Daśaratha. To help the administration of the demigods, He killed fourteen thousand demons, and by the intrigues of the demons, His wife, Sītādevī, was kidnapped by Rāvaṇa. He made friendship with Sugrīva, who was helped by the Lord to kill Vali, brother of Sugrīva. By the help of Lord Rāma, Sugrīva became the king of the Vānaras (a race of gorillas). The Lord built a floating bridge of stones on the Indian Ocean and reached Laṅkā, the kingdom of Rāvaṇa, who had kidnapped Sītā. Later on Rāvaṇa was killed by Him, and Rāvaṇa's brother Vibhīṣaṇa was installed on the throne of Laṅkā. Vibhīṣaṇa was one of the brothers of Rāvaṇa, a demon, but Lord Rāma made him immortal by His blessings. On the expiry of fourteen years, after settling the affairs at Laṅkā, the Lord came back to His kingdom, Ayodhyā, by flower plane. He instructed His brother Śatrughna to attack Lavaṇāsura, who reigned at Mathurā, and the demon was killed. He performed ten *aśvamedha* sacrifices, and later on He disappeared while taking a bath in the Śarayu River. The great epic *Rāmāyaṇa* is the history of Lord Rāma's activities in the world, and the authoritative *Rāmāyaṇa* was written by the great poet Vālmīki.

TEXT 20

एष दाता शरण्यश्च यथा ह्यौशीनरः शिबिः ।
यशो वितनिता स्वानां दौष्यन्तिरिव यज्वनाम् ॥२०॥

eṣa dātā śaraṇyaś ca
yathā hy auśīnaraḥ śibiḥ
yaśo vitanitā svānāṁ
dauṣyantir iva yajvanām

eṣaḥ—this child; *dātā*—donor in charity; *śaraṇyaḥ*—protector of the surrendered; *ca*—and; *yathā*—as; *hi*—certainly; *auśīnaraḥ*—the country named Uśīnara; *śibiḥ*—Śibi; *yaśaḥ*—fame; *vitanitā*—disseminator; *svānām*—of the kinsmen; *dauṣyantiḥ iva*—like Bharata, the son of Duṣyanta; *yajvanām*—of those who have performed many sacrifices.

TRANSLATION

This child will be a munificent donor of charity and protector of the surrendered, like the famous King Śibi of the Uśīnara country. And he will expand the name and fame of his family like Bharata, the son of Mahārāja Duṣyanta.

PURPORT

A king becomes famous by his acts of charity, performances of *yajñas*, protection of the surrendered, etc. A *kṣatriya* king is proud to give protection to the surrendered souls. This attitude of a king is called *īśvara-bhāva,* or factual power to give protection in a righteous cause. In the *Bhagavad-gītā* the Lord instructs living beings to surrender unto Him, and He promises all protection. The Lord is all-powerful and true to His word, and therefore He never fails to give protection to His different devotees. The king, being the representative of the Lord, must possess this attitude of giving protection to the surrendered souls at all risk. Mahārāja Śibi, the King of Uśīnara, was an intimate friend of Mahārāja Yayāti, who was able to reach the heavenly planets along with Mahārāja Śibi. Mahārāja Śibi was aware of the heavenly planet where he was to be transferred after his death, and the description of this heavenly planet is given in the *Mahābhārata* (*Ādi-parva*, 96.6–9). Mahārāja Śibi was so charitably disposed that he wanted to give over his acquired position in the heavenly kingdom to Yayāti, but he did not accept it. Yayāti went to the heavenly planet along with great *ṛṣis* like Aṣṭaka and others. On inquiry from the *ṛṣis*, Yayāti gave an account of Śibi's pious acts when all of them were on the path to heaven. He has become a member of the assembly of Yamarāja, who has become his worshipful deity. As confirmed in the *Bhagavad-gītā*, the worshiper of the demigods goes to the planets of the demigods (*yānti deva-vratā devān*); so Mahārāja Śibi has become an associate of the great Vaiṣṇava authority Yamarāja on that particular planet. While he was on the earth he became very famous as a protector of surrendered souls and a donor of charities. The King of heaven once took the shape of a pigeon-hunter bird (eagle), and Agni, the fire-god, took the shape of a pigeon. The pigeon, while being chased by the eagle, took shelter on the lap of Mahārāja Śibi, and the hunter eagle wanted the pigeon back from the King. The King wanted to give it some other meat to eat and requested the bird not to kill the pigeon. The hunter bird refused to accept the King's offer, but it was settled later on that the eagle would accept flesh from the body of the King of the pigeon's equivalent weight. The King began to cut flesh from his body to weigh in the balance equivalent to the weight of the pigeon, but the mystic pigeon always remained heavier. The King then put himself on the balance to equate with the pigeon, and the demigods were pleased with him. The King of heaven and the fire-god disclosed their identity, and the King was blessed by them. Devarṣi Nārada also glorified Mahārāja Śibi for his great achievements, specifically in charity and protection. Mahārāja Śibi sacrificed his own son for the satisfaction of human beings in his kingdom. And thus child Parīkṣit was to become a second Śibi in charity and protection.

Dauṣyanti Bharata: There are many Bharatas in history, of which Bharata the brother of Lord Rāma, Bharata the son of King Ṛṣabha, and Bharata the son of Mahārāja Duṣyanta are very famous. And all these

Bharatas are historically known to the universe. This earth planet is known as Bhārata, or Bhārata-varṣa, due to King Bharata the son of Ṛṣabha, but according to some this land is known as Bhārata due to the reign of the son of Duṣyanta. So far as we are convinced, this land's name Bhārata-varṣa was established from the reign of Bharata the son of King Ṛṣabha. Before him the land was known as Ilāvṛta-varṣa, but just after the coronation of Bharata, the son of Ṛṣabha, this land became famous as Bhārata-varṣa.

But despite all this, Bharata, the son of Mahārāja Duṣyanta was not less important. He is the son of the famous beauty Śakuntalā. Mahārāja Duṣyanta fell in love with Śakuntalā in the forest, and Bharata was conceived. After that, Mahārāja forgot his wife Śakuntalā by the curse of Kaṇva Muni, and the child Bharata was brought up in the forest by his mother. Even in his childhood he was so powerful that he challenged the lions and elephants in the forest and would fight with them as little children play with cats and dogs. Because of the boy's becoming so strong, more than the so-called modern Tarzan, the *ṛṣis* in the forest called him Sarvadamana, or one who is able to control everyone. A full description of Mahārāja Bharata is given in the *Mahābhārata, Ādi-parva.* The Pāṇḍavas, or the Kurus, are sometimes addressed as Bhārata due to being born in the dynasty of the famous Mahārāja Bharata, the son of King Duṣyanta.

TEXT 21

धन्विनामग्रणीरेष तुल्यश्चार्जुनयोर्द्वयोः ।
हुताश इव दुर्धर्षः समुद्र इव दुस्तरः ॥२१॥

dhanvinām agraṇīr eṣa
tulyaś cārjunayor dvayoḥ
hutāśa iva durdharṣaḥ
samudra iva dustaraḥ

dhanvinām—of the great bowmen; *agraṇīḥ*—the foreman; *eṣaḥ*—this child; *tulyaḥ*—equally good; *ca*—and; *arjunayoḥ*—of the Arjunas; *dvayoḥ*—of the two; *hutāśaḥ*—fire; *iva*—like; *durdharṣaḥ*—irresistible; *samudraḥ*—ocean; *iva*—like; *dustaraḥ*—unsurpassable.

TRANSLATION

Amongst great bowmen, this child will be as good as Arjuna. He will be as irresistible as fire and as unsurpassable as the ocean.

PURPORT

In history there are two Arjunas. One is Kārtavīrya Arjuna, the King of Haihaya, and the other is the grandfather of the child. Both the Arjunas are famous for their bowmanship, and the child Parīkṣit is foretold to be equal to both of them, particularly in fighting. A short description of the Pāṇḍava Arjuna is given below:

Pāṇḍava Arjuna: The great hero of the *Bhagavad-gītā*. He is the *kṣatriya* son of Mahārāja Pāṇḍu. Queen Kuntīdevī could call for any one of the demigods, and thus she called Indra, and Arjuna was born by him. Arjuna is therefore a plenary part of the heavenly King Indra. He was born in the month of Phalguna (February–March), and therefore he is also called Phālguni. When he appeared as the son of Kuntī, his future greatness was proclaimed by air messages, and all the important personalities from different parts of the universe, such as the demigods, the Gandharvas, the Ādityas (from the sun globe), the Rudras, the Vasus, the Nāgas, the different *ṛṣis* (sages) of importance, and the Apsarās (the society girls of heaven), all attended the ceremony. The Apsarās pleased everyone by their heavenly dances and songs. Vasudeva, the father of Lord Kṛṣṇa and the maternal uncle of Arjuna, sent his priest representative Kaśyapa to purify Arjuna by all the prescribed *saṁskāras*, or reformatory processes. His *saṁskāra* of being given a name was performed in the presence of the *ṛṣis*, residents of Śataśṛṅga. He married four wives, Draupadī, Subhadrā, Citrāṅgadā and Ulūpī, from whom he got four sons of the names Śrutakīrti, Abhimanyu, Babhruvāhana and Irāvān respectively.

During his student life he was entrusted to study under the great professor Droṇācārya, along with other Pāṇḍavas and the Kurus. But he excelled everyone by his studious intensity, and Droṇācārya was especially attracted by his disciplinary affection. Droṇācārya accepted him as a first-grade scholar and loved heartily to bestow upon him all the blessings of military science. He was so ardent a student that he used to practice bowmanship even at night, and for all these reasons Professor

Droṇācārya was determined to make him the topmost bowman of the world. He passed very brilliantly the examination in piercing the target, and Droṇācārya was very pleased. Royal families at Maṇipura and Tripura are descendants of Arjuna's son Babhruvāhana. Arjuna saved Droṇācārya from the attack of a crocodile, and the Ācārya, being pleased with him, rewarded him with a weapon of the name *brahmaśiras.* Mahārāja Drupada was inimical toward Droṇācārya, and thus when he attacked the Ācārya, Arjuna got him arrested and brought him before Droṇācārya. He besieged a city of the name Ahicchatra, belonging to Mahārāja Drupada, and after taking it over he gave it to Droṇācārya. The confidential treatment of the weapon *brahmaśiras* was explained to Arjuna, and Droṇācārya was promised by Arjuna that he would use the weapon if necessary when he (Droṇācārya) personally became an enemy of Arjuna. By this, the Ācārya forecasted the future battle of Kurukṣetra, in which Droṇācārya was on the opposite side. Mahārāja Drupada, although defeated by Arjuna on behalf of his professor Droṇācārya, decided to hand over his daughter Draupadī to his young combatant, but he was disappointed when he heard the false news of Arjuna's death in the fire of a shellac house intrigued by Duryodhana. He therefore arranged for Draupadī's personal selection of a groom who could pierce the eye of a fish hanging on the ceiling. This trick was especially made because only Arjuna could do it, and he was successful in his desire to hand over his equally worthy daughter to Arjuna. Arjuna's brothers were at that time living incognito under agreement with Duryodhana, and Arjuna and his brothers attended the meeting of Draupadī's selection in the dress of *brāhmaṇas.* When all the *kṣatriya* kings assembled saw that a poor *brāhmaṇa* had been garlanded by Draupadī for her lord, Śrī Kṛṣṇa disclosed his identity to Balarāma.

He met Ulūpī at Haridvāra (Hardwar), and he was attracted by a girl belonging to Nāgaloka, and thus Iravān was born. Similarly, he met Citrāṅgadā, a daughter of the King of Maṇipura, and thus Babhruvāhana was born. Lord Śrī Kṛṣṇa made a plan to help Arjuna to kidnap Subhadrā, sister of Śrī Kṛṣṇa, because Baladeva was inclined to hand her over to Duryodhana. Yudhiṣṭhira also agreed with Śrī Kṛṣṇa, and thus Subhadrā was taken by force by Arjuna and then married to him. Subhadrā's son is Abhimanyu, the father of Parīkṣit Mahārāja, the posthumous child. Arjuna satisfied the fire-god by setting fire to the

Khāṇḍava Forest, and thus the fire-god gave him one weapon. Indra was angry when the fire was set in the Khāṇḍava Forest, and thus Indra, assisted by all other demigods, began fighting with Arjuna for his great challenge. They were defeated by Arjuna, and Indradeva returned to his heavenly kingdom. Arjuna also promised all protection to one Mayāsura, and the latter presented him one valuable conchshell celebrated as the Devadatta. Similarly, he received many other valuable weapons from Indradeva when he was satisfied to see his chivalry.

When Mahārāja Yudhiṣṭhira was disappointed in defeating the King of Magadha, Jarāsandha, it was Arjuna only who gave King Yudhiṣṭhira all kinds of assurances, and thus Arjuna, Bhīma and Lord Kṛṣṇa started for Magadha to kill Jarāsandha. When he went out to bring all other kings of the world under the subjection of the Pāṇḍavas, as was usual after the coronation of every emperor, he conquered the country named Kelinda and brought in subjugation King Bhagadatta. Then he traveled through countries like Antagiri, Ulūkapura and Modāpura and brought under subjugation all the rulers.

Sometimes he underwent severe types of penances, and later on he was rewarded by Indradeva. Lord Śiva also wanted to try the strength of Arjuna, and in the form of an aborigine, Lord Śiva met him. There was a great fight between the two, and at last Lord Śiva was satisfied with him and disclosed his identity. Arjuna prayed to the lord in all humbleness, and the lord, being pleased with him, presented him the *pāśupata* weapon. He acquired many other important weapons from different demigods. He received *daṇḍāstra* from Yamarāja, *pāśāstra* from Varuṇa, and *antardhānāstra* from Kuvera, the treasurer of the heavenly kingdom. Indra wanted him to come to the heavenly kingdom, the Indraloka planet beyond the moon planet. In that planet he was cordially received by the local residents, and he was awarded reception in the heavenly parliament of Indradeva. Then he met Indradeva, who not only presented him with his *vajra* weapon, but also taught him the military and musical science as used in the heavenly planet. In one sense, Indra is the real father of Arjuna, and therefore indirectly he wanted to entertain Arjuna with the famous society girl of heaven, Urvaśī, the celebrated beauty. The society girls of heaven are lusty, and Urvaśī was very eager to contact Arjuna, the strongest human being. She met him in his room and expressed her desires but Arjuna sustained his unimpeachable character by closing his eyes before Urvaśī, addressing her as mother of the Kuru dynasty and placing her in the category of his mothers Kuntī, Mādrī and Śacīdevī, wife of Indradeva. Disappointed, Urvaśī cursed Arjuna and left. In the heavenly planet he also met the great celebrated ascetic Lomaśa and prayed to him for the protection of Mahārāja Yudhiṣṭhira.

When his inimical cousin Duryodhana was under the clutches of the Gandharvas, he wanted to save him and requested the Gandharvas to release Duryodhana, but the Gandharvas refused, and thus he fought with them and got Duryodhana released. When all the Pāṇḍavas lived incognito, he presented himself in the court of King Virāṭa as a eunuch and was employed as the musical teacher of Uttarā, his future daughter-in-law, and was known in the Virāṭa court as the Bṛhannala. As Bṛhannala, he fought on behalf of Uttara, the son of King Virāṭa, and thus defeated the Kurus in the fight incognito. His secret weapons were safely kept in the custody of a *somi* tree, and he ordered Uttarā to get them back. His identity and his brothers' identity were later on disclosed to Uttarā. Droṇācārya was informed of Arjuna's presence in the fight of the Kurus and the Virāṭas. Later, on the Battlefield of Kurukṣetra, Arjuna killed many great generals like Karṇa and others. After the Battle of Kurukṣetra, he punished Aśvatthāmā, who had killed all the five sons of Draupadī. Then all the brothers went to Bhīṣmadeva.

It is due to Arjuna only that the great philosophical discourses of the *Bhagavad-gītā* were again spoken by the Lord on the Battlefield of Kurukṣetra. His wonderful acts on the Battlefield of Kurukṣetra are vividly described in the *Mahābhārata*. Arjuna was defeated, however, by his son Babhruvāhana at Maṇipura and fell unconscious when Ulūpī saved him. After the disappearance of Lord Kṛṣṇa, the message was brought by Arjuna to Mahārāja Yudhiṣṭhira. Again, Arjuna visited Dvārakā, and all the widow wives of Lord Kṛṣṇa lamented before him. He took them all in the presence of Vasudeva and pacified all of them. Later on, when Vasudeva passed away, he performed his funeral ceremony in the absence of Kṛṣṇa. While Arjuna was taking all the wives of Kṛṣṇa to Indraprastha, he was attacked on the way, and he could not protect the ladies in his custody. At last, advised by Vyāsadeva, all the

brothers headed for Mahāprasthāna. On the way, at the request of his brother, he gave up all important weapons as useless, and he dropped them all in the water.

TEXT 22

मृगेन्द्र इव विक्रान्तो निषेव्यो हिमवानिव ।
तितिक्षुर्वसुधेवासौ सहिष्णुः पितराविव ॥२२॥

mṛgendra iva vikrānto
niṣevyo himavān iva
titikṣur vasudhevāsau
sahiṣṇuḥ pitarāv iva

mṛgendraḥ—the lion; *iva*—like; *vikrāntaḥ*—powerful; *niṣevyaḥ*—worthy of taking shelter; *himavān*—the Himalaya Mountains; *iva*—like; *titikṣuḥ*—forbearance; *vasudhā iva*—like the earth; *asau*—the child; *sahiṣṇuḥ*—tolerant; *pitarau*—parents; *iva*—like.

TRANSLATION

This child will be as strong as a lion, and as worthy a shelter as the Himalaya Mountains. He will be forbearing like the earth, and as tolerant as his parents.

PURPORT

One is compared to the lion when one is very strong in chasing an enemy. One should be a lamb at home and a lion in the chase. The lion never fails in the chase of an animal; similarly, the head of the state should never fail in chasing an enemy. The Himalaya Mountains are famous for all richness. There are innumerable caves to live in, numberless trees of good fruits to eat, good springs to drink water from and profuse drugs and minerals to cure diseases. Any man who is not materially prosperous can take shelter of these great mountains, and he will be provided with everything required. Both the materialist and the spiritualist can take advantage of the great shelter of the Himalayas. On the surface of the earth there are so many disturbances caused by the inhabitants. In the modern age the people have begun to detonate atomic weapons on the surface of the earth, and still the earth is forbearing to the inhabitants, like a mother who excuses a little child. Parents are al-

ways tolerant to children for all sorts of mischievous acts. An ideal king may be possessed of all these good qualities, and the child Parīkṣit is foretold to have all these qualities in perfection.

TEXT 23

पितामहसमः साम्ये प्रसादे गिरिशोपमः ।
आश्रयः सर्वभूतानां यथा देवो रमाश्रयः ॥२३॥

pitāmaha-samaḥ sāmye
prasāde giriśopamaḥ
āśrayaḥ sarva-bhūtānāṁ
yathā devo ramāśrayaḥ

pitāmaha—the grandfather, or Brahmā; *samaḥ*—equally good; *sāmye*—in the matter; *prasāde*—in charity or in munificence; *giriśa*—Lord Śiva; *upamaḥ*—comparison of equilibrium; *āśrayaḥ*—resort; *sarva*—all; *bhūtānām*—of the living beings; *yathā*—as; *devaḥ*—the Supreme Lord; *ramā-āśrayaḥ*—the Personality of Godhead.

TRANSLATION

This child will be like his grandfather Yudhiṣṭhira or Brahmā in equanimity of mind. He will be munificent like the lord of the Kailāsa Hill, Śiva. And he will be the resort of everyone, like the Supreme Personality of Godhead Nārāyaṇa, who is even the shelter of the goddess of fortune.

PURPORT

Mental equanimity refers both to Mahārāja Yudhiṣṭhira and to Brahmā, the grandfather of all living beings. According to Śrīdhara Svāmī, the grandfather referred to is Brahmā, but according to Viśvanātha Cakravartī, the grandfather is Mahārāja Yudhiṣṭhira himself. But in both cases the comparison is equally good because both of them are recognized representatives of the Supreme Lord, and thus both of them have to maintain mental equanimity, being engaged in welfare work for the living being. Any responsible executive agent at the top of administration has to tolerate different types of onslaughts from the very persons for whom he works. Brahmājī was criticized even by the *gopīs*, the highest perfectional devotees of the Lord. The *gopīs* were dissatisfied with the work of Brahmājī because Lord Brahmā, as creator of this particular universe, created eyelids which obstructed their seeing Lord Kṛṣṇa. They could not tolerate a moment's blinking of the eyes, for it kept them from seeing their beloved Lord Kṛṣṇa. So what to speak of others, who are naturally very critical of every action of a responsible man? Similarly, Mahārāja Yudhiṣṭhira had to cross over many difficult situations created by his enemies, and he proved to be the most perfect maintainer of mental equanimity in all critical circumstances. Therefore the example of both grandfathers for maintaining equanimity of mind is quite fitting.

Lord Śiva is a celebrated demigod who awards gifts to beggars. His name is therefore Āśutoṣa, or one who is pleased very easily. He is also called the Bhūtanātha, or the lord of the common folk, who are mainly attached to him because of his munificent gifts, even without consideration of the aftereffects. Rāvaṇa was very attached to Lord Śiva, and by easily pleasing him, Rāvaṇa became so powerful that he wanted to challenge the authority of Lord Rāma. Of course, Rāvaṇa was never helped by Lord Śiva when he fought with Rāma, the Supreme Personality of Godhead and the Lord of Lord Śiva. To Vṛkāsura, Lord Śiva awarded a benediction which was not only awkward, but also disturbing. Vṛkāsura became empowered, by the grace of Lord Śiva, to vanish anyone's head simply by touching it. Although this was awarded by Lord Śiva, the cunning fellow wanted to make an experiment of the power by touching the head of Lord Śiva. Thus the lord had to take shelter of Viṣṇu to save himself from trouble, and the Lord Viṣṇu, by His illusory potency, asked Vṛkāsura to make an experiment with his own head. The fellow did it and was finished himself, and so the world was saved from all sorts of trouble by such a cunning beggar of the demigods. The excellent point is that Lord Śiva never denies anyone any sort of gift. He is therefore the most generous, although sometimes some kind of a mistake is made.

Ramā means the goddess of fortune. And her shelter is Lord Viṣṇu. Lord Viṣṇu is the maintainer of all living beings. There are innumerable living beings, not only on the surface of this planet but also in all other hundreds of thousands of planets. All of them are provided with all necessities of life for the progressive march towards the end of self-realization, but on the path of sense gratification they are put into difficulty by the agency of *māyā*, the illusory energy, and so travel the path of a false plan of economic development. Such economic development is never successful because it is illusory. These men are always after the mercy of the illusory goddess of fortune, but they do not know that the goddess of fortune can live only under the protection of Viṣṇu. Without Viṣṇu, the goddess of fortune is an illusion. We should therefore seek the protection of Viṣṇu instead of directly seeking the protection of the goddess of fortune. Only Viṣṇu and the devotees of Viṣṇu can give protection to all, and because Mahārāja Parīkṣit was himself protected by Viṣṇu, it was quite possible for him to give complete protection to all who wanted to live under his rule.

TEXT 24

सर्वसद्गुणमाहात्म्ये एष कृष्णमनुव्रतः ।
रन्तिदेव इवोदारो ययातिरिव धार्मिकः ॥२४॥

sarva-sad-guṇa-māhātmye
eṣa kṛṣṇam anuvrataḥ
rantideva ivodāro
yayātir iva dhārmikaḥ

sarva-sat-guṇa-māhātmye—glorified by all godly attributes; *eṣaḥ*—this child; *kṛṣṇam*—like Lord Kṛṣṇa; *anuvrataḥ*—a follower in His footsteps; *rantidevaḥ*—Rantideva; *iva*—like; *udāraḥ*—in the matter of magnanimity; *yayātiḥ*—Yayāti; *iva*—like; *dhārmikaḥ*—concerning religion.

TRANSLATION

This child will be almost as good as Lord Śrī Kṛṣṇa by following in His footsteps. In magnanimity he will become as great as King Rantideva. And in religion he will be like Mahārāja Yayāti.

PURPORT

The last instruction of Lord Śrī Kṛṣṇa in the *Bhagavad-gītā* is that one should give up everything and should follow in the footsteps of the Lord alone. Less intelligent persons do not agree to this great instruction of the Lord, as ill luck would have it, but one who is actually intelligent catches up this sublime instruction and is immensely benefited. Foolish people do not know that association is the cause of acquiring qualities. Association with fire makes an object hot, even in the material sense. Therefore, association with the Supreme Personality of Godhead makes one qualified like the Lord. As we have discussed previously, one can achieve seventy-eight percent of the godly qualities by the Lord's intimate association. To follow the instructions of the Lord is to associate with the Lord. *The Lord is not a material object whose presence one has to feel for such association.* The Lord is present everywhere and at all times. It is quite possible to have His association simply by following His instruction because the Lord and His instruction and the Lord and His name, fame, attributes and paraphernalia are all identical with Him, being absolute knowledge. Mahārāja Parīkṣit associated with the Lord even from the womb of his mother up to the last day of his valuable life, and thus he acquired all the essential good qualities of the Lord in all perfection.

Rantideva: An ancient king prior to the *Mahābhārata* period, referred to by Nārada Muni while instructing Sañjaya, as mentioned in *Mahābhārata* (*Droṇa-parva* 67). He was a great king, liberal for hospitality and distribution of foodstuff. Even Lord Śrī Kṛṣṇa praised his acts of charity and hospitality. He was blessed by the great Vasiṣṭha Muni for supplying him cold water, and thus he achieved the heavenly planet. He used to supply fruits, roots and leaves to the *ṛṣis*, and thus he was blessed by them with fulfillment of his desires. *Although a kṣatriya by birth, he never ate flesh in his life.* He was especially hospitable to Vasiṣṭha Muni, and by his blessings only he attained the higher planetary residence. He is one of those pious kings whose names are remembered in the morning and evening.

Yayāti: The great emperor of the world and the original forefather of all great nations of the world who belong to the Āryan and Indo-European stock. He is the son of Mahārāja Nahuṣa, and he became the emperor of the world due to his elder brother's becoming a great and liberated saintly mystic. He ruled over the world for several thousands of years and performed many sacrifices and pious activities recorded in history, although his early youth was very lustful and full of romantic stories. He fell in love with Devayānī, the most beloved daughter of

Śukrācārya. Devayānī wished to marry him, but at first he refused to accept her because of her being a daughter of a *brāhmaṇa.* According to *śāstras,* a *brāhmaṇa* could marry the daughter of a *brāhmaṇa.* They were very much cautious about *varṇa-saṅkara* population in the world. Śukrācārya amended this law of forbidden marriage and induced Emperor Yayāti to accept Devayānī. Devayānī had a girl friend named Śarmiṣṭhā, who also fell in love with the emperor and thus went with her friend Devayānī. Śukrācārya forbade Emperor Yayāti to call Śarmiṣṭhā into his bedroom, but Yayāti could not strictly follow his instruction. He secretly married Śarmiṣṭhā also and begot sons by her. When this was known by Devayānī, she went to her father and lodged a complaint. Yayāti was much attached to Devayānī, and when he went to his father-in-law's place to call her, Śukrācārya was angry with him and cursed him to become impotent. Yayāti begged his father-in-law to withdraw his curse, but the sage asked Yayāti to ask youthfulness from his sons and let them become old as the condition of his becoming potent. He had five sons, two from Devayānī and three from Śarmiṣṭha. From his five sons, namely (1) Yadu, (2) Turvasu, (3) Druhyu, (4) Anu and (5) Pūru, five famous dynasties, namely (1) the Yadu dynasty, (2) the Yavana (Turk) dynasty, (3) the Bhoja dynasty, (4) the Mleccha dynasty (Greek) and (5) the Paurava dynasty, all emanated to spread all over the world. He reached the heavenly planets by dint of his pious acts, but he fell down from there because of his self-advertisement and criticizing other great souls. After his fall, his daughter and grandson bestowed upon him their accumulated virtues, and by the help of his grandson and friend Śibi, he was again promoted to the heavenly kingdom, becoming one of the assembly members of Yamarāja, with whom he is staying as a devotee. He performed more than one thousand different sacrifices, gave in charity very liberally and was a very influential king. His majestic power was felt all over the world. His youngest son agreed to award him his youthfulness when he was troubled with lustful desires, even for one thousand years. Finally he became detached from worldly life and returned the youthfulness again to his son Pūru. He wanted to hand over the kingdom to Pūru, but his noblemen and the subjects did not agree. But when he explained to his subjects the greatness of Pūru, they agreed to accept Pūru as the King, and thus Emperor Yayāti retired from family life and left home for the forest.

TEXT 25

**धृत्या बलिसमः कृष्णे प्रह्राद इव सद्ग्रहः ।
आहर्तैषोऽश्वमेधानां वृद्धानां पर्युपासकः ॥२५॥**

dhṛtyā bali-samaḥ kṛṣṇe
prahrāda iva sad-grahaḥ
āhartaiṣo 'śvamedhānāṁ
vṛddhānāṁ paryupāsakaḥ

dhṛtyā—by patience; *bali-samaḥ*—like Bali Mahārāja; *kṛṣṇe*—unto Lord Śrī Kṛṣṇa; *prahrāda*—Prahlāda Mahārāja; *iva*—like; *sat-grahaḥ*—devotee of; *āhartā*—performer; *eṣaḥ*—this child; *aśva-medhānām*—of Aśvamedha sacrifices; *vṛddhānām*—of the old and experienced men; *paryupāsakaḥ*—follower.

TRANSLATION

This child will be like Bali Mahārāja in patience, a staunch devotee of Lord Kṛṣṇa like Prahlāda Mahārāja, a performer of many aśvamedha [horse] sacrifices and a follower of the old and experienced men.

PURPORT

Bali Mahārāja: One of the twelve authorities in the devotional service of the Lord. Bali Mahārāja is a great authority in devotional service because he sacrificed everything to please the Lord and relinquished the connection of his so-called spiritual master who obstructed him on the path of risking everything for the service of the Lord. The highest perfection of religious life is to attain to the stage of unqualified devotional service of the Lord without any cause or without being obstructed by any kind of worldly obligation. Bali Mahārāja was determined to give up everything for the satisfaction of the Lord, and he did not care for any obstruction whatsoever. He is the grandson of Prahlāda Mahārāja, another authority in the devotional service of the Lord. Bali Mahārāja and the history of his dealings with Viṣṇu Vāmanadeva are described in the Eighth Canto of *Śrīmad-Bhāgavatam* (Chapter 11–24).

Prahlāda Mahārāja: A perfect devotee of Lord Kṛṣṇa (Viṣṇu). His father, Hiraṇyakaśipu, chastised him severely when he was only five years old for his becoming an unalloyed devotee of the Lord. He was the first son of Hiraṇyakaśipu, and his mother's name was Kayādhu. Prahlāda Mahārāja was an authority in the devotional service of the Lord because he had his father killed by Lord Nṛsiṁhadeva, setting the example that even a father should be removed from the path of devotional service if such a father happens to be an obstacle. He had four sons, and the eldest son, Virocana, is the father of Bali Mahārāja, mentioned above. The history of Prahlāda Mahārāja's activities is described in the Seventh Canto of *Śrīmad-Bhāgavatam.*

TEXT 26

राजर्षीणां जनयिता शास्ता चोत्पथगामिनाम् ।
निग्रहीता कलेरेष भुवो धर्मस्य कारणात् ॥२६॥

rājarṣīṇāṁ janayitā
śāstā cotpatha-gāminām
nigrahītā kaler eṣa
bhuvo dharmasya kāraṇāt

rāja-ṛṣīnām—of kings as good as sages; *janayitā*—producer; *śāstā*—chastiser; *ca*—and; *utpatha-gāminām*—of the upstarts; *nigrahītā*—molester; *kaleḥ*—of the quarrelsome; *eṣaḥ*—this; *bhuvaḥ*—of the world; *dharmasya*—of religion; *kāraṇāt*—on account of.

TRANSLATION

This child will be the father of kings who will be like sages. For world peace and for the sake of religion, he will be the chastiser of the upstarts and the quarrelsome.

PURPORT

The wisest man in the world is a devotee of the Lord. The sages are called wise men, and there are different types of wise men for different branches of knowledge. Unless, therefore, the king or the head of the state is the wisest man, he cannot control all types of wise men in the state. In the line of royal succession in the family of Mahārāja Yudhiṣṭhira, all the kings, without exception, were the wisest men of their times, and so also it is foretold about Mahārāja Parīkṣit and his son Mahārāja Janamejaya, who was yet to be born. Such wise kings can become chastisers of upstarts and uprooters of Kali, or quarrelsome elements. As will be clear in the chapters ahead, Mahārāja Parīkṣit wanted to kill the personified Kali, who was attempting to kill a cow, the emblem of peace and religion. The symptoms of Kali are (1) wine, (2) women, (3) gambling and (4) slaughterhouses. Wise rulers of all states should take lessons from Mahārāja Parīkṣit in how to maintain peace and morality by subduing the upstarts and quarrelsome people who indulge in wine, illicit connection with women, gambling and meat-eating supplied by regularly maintained slaughterhouses. In this age of Kali, regular license is issued for maintaining all of these different departments of quarrel. So how can they expect peace and morality in the state? The state fathers, therefore, must follow the principles of becoming wiser by devotion to the Lord, by chastising the breaker of discipline and by uprooting the symptoms of quarrel, as mentioned above. If we want blazing fire, we must use dry fuel. Blazing fire and moist fuel go ill together. Peace and morality can prosper only by the principles of Mahārāja Parīkṣit and his followers.

TEXT 27

तक्षकादात्मनो मृत्युं द्विजपुत्रोपसर्जितात् ।
प्रपत्स्यत उपश्रुत्य मुक्तसङ्गः पदं हरेः ॥२७॥

takṣakād ātmano mṛtyuṁ
dvija-putropasarjitāt
prapatsyata upaśrutya
mukta-saṅgaḥ padaṁ hareḥ

takṣakāt—by the snakebird; *ātmanaḥ*—of his personal self; *mṛtyum*—death; *dvija-putra*—the son of a *brāhmaṇa; upasarjitāt*—being sent by; *prapatsyate*—having taken shelter of; *upaśrutya*—after hearing; *mukta-saṅgaḥ*—freed from all attachment; *padam*—position; *hareḥ*—of the Lord.

TRANSLATION

After hearing about his death, which will be caused by the bite of a snakebird sent by a son of a brāhmaṇa, he will get himself

freed from all material attachment and surrender unto the Personality of Godhead, taking shelter of Him.

PURPORT

Material attachment and taking shelter of the lotus feet of the Lord go ill together. Material attachment means ignorance of transcendental happiness under the shelter of the Lord. Devotional service to the Lord, while existing in the material world, is a way to practice one's transcendental relation with the Lord, and when it is matured, one gets completely free from all material attachment and becomes competent to go back home, back to Godhead. Mahārāja Parīkṣit, being especially attached to the Lord from the beginning of his body in the womb of his mother, was continuously under the shelter of the Lord, and the so-called warning of his death within seven days from the date of the curse by the *brāhmaṇa's* son was a boon to him to enable him to prepare himself to go back home, back to Godhead. Since he was always protected by the Lord, he could have avoided the effect of such a curse by the grace of the Lord, but he did not take such undue advantage for nothing. Rather, he made the best use of a bad bargain. For seven days continuously he heard *Śrīmad-Bhāgavatam* from the right source, and thus he got shelter at the lotus feet of the Lord by that opportunity.

TEXT 28

जिज्ञासितात्मयाथार्थ्यो मुनेर्व्याससुतादसौ ।
हित्वेदं नृप गङ्गायां यास्यत्यद्धाकुतोभयम् ॥२८॥

jijñāsitātma-yāthārthyo
muner vyāsa-sutād asau
hitvedaṁ nṛpa gaṅgāyāṁ
yāsyaty addhākutobhayam

jijñāsita—having inquired of; *ātma-yāthārthyaḥ*—right knowledge of one's own self; *muneḥ*—from the learned philosopher; *vyāsa-sutāt*—the son of Vyāsa; *asau*—he; *hitvā*—quitting; *idam*—this material attachment; *nṛpa*—O King; *gaṅgāyām*—on the bank of the Ganges;

yāsyati—will go; *addhā*—directly; *akutaḥ-bhayam*—the life of fearlessness.

TRANSLATION

After inquiring about proper self-knowledge from the son of Vyāsadeva, who will be a great philosopher, he will renounce all material attachment and achieve a life of fearlessness.

PURPORT

Material knowledge means ignorance of the knowledge of one's own self. Philosophy means to seek after the right knowledge of one's own self, or the knowledge of self-realization. Without self-realization, philosophy is dry speculation or a waste of time and energy. *Śrīmad-Bhāgavatam* gives the right knowledge of one's own self, and by hearing *Śrīmad-Bhāgavatam* one can get free from material attachment and enter into the kingdom of fearlessness. This material world is fearfulness. Its prisoners are always fearful as within a prison house. In the prison house no one can violate the jail rules and regulations, and violating the rules means another term for extension of prison life. Similarly, we in this material existence are always fearful. This fearfulness is called anxiety. Everyone in the material life, in all species and varieties of life, is full of anxieties, either by breaking or without breaking the laws of nature. Liberation, or *mukti*, means getting relief from these constant anxieties. This is possible only when the anxiety is changed to the devotional service of the Lord. *Śrīmad-Bhāgavatam* gives us the chance to change the quality of anxiety from matter to spirit. This is done in the association of a learned philosopher like the self-realized Śukadeva Gosvāmī, the great son of Śrī Vyāsadeva. Mahārāja Parīkṣit, after receiving warning of his death, took advantage of this opportunity by association with Śukadeva Gosvāmī and achieved the desired result.

There is a sort of imitation of this reciting and hearing of *Śrīmad-Bhāgavatam* by professional men, and their foolish audience thinks that they will get free from the clutches of material attachment and attain the life of fearlessness. Such imitative hearing of *Śrīmad-Bhāgavatam* is a caricature only, and one should not be misled by such a performance of *bhāgavatam saptāha* undertaken by ridiculous greedy fellows to maintain an establishment of material enjoyment.

TEXT 29

इति राज्ञ उपादिश्य विप्रा जातककोविदाः ।
लब्धापचितयः सर्वे प्रतिजग्मुः स्वकान् गृहान्॥२९॥

iti rājña upādiśya
viprā jātaka-kovidāḥ
labdhāpacitayaḥ sarve
pratijagmuḥ svakān gṛhān

iti—thus; *rājñe*—unto the King; *upādiśya*—having advised; *viprāḥ*—persons well versed in the *Vedas; jātaka-kovidāḥ*—persons expert in astrology and in the performance of birth ceremonies; *labdha-apacitayaḥ*—those who had received sumptuously as remuneration; *sarve*—all of them; *pratijagmuḥ*—went back; *svakān*—their own; *gṛhān*—houses.

TRANSLATION

Thus those who were expert in astrological knowledge and in performance of the birth ceremony instructed King Yudhiṣṭhira about the future history of his child. Then, being sumptuously remunerated, they all returned to their respective homes.

PURPORT

The *Vedas* are the storehouse of knowledge, both material and spiritual. But such knowledge aims at perfection of self-realization. In other words, the *Vedas* are the guides for the civilized man in every respect. Since human life is the opportunity to get free from all material miseries, it is properly guided by the knowledge of the *Vedas*, in the matters of both material needs and spiritual salvation. The specific intelligent class of men who were devoted particularly to the knowledge of the *Vedas* were called the *vipras*, or the graduates of the Vedic knowledge. There are different branches of knowledge in the *Vedas*, of which astrology and pathology are two important branches necessary for the common man. So the intelligent men, generally known as the *brāhmaṇas*, took up all the different branches of Vedic knowledge to guide society. Even the department of military education (*Dhanur-veda*) was also taken up by such intelligent men, and the *vipras* were also teachers of this section of knowledge, as were Droṇācārya, Kṛpācārya, etc.

The word *vipra* mentioned herein is significant. There is a little difference between the *vipras* and the *brāhmaṇas*. The *vipras* are those who are expert in *karma-kāṇḍa*, or fruitive activities, guiding the society towards fulfilling the material necessities of life, whereas the *brāhmaṇas* are expert in spiritual knowledge of transcendence. This department of knowledge is called *jñāna-kāṇḍa*, and above this there is the *upāsanā-kāṇḍa*. The culmination of *upāsanā-kāṇḍa* is the devotional service of the Lord Viṣṇu, and when the *brāhmaṇas* achieve perfection, they are called Vaiṣṇavas. Viṣṇu worship is the highest of the modes of worship. Elevated *brāhmaṇas* are Vaiṣṇavas engaged in the transcendental loving service of the Lord, and thus *Śrīmad-Bhāgavatam*, which is the science of devotional service, is very dear to the Vaiṣṇavas. And as explained in the beginning of the *Śrīmad-Bhāgavatam*, it is the mature fruit of Vedic knowledge and is superior subject matter, above the three *kāṇḍas*, namely *karma*, *jñāna* and *upāsanā*.

Amongst the *karma-kāṇḍa* experts, the *jātaka* expert *vipras* were good astrologers who could tell all the future history of a born child simply by the astral calculations of the time (*lagna*). Such expert *jātaka-vipras* were present during the birth of Mahārāja Parīkṣit, and his grandfather, Mahārāja Yudhiṣṭhira, awarded the *vipras* sufficiently with gold, land, villages, grains and other valuable necessaries of life, which also include cows. There is a need of such *vipras* in the social structure, and it is the duty of the state to maintain them comfortably, as designed in the Vedic procedure. Such expert *vipras*, being sufficiently paid by the state, could give free service to the people in general, and thus this department of Vedic knowledge could be available for all.

TEXT 30

स एष लोके विख्यातः परीक्षिदिति यत्प्रभुः ।
पूर्वं दृष्टमनुध्यायन् परीक्षेत नरेष्विह ॥३०॥

sa eṣa loke vikhyātaḥ
parīkṣid iti yat prabhuḥ
pūrvaṁ dṛṣṭam anudhyāyan
parīkṣeta nareṣv iha

saḥ—he; *eṣaḥ*—in this; *loke*—world; *vikhyātaḥ*—famous; *parīkṣit*—one who examines; *iti*—thus; *yat*—what; *prabhuḥ*—O my King; *pūrvam*—before; *dṛṣṭam*—seen; *anudhyāyan*—constantly contemplating; *parīkṣeta*—shall examine; *nareṣu*—unto every man; *iha*—here.

TRANSLATION

So his son would become famous in the world as Parīkṣit [examiner] because he would come to examine all human beings in his search after that personality whom he saw before his birth. Thus he would come to constantly contemplate Him.

PURPORT

Mahārāja Parīkṣit, fortunate as he was, got the impression of the Lord even in the womb of his mother, and thus his contemplation on the Lord was constantly with him. Once the impression of the transcendental form of the Lord is fixed in one's mind, one can never forget Him in any circumstance. Child Parīkṣit, after coming out of the womb, was in the habit of examining everyone to see whether he was the same personality whom he first saw in the womb. But no one could be equal to or more attractive than the Lord, and therefore he never accepted anyone. But the Lord was constantly with him by such examination, and thus Mahārāja Parīkṣit was always engaged in the devotional service of the Lord by remembrance.

Śrīla Jīva Gosvāmī remarks in this connection that every child, if given an impression of the Lord from his very childhood, certainly becomes a great devotee of the Lord like Mahārāja Parīkṣit. One may not be as fortunate as Mahārāja Parīkṣit to have the opportunity to see the Lord in the womb of his mother, but even if he is not so fortunate, he can be made so if the parents of the child desire him to be so. There is a practical example in my personal life in this connection. My father was a pure devotee of the Lord, and when I was only four or five years old, my father gave me a couple of forms of Rādhā and Kṛṣṇa. In a playful manner, I used to worship these Deities along with my sister, and I used to imitate the performances of a neighboring temple of Rādhā-Govinda. By constantly visiting this neighboring temple and copying the ceremonies in connection with my own Deities of play, I developed a natural affinity for the Lord. My father used to observe all the ceremonies befitting my position.

Later on, these activities were suspended due to my association in the schools and colleges, and I became completely out of practice. But in my youthful days, when I met my spiritual master, Śrī Śrīmad Bhaktisiddhānta Sarasvatī Gosvāmī Mahārāja, again I revived my old habit, and the same playful Deities became my worshipful Deities in proper regulation. This was followed up until I left the family connection, and I am pleased that my generous father gave the first impression which was developed later into regulative devotional service by His Divine Grace. Mahārāja Prahlāda also advised that such impressions of a godly relation must be impregnated from the beginning of childhood, otherwise one may miss the opportunity of the human form of life, which is very valuable although it is temporary like others.

TEXT 31

स राजपुत्रो ववृधे आशु शुक्ल इवोडुपः ।
आपूर्यमाणः पितृभिः काष्ठाभिरिव सोऽन्वहम् ॥३१॥

sa rāja-putro vavṛdhe
āśu śukla ivoḍupaḥ
āpūryamāṇaḥ pitṛbhiḥ
kāṣṭhābhir iva so 'nvaham

saḥ—that; *rāja-putraḥ*—the royal prince; *vavṛdhe*—grew up; *āśu*—very soon; *śukle*—waxing moon; *iva*—like; *uḍupaḥ*—the moon; *āpūryamāṇaḥ*—luxuriantly; *pitṛbhiḥ*—by the parental guardians; *kāṣṭhābhiḥ*—plenary development; *iva*—like; *saḥ*—he; *anvaham*—day after day.

TRANSLATION

As the moon, in its waxing fortnight, develops day after day, so the royal prince [Parīkṣit] very soon developed luxuriantly under the care and full facilities of his guardian grandfathers.

TEXT 32

यक्ष्यमाणोऽश्वमेधेन ज्ञातिद्रोहजिहासया ।
राजालब्धधनो दध्यौ नान्यत्र करदण्डयोः ॥३२॥

yakṣyamāṇo 'śvamedhena
jñāti-droha-jihāsayā
rājā labdha-dhano dadhyau
nānyatra kara-daṇḍayoḥ

yakṣyamāṇaḥ—desiring to perform; *aśvamedhena*—by the horse sacrifice ceremony; *jñāti-droha*—fighting with kinsmen; *jihāsayā*—for getting free; *rājā*—King Yudhiṣṭhira; *labdha-dhanaḥ*—for getting some wealth; *dadhyau*—thought about it; *na anyatra*—not otherwise; *kara-daṇḍayoḥ*—taxes and fines.

TRANSLATION

Just at this time, King Yudhiṣṭhira was considering performing a horse sacrifice to get freed from sins incurred from fighting with kinsmen. But he became anxious to get some wealth, for there were no surplus funds outside of fines and tax collection.

PURPORT

As the *brāhmaṇas* and *vipras* had a right to be subsidized by the state, the state executive head had the right to collect taxes and fines from the citizens. After the Battle of Kurukṣetra the state treasury was exhausted, and therefore there was no surplus fund except the fund from tax collection and fines. Such funds were sufficient only for the state budget, and having no excess fund, the King was anxious to get more wealth in some other way in order to perform the horse sacrifice. Mahārāja Yudhiṣṭhira wanted to perform this sacrifice under the instruction of Bhīṣmadeva.

TEXT 33

तदभिप्रेतमालक्ष्य भ्रातरोऽच्युतचोदिताः ।
धनं प्रहीणमाजह्रुरुदीच्यां दिशि भूरिशः ॥३३॥

tad abhipretam ālakṣya
bhrātaro 'cyuta-coditāḥ
dhanaṁ prahīṇam ājahrur
udīcyāṁ diśi bhūriśaḥ

tat—his; *abhipretam*—wishes of the mind; *ālakṣya*—observing; *bhrātaraḥ*—his brothers; *acyuta*—the infallible (Lord Śrī Kṛṣṇa); *coditāḥ*—being advised by; *dhanam*—riches; *prahīṇam*—to collect; *ājahruḥ*—brought about; *udīcyām*—northern; *diśi*—direction; *bhūriśaḥ*—sufficient.

TRANSLATION

Understanding the hearty wishes of the King, his brothers, as advised by the infallible Lord Kṛṣṇa, collected sufficient riches from the North [left by King Marutta].

PURPORT

Mahārāja Marutta: one of the great emperors of the world. He reigned over the world long before the reign of Mahārāja Yudhiṣṭhira. He was the son of Mahārāja Avikṣit and was a great devotee of the son of the sun-god, known as Yamarāja. His brother Samvarta was a rival priest of the great Bṛhaspati, the learned priest of the demigods. He conducted one sacrifice called Saṅkara-yajña by which the Lord was so satisfied that He was pleased to hand over to him the charge of a mountain peak of gold. This peak of gold is somewhere in the Himalaya Mountains, and modern adventurers may try to find it there. He was so powerful an emperor that at the day's end of sacrifice, the demigods from the other planets like Indra, Candra and Bṛhaspati used to visit his palace. And because he had the gold peak at his disposal, he had sufficient gold in his possession. The canopy of the sacrificial altar was completely made of gold. In his daily performances of the sacrificial ceremonies, some of the inhabitants of the Vāyuloka (airy planets) were invited to expedite the cooking work of the ceremony. And the assembly of the demigods in the ceremony was led by Viśvadeva.

By his constant pious work he was able to drive out all kinds of diseases from the jurisdiction of his kingdom. All the inhabitants of higher planets like Devaloka and Pitṛloka were pleased with him for his great sacrificial ceremonies. Every day he used to give in charity to the learned *brāhmaṇas* such things as beddings, seats, conveyances and sufficient quantities of gold. Because of munificent charities and performances of innumerable sacrifices, the King of heaven, Indradeva, was fully satisfied with him and always wished for his welfare. Due to his pious activities, he remained a young man throughout his life and reigned over the world for one thousand years, surrounded by his satisfied subjects, ministers, legitimate wife, sons and brothers. Even Lord Śrī Kṛṣṇa praised his spirit of pious activities. He handed over his only daughter to Maharṣi Aṅgirā, and by his good blessings, he was elevated to the kingdom of heaven. First of all, he wanted to offer the priesthood of his sacrifices to learned Bṛhaspati, but the demigod refused to accept the post because of the King's being a human being, a man of this earth. He was very sorry for this, but on the advice of Nārada Muni he appointed Samvarta to the post, and he was successful in his mission.

The success of a particular type of sacrifice completely depends on the priest in charge. In this age, all kinds of sacrifice are forbidden because there is no learned priest amongst the so-called *brāhmaṇas*, who go by the false notion of becoming sons of *brāhmaṇas* without brahminical qualifications. In this age of Kali, therefore, only one kind of sacrifice is recommended, *saṅkīrtana-yajña*, as inaugurated by Lord Śrī Caitanya Mahāprabhu.

TEXT 34

तेन सम्भृतसम्भारो धर्मपुत्रो युधिष्ठिरः ।
वाजिमेधैस्त्रिभिर्भीतो यज्ञैः समयजद्धरिम् ॥३४॥

tena sambhṛta-sambhāro
dharma-putro yudhiṣṭhiraḥ
vājimedhais tribhir bhīto
yajñaiḥ samayajad dharim

tena—with that wealth; *sambhṛta*—collected; *sambhāraḥ*—ingredients; *dharma-putraḥ*—the pious king; *yudhiṣṭhiraḥ*—Yudhiṣṭhira; *vājimedhaiḥ*—by horse sacrifices; *tribhiḥ*—three times; *bhītaḥ*—being greatly afraid after the Battle of Kurukṣetra; *yajñaiḥ*—sacrifices; *samayajat*—perfectly worshiped; *harim*—the Personality of Godhead.

TRANSLATION

By those riches, the King could procure the ingredients for three horse sacrifices. Thus the pious King Yudhiṣṭhira, who was

very fearful after the Battle of Kurukṣetra, pleased Lord Hari, the Personality of Godhead.

PURPORT

Mahārāja Yudhiṣṭhira was the ideal and celebrated pious King of the world, and still he was greatly afraid after the execution of the Battle of Kurukṣetra because of the mass killing in the fight, all of which was done only to install him on the throne. He therefore took all the responsibility for sins committed in the warfare, and to get rid of all these sins, he wanted to perform three sacrifices in which horses are offered at the altar. Such a sacrifice is very costly. Even Mahārāja Yudhiṣṭhira had to collect the necessary heaps of gold left by Mahārāja Marutta and the *brāhmaṇas* who were given gold in charity by King Marutta. The learned *brāhmaṇas* could not take away all the loads of gold given by Mahārāja Marutta, and therefore they left behind the major portion of the gift. And Mahārāja Marutta also did not again collect such heaps of gold given away in charity. Besides that, all the golden plates and utensils which were used in the sacrifice were also thrown in the dustbins, and all such heaps of gold remained unclaimed property for a long time, till Mahārāja Yudhiṣṭhira collected them for his own purposes. Lord Śrī Kṛṣṇa advised the brothers of Mahārāja Yudhiṣṭhira to collect the unclaimed property because it belonged to the King. The more astonishing thing is that no subject of the state also collected such unclaimed gold for industrial enterprise or anything like that. This means that the state citizens were completely satisfied with all necessities of life and therefore not inclined to accept unnecessary productive enterprises for sense gratification. Mahārāja Yudhiṣṭhira also requisitioned the heaps of gold for performing sacrifices and for pleasing the Supreme Hari Personality of Godhead. Otherwise he had no desire to collect them for the state treasury.

One should take lessons from the acts of Mahārāja Yudhiṣṭhira. He was afraid of sins committed on the battlefield, and therefore he wanted to satisfy the supreme authority. This indicates that unintentional sins are also committed in our daily occupational discharge of duties, and to counteract even such unintentional crimes, one must perform sacrifices as they are recommended in the revealed scriptures. The Lord says in *Bhagavad-gītā* (*yajñārthāt karmaṇo 'nyatra loko 'yaṁ karma-bandhanaḥ*) that one must perform sacrifices recommended in the scriptures in order to get rid of commitments of all unauthorized work, or even unintentional crimes which we are apt to commit. By doing so, one shall be freed from all kinds of sins. And those who do not do so but work for self-interest or sense gratification have to undergo all tribulations accrued from committed sins. Therefore, the main purpose of performing sacrifices is to satisfy the Supreme Personality Hari. The process of performing sacrifices may be different in terms of different times, places and persons, but the aim of such sacrifices is one and the same at all times and in all circumstances, *viz.*, satisfaction of the Supreme Lord Hari. That is the way of pious life, and that is the way of peace and prosperity in the world at large. Mahārāja Yudhiṣṭhira did all these as the ideal pious king in the world.

If Mahārāja Yudhiṣṭhira is a sinner in his daily discharge of duties, in royal administration of state affairs, wherein killing of man and animals is a recognized art, then we can just imagine the amount of sins committed consciously or unconsciously by the untrained population of the Kali-yuga who have no way to perform sacrifice to please the Supreme Lord. The *Bhāgavatam* says, therefore, that the prime duty of the human being is to satisfy the Supreme Lord by the performance of one's occupational duty (*Bhāg.* 1.2.13).

Let any man of any place or community, caste or creed be engaged in any sort of occupational duty, but he must agree to perform sacrifices as it is recommended in the scriptures for the particular place, time and person. In the Vedic literatures it is recommended that in Kali-yuga people engage in glorifying the Lord by chanting the holy name of Kṛṣṇa (*kīrtanād eva kṛṣṇasya mukta-saṅgaḥ paraṁ vrajet*) without offense. By doing so one can be freed from all sins and thus can attain the highest perfection of life by returning home, back to Godhead. We have already discussed this more than once in this great literature in different places, especially in the introductory portion by sketching the life of Lord Śrī Caitanya Mahāprabhu, and still we are repeating the same with a view to bring about peace and prosperity in society.

The Lord has declared openly in *Bhagavad-gītā* how He becomes pleased with us, and the same process is practically demonstrated in the life and preaching work of Lord Śrī Caitanya Mahāprabhu. The perfect process of performing *yajñas*, or sacrifice, to please the Supreme Lord Hari (the Personality of Godhead, who gets us free from all miseries of existence) is to follow the ways of Lord Śrī Caitanya Mahāprabhu in this dark age of quarrel and dissension.

Mahārāja Yudhiṣṭhira had to collect heaps of gold to secure the paraphernalia for the horse sacrifice *yajñas* in days of sufficiency, so we can hardly think of such performance of *yajñas* in these days of insufficiency and complete scarcity of gold. At the present moment we have heaps of papers and promises of their being converted into gold by economic development of modern civilization, and still there is no possibility of spending riches like Mahārāja Yudhiṣṭhira, either individually or collectively or by state patronization. Just suitable, therefore, for the age, is the method recommended by Lord Śrī Caitanya Mahāprabhu in terms of the *śāstra.* Such a method requires no expenditure at all and yet can award more benefit than other expensive methods of *yajña* performances.

The horse sacrifice *yajña* or cow sacrifice *yajña* performed by the Vedic regulations shouldn't be misunderstood as a process of killing animals. On the contrary, animals offered for the *yajña* were rejuvenated to a new span of life by the transcendental power of chanting the Vedic hymns, which, if properly chanted, are different from what is understood by the common layman. The *Veda-mantras* are all practical, and the proof is rejuvenation of the sacrificed animal.

There is no possibility of such methodical chanting of the Vedic hymns by the so-called *brāhmaṇas* or priests of the present age. The untrained descendants of the twice-born families are no more like their forefathers, and thus they are counted amongst the *śūdras*, or once-born men. The once-born man is unfit to chant the Vedic hymns, and therefore there is no practical utility of chanting the original hymns.

And to save them all, Lord Śrī Caitanya Mahāprabhu propounded the *saṅkīrtana* movement or *yajña* for all practical purposes, and the people of the present age are strongly recommended to follow this sure and recognized path.

TEXT 35

आहूतो भगवान् राज्ञा याजयित्वा द्विजैर्नृपम् ।
उवास कतिचिन्मासान् सुहृदां प्रियकाम्यया ॥३५॥

āhūto bhagavān rājñā
yājayitvā dvijair nṛpam

uvāsa katicin māsān
suhṛdāṁ priya-kāmyayā

āhūtaḥ—being called by; *bhagavān*—Lord Kṛṣṇa, the Personality of Godhead; *rājñā*—by the King; *yājayitvā*—causing to be performed; *dvijaiḥ*—by the learned *brāhmaṇas; nṛpam*—on behalf of the King; *uvāsa*—resided; *katicit*—a few; *māsān*—months; *suhṛdām*—for the sake of the relatives; *priya-kāmyayā*—for the pleasure.

TRANSLATION

Lord Śrī Kṛṣṇa, the Personality of Godhead, being invited to the sacrifices by Mahārāja Yudhiṣṭhira, saw to it that they were performed by qualified [twice-born] brāhmaṇas. After that, for the pleasure of the relatives, the Lord remained a few months.

PURPORT

Lord Śrī Kṛṣṇa was invited by Mahārāja Yudhiṣṭhira to look into the supervision of the performances of *yajña*, and the Lord, to abide by the orders of His elderly cousin, caused the performance of *yajñas* by learned twice-born *brāhmaṇas*. Simply taking birth in the family of a *brāhmaṇa* does not make one qualified to perform *yajñas*. One must be twice-born by proper training and initiation from the bona fide *ācārya*. The once-born scions of *brāhmaṇa* families are equal with the once-born *śūdras*, and such *brahma-bandhus*, or unqualified once-born scions, must be rejected for any purpose of religious or Vedic function. Lord Śrī Kṛṣṇa was entrusted to look after this arrangement, and perfect as He is, He caused the *yajñas* to be performed by the bona fide twice-born *brāhmaṇas* for successful execution.

TEXT 36

ततो राज्ञाभ्यनुज्ञातः कृष्णया सह बन्धुभिः ।
ययौ द्वारवतीं ब्रह्मन् सार्जुनो यदुभिर्वृतः ॥३६॥

tato rājñābhyanujñātaḥ
kṛṣṇayā saha-bandhubhiḥ
yayau dvāravatīṁ brahman
sārjuno yadubhir vṛtaḥ

tataḥ—thereafter; *rājñā*—by the King; *abhyanujñātaḥ*—being permitted; *kṛṣṇayā*—as well as by Draupadī; *saha*—along with; *bandhubhiḥ*—other relatives; *yayau*—went to; *dvāravatīm*—Dvārakā-dhāma; *brahman*—O *brāhmaṇas; sa-arjunaḥ*—along with Arjuna; *yadubhiḥ*—by the members of the Yadu dynasty; *vṛtaḥ*—surrounded.

TRANSLATION

O Śaunaka, thereafter the Lord, having bade farewell to King Yudhiṣṭhira, Draupadī and other relatives, started for the city of Dvārakā, accompanied by Arjuna and other members of the Yadu dynasty.

Thus end the Bhaktivedanta purports of the First Canto, Twelfth Chapter, of the Śrīmad-Bhāgavatam, *entitled "Birth of Emperor Parīkṣit."*

Appendixes

The Author

His Divine Grace A. C. Bhaktivedanta Swami Prabhupāda appeared in this world in 1896 in Calcutta, India. He first met his spiritual master, Śrīla Bhaktisiddhānta Sarasvatī Gosvāmī, in Calcutta in 1922. Bhaktisiddhānta Sarasvatī, a prominent devotional scholar and the founder of sixty-four Gauḍīya Maṭhas (Vedic institutes), liked this educated young man and convinced him to dedicate his life to teaching Vedic knowledge. Śrīla Prabhupāda became his student, and eleven years later (1933) at Allahabad he became his formally initiated disciple.

At their first meeting, in 1922, Śrīla Bhaktisiddhānta Sarasvatī Ṭhākura requested Śrīla Prabhupāda to broadcast Vedic knowledge through the English language. In the years that followed, Śrīla Prabhupāda wrote a commentary on the *Bhagavad-gītā*, assisted the Gauḍīya Maṭha in its work and, in 1944, without assistance, started an English fortnightly magazine, edited it, typed the manuscripts and checked the galley proofs. He even distributed the individual copies freely and struggled to maintain the publication. Once begun, the magazine never stopped; it is now being continued by his disciples in the West.

Recognizing Śrīla Prabhupāda's philosophical learning and devotion, the Gauḍīya Vaiṣṇava Society honored him in 1947 with the title "Bhaktivedanta." In 1950, at the age of fifty-four, Śrīla Prabhupāda retired from married life, and four years later he adopted the *vānaprastha* (retired) order to devote more time to his studies and writing. Śrīla Prabhupāda traveled to the holy city of Vṛndāvana, where he lived in very humble circumstances in the historic medieval temple of Rādhā-Dāmodara. There he engaged for several years in deep study and writing. He accepted the renounced order of life (*sannyāsa*) in 1959. At Rādhā-Dāmodara, Śrīla Prabhupāda began work on his life's masterpiece: a multivolume translation and commentary on the eighteen thousand verse *Śrīmad-Bhāgavatam* (*Bhāgavata Purāṇa*). He also wrote *Easy Journey to Other Planets*.

After publishing three volumes of *Bhāgavatam*, Śrīla Prabhupāda came to the United States, in 1965, to fulfill the mission of his spiritual master. Since that time, His Divine Grace has written over forty volumes of authoritative translations, commentaries and summary studies of the philosophical and religious classics of India.

In 1965, when he first arrived by freighter in New York City, Śrīla Prabhupāda was practically penniless. It was after almost a year of great difficulty that he established the International Society for Krishna Consciousness in July of 1966. Under his careful guidance, the Society has grown within a decade to a worldwide confederation of almost one hundred *āśramas*, schools, temples, institutes and farm communities.

In 1968, Śrīla Prabhupāda created New Vṛndāvana, an experimental Vedic community in the hills of West Virginia. Inspired by the success of New Vṛndāvana, now a thriving farm community of more than one thousand acres, his students have since founded several similar communities in the United States and abroad.

In 1972, His Divine Grace introduced the Vedic system of primary and secondary education in the West by founding the Gurukula school in Dallas, Texas. The school began with 3 children in 1972, and by the beginning of 1975 the enrollment had grown to 150.

Śrīla Prabhupāda has also inspired the construction of a large international center at Śrīdhāma Māyāpur in West Bengal, India, which is also the site for a planned Institute of Vedic Studies. A similar project is the magnificent Kṛṣṇa-Balarāma Temple and International Guest House in Vṛndāvana, India. These are centers where Westerners can live to gain firsthand experience of Vedic culture.

Śrīla Prabhupāda's most significant contribution, however, is his books. Highly respected by the academic community for their authoritativeness, depth and clarity, they are used as standard textbooks in numerous college courses. His writings have been translated into eleven languages. The Bhaktivedanta Book Trust, established in 1972 exclusively to publish the works of His Divine Grace, has thus become the world's largest publisher of books in the field of Indian religion and philosophy. Its latest project is the publishing of Śrīla Prabhupāda's most recent work: a seventeen-volume translation and commentary—completed by Śrīla Prabhupāda in only eighteen months—on the Bengali religious classic *Śrī Caitanya-caritāmṛta.*

In the past ten years, in spite of his advanced age, Śrīla Prabhupāda has circled the globe twelve times on lecture tours that have taken him to six continents. In spite of such a vigorous schedule, Śrīla Prabhupāda continues to write prolifically. His writings constitute a veritable library of Vedic philosophy, religion, literature and culture.

References

The purports of *Śrīmad-Bhāgavatam* are all confirmed by standard Vedic authorities. The following authentic scriptures are specifically cited in this volume.

References

The purports of *Śrīmad-Bhāgavatam* are all confirmed by standard Vedic authorities. The following authentic scriptures are specifically cited in this volume:

Bhagavad-gītā, 6, 14, 15, 19, 20, 29, 33, 37, 43, 45, 49, 56, 66, 91, 98, 102, 106, 110, 112–113, 116, 120, 122, 124, 133, 134, 135, 142, 153, 169, 171, 173, 174, 175, 176, 180, 182, 201, 219, 222, 239–240, 247, 256, 257–258, 258, 259, 263, 264, 266, 277, 279, 280, 289, 301

Brahma-saṁhitā, 22, 171, 201, 227, 237, 262

Īśopaniṣad, 147

Kaṭha Upaniṣad, 115, 162, 278

Mahābhārata, 60, 68, 76, 79, 84, 162, 230, 231, 235, 290

Rāmāyaṇa, 278

Skanda Purāṇa, 120

Śrīmad-Bhāgavatam, 41, 73, 92, 94, 170, 243, 254, 292, 294, 303

Upaniṣads, 22, 126

Vedas, 217

Glossary

A

Ācārya—a spiritual master who teaches by example.

Ahiṁsā—nonviolence.

Ārati—a ceremony for greeting the Lord with offerings of food, lamps, fans, flowers and incense.

Arcanā—the devotional process of Deity worship.

Āśrama—the four spiritual orders of life: celibacy, household life, retirement and renunciation.

Asuras—atheistic demons.

Aśvamedha-yajña—Vedic horse sacrifice.

Avatāra—a descent of the Supreme Lord.

B

Bhagavad-gītā—the basic directions for spiritual life spoken by the Lord Himself.

Bhakta—a devotee.

Bhakti-yoga—linking with the Supreme Lord by devotional service.

Bhāva—the preliminary stage of love of Godhead.

Brahmacarya—celibate student life; the first order of Vedic spiritual life.

Brahman—the Absolute Truth; especially the impersonal aspect of the Absolute.

Brāhmaṇa—one wise in the *Vedas* who can guide society; the first Vedic social order.

Brahmānanda—the pleasure of merging into the spiritual effulgence of the Lord.

C

Caṇḍālas—dog-eaters, the lowest class of human beings.

D

Daridra-Nārāyaṇa—a nonsensical term meaning "poor Nārāyaṇa"; used by Māyāvādī *sannyāsīs* to refer to themselves and also the poverty stricken.

Dharma—eternal occupational duty; religious principles.

E

Ekādaśī—a special fast day for increased remembrance of Kṛṣṇa, which comes on the eleventh day of both the waxing and waning moon.

G

Garbhādhāna-saṁskāra—Vedic purificatory ritual for obtaining good progeny; performed by husband and wife before child's conception.

Goloka (Kṛṣṇaloka)—the highest spiritual planet, containing Kṛṣṇa's personal abodes, Dvārakā, Mathurā and Vṛndāvana.

Gopīs—Kṛṣṇa's cowherd girl friends, His most confidential servitors.

Gṛhastha—regulated householder life; the second order of Vedic spiritual life.

Guru—a spiritual master.

H

Hare Kṛṣṇa mantra—*See: Mahā-mantra*

Harināma-yajña—congregational chanting of the holy names of the Lord, the recommended sacrifice for this age.

J

Jīva-tattva—the living entities, atomic parts of the Lord.

K

Kaivalya—oneness with the Supreme.

Kali-yuga (Age of Kali)—the present age, the age of quarrel. It is last in the cycle of four, and began five thousand years ago.

Kāmadhenu—spiritual cows, in the spiritual world, which yield unlimited quantities of milk.

Karatālas—hand cymbals used in *kīrtana.*

Karma—fruitive action, for which there is always reaction, good or bad.

Karmī—a person satisfied with working hard for flickering sense gratification.

Kīrtana—chanting the glories of the Supreme Lord.
Kṛṣṇaloka—*See:* Goloka
Kṣatriyas—a warrior or administrator; the second Vedic social order.

M

Mahājanas—great self-realized souls, authorities on the science of Kṛṣṇa consciousness.
Mahā-mantra—the great chanting for deliverance:
Hare Kṛṣṇa, Hare Kṛṣṇa, Kṛṣṇa Kṛṣṇa, Hare Hare
Hare Rāma, Hare Rāma, Rāma Rāma, Hare Hare
Mahātmā—a self-realized soul.
Mantra—a sound vibration that can deliver the mind from illusion.
Mathurā—Lord Kṛṣṇa's abode, surrounding Vṛndāvana, where He took birth and later returned to after performing His Vṛndāvana pastimes.
Māyā—(*mā*—not; *yā*—this), illusion; forgetfulness of one's relationship with Kṛṣṇa.
Māyāvādīs—impersonal philosophers who say that the Lord cannot have a transcendental body.
Muni—a learned sage.
Mṛdaṅga—a clay drum used for congregational chanting.

N

Nirguṇa—possessing no material qualities.

P

Parakīyā—the relationship between a married woman and her paramour; particularly the relationship between Kṛṣṇa and the damsels of Vṛndāvana.
Parameśvara—the supreme controller, Lord Śrī Kṛṣṇa.
Paramparā—the chain of spiritual masters in disciplic succession.
Prasāda—food spiritualized by being offered to the Lord.

R

Rāma-rājya—a perfect, Vedic kingdom following the example of Lord Rāmacandra, the incarnation of God appearing as the perfect king.

S

Sac-cid-ānanda-vigraha—the Lord's transcendental form, which is eternal, full of knowledge and bliss.

Sampradāya—a disciplic succession of spiritual masters.

Saṁskāras—Vedic rituals for purifying a human being from the time of conception until death.

Sanātana-dharma—the eternal occupation of all living beings, rendering devotional service to the Supreme Lord.

Saṅkīrtana—public chanting of the names of God, the approved *yoga* process for this age.

Sannyāsa—renounced life; the fourth order of Vedic spiritual life.

Śāstras—revealed scriptures.

Sāyujya—the liberation of merging into the spiritual effulgence of the Lord.

Śravaṇaṁ kīrtanaṁ viṣṇoḥ—the devotional processes of hearing and chanting about Lord Viṣṇu.

Śūdra—a laborer; the fourth of the Vedic social orders.

Surabhi—*See:* Kāmadhenu

Svāmī—one who controls his mind and senses; title of one in the renounced order of life.

T

Tapasya—austerity; accepting some voluntary inconvenience for a higher purpose.

Tilaka—auspicious clay marks that sanctify a devotee's body as a temple of the Lord.

V

Vaikuṇṭha—the spiritual world.

Vaiṣṇava—a devotee of Lord Viṣṇu, Kṛṣṇa.

Vaiśyas—farmers and merchants; the third Vedic social order.

Vānaprastha—one who has retired from family life; the third order of Vedic spiritual life.

Varṇa-saṅkara—children born of parents who did not follow Vedic purificatory rules for procreation.

Varṇāśrama—the Vedic social system of four social and four spiritual orders.

Vedas—the original revealed scriptures, first spoken by the Lord Himself.

Viṣṇu, Lord—Kṛṣṇa's first expansion for the creation and maintenance of the material universes.

Viṣṇu-tattva—primary, personal expansions of the Lord.

Vṛndāvana—Kṛṣṇa's personal abode, where He fully manifests His quality of sweetness.

Vyāsadeva—Kṛṣṇa's incarnation, at the end of Dvāpara-yuga, for compiling the *Vedas*.

Y

Yajña—sacrifice; work done for the satisfaction of Lord Viṣṇu.

Yātrā—a journey.

Yogī—a transcendentalist who, in one way or another, is striving for union with the Supreme.

Yugas—ages in the life of a universe, occurring in a repeated cycle of four.

Z

Zamindar—landholder.

Varṇāśrama—the Vedic social system of four social and four spiritual orders.

Vedas—the original revealed scriptures, first spoken by the Lord Him-

Viṣṇu, Lord—Kṛṣṇa's first expansion for the creation and maintenance of the material universes.

Viṣṇu-tattva—primary, personal expansions of the Lord.

Vṛndāvana—Kṛṣṇa's personal abode, where He fully manifests His quality of sweetness.

Vyāsadeva—Kṛṣṇa's incarnation, at the end of Dvāpara-yuga, for compiling the *Vedas*.

Y

Yajña—sacrifice; work done for the satisfaction of Lord Viṣṇu.

Yātrā—a journey.

Yogī—a transcendentalist who, in one way or another, is striving for union with the Supreme.

Yugas—ages in the life of a universe, occurring in a repeated cycle of four.

Z

Zamindar—landholder.

Sanskrit Pronunciation Guide

Vowels

अ a आ ā इ i ई ī उ u ऊ ū ऋ ṛ ॠ ṝ
ऌ ḷ ए e ऐ ai ओ o औ au

ं ṁ *(anusvāra)* ः ḥ *(visarga)*

Consonants

Gutturals:	क ka	ख kha	ग ga	घ gha	ङ ṅa
Palatals:	च ca	छ cha	ज ja	झ jha	ञ ña
Cerebrals:	ट ṭa	ठ ṭha	ड ḍa	ढ ḍha	ण ṇa
Dentals:	त ta	थ tha	द da	ध dha	न na
Labials:	प pa	फ pha	ब ba	भ bha	म ma
Semivowels:	य ya	र ra	ल la	व va	
Sibilants:	श śa	ष ṣa	स sa		
Aspirate:	ह ha	ऽ ' *(avagraha)* – the apostrophe			

The vowels above should be pronounced as follows:

a – like the *a* in org*a*n or the *u* in b*u*t.
ā – like the *a* in f*a*r but held twice as long as short *a*.
i – like the *i* in p*i*n.
ī – like the *i* in p*i*que but held twice as long as short *i*.
u – like the *u* in p*u*sh.
ū – like the *u* in r*u*le but held twice as long as short *u*.

ṛ – like the *ri* in *ri*m.
ṝ – like *ree* in *ree*d.
ḷ – like *l* followed by *ṛ* (*lṛ*).
e – like the *e* in th*ey*.
ai – like the *ai* in *ai*sle.
o – like the *o* in g*o*.
au – like the *ow* in h*ow*.
ṁ (*anusvāra*) – a resonant nasal like the *n* in the French word *bon*.
ḥ (*visarga*) – a final *h*-sound: *aḥ* is pronounced like *aha; iḥ* like *ihi*.

The consonants are pronounced as follows:

k – as in *k*ite
kh – as in Ec*kh*art
g – as in *g*ive
gh – as in di*g-h*ard
ṅ – as in si*ng*
c – as in *ch*air
ch – as in staun*ch-h*eart
j – as in *j*oy
jh – as in he*dgeh*og
ñ – as in ca*ny*on
ṭ – as in *t*ub
ṭh – as in ligh*t-h*eart
ḍ – as in *d*ove
ḍha- as in re*d-h*ot
ṇ – as r*na* (prepare to say the *r* and say *na*).

Cerebrals are pronounced with tongue to roof of mouth, but the following dentals are pronounced with tongue against teeth:

t – as in *t*ub but with tongue against teeth.
th – as in ligh*t-h*eart but with tongue against teeth.
d – as in *d*ove but with tongue against teeth.
dh – as in re*d-h*ot but with tongue against teeth.
n – as in *n*ut but with tongue between teeth.

p – as in *p*ine
ph – as in u*ph*ill (not *f*)
b – as in *b*ird
bh – as in ru*b-h*ard
m – as in *m*other
y – as in *y*es
r – as in *r*un
l – as in *l*ight
v – as in *v*ine
ś (palatal) – as in the *s* in the German word *sprechen*
ṣ (cerebral) – as the *sh* in *sh*ine
s – as in *s*un
h – as in *h*ome

There is no strong accentuation of syllables in Sanskrit, only a flo ing of short and long (twice as long as the short) syllables.

Index of Sanskrit Verses

This index constitutes a complete listing of the first and third lines of each of the
nskrit poetry verses of this volume of *Śrīmad-Bhāgavatam*, arranged in English
phabetical order. The first column gives the Sanskrit transliteration, and the second and
ird columns, respectively, list the chapter-verse reference and page number for each
rse.

General Index

Numerals in boldface type indicate references to translations of the verses of *Śrīmad-Bhāgavatam.*

A

Abhimanyu
  as Subhadrā's son, 157
  as Uttarā's husband, 10
Absolute Truth
  demons reject, 20
  features of, three, 134–35
  Kṛṣṇa as, 134
  See also: Supreme Lord
Ācārya. See: Spiritual master(s)
Activities
  absolute compared with mundane, 121
  body given according to, 266–67
  devotional service transforms, 56
  of Kṛṣṇa. *See:* Kṛṣṇa, pastimes of
  pious, 266–67
  See also: Karma; Work
Age of Kali. *See:* Kali-yuga
Aghāsura, 179
Agnideva
  as pigeon, 280
  Sudarśana given to Kṛṣṇa by, 79
Ahaṅkāra. See: False ego
Akrūra, historical accounts on, 213
Akṣauhiṇī defined, 63
Ambā, 77
Analogies
  of bees & devotees, 228
  of desire trees & Lord, 200
  of fire & women, 165
  of forest fire & world, 149
  of Ganges & devotees, 187
  of Himalaya mountains & Parīkṣit, 286
  of lion & Parīkṣit, 286
  of lotus & Lord, 197
Analogies (*continued*)
  of moon's waxing & Parīkṣit's growing, **300**
  of nature & Lord's smile, 227
  of prison shackles & gravity, 242
  of sandalwood & Kṛṣṇa, 42
  of sun & Kṛṣṇa, 7, 16, 36, 37, 42, 96, 114, 180, 205, 206
  of sunrise & Kṛṣṇa's advent, 42, 180
  of sun's rays & living entities, 206
  of sun's rays & Lord's energy, 96
  of sun's rays & Lord's mercy, 7, 36
  of swan & *paramahaṁsa*, 197
  of wind & Lord's power, 239
Anartha defined, 32–33
Anātha defined, 49
Andhaka, **207**
Anger, freedom from, 108
Aṅgirā Maharṣi, 81, 303
Āṅgirasa, 81
Animals
  activities of, four, 102–3
  as citizens, 256
  demons degraded to, 258
  Lord incarnates in forms of, 38
  protection of, 104, 152, 153, 276–77
  sacrifice of, 67, 306
  See also: specific animals
Animal slaughter
  animal sacrifice compared with, 67, 306
  as barbaric, 104
  condemned, 53, 104, 153, 156
  as Satan's philosophy, 156
  war caused by, 156
Aniruddha, 92
Annihilation of the universe, 170, 173

C

D

E

L

O

P

W

Z